Native Americans and the Criminal Justice System

NATIVE AMERICANS AND THE CRIMINAL JUSTICE SYSTEM

edited by

Jeffrey Ian Ross and Larry Gould
with a foreword by Duane Champagne

Paradigm Publishers
Boulder • London

Copyright © 2006 Jeffrey Ian Ross and Larry Gould

Published in the United States by Paradigm Publishers, 3360 Mitchell Lane Suite E, Boulder, Colorado 80301 USA

Paradigm Publishers is the trade name of Birkenkamp & Company, LLC, Dean Birkenkamp, President and Publisher.

Library of Congress Cataloging-in-Publication Data
Native Americans and the criminal justice system : theoretical and policy directions / edited by Jeffrey Ian Ross and Larry Gould / with a foreword by Duane Champagne.
     p. cm.
   Includes bibliographical references and index.
   ISBN-13: 978-1-59451-179-0 (hc : alk. paper)
   ISBN-10: 1-59451-179-9 (hc : alk. paper)
   ISBN-13: 978-1-59451-180-6 (pbk : alk. paper)
   ISBN-10: 1-59451-180-2 (pbk : alk. paper)   1. Indians of North America—Legal status, laws, etc.   2. Criminal justice, Administration of—United States.   I. Ross, Jeffrey Ian.
II. Gould, Larry Allen, 1950–
   KF8210.C7N38   2006
   364.3'497073—dc22

                                                            2006002093

Printed and bound in the United States of America on acid-free paper that meets the standards of the American National Standard for Permanence of Paper for Printed Library Materials.

Designed and Typeset by Straight Creek Bookmakers.

10 09 08 07   2   3   4   5

Destiny
by Keanu Ross-Cabrera

What we know and we don't is doomed to remain that way
unless we take control of our futures and steer them toward a goal.
Some things remain uncovered, unknown, and unsaid.
Move towards them and stride for goals unknown.
Several paths not taken.
So many lives destroyed.
All for things unseen or unheard
but still there for some to uncover.
Your destiny is yours to take
and everyone should know.

Contents

Foreword

Since the beginning of the self-determination policy in the 1970s, American Indian nations have been seeking restoration of more autonomous governing powers and cultural renewal. Starting in the early 1960s, much of this struggle has focused on native activism, the mobilization of reservation communities and leadership, and many legal battles fought in U.S. courts. From the early 1960s to the early 1980s, the courts handed down many decisions that affirmed limited powers of Indian self-government under U.S. law. During the late 1960s and 1970s, Congress passed many legislative acts that supported greater funding and decisionmaking powers for tribal governments. Since the early 1980s, the courts have become less supportive of Indian sovereignty issues, and Congress has encountered fiscal constraints that have diminished its direct impact on institution building in Indian country. Nevertheless, many Indian communities have firmly embraced sovereignty and self-government concepts and are actively engaged in institution building. They seek to create stronger tribal governments that reflect the interests, values, and culture of their communities. In a recent book, *Blood Struggle,* Charles Wilkinson says that the Indian self-determination movement is as important to U.S. history as the civil rights movement, although the Indian movement is by far less well known.

Many believe that tribal governments cannot exercise meaningful self-government unless they develop market economies. Government programs have encouraged economic development in Indian country with mixed success, and the current Indian gaming industry fills the gap to a certain extent but is unevenly distributed across Indian country. The U.S. federal court system has upheld treaties and tribal sovereignty issues enough to create a de facto Indian government within the federal system of state, national, and local governments, but it is based on treaties, legal decisions, and congressional policy. While in recent decades the congressional and judicial branches of the U.S. government have become less attentive to Indian aspirations for greater self-government and culturally based institution building, Indian communities have sought to define and protect their rights and are seeking to strengthen traditional and American-based tribal governments.

Relatively little attention in Indian country has been given to police regimes and justice issues, and if tribal communities are going to become whole again, they need to manage their own forms of justice, police, and court systems. In many ways, Indians have been classified as an ethnic group, and crime statistics are often cited without regard to reservation or cultural context. Indians show disproportionate rates of imprisonment, substance abuse, victimization from violent crimes, and other signs of social distress. The chapters in this book outline many of these issues; introduce concepts of colonization and criminalization of culture that help explain more effectively the nature of life and justice on Indian reservations; provide a starting point for the explanation of crime on reservations and policies for change; and develop new possibilities for strengthening tribal self-government and community accountability.

Max Weber, the German sociologist, makes a classic definition of the state as the institution that controls the legitimate use of force. Do tribal governments manage the legitimate use of force on reservations? In many states where Public Law 280 (PL 280) prevails, often the legitimate use of force is exercised by state police and courts, and the tribal governments have little input. Similarly, in non–PL 280 reservations, where federal and tribal law prevails, Bureau of Indian Affairs (BIA) police and often courts are not administered by or responsible to tribal governments. Many tribes have sought to gain management of courts and police through 638 contracting. And in many cases, tribes with successful gaming casinos have moved to establish and support more police officers, not only to protect casino patrons but also to provide greater service and protection to reservation tribal members. The gaming tribes, however, have been less willing to establish courts, at least in the American style.

Similarly, the French sociologist Emile Durkheim, in his book on the division of labor, commented that government is not about efficiency but is mainly concerned with the management and distribution of justice. In order to establish self-government, tribal governments need to restore the power of the legitimate use of force and accountability and concentrate on the management of justice in their communities. Ever since the Crow Dog ex parte case and the resulting Major Crimes Act of the mid-1880s, the federal government and U.S. courts have restricted Indian control and management of justice within reservation communities. Tribal institution building has to be more than economic development and legal negotiation over jurisdiction with the federal government; it must also include the culturally informed administration of justice within the tribal community. Tribal governments have been restricted from exercising justice and most likely will not be able to heal their communities from present-day social and criminal depression without exercising legitimate force, greater cultural and community control over the administration of justice, and accountability to the reservation community over issues of police protection and service. Communities that do not have control over their institutions of justice and are subject to external, colonial, and culturally incompatible control show higher rates of alienation, anomie, lawlessness, and criminality. Without solving the sovereignty and management of justice in Indian country, Indian people will continue to show relatively high rates of crime, imprisonment, substance abuse, and other signs of social disruption. The path to tribal sovereignty is not easy, but the administration of justice must be one major element combined with legal, political, and economic development. Without growing economies, effective tribal governments, and tribally accountable administration of justice, there is little hope of creating wholesome tribal communities.

Native Americans and the Criminal Justice System: Theoretical and Policy Directions explores the cultural, colonized, and tribal sovereignty issues of criminal justice in Indian country. The chapters reflect recent and changing directions in understanding law and criminality on Indian reservations. There is relative little systematic literature on this important subject, and much of it has been done with relatively little attention to issues of tribal sovereignty and culture. The collection presents summaries of past criminal behavior and significant new cultural and political contextualizations that provide greater understanding of the complex effects of sovereignty, culture, and colonization on crime and criminalization on Indian reservations.

Duane Champagne
University of California at Los Angeles

Preface and Acknowledgments

Why would two scholars of European ancestry take on a project that involved Native American issues? Each of us has taken a bit different path to this end.

Jeff: From an early age, I felt an affinity for Native American history and culture. As a college student at the University of Toronto, and working as a part-time reporter for the *Toronto Clarion,* I learned about native people's issues and their plight. When I attended graduate school in Colorado, I quickly received both a scholarly and an activist introduction to Native American politics and how they play out in real-life contexts. Later, as an assistant professor at the University of Lethbridge in the early 1990s, I lived in a community with a large number of First Nations people. I taught Native American students, periodically socialized with native peoples, and attended a considerable number of powwows and other Native American cultural events. In these diverse contexts, which ranged from the classroom to the community at large, I was routinely exposed to the daily problems facing native peoples.

In this milieu, there are a number of experiences that I will never forget. It seemed that almost every night a police paddy wagon would appear in the small city park in an effort to arrest the ostensibly harmless "drunken Indians" who were spending the night there. I observed countless legal proceedings where native people were charged and routinely convicted of minor offenses because they were not equipped with an attorney who could provide an adequate defense. In the dead of winter, I recall picking up native hitchhikers and wondering how long they had been waiting in the bitter cold before being helped by a stranger. These memories speak to the injustices that Native Americans experience on a daily basis in Indian Country.

While in Lethbridge, I began to research and lecture on the role of Native Americans in violent protest, but it was not until 1996—when I was working for the National Institute of Justice—that my writings finally crystallized into what became the basis for this book. While at the Department of Justice, I began to outline this book and struggled to find resources to get it done. For a variety of reasons, ranging from personal to academic, it has taken me nine years to bring this project to a close. In the end it is something worth the wait, because I believe this is the most comprehensive book on the subject.

Larry: Whether it was marching in civil rights parades, fighting for gay and lesbian rights, seeking social justice for those who are oppressed, or (in my youth) standing up to Klan members in the South, I have always felt the need to speak out or at least create a venue for others to speak out on human rights. For the last thirteen years, I have been immersed in the native culture of the Southwest. I did not do this because it was the politically correct thing, because it has been a fad among some researchers of late, or because it was convenient. I did it because there is an unfilled need for which I might be able to provide some small amount of resources and knowledge. It is interesting to note that of the major academic meetings held each year, only the Western Social Science Association has a large number of sessions (fifteen to twenty sessions over a three day period) committed to Native American issues. The subject is largely ignored by other associations including the American Society of Criminology, the Academy of Criminal Justice Sciences, the American Sociological Association, and the American Political Science Association.

As this book is a collective enterprise, we offer both our joint words of thanks and a few individual ones. This project has been a long time in coming, in part as a result of trying to expound on the native voice rather than simply finding generalists who could write in this area. We must give credit to our contributors who stuck with us for so long; scholarly publishing is often full of surprises, and this manuscript is no exception.

Our expression of thanks for this collection also extends to the people who were willing to share their stories, to the individuals who have suffered for no other reason than because somebody with greater power could make them suffer, and to the people who have strived to make things a little better in Indian Country. Our gratitude also extends to the people who collected and compiled these stories. We recognize that it is not easy working, conducting research in, and/or living in Indian Country.

Additionally, we give thanks to Catherine Leidemer, who performed an initial copyedit of this manuscript, and to Kim Berger for keying in the majority of the edits. We are also thankful to Dean Birkenkamp, a truly enlightened publisher, for finding exceptional merit in this project, and to his team, including Melanie Stafford and Alison Sullenberger, who shepherded it through the production and marketing process, respectively. We also thank our anonymous reviewers for their careful read of the manuscript and Jon Resh for an excellent cover.

Jeff expresses his gratitude to Larry Gould and to Marianne Nielsen. Larry stepped up to the plate at a critical point in time to marshal that extra energy that was necessary. He has a work schedule and style that jived really nicely with Jeff's. And Marianne has been in the background as a virtual cheerleader and adviser of sorts.

Jeff also extends his thanks to his wife, Natasha J. Cabrera, who provided encouragement and feedback at several critical times, and to his children, Keanu and Dakota, who tolerated their father's divided attention more times than necessary.

Larry would like to specifically acknowledge the impact of Marianne Nielsen and Linda Robyn, who in their very different ways have contributed significantly to this work in terms of moral support. He would also like to thank Dorothy Fulton, head of the Department of Public Safety at the Navajo Nation; Daniel Benally, captain of investigation (retired) at the Navajo Police Department; Thomas Yazzie, Criminal Investigations Supervisor with the Navajo Nation Divison of Public Safety; Freddie Miller, Navajo Peacemakers Division; and Phil Bluehouse, Navajo Peacemakers Division (retired) for taking the time and effort to guide him as he learned more about Indian Country.

I

Introduction

I

Native Americans, Criminal Justice, Criminological Theory, and Policy Development

Jeffrey Ian Ross and Larry Gould

The study of law, justice, and criminal justice issues in Indian Country is complex and laden with cultural, economic, emotional, political, and social undertones that are bound in a deeply rooted historical context. In order to understand the relationship between the Native American and the U.S. criminal justice system (typically law enforcement, courts, corrections, and juvenile justice), it is necessary to appreciate the complexities of the European approach to deviance, justice, and social control. In short, the European system rests on punishment and retribution, whereas the Native American more often relies on cooperation and consensus building. One must also recognize the changing Native American responses to these processes, both before and after their contact with Europeans.

In their discussion of the fundamentally different concepts of sovereignty in European-based development and Native American tradition, Menno Boldt and J. Anthony Long (1984: 537–547) identify European-based concepts such as authority, hierarchy, and ruling entity as conflicting with the Native American concepts of spiritual compact, tribal will, and customary/traditional worldview. This systemic conflict sets the stage for both individual and organizational conflict, particularly among those native peoples who must work in both the native and European-based legal systems and cultures (Gould, 2002).

These conflicts are based on two very different ways of approaching these concepts and processes, which in their most basic characteristics are fundamentally at odds with each other. Even the briefest review of the literature suggests a constant attempt on the part of many Europeans to oppress, control, forcefully assimilate, and in many cases eliminate Native Americans through the creation and use of European-based laws (Boldt and Long, 1984: 537–547; Gould, 1998a; 1998b). The result, in most instances, was the criminalization of various native behaviors that were acceptable or controlled through different means prior to colonization along with the disruption of family structures and traditional tribal controls over individuals. Additionally, when Native Americans attempted to protect their rights and stand up for their traditional ways, this behavior was also criminalized.

The relationship between Native Americans and local, state/provincial, and federal branches of the criminal justice system is in a constant state of flux, often resulting in conflict and misunderstanding. This outcome has to do with the deeply rooted religious and spiritual underpinnings on which the various European and native cultures are based. Also in conflict is the two sides' basic understanding of the nature of human beings and their relationship with one another. European culture is rooted in the predominant belief of the superiority of one people over another, with the winners of the conflict being able to force their superiority on the losers. The status of Native American tribes, in terms of the view the U.S. government has of them, seems to change constantly, varying from attempting to assimilate all native peoples to considering them as sovereign nations, from treatment of a geographic tribal area as one nation to requiring the allotment of land to individuals of the tribe. This treatment may result from a feeling of superiority that Europeans have long held over other cultures and societies. This attitude is directly traceable to and can account in large part for the relationship between the U.S. government and the various tribes, as well as the position of Native Americans in the criminal justice system. This includes the enactment of laws by the federal and state governments that negatively affect Native Americans, whose treatment of natives as noncitizens, incorrect interpretations of intent on both sides, racism, and differing and sometimes conflictual definitions of terms such as justice, sovereignty, spirituality, religion, and self-determination.

Many of the problems faced by Native Americans as they come into conflict with European-based justice—the basic foundation of U.S. justice—can be traced to the "Discovery Doctrine" (Jennings, 1975; and Washburn, 1988; Wilkins and Lomawaima, 2001; Williams, 1990; 1991). This approach, finding its origins in Aristotle's *Politics*, was formalized in the late eleventh century and was based on "starkly prejudiced European religious and cultural biases, rather than on equitable or 'just' international laws" (Utter, 2001). Aristotle (384 to 322 B.C.) suggested that there are those who need to be ruled by their rational betters. This certainly seems to have been the philosophy and policy of early European colonists, as well as their descendants. Jack Utter (2001) provides a more comprehensive illustration of the "Discovery Doctrine," but simply stated, it is the institutionalized superiority of one people over another. The doctrine practiced by Europeans from the moment of first contact was formalized in *Johnson v. McIntosh* (1823):

> The United States, then, have unequivocally acceded to that great and broad rule by which its civilized inhabitants now hold this country. They hold, and assert in themselves, the title by which it was acquired. They maintain, as all others have maintained, that discovery gave an exclusive right to extinguish the Indian title of occupancy, either by purchase or by conquest: and gave also a right to such a degree of sovereignty [over Indians and their land], as the circumstances of the people [of the United States] would allow them to exercise. (*Johnson v. McIntosh*, 1823, 21 U.S. 543)

The Wheeler-Howard Indian Reorganization Bill (1934), which would have created separate Indian courts and self-governing communities that were empowered to make their own law and make contracts with the federal and state governments, was vehemently opposed by leading missionary groups and other advocates who favored assimilation by "civilizing" and "Christianizing" Native Americans. The missionaries were probably acting on their racist feelings of superiority based in their own religion and heritage. The halls of Congress and the Bureau of Indian Affairs have repeatedly resounded with debates over the protection of Native Americans' civil rights, as well as debates over the restoration of traditional culture versus assimilation. Much of the conflict began to come to a head just prior to and after World War II, although native participation in the war presented its own set of problems.

During World War II there was much debate over the idea of Native Americans being drafted. The military needed cannon fodder, but to this point Native Americans had been denied many of the basic rights given to other peoples living within the continental United States. At that time most Native Americans could not vote, particularly those in New Mexico and Arizona. One young Paiute from Utah complained to the federal government in Washington, "The gent here is signing up all the young boys in the Army.... The young Indian boys aren't citizens and they don't buy whiskey.... We wanted to know if all of us Indian boys are going to fight for the white people." A Mississippi Choctaw chief argued that his tribe "never vote or pay poll tax. The whites here say we not allowed to vote.... If we are not citizens, will it be right for Choctaws to go to war?"(Bernstein, 1991).

In another story—one that reflects the paternalistic ways in which those of European heritage have treated Native Americans—shared with one of the editors, a young Native American woman wanted to sell some of her calves. She had to apply to the secretary of the interior for permission to make the sale. The sale was approved after about three years, but by then the calves were cattle.

Even after the Indian Citizenship Act of 1924, a number of states continued to prohibit Native Americans from voting. The states' legal arguments were (1) that Indians were "under guardianship" and therefore not competent to vote or (2) that Indians were not residents of the states in which they lived if they resided on reservations (Bernstein, 1991). The last states to fully extend voting rights to Indians were Arizona (1948), Maine (1954), Utah (1956), and New Mexico (1962) (Utter, 2001).

Another provocative issue in the relationship between Native Americans and the U.S. government, and one that relates to crime and the criminal justice system, involves the lingering effects of the boarding schools. If one assumes that stability in the family structure has a positive impact that serves to decrease criminality, boarding schools have had a particularly destructive influence on the children that attended and fostered increases in their criminality (Unger, 1977). Although the following quote from "Kid Catching" on the Navajo Reservation might not be directly related to the subject matter of this book, it does provide a poignant example of the attitude of the government and its representatives toward Native Americans.

> I am making a brief statement of my experience with what I consider the greatest shame of the Indian Service (BIA)—the rounding up of Indian children to be sent away to government schools. ... Stockmen, Indian police, and other mounted men are sent ahead [of the trucks] to round them up. The children are caught, often roped like cattle, and taken away from their parents, many times never to return. (in Unger, 1977, unnamed respondent)

There is little doubt that this type of treatment—the removal of a whole generation of people from their respective communities—has had a long-lasting impact on crime and criminality in Indian Country. As a result of this experience, many Native Americans developed institutionalized personalities, lost touch with family and their tribes, and were never prepared for life either on or off the reservation (Dumont, 1996a).

Yet another issue concerns sovereignty and its implementation and practice. At its most basic level, sovereignty means separateness. Any action by the county, state, or federal governments that threatens the autonomy of an Indian nation also impacts the sovereignty of the tribal government and thus the rights of Indian people. Common threats result from the suppression of culture, assimilative education, assimilative tribal government structures, destructive federal legislation, damaging state and federal court decisions, the loss of native language, and the acceptance of capitalism as the primary worldview to the exclusion of tribalism (Utter, 2001). Sovereignty also means the inherent right to or power of self-government. Indeed, sovereignty is a complex construct. Tribal sovereignty is closely related to tribal self-determination in terms of economic, political, legal, and cultural matters and not only guides how tribes interact with external systems but is also constrained by those systems.

Although each of the issues addressed above and many more not covered by scholars have had an impact on both the criminal justice system and the Native Americans who pass through or use it, the underlying causes of the conflicts are predominantly cultural. For example, something as seemingly simple as developing a common set of definitions for the discussion of native versus European systems of social control can set the stage for much debate and conflict. In their discussion of the fundamentally different concepts of sovereignty in European-based development and Native American tradition, Boldt and Long (1984: 537–547) identify European-based concepts such as authority, hierarchy, and ruling entity as conflicting with the Native American concepts of spiritual compact, tribal will, and customary/traditional worldview.

This systemic conflict sets the stage for both individual and organizational conflict (Gould, 2000; 2002) between two general types of legal systems: adjudicatory justice (in this case, the crime control model) and restorative justice. The European-based concepts of authority, hierarchy, and power differ fundamentally from the Native American concept of sovereignty or responsible and egalitarian government social control. The European system is most often based on the use of power and authority, involving adversarial methods of coercion and force to control the behavior of individuals (Yazzie, 1994), whereas the foundation for most native-based systems results from a healing process (Gould, 2000).

The specific points of conflict, according to Boldt and Long (1984), stem from the European concept of authority based on a belief in the inherent inequality of human beings. Adding to the conflict with Native American systems of justice and social control are the concepts of personal authority, hierarchical relationships, and a separate ruling entity, all based on European thought (Dumont, 1996b). In European-based societies, individual autonomy is regarded as the foundation for the successful acquisition of private property and achievement through competitive pursuits. Social control in terms of authority is deemed necessary to protect society against rampant individual self-interest; thus authoritative power is essential to maintain the integrity of a sovereign society. In this worldview, hierarchical power structures are necessary to ensure the distribution of privileges and the maintenance of order from the most authoritative to the most powerless (Brown, 1982; Dumont, 1993).

Furthermore, the adversarial approach to resolving issues on which the European system is based puts the different parties in a conflictual relationship. This is the kind of system that was imposed upon Indian nations toward the close of the nineteenth century. In traditional Native American society, self-interest is inextricably intertwined with tribal interest (Boldt and Long, 1984; Brown, 1982; Dumont, 1993). One of the strongest tenets of European-based forms of social control is the social contract, a concept of how authorities might more humanely exercise the right to govern others and devise egalitarian methods of extending authoritative rule from the ruler to the ruled (Rousseau, 1762/1998). In traditional native societies, it is believed that no human being rightfully has control over the life of another (Boldt and Long, 1984). According to native belief, social control has been viewed as a "spiritual compact, while the European-based means of social control derive from personal authority, hierarchical relationship and the concept of a separate ruling entity" (Boldt and Long, 1984; Dumont, 1993). As noted by James Dumont (1996b), European and native differences in the basic understanding of justice have had profound implications for the relationship of Native Americans to the justice system imposed upon them by European settlers and their descendants.

The impact of these numerous conflicts are evidenced in the simple fact that "native peoples are overrepresented in the criminal justice system statistics in the United States and Canada.... Native people, who make up 15.6 percent of the population of the state of Alaska ... actually make up 31 percent of that state's prison population" (U.S. Department of Justice, 1993). In other states, "the over-representation is less dramatic, being concentrated in specific categories such as substance abuse–related crime.... Furthermore, in some states, native offenders are not only overrepresented in terms of their numbers in prison but also receive longer sentences and serve more of their sentence than any other group.... This situation is even more pronounced in Canada, where native peoples are the largest minority group (about 4 percent of the total population). Native peoples make up about 8 percent of the federal prison population and make up an average of 20 percent of the provincial prison populations" (Nielsen, 1996: 12–13).

Additionally, "native societies are still in the process of adapting to the cataclysmic changes that colonization by Europeans produced. As part of this adaptation, native peoples are developing innovative criminal justice (and other) services from which the dominant society could learn a great deal" (Nielsen, 1996: 12). Since the 1980s, a number of experiments in native criminal justice have been introduced. Some appear helpful, whereas others simply replace old, traditional European values. After September 11, 2001, and the tightness of state budgets in law enforcement, it is difficult to determine what sort of effects the war on terror may have on or how it may trickle down to native communities. With recent decisions in several important Supreme Court cases (*Chickasaw Nation v. United States* (Docket No. 00–50) 534 U.S. 84 (2001), *United States v. Navajo Nation* (Docket No. 01–1375) 263 F.3d 1325 (2003), *United States v. White Mountain Apache* (Docket No. 01–1067) (2003), the law in Indian Country continues to evolve.

Although a considerable amount of research has been conducted on Native Americans and the criminal justice system, it is generally unintegrated with both the general criminology and criminal justice literature, that on law and jurisprudence, or that in native studies. Granted, periodically this material appears in well-known criminology and criminal justice journals. Until recently, though, only a few books existed that were devoted to this subject matter.

OVERVIEW OF THE CHAPTERS

There are several reasons to study the relationship between Native Americans and the criminal justice system (e.g., Nielsen, 1996: 12–13; Snipp, 1989: 2–3). Perhaps the most important factors involve the study of the confluence of the two sometimes competing systems of social control along with the study of the causes of the overrepresentation of Native Americans in the justice system.

This book, containing sixteen chapters including the introduction and conclusion, incorporates the contributions of well-respected researchers, administrators, consultants, and activists. Many of these individuals have both field and academic experience covering the relationship of the major branches of the criminal justice system with Native American communities in the United States. At least half of the contributors are Native American, and the remainder of the authors have worked or lived in Indian Country and have gained the respect of the communities in which they conducted their research. The authors' academic credentials span many different disciplines, including political science, anthropology, sociology, criminology, criminal justice, Native American studies, and the law. They are noted for taking a critical stance on the subjects about which they write. This approach is often sadly lacking from previous research and edited collections.

The book is organized into four sections: an introduction; theoretical issues in the area of criminology, criminal justice, and Native Americans; contemporary policy issues; and a conclusion. The contributors examine the four major branches of criminal justice: the courts, police, corrections, and juvenile justice. The book's goal is to be more theoretical and policy-oriented than other currently available readers (e.g., Nielsen and Silverman, 1992) or out of print readers (French, 1982a; Nielsen and Silverman, 1996) in order to complement and not necessarily compete with them. It also tries to avoid case studies and aims at more general issues and processes that native communities in Canada and the United States have in common. *Native Americans and the Criminal Justice System: Theoretical and Policy Directions* will be accessible to students, scholars, and the general public.

Much can be learned from Native American culture by studying its interaction with the criminal justice system, particularly in the areas of critical/radical criminology (e.g., Ross, 1998), restorative justice (Utter, 2001), violent crime (e.g., Gurr, 1998; Ross, 2004/1995), and state crime (e.g., Ross, 2000a/1995; 2000b). As others before us have suggested, the problem of Native Americans and the criminal justice system cannot be understood without taking into consideration other important factors affecting the lives of native peoples, such as "political power, land, economic development, and individual despair" (Nielsen, 1996: 10).

THEORETICAL ISSUES IN THE AREA OF NATIVE AMERICANS AND CRIMINAL JUSTICE

This section encompasses chapters that examine old or new (emerging) theoretical perspectives on Native Americans and the criminal justice system. It is intended to widen the readers' knowledge with respect to interpreting the relationship in this subject area.

In Chapter 2, "Navajo Criminal Justice: A Jungian Perspective," by Marilyn Holly, the Navajo concept of *hozho* is reviewed. *Hozho* relates closely to the Navajo philosophy or metaphysics of nature and provides a guide for the goals of the criminal justice system as related to Navajo healing methods. Justice, as the goal of the Navajo Peacemaker Courts, is seen as restoring an offender's harmony with the community (where the community includes not only humans but also the creatures and entities of nature), as well as restoring his or her own inner harmony. Appropriate restitution to the victim(s) is a desideratum, and this restitution has to be agreed upon by all those affected by the offense and must be in accord with traditional Navajo values. The restitution is kept track of by all those concerned.

The concept of *hozho* lends itself fruitfully to a Jungian interpretation about the relations of the individual to the community and to nature, as well as to his or her own internal integration. The concept of *hozho,* after being given a philosophical and practical explanation in Holly's chapter, is then interpreted from a Jungian perspective. Both Jung's and the Navajos' conception of "evil" are discussed as having something in common. The relevant traditional Navajo personal and community values are considered, as are the effects brought about by urbanization on the values of some Navajos who later return to the reservation. The chapter also includes an evaluation of whether and to what extent Navajo Peacemaker Court methods could be successfully adapted to the mainstream criminal justice system.

Dorothy H. Bracey, in Chapter 3, "Criminalizing Culture: An Anthropologist Looks at Native Americans and the U.S. Legal System," examines crime among Native Americans. She says it can be explained through standard criminological theories, but only when the elements of these explanations are interpreted in light of their particular cultural and historical circumstances. Chapter 3 examines the legal and social histories of several attempts to weaken or destroy important aspects of Indian culture, primarily religion, family, and community justice. The irony of these past and continuing efforts at assimilation is that they have criminalized those very institutions that best control crime and deviant behavior.

In Chapter 4, "Justice as Phoenix: Traditional Indigenous Law, Restorative Justice, and the Collapse of the State," James W. Zion examines the rise of restorative justice and the rebirth of traditional indigenous justice. He examines why the two movements have spontaneously emerged, linking the emergence of the two movements to the collapse of the state (or its irrelevance in modern life). He compares the two movements to the mythical phoenix, rising from the ashes of the state, and describes the rise of parallel movements. The chapter also discusses their directions, highlights similarities and differences, and proposes a relationship model of the two movements as voluntary alternatives to state adjudication, power, and force.

Chapter 5, "The Link between Environmental Policy and the Colonization Process and Its Effects on American Indian Involvement in Crime, Law, and Society," written by Lynda Robyn and Thom Alcoze, argues that native people as a whole have been denied equal access to economic power in the past throughout the United States and Canada. Indigenous peoples have not been included in decisionmaking concerning the environmental impact of corporate intrusion upon their lands. This fact is changing, and today, native peoples are calling for inclusion by challenging the most powerful institutions across the North American continent through a critical perspective on power and control.

The loss of power and autonomy through the process of colonialism has relegated indigenous peoples to a position on the lower end of the hierarchical scale in society. It comes as no surprise, then, that indigenous knowledge and perspectives have been ignored and denigrated in the past by colonial powers and through contemporary government policies that sought to exploit indigenous resources. Today, indigenous knowledge is emerging as a mechanism to empower and decolonize the dynamics of Native American communities. Contemporary research in a wide array of academic fields demonstrates that indigenous peoples and their cultures represent examples of highly developed social and environmental knowledge. Chapter 5 illustrates positive and effective ways to open a new era of research into and understanding of how to enhance criminal, social, and environmental justice systems.

CURRENT POLICY ISSUES AFFECTING NATIVE AMERICANS AND CRIMINAL JUSTICE

Section 3 consists of chapters that critically explore the effects of dominant criminal justice policy issues (e.g., prison, religious freedom in prisons, fishing and hunting rights, alcoholism and drugs, gangs, land claims, and discrimination) affecting Native Americans as they relate to or interact with the criminal justice system. This part strays from causal studies and looks more at the effects of these social and policy problems on the maintenance of and change in the various aspects of the criminal justice system. Each chapter takes a particular issue and traces its history, focusing primarily on the success and failure of trying to address the problem.

In Chapter 6, "Alcoholism, Colonialism, and Crime," Larry Gould argues that alcohol abuse influences the majority of crimes in the United States and that the impact of alcohol and crime is no less evident in Indian Country, particularly in intimate homicide and domestic abuse situations. Gould reviews the social, political, individual, cultural, and economic impact of alcohol on indigenous populations, which has had a long-term negative impact on the social structures of indigenous peoples. This research suggests that Europeans used alcohol not only as a means of profit but also as a tool of colonialization and subjugation. Gould also argues that, in some segments of the European-based population, alcohol continues to be used as a tool to demoralize, demean, and disenfranchise indigenous peoples. Generally, female prisoners are at particular risk because they have more intensive involvement with addictive drugs, and there are few specialized programs for women offenders who may have affective disorders and/or substance abuse problems. The author argues that these difficulties are highlighted for Native American women and discusses methods to solve this problem.

In Chapter 7, "Examining the Interpretation and Application of the Indian Child Welfare Act of 1978," Tracy M. Bouvier discusses the circumstances surrounding the implementation of the law, including the gross inequities that Native Americans have endured since Europeans first arrived on this continent. The express purpose of this federal legislation is the establishment of minimum federal standards in the removal of Native American children from their families to ensure that the best interests of the children are protected and, further, that the stability and security of Indian tribes and families are promoted (25 U.S.C. 1902). The chapter explores the interpretation, application, and overall compliance with this significant federal mandate.

Because state courts are charged with these responsibilities, court decisions involving the interpretation of this act vary from state to state. Chapter 7 focuses on the examination of decisions by Arizona state courts, presents a historical backdrop for the enactment of this legislation, and reviews federal policy standards in an attempt to gain an understanding of the spirit of the act and its intended purpose. Arizona case law is examined in this context to demonstrate the procedural and substantive interpretations of the act by Arizona courts and the impact of these interpretations on Native American tribes and families in Arizona. Finally, the chapter explores the implications of these findings, including the need for effective compliance strategies and the need for further research in this area.

In Chapter 8, "Law Enforcement and the American Indian: Challenges and Obstacles to Effective Law Enforcement," Eileen Luna and Samuel Walker point out how, subsequent to the passage of the Indian Self-Determination and Education Assistance Act, American Indian tribal governments have the opportunity to expand tribal sovereignty in important ways. Many tribes are using funds obtained directly from the federal government to develop and implement tribal law enforcement services. Tribal governments and law enforcement personnel must operate within a legal minefield and a jurisdictional maze. They must be successfully negotiated, however, if tribal sovereignty and essential services to Indian tribal members are to be advanced through the assertion of police authority.

Chapter 9, Jeffrey Ian Ross's "Policing Native Americans Off the Rez" is the companion piece to the previous chapter. It reviews the relationship between police and Native Americans in large U.S. cities. Ross explains the subject's importance, outlines the paucity of academic and policy research, and reviews the results from a questionnaire he distributed. He also examines potential areas for future research to address how to improve municipal policing for Native Americans.

In Chapter 10, "Imprisonment and American Indian Medicine Ways: A Comparative Analysis of Conflicting Cultural Beliefs, Values, and Practices," William Archambeault suggests that the totalitarian nature of prisons in the United States creates an alien environment in which to conduct traditional Native American healing ceremonies that evolved over many millennia in the freedom of the woodlands, plains, deserts, and mountains of "Turtle Island" (a native American term to explain the world). Yet, where permitted, mentors and medicine people from many different Native American cultural traditions are attempting to bring the healing ways and teachings of their ancestors to native prisoners. Even under the best of circumstances, in which prison officials and religious coordinators try to accommodate native healing traditions in the prison structure, antithetical differences exist between native and prison management subcultures. These differences negatively affect the delivery of traditional healing ceremonies to confined inmates. Chapter 10 presents a schema for analyzing and understanding some of these critical differences. It also discusses the types of traditional ceremonies that might be found in prisons, as well as those that are normally banned.

In Chapter 11, "Criminalization of the Treaty Right to Fish: Response to the Great Lakes Chippewa," Linda Robyn argues that lands ceded to the U.S. government by the Chippewa in the Treaty of 1837 guaranteed the continued privilege of hunting, fishing, and gathering wild rice upon the lands, rivers, and lakes included in the territory area. But as non-Indians began to move into ceded territory that was previously home to the Chippewa, it became increasingly easier to restrict their hunting and fishing rights. As the government exercised its paternalistic powers over the Chippewa, treaty rights that promised the continuance of fishing, hunting, and gathering were severely eroded.

The political assault against Indian treaties began in 1973, when two Chippewa men were arrested for ice fishing on off-reservation waters. With this arrest, the knowledge and methods of hunting and fishing passed down from elders through the ages became criminalized, and the Chippewa were punished for continuing their traditions. This chapter outlines the *Voigt* decision reaffirming Chippewa treaty rights and the ensuing intense racial hostilities that pitted whites against Indians both in court and at the boat landings with the beginning of each new fishing season every spring.

Chapter 12, "Indian Gaming and the American Indian Criminal Justice System," by Nicholas C. Peroff, argues that although there has been limited interest in a relationship between Indian gaming and American Indian criminal justice, one exception is a growing amount of research that has sought to explore possible associations between Indian casinos and criminal behavior, both on Indian reservations and in adjacent, non-Indian communities. Chapter 12 reviews the available literature on the relationship between Indian gaming and the criminal justice system, offers some insight into what American Indians themselves think about possible linkages between casinos and crime within their communities, and concludes with a consideration of the mixed positive and negative impacts of Indian gaming and their connection to criminal justice in Indian Country.

In Chapter 13, "Research on Juvenile Delinquency in Indian Communities: Resisting Generalization," by Lisa Bond-Maupin, Taka X. GoodTracks, and James R. Maupin, the authors outline how early researchers on American Indians and crime concluded, based largely on off-reservation arrests for public drunkenness, that Indian peoples were disproportionately criminal. Recently, due to the publication of a national study entitled *American Indians and Crime* (Bureau of Justice Statistics, 1999), newspapers in the United States have suggested that crime in "Indian Country" is out of control. This study primarily uses off-reservation data and focuses on interpersonal violence. Consequently, its conclusions are limited as a source of information about crime by Indian peoples, given that (1) the majority of Native Americans reside on or near reservations, (2) most of the violence in the report is perpetrated by non-Indians, and (3) Indian populations are younger overall than the rest of the U.S. population. Also, little information is provided about youths and crime.

In Chapter 13, the authors examine research on crime and American Indian youths, utilizing reservation-based data and providing a case study of juvenile delinquency in a western reservation not previously studied. Their data do not support the national picture of a rise in crime or violence by Indian youths. They discuss the results in the context of the limitations of national studies and argue that culturally specific, community-based, collaborative research will yield meaningful information about Indian youths' involvement in crime. They also point out that this research will provide tribes and nations with more relevant information for self-governance and policymaking.

In Chapter 14, "Recent Trends in Community-Based Strategies for Dealing with Juvenile Crime in the Navajo Nation," by Marianne O. Nielsen, Dorothy Fulton, and Ivan Tsosie, the authors argue that although juvenile crime in the rest of the country has been dropping, in many Native American communities, the rate of crime by juveniles has been rising steadily. Unfortunately, the Navajo Nation is no exception. Although data on Native American delinquency are difficult to collect, the data presented here are collected directly from the files of the Navajo Nation Department of Criminal Investigation. The chapter provides an overview of crime by Navajo Nation youth and describes some of the innovative strategies that have been developed to prevent crime and recidivism. These new strategies focus on providing culturally knowledgeable and sensitive services to youth, their families, and the community.

In Chapter 15, "Scattered Like Reindeer: Alaska Natives and the Loss of Autonomy," by Nella Lee, the author outlines how the indigenous peoples of Alaska have been subordinated to the dominant Western sociocultural/legal system. Once autonomous and fully self-sufficient groups with little historically recorded crime, most native peoples in Alaska have become victims of violent crime and suicide—most of which is linked to alcohol. Rural villages are in a state of social disorganization, that is the result of state policies stemming from colonialism. Lee discusses remedies to the current situation, as well as the political ramifications of state policy.

Finally, in Chapter 16, "Integrating the Past, Present, and Future," by Larry Gould and Jeffrey Ian Ross, the authors summarize the diverse threads of literature and thoughts that have been woven throughout the book. They focus on neglected topics, enduring dilemmas, the integration and adoption of technology, funding, blind spots, and the ownership of the problem.

II

Theoretical Issues in the Area of Native Americans and Criminal Justice

2

Navajo Criminal Justice: A Jungian Perspective

Marilyn Holly

Although the Navajos and other Indian peoples have been given U.S. federal approval to run their own tribal courts for close to a century, the Navajo tribal courts are said to have been able to maintain traditional values to a greater extent than has been the case with tribal courts in many other American Indian nations (Yazzie, 1994). The Navajo tribal courts have been more resistant to assimilation of non-Navajo conceptions and methods of criminal justice.

However, until the early 1980s a Western "vertical" model of justice prevailed in principle in Navajo tribal courts. According to the present chief justice of the Navajo Supreme Court (Yazzie, 1994), a vertical system of justice is adversarial and is based on a win-lose model. One party is "bad" and wrong; the other party is "good" and right. Vertical justice relies on hierarchies, coercive power, and punishment. Judges have more authority and power in judicial settings than do lawyers, jurors, or any of the other participants. The parties have limited power and control and must obey the judges' decisions. Emotions are not allowed to be expressed. Underlying problems are not addressed, and the needs and feelings of victims are often ignored. There are many victims of a crime, including family, relatives, and the community. The perpetrator may be a victim too, of lost hope, alcohol, and other means of escaping problems.

The traditional Navajo model of justice was and is "horizontal"; that is, no person is above another. Victim, offender, and all those affected by the crime discuss the situation, express their feelings, get to the underlying problems, and arrive at a consensus about what compensation would restore good harmony to all concerned. A respected elder reminds participants of Navajo values, and prayers are addressed to the divinities for guidance. Moral fault, guilt, and punishment are not a part of horizontal justice, and a win-win model is used in which the focus is on ensuring well-being for everyone. The horizontal model of justice is related to healing, and many of the principles are the same (Yazzie, 1994).

Since the vertical model was difficult for traditional Navajo people to understand, it afforded little satisfaction or else was contravened in actual practice quietly for fear that the mainstream adversarial system would try to eliminate or change it. But in 1982, the Judicial Conference of the Navajo Nation created what is called the Navajo Peacemaker Court method of "horizontal" conflict resolution. It incorporates the traditional horizontal model into the vertical model; a district tribal judge can now avoid adjudication by referring cases to a peacemaker court for the traditional Navajo method of conflict resolution, which is known as the Navajo Peacemaker Court Healing and Justice Ceremony (Yazzie, 1994).

To understand something about the Navajo Peacemaker Court way of conflict resolution, it is important to consider Navajo philosophy. This discussion, in addition to a survey of the Navajo method and goal of healing, will help us to see how Navajo justice is a form of healing. Additionally, this chapter will show how some Jungian ideas can be applied in interpreting Navajo concepts relevant to healing.

CENTRAL NAVAJO VALUES AND THE METHOD AND GOAL OF NAVAJO HEALING

Witherspoon points to *hozho* as both a key word and the central concept in Navajo culture (1974; 1975). A pair of Navajo concepts—*hozho* and its opposite, *hochxo*—are core elements in Navajo philosophy, healing, and justice and are used in everyday speech. In the concept of *hozho,* the stem *-zho* refers to harmony, beauty, order, good, and excellence. The prefix *ho* refers to the total environment, including other people. The stem and prefix together express everything that is favorable to humans in the way of well-being, order, and beautiful and harmonious living. The prefix *ho* can also occur with the stem *-chxo* in the term *hochxo* to signify an ugly, disharmonious, and disordered environment, including other people, that is bad and unfavorable to humans in the way of well-being, order, and harmony (Farella, 1984).

There has been a disagreement among commentators as to whether the terms *hozho* and *hochxo* refer to moral good and moral evil, respectively. For example, Gladys Reichard (1970) and Father Berard Haile (1982) have at times regarded the terms in this respect and have interpreted Navajo philosophy as incorporating a fundamental moral dualism in which moral good will eventually prevail. But more recent analyses by John Farella (1984) and Trudy Griffin-Pierce (1992) construe *hozho* and *hochxo* as something closer to aesthetic categories. Farella, in particular, asserts that Western notions of moral good and evil, as incorporating ideas of the presence or absence of guilt, have little relevance or use in the worldview of Navajo people, although this does not imply that Navajo people are not guided by standards of appropriate and worthwhile conduct. Griffin-Pierce, who had the advantage of living for a time with a Navajo family as an adolescent, as well as later doing extensive fieldwork with the Navajo people, agrees with Farella on these points.

I am persuaded by Farella and Griffin-Pierce that the ascription to the Navajo worldview of a good/evil dualism involving Western Judeo-Christian ideas about the presence or absence of guilt is not an accurate way of interpreting Navajo healing and Navajo justice. But to substitute so-called aesthetic categories for Western guilt-based categories does not seem to me to aid in understanding Navajo healing and Navajo justice.

I shall offer what seems to me to be a preferable Jungian interpretation of *hozho* and *hochxo*. In this latter interpretation, one can construe "good" as describing that which is beneficial to human personal or social well-being or health. I argue later that we can retain the idea of the good/evil dualism as characterizing Navajo thought. Yet, this good/evil dualism does not for Navajos involve Western ideas of guilt or sin on the part of human agents. The Navajo idea of moral responsibility and legal accountability for and rectification of misdeeds can and does make sense in the latter view.

The question of how to interpret *hozho* and *hochxo* becomes very important when we try to understand the traditional goals of Navajo healing and Navajo justice. The goal of Navajo healing is to help the patient achieve physical and/or psychological *hozho*. The goal of Navajo justice is also to achieve *hozho* within the psyche of an agent of socially disruptive action, between such an agent and the victim, and between the agent and his or her community. *Hozho* is not a fixed, or permanent, state. The Navajo worldview is one of process in which change is always taking place (Griffin-Pierce, 1992), and a person must constantly adapt to it. This process-oriented philosophy of change may have been derived in part from frequent changes—some very traumatic changes—in Navajo history and may have contributed to their success in adapting as a people to these changes.

Psychological as well as external factors have contributed to the rise in crime on the Navajo reservation. According to Nathanson (1992), the feeling continuum of shame-humiliation is brought about in persons whose positive feelings are interrupted by external causes when this is accompanied by social assumptions in which the victim is seen by self and others as shameful and unworthy. Nathanson describes four ways in which the victim can deal with shame-humiliation, including an "attack self" mode, withdrawal, an "attack other" mode, and the use of alcohol as a temporary shame-avoiding technique (a "shame avoider"). "It is in the cultures that are the most affected by shame that we see the greatest amount of personality change with alcohol," he says (Nathanson, 1992: 356).

The deeply traumatic experiences of the Navajos who were incarcerated in Fort Sumner for four years in the 1860s, as well as their later experiences connected with the U.S. government's forcing an unwanted stock reduction program on them in the 1930s, brought about the massive interruption of positive affect and then led to a massive collapse of self-esteem (i.e., shame-humiliation). These events can be seen as playing an important role in the rise of crime (the "attack other" mode of dealing with shame) and the use of alcohol (a "shame avoider"), which contributes to the rate at which individuals commit crimes. The Navajos have nevertheless shown resilience in maintaining their traditional aims and process of justice, despite many changes (both voluntary and forced) and many external and psychological problems.

Navajo moral values form the core of the present-day peacemaker courts, and are identified by John Ladd as follows: (1) knowledge, especially of patterns of nature's energy, including one's own and other people's energy patterns; (2) talking things over and thinking about them, especially in settling disputes, with no undeliberated action; (3) individuality, as in "let him decide it"; (4) attention to relationships and concomitant obligations ("he acts as if he has no relatives" is regarded as serious criticism); (5) prosperity, but not at the expense of others—don't get too rich; (6) harmony with others, with the environment, and within yourself; (7) reciprocity (you give as well as receive) and respect; (8) the cultivation of the virtues of honesty, truthfulness, sobriety, hard work, helpfulness to others, generosity, refraining from stealing; (9) compensation for wrongdoing, including appropriate payment in goods or services to the injured party; and, (10) care for yourself and your possessions. In addition, there are proscriptions of many acts that make people angry and provoke either retaliation by the victim and his or her friends or public disapproval. All this brings about disorder, or *hochxo*. Social disapproval is to be avoided. (Talking things over, by the way, is exemplified in the Navajo creation story.)

Father Berard Haile (1943) describes the traditional Navajo justice process as being under the guidance of a wise and respected elder, mentioning that such elders might convene with one another to reach agreement about general policies. The justice process is characterized as being one of persuasion rather than of force, aimed at a successful negotiation between offender and victim about recompense. Haile says that according to Navajos, we cannot truly know whether the inner soul of an offender is good or evil—for witchcraft or other unknown causes may have led to a misdeed—hence it is the misdeed itself that must be rectified by the offender. This gives Navajo justice a practical focus rather than a morally condemnatory orientation.

Since the Navajo criminal justice system is based on traditional Navajo moral values, this community's conception of legal accountability reflects its ideas about personal moral responsibility. There has been much erosion and loss of traditional Navajo moral ideology among many Navajo people today, causing loss of a sense of legal accountability for one's behavior. That one is responsible for one's own character development and deeds is easily lost sight of; it is easier to say and think that "everybody does this" or "somebody (or something) made me do this" (Yazzie, 1994; 1995; Zion, 1994a). The Navajo Peacemaker Courts in their educative function with respect to offender, victim, and all those concerned in a criminal case make use of the traditional philosophy. This helps people to sort out what they are responsible for morally and legally.

Maureen Schwartz's (1997) discussion of the Navajo principles of (1) *homology* (the belief in structural analogies between all creatures and entities, as well as their sharing in common the same elements of nature, albeit combined differently), (2) *complementarity* (the seeing of opposites and their interactions at work in human personality, as well as in the cosmos), and (3) *synecdoche* (the attribution of the effects of a whole to a part of the whole and vice versa) helps in understanding Navajo views about (1) the kinship of humans with all creatures and entities, (2) the workings of the opposites of *hozho* and *hochxo* in the human personality and the cosmos, and (3) the efficacy of healing ceremonies in which the event itself is seen as affecting and being affected by relevant energies of nature.

Further aspects of Navajo philosophy found in the myths, especially the creation story, are used in peacemaker courts to educate people about law. Law is seen in these myths as laid down in the very foundations of the natural creation and as absolute. The Navajo creation story includes a story about male twins who conquer dreadful and grotesque monsters who are destroying human beings. The twins overpower most of the monsters but cannot overcome at least two of them—one being old age and the other being poverty. For a long time, Navajos have bestowed metaphorical and psychological meaning upon the story of the conquest of the monsters, who nowadays are understood to denote such intrapsychic conditions as hatred, jealousy, ignorance due to bad socialization, inner conflict, denial of reality, attempts to minimize the importance of what one is doing to others, and the blaming of others for one's own faults. The peacemaker courts discuss and expose the influence of such metaphorical monsters on criminal offenders (Yazzie, 1995).

In the creation story or myth, human beings are instructed from the start by what the Navajos call the Holy People in what are considered by traditional Navajos to be absolute laws. These Holy People are not human beings; each one possesses special supernatural powers. Navajos view these powers not as dwelling in a remote realm far from humans but as near to us and aware of what we go through. Such beings include Navajo deities such as a creator figure or figures, Sun, Changing Woman (or earth), various heroes, and the trickster Coyote, as well as rocks, minerals, thunder, air, dawn, animals, and so on. Every type of creature and entity has its Holy People (Albanese, 1980; Griffin-Pierce, 1992). They are believed to have created absolute law, including the law about how humans can best achieve inward harmony as well as social harmony and harmony with nature. The absoluteness of the laws means that they are, for Navajos, not man-made, and they hold for all people at all times. These laws include respect for other people and for all creatures and entities of nature, reciprocity of obligations, and other fundamental laws that make it possible for individuals and society to attain a state of *hozho* (inner beauty, harmony, and order) as well as social beauty, harmony, and order. It is the Holy People that send little "messenger winds" to erring humans to warn them of their departure from these eternal and absolute laws (McNeley, 1981). The peacemaker court reacquaints those Navajos who commit crimes as a result of forgetting or losing their tradition with the absolute teachings of the Holy People that the creation myth describes.

If we do not give a guilt-based interpretation to *hozho* or *hochxo,* (harmony, order, and good as conducive to human well-being versus disharmony, disorder, and evil as inimical to human well-being), ought these "criminals" to be considered morally evil? We have previously seen that the Navajos have a concept of personal responsibility and accountability for one's character and one's deeds, but we have also seen that the Western notion of moral evil as incorporating the idea of guilt and punishment does not apply to crime in view of the Navajo connection between healing and justice. There is no term in the Navajo language that precisely expresses the Western idea of "guilt." Since the agent of crime is not adjudged to be morally guilty but rather is seen as needing healing, then instruction for the purpose of building the agent's knowledge of self and society, psychological rehabilitation as preventive of further offenses, [1] loving support from family and community, and sufficient restitution to the victim and his or her family to restore good feeling are seen as the appropriate goals for the Navajo criminal justice system, rather than jail or punishment. However, if the agent of the crime has done something that, if repeated, would constitute a danger to the community (e.g., murder), then this person must be isolated from the community.

In Farella's construction of *hozho* and *hochxo* as aesthetic categories mentioned earlier, the creator devised *hochxo* (disorder), or the possibility of it, from the beginning, in addition to creating *hozho* (order), or the possibility of it, from the start of creation. Humans would not grow in life wisdom and knowledge if these correlatives did not exist; thus it is unnecessary, according to Farella, to construe them as denoting a good/evil dualism involving a struggle between them. However, I do not think that an aesthetic/epistemological view of *hozho* and *hochxo* such as Farella develops is sufficient to explain Navajo justice. In the aesthetic/epistemological view, justice would imply the correction of a person's aesthetic and epistemological mistakes. But the Navajo Peacemaker Court's Healing and Justice Ceremony is more profound than this, for it has the aim of healing all parties involved in and affected by a crime. Such healing would be a condition of *hozho,* manifested both in intrapsychic harmony and harmony with the community, with nature, and with absolute law as laid down by the supernaturals, or Holy People.

The Navajo creation story, which has been rather differently narrated by a variety of individuals, nevertheless in most of the extant versions depicts the presence of Coyote from the beginning, along with the creator figures First Man and First Woman and one or more additional figures, including additional creator figures (for example, Haile [1943] and Levy [1998] discern two different aspects of Coyote as still being present in the various Navajo healing ceremonies that may be derived from different periods in the Navajo past). Versions of the creation stories show one Coyote with both constructive and destructive aspects, but other versions show two Coyotes—one more constructive and the other more destructive. If we think of Coyote as one figure with two aspects, we can see him—the stories attribute the male gender to Coyote—as a trickster (also called a witch in some versions) who is also a wise philosopher at times. In short, Coyote brings disorder into order (Griffin-Pierce, 1992).

This theme illuminates Navajo attitudes in a way that neither Farella's aesthetic construction of *hozho* or *hochxo* nor the Reichard and Haile guilt-based good/evil dualism manage. A Jungian perspective can help us to see the Navajo view of what Westerners call crime as an outbreak of the destructive Shadow part (i.e., the destructive Coyote part) of the personality, and criminal justice as a way of dealing with the Shadow implies neither a guilt-based good/evil dualism nor aesthetic/epistemological categories. It is also very important to note that Levy's accounts as well as many other descriptions of the Navajo creation story show First Man and First Woman as witches as well as creators; that is, as having what may be called both a destructive and constructive aspect, or an evil as well as a good aspect. One way to think about all this, for a Westerner, is that the creative energies of nature can at times be inimical to or destructive of the sorts of order that further human well-being and at other times can be conducive to the sorts of order that further human well-being. In this sense, evil and good can be seen as two aspects of the same energy process.

Navajo philosophy, as expressed in the creation narrative or myth, thus incorporates disorder and disharmony as well as order and harmony into the fundamental structure of reality, present from the beginning of everything. It is important to understand this in order to see that a criminal—seen as violating the social order and harmony—is nevertheless not judged to be guilty or sinful by Navajos. Such persons are only to be expected in a universe where disorder is as fundamental as order. They are living out an aspect of reality that is perennially going to manifest itself. However, the Navajo view holds that it is within human powers to support the order and harmony that make community possible, even though there is always the possibility that disorder (crime) may break out again.

CONFLICT RESOLUTION IN THE NAVAJO PEACEMAKER COURT HEALING AND JUSTICE CEREMONY

Navajo Peacemaker Courts are based on the traditional ways of settling socially major disputes. The aim of Navajo traditional law is to heal, not to punish or hurt. To be healed is to be restored to *hozho*. The peacemaker court attempts to restore *hozho*, or harmony, both in the offender's psyche and in the relations of the offender with his or her community. As emphasized before, healing and justice share many of the same concepts in Navajo thought. Healing brings an ill person back to good relations in solidarity with self and surroundings. Justice too restores an individual to good relations in solidarity with everyone and everything else (Yazzie, 1994).

The present-day Navajo Nation has a dual court system (LeResche, 1993), including district courts that operate on the Western "vertical" model in which there is an adversarial relation between the offender and victim, lawyers speak for each side, and a judge hands down a verdict about punishment for the guilty party; and peacemaker courts that use a "horizontal" model in which there are no lawyers or judges in the courtroom. In this case, all affected by the situation enter into a fact-finding discussion and negotiation about an appropriate compensation to the victim, and the offender is not seen as guilty but rather as in need of healing. A district judge can direct a given case of civil or criminal justice to a peacemaker court for conflict resolution as long as this is voluntary on the part of the offender, who must sign a paper indicating consent (Zion, 1994b). If an offender does not want his or her case to be dealt with in a peacemaker court, then the district court with its Western, vertical justice method is used. The peacemaker court, if chosen by the offender, makes reports to the district court. Cases can be appealed to the Navajo Supreme Court.

Peacemaker courts also have an educative function. In 1991 the Navajo Peacemaker Courts got a grant from the Bureau of Indian Affairs (BIA) to enhance their work through public education and discussion (Austin, 1993). There is also what I would call a preventive function that involves what mainstream people might think of as emotional or psychological diagnosis and counseling in the peacemaker court's healing of an offender's relation to himself or herself. Some procedures in the peacemaker court are themselves intended to restore the emotional health of the offender, and in other cases the offender may be referred to a traditional Navajo healing ceremony.

The Navajo Peacemaker Court also provides a Healing and Justice Ceremony, which is based not on a model in which an individual wins or loses, but rather on a win-win model (Yazzie, 1994; 1995). Navajo traditional shared morals and shared feelings indicate to people how to do things in a good way; if someone does wrong, the one who is wronged demands enough compensation so there will be no hard feelings, which is a shared value. The measure here is not necessarily the exact compensation that will balance out the offense, but rather the amount of compensation that works in the restoration of harmonious relations between the offender and the community. Sometimes the victim and his or her family will lower their demand for compensation to a level that is feasible for the offender and his or her family (Yazzie, 1994).

Force and punishment are not used in the Peacemaker Court's Healing and Justice Ceremony. Instead, traditional Navajo ideas about appropriate relationship roles are used in the courtroom, and people come to an agreement that everyone present knows and follows without force. The agreement works because it is based on *k'e,* or respect for others, for group decisions, and for an individual's right to decide what to do. Navajo justice respects the individual's freedom, but the idea of freedom is also seen as connected with responsibility, with the feeling that one must relate well with others. Although people say, "It's up to him" of an individual's right to decide on action, they also say, "He acts as if he has no relatives" when an individual lacks respect for others. *K'e* is a deep emotion that Navajos learn early on in life that expresses all this. There are ceremonies that teach *k'e* as life in relationships, and they help Navajo law to work (Manlove, Warren, and Holgate, 1993; Yazzie, 1995).

Peacemaking guidelines originated in the Navajo creation story. In the context of criminal justice, everyone who is affected by the dispute in question comes to the courtroom and participates in the proceedings. Navajo relationships, particularly clan relationships, work as a legal system. Clan relationships define rights, duties, and mutual obligations in relationships, and clan members enforce them (Austin, 1993).

The Navajo Peacemaker Court Healing and Justice Ceremony begins with prayer to the Holy People, asking for their help. The Navajo worldview incorporates the beliefs that thought is the power source of all creation, transformation, and regeneration and that ritual language is performative, that is, it brings about or restores or maintains its goal (in this case, *hozho*). Thus, the ceremonial prayer involving thought and speech by some or all participants helps to bring about the desired goal restoring *hozho*, and since the prayer is addressed to the Holy People, it invokes their presence, which will be instrumental in achieving *hozho* (Witherspoon, 1975). The presence of these supernatural forces arouses, focuses, and energizes people's intentions; helps to identify the disharmony that creates disputes; heals the parties; and restores their relationships.

Next, all present are encouraged to express their feelings and to say what they think caused the problem, even recounting events that may go back some generations. Everyone present now knows each other's attitudes and feelings about the problem. The elder, or peacemaker, called a *naat'aanii*, at this point gives his or her guidance in the form of a lecture to the disputants, bringing in stories, prayers, traditions, and ceremonies that apply to the situation. He or she shares the Navajo values and how they relate to the dispute and shows how people's attitudes and emotions at present vary from traditional Navajo values. People now have the information they need to discuss the situation with each other and with the elder until a satisfactory plan is made to restore damaged relations and regain *hozho*. To achieve this, the root cause of the offender's conduct must be determined and a solution found. This is similar to what occurs in Navajo healing, where an illness must be diagnosed before an effective solution or healing method can be applied (Tso, 1992).

The plan includes concrete ways in which compensation, sufficient to restore good feeling to all concerned, will be made by the offender to the victim. If the offender does not agree, he or she can explain why and continue the discussion until consensus is reached. Consensus on a good plan about compensation, as an important component of the Navajo Peacemaker Court process, relies on *k'e* (respect) and makes reconciliation and a continued relationship possible.

When a mutually acceptable plan has been agreed upon, it is then followed by a closing prayer to the Holy People that motivates everyone to remember and carry out what was agreed upon. A shift in the direction of *hozho* has now begun. All those affected by the offense will in the subsequent weeks and months keep a watchful eye upon the actual making of compensation by the offender, who may be assisted by his or her family. Compensation, or restitution, is key to Navajo civil and criminal law, as is apology (Tso, 1992).

Communities are encouraged by the tribal district courts (which refer cases to the peacemaker courts) to select their own peacemakers and can agree to appoint any individual as a peacemaker. Such an individual must not act as a judge but must be seen by all parties as having the moral authority to mediate if the parties disagree. He or she assembles the disputants and participants and coordinates activities with the tribal district court. The latter takes care of any paperwork, makes reports to a centralized records office, notifies peacemakers of their appointments, and acts as an information and assistance resource (Zion, 1994b).

In the discussion phase of the Navajo Peacemaker Court's Healing and Justice Ceremony, the Navajo creation story account of the twins who slay monsters helps people identify the metaphorical monsters of denial, minimization, and externalization, which all get in the way of good, successful living. Monsters also include depression. There are new monsters today, including (1) domestic violence (spousal abuse and elder abuse); (2) gang violence; (3) alcohol-related crime such as disorderly conduct, especially fighting among families and neighbors; (4) child abuse and neglect; and (5) the breakup of families in divorce and separations. Loss of hope and self-respect is an emotional state that frequently underlies all these situations.

These newer problems are imports from the mainstream culture, and since many Navajos today have lost their language, tradition, and religion, they do not have a clear idea of traditional values with which to counteract harmful influences. Hence, the information given by the presiding elder and the discussion following it have an educative function, and the identification of metaphorical monsters is a necessary step in the healing of both the offender and any other affected parties.

The offender's relatives help him or her to recognize his or her "monsters" and offer emotional support to help overcome them. Common offenses, such as drunken driving and domestic violence, are seen more clearly by the offender when his or her monsters are identified by relatives. The relatives also help the victims and protect them from further abuse. If the convicted individuals' psychological healing requires a procedure that exceeds the courtroom's resources, such as the traditional Navajo Enemyway healing ceremony for returned war veterans with post-traumatic stress syndrome, it will be recommended. I cannot emphasize enough that what mainstream people would think of as psychological diagnosis and emotional healing methods are a part of the Navajo Peacemaker Court's criminal justice system. Emotional health is seen as a criminal justice issue in the sense that it is part of the healing that Navajo justice requires. We can see this as an important preventive function of this sort of justice.

Since *hozho* is not a constant state, there may sometimes be repeat offenders. Various influences and circumstances can cause someone to move out of *hozho* to *hochxo.* The traditional Navajo approach, as exemplified in the Navajo Peacemaker Court Healing and Justice Ceremony may not work with those Navajos who have lost their language, culture, or religion. The peacemaker ceremony can then be tried again with such a person. If peacemaking still fails, the repeat offender is sent back to the Western court system with its rules and punishments.

After the Navajo Peacemaker Courts were established in 1982, officials and leaders from Australia, New Zealand, Canada, and South Africa studied them as a model they might use (Goldberg, 1997). In the U.S. criminal justice system, however, few equivalents exist to the procedures and aims of the Navajo Peacemaker Courts. Victim-offender reconciliation programs have some rather limited similarity (Volpe, 1991) but are largely short-term, with one session of an hour or two. A mediator helps disputing parties to resolve differences informally, face-to-face. The mediators do not act as judges or lawyers, and in principle they encourage the parties to speak for themselves, look at relevant information, air emotions, consider possible settlements, and make a mutually satisfactory, signed agreement for restitution. The mediator usually talks to the parties separately at the beginning and ensures that the subsequent discussion is nonabusive without taking sides.

On the basis of a number of empirical studies, Mark Umbreit (1994) reports a high degree of victim and offender satisfaction, although recidivism has not been found to improve. The latter may be accounted for by factors in an offender's life unrelated to the victim-offender reconciliation procedures. Richard Quinney (1991) supports the creation of a better criminology based on compassion, forgiveness, and love, rather than on the concepts of guilt and retribution. He favors alternate dispute resolution, such as victim-offender programs, as exemplifying a better criminology. But Umbreit's finding that victim-offender programs do not affect recidivism suggest that perhaps Anne Kass's recommendation (1993)—that mainstream persons involved in administering the U.S. court system undertake Navajo peacemaker training to reduce the "revolving door" phenomenon—seems worth considering. However, victim-offender programs lack important features of Navajo peacemaking, such as emotional healing of the offender and identification of the underlying causes of his or her offense, shared spirituality and references to shared moral values, prolonged airing of feelings and differing perceptions of fact, and the supportive presence of extended family and affected members of the community. Furthermore, Navajo peacemaking takes as long as it takes, unlike the usual one- or two-hour single sessions of victim-offender reconciliation.

Just how much of the fuller Navajo peacemaking ideology and procedure could be incorporated into present-day mainstream victim-offender programs is problematic, although Kass's recommendations about this should surely be given further serious consideration. Carole Goldberg (1997) suggests that borrowing from Native American dispute resolution by non-Indians is a mistake, even though alternatives to the prevailing U.S. legal system may be desirable. She argues that tribal peacemaking is embedded in a cultural and religious framework that finds no parallel in contemporary non-Indian American life. According to her, if the mainstream legal system wants to become less adversarial and more effective, it will have to find features already in mainstream American culture that will bring about that result.

Harry Blagg (1997) also argues that the assumption that any particular indigenous method of conflict resolution will work in another cultural context is likely to be unjustified and to lead to failure. He states that a particular indigenous method cannot fruitfully be denuded of its indigenous history and that the social and ceremonial structure of a particular indigenous society is relevant to the success of its method of conflict resolution. The totality of the particular indigenous experience needs to be attended to, rather than assuming that one can extract from it some universalizable "essence" that can be successfully applied in a different context. Such an assumption is called "Orientalism." Orientalism, as Blagg points out, further has the unsavory accompaniment of being used by Western nations to appropriate or consume some aspects of the wisdom of cultures considered in other respects to be inferior, in such a way as to bolster the assumed superiority of the appropriating culture.

Nevertheless, it does not seem useful to argue a priori that Western methods of achieving justice cannot borrow anything from the Navajo peacemaking ideas and procedures. There may well be mainstream situations in which the social dynamics and structure have enough in common with the Navajo social healing dynamics and structure that "borrowing" from the peacemaking ideology and methods could prove to be valuable. One must, for example, take seriously Judge Kass's assertion that in mainstream domestic relations courts, peacemaking methods have value, and one must also take seriously Navajo Supreme Court chief justice Robert Yazzie's encouragement of such borrowing. Judge Yazzie has a law degree from a mainstream law school, and earlier he practiced law in mainstream settings before devoting himself to Navajo peacemaking. Also, once we are aware of the danger of Orientalism, we need not naively fall victim to it. As previously mentioned, some other countries are already studying Navajo peacemaking to see what can be learned from it. The Navajo Peacemaker Courts are themselves being tried out on an experimental basis (Zion, 1994), so we need to await further information as to what degree of recidivism will actually take place over time.

THE APPLICATION OF SOME JUNGIAN IDEAS
TO NAVAJO CONCEPTS ABOUT HEALING

In view of Carl Jung's interest in American Indians, triggered first by reading *Black Elk Speaks* (1932) in the early 1930s and further evoked by two of his visits to the United States to visit and talk with American Indians of the Southwest, it should come as no surprise that present-day Jungians in the United States are very much interested in American Indian concepts and process of healing. The Jung Institute in Chicago has for some time invited various Indian speakers to give presentations, and at least one non-Indian physician who is also a Jungian analyst, Dr. Donald Sander, has written about and also presented a long audiotaped lecture on concepts and methods used in Navajo healing. Since the Navajo view of and method of administering criminal justice is so centrally connected to their idea of healing, Dr. Sander's 1990 lecture on healing is particularly helpful and relevant: it reflects a Jungian view that seems to me to illuminate the current Navajo Peacemaker Court ideas and procedures as practiced openly since 1982 (Moon, 1970; Oakes, King, and Campbell, 1943; Sander, 1979; Schevill Link, 1956).

Navajo justice includes both personal and social healing, so let us now see what Navajo personal healing involves before exploring what justice as personal and social healing involves. The Navajo healing procedure, extensively detailed with helpful illustrations by Griffin-Pierce, involves a four- to nine-night ceremony to cure the patient, who may be suffering an illness either of the body or of the mind. The cause of the ailment is diagnosed by a shamanic diagnostician who uses special diagnostic methods. At one point in the healing process, the patient is seated in a newly completed sandpainting supervised by the chanter, or medicine man. The sandpainting (made inside a circular building called a hogan using colored sands), condenses life into images so that the patients can open themselves to the images, which serve as an inner map. Every Holy Person and myth included in the creation story is a guide for how to live. Joseph Campbell (cited by Sander) holds that a "god" (e.g., one of the Navajo Holy People) represents an energetic pattern coming from both inside the psyche and from outside nature; a Holy Person or god represents a way of being and brings his or her eternal energy into a person's temporal life through the images. The Holy People want to give help to humans, in a proper ceremonial context. The ceremonial contact with them enables the patient to descend into his or her psyche and experience the primordial energetic patterns there. The sandpaintings come from the deep mythic level (which stems originally from the collective level of the psyche, that is, from the collective unconciousness previously mentioned) that Jung believed all humans share.

In an individual's healing ceremony, some aspect of the creation story that is deemed relevant to the patient's complaint is emphasized in a sandpainting depicting the cosmos. Here, the patient sits and feels himself or herself surrounded by the energetic powers of the cosmos and especially by the energetic powers that can be of special help healing his or her ailment. The chanter recites word-for-word a long, special chant relevant to the ailment in which a hero overcomes a problem. There are special chantways for different sorts of ailments, and each chantway focuses on one of the great natural forces or energetic patterns. Plumed prayer sticks are placed around the painting to draw the attention and presence of particular Holy People who can help. The sandpainting is imbued with energy; the medicine person transfers this energy to the patient by pressing his or her hands on the patient's body. The patient's extended family stands around the periphery of the hogan to lend their supportive presence to the ceremony. Afterward, the sandpainting is effaced. The hogan where the healing ceremony took place becomes a sacred space that contains the ceremony.

The complete ceremony is, of course, much more complex and detailed than this description indicates, but the latter suffices for our purposes here. The ceremony aims to create a focused mind in the patient, whose thoughts are cleansed of any imbalance—that is, of any neglect or violation or absence or excess of some of nature's vital energies. Since, for Navajos, the patient's train of thought is not wholly separable from action, the patient's return to psychological *hozho* (balance or order or harmony with neglected or violated natural energies) is the beginning of a cure of the illness.

The Jungians make use of their understanding of archetypes in their myth and dream interpretation. For the time being let us say that archetypes are primordial organizing tendencies in the psyche derived from human beings' long adaptation to the natural energy patterns we experience in our life on this planet. This point will be further developed below. In Jung's way of interpreting a myth or dream, one has a dialogue when awake with dream or myth figures as the images of those archetypes that are particularly relevant to one's life, with the aim of reducing inner conflict and improving inner harmony. This process resembles what the Navajo patient undergoes in a healing ceremony when he or she feels the presence of the most personally relevant Holy People (which Sander recognizes as Jungian archetypes). The patient gets in touch with them via the chanter's recitation and via the patient's own vivid imagining of their presence.

Navajo Peacemaker Court procedures include prayer to the Holy People both before and after the proceedings. These prayers are intended to bring about contact with the energies of what Jungians would call relevant archetypes, thus producing less hurt, less conflict, and a more stable, orderly, and harmonious emotional condition in the offender, the victim, and others present, as the first step in helping both the offender and the victim achieve *hozho* both inwardly and with the community. The Navajo theory of criminal justice incorporates procedures to restore *hozho* within both the offender's and the victim's psyches, as well as between the offender and his or her society, as previously discussed. Thus criminal justice as administered by the Healing and Justice Ceremony of the peacemaker courts incorporates both religion and psychology as essential components of the healing aspect of justice, as well as providing a means of conflict resolution in criminal cases (and civil cases too). For Jungians as well, both spiritual and psychological well-being are important components of healing. The Navajo aim is to bring about *hozho,* and from a Jungian perspective *hozho* means health as restoration of both the emotional health of the individual and the social health of the community. Inner emotional ill-being and disorder, as well as social ill-being and disorder (*hochxo*), are replaced by health, well-being, and order (*hozho*). The underlying root causes of an offender's crime, seen by Navajos as at least in part an offender's emotional illness, have been healed.

Although sometimes misunderstood as "mystical" by U.S. psychologists, Jung's theory of archetypes makes good sense philosophically, psychologically, and biologically. Human beings, despite differences in sex, race, ethnicity, geography, and regional history, have in common an anatomy and a physiology that distinguishes them from other animals. They also share in common some planetwide phenomena as well as some planetwide aspects of human life (e.g., gravity; day and night; earth, air, fire, and water; rocks; sky; the celestial panoply of sun, moon, planets, and stars in constellations; nonhuman animals; kinship; dangers; heroes and villains; illness, birth, and death; etc.). In addition, we humans have a similar neural wiring that helps us organize our thoughts, emotions, and imagination in ways common to all humans. These deep-seated, similar organizational patterns, in operation in a life field that affects all of us, are called by Jung the archetypes of the collective unconscious. They are "collective" because human beings have them in common (albeit with some differences because of culture), and they are "unconscious," at least until they are called to our attention in artworks, myths, dreams, and so on. As a physician and psychiatrist, Jung was well versed in scientific method, and he found the latter consistent with the formation of hypotheses in medical, psychiatric, and biological science (Jung, 1973). Although we do not directly observe archetypes, Jung thought it was reasonable to postulate them as hypotheses that help us to explain and predict some important aspects of human behavior, such as thought, emotion, imagery, myth, art, religion, and science.

To these considerations, I would add the following: The Navajos' Holy People can be thought of as the archetypal imagery generated by the organizing tendencies of human minds as manifested within the context of the distinctive history and geography of the Navajos. The Holy People, as Navajo archetypes, are from a Jungian perspective a recognition of the various energy patterns of nature seen as containing much valuable, primordial wisdom from which humans can learn if they are attentive. Since we humans have emerged from a long period of evolution of prehuman animal life on this planet, Jung hypothesizes that we contain within us various prehuman animal archetypes as well as human archetypes. (Consider, e.g., the fishlike state of the fetus in amniotic fluid or the reptile and mammalian levels of the several parts of our brains.) The impulses that come to us from prehuman archetypes may not accord with frontal-lobe-derived and distinctively human archetypes that offer, among other things, human adaptive wisdom that lends itself to a human level of moral evaluation. especially because we tend to consider prehuman life amoral. Thus, for Jung a blind and unreflective living out of all our archetypes would lead to an unbalanced and inharmonious life, with prehuman amoral energies coming into conflict with human standards as the necessary bases of social and community life. Furthermore, some human archetypes are inimical to the well-being of society (some patterns of human energy are antisocial, or in a Navajo conceptual scheme are "witchlike") and can also require a human agent's moral evaluation.

One archetype in particular, called the Shadow, must be dealt with if one is to live well, both inwardly in one's psyche or outwardly with one's society. Every organized order, whether in the individual human psyche or in a particular human society, excludes some things in order to achieve order. What is excluded is what does not fit into the order. Order is purchased at the expense of noninclusion of what is left out because the latter does not function in harmony with the structure and dynamics of what is subject to order. It is always still there, just beyond the boundaries of what is ordered, and always threatens to break in upon the order to create disruption. Jung calls what is excluded from one's individual psychic internal order or from the collective order imposed by a particular human society the "Shadow side" of an individual or of a collective society. The Shadow is an archetype that has a somewhat different makeup in each individual person. Let us keep in mind a point previously made—one's Shadow may include traits that could be conducive to or inimical to both one's own personal well-being and the well-being of society. It would be a mistake to see the Shadow side of a person solely as one or the other. For Jung, one must always evaluate one's Shadow side when one becomes aware of it, rather than just blindly living it out, if one is also to achieve a balanced and harmonious (i.e., healthy) life.

For Navajos too, a balanced, harmonious, and healthy life also requires evaluation of the long-range consequences of living out the prompting of one particular archetype, namely Coyote. Coyote is the archetype that includes but is not limited to those energies that are disruptive to social order, as well as those energies within each of us that are disruptive to our sense of what sort of people we are. We must keep in mind here that Coyote, like Jung's Shadow, is not always destructive but can at times represent a need to live out potentially constructive energies that one has suppressed. From a Jungian perspective, Coyote is a deeply significant figure. Sander sees Coyote as the archetype of the Shadow side of order, namely, what is excluded from an individual's sense of his or her inner order or that of a society.[2] A Navajo can be possessed by Coyote (i.e., find himself or herself invaded, as it were), by urges that he or she has felt to be unacceptable or that he or she has been taught by society are unacceptable.

Such urges may or may not lead to wrongdoing to others. If they do not, and if the urges are inimical to one's health, a healing ceremony can bring such a person back to emotional and physical health, order, and harmony. But if they do lead to wrongdoing to others, the person needs to be restored not only to emotional health but also to *hozho* with the community. In this case, the Navajo Peacemaker Court's Healing and Justice Ceremony would be required. Both the healing ceremonies used to heal illness inside the hogan, such as Enemyway, and the Peacemaker Court's Healing and Justice Ceremony help a Navajo become conscious of the destructive aspects of his or her Shadow side and deal with it in conscious awareness.

The Navajo healing ceremony seeks an inner integration not unlike the aim of Jungian therapy. In both cases, contact with relevant archetypes or Holy People helps people to get the necessary energy to evaluate and deal with what the Shadow or Coyote is bringing into their consciousness by means of an invasion of disorder into the personality. The Peacemaker Court's Healing and Justice Ceremony helps offenders to become aware of the ways in which the Shadow or Coyote has led them to engage in practices harmful to the social order and to be healed of those practices, as well as to make restoration to those who have been injured. For Navajos, the difference between being merely sick and being an agent of what the West calls crime depends on whether an inner destructive disharmony does or does not bring about harm to others. Since disorder—or the Shadow or Coyote—is always going to be present in a world in which disorder is just as fundamental an aspect of reality as order, anyone—as far as we can tell—could be invaded or possessed by Coyote, since that is the way reality is. As suggested earlier, one is not judged as sinful or guilty when this happens, but one is responsible and accountable for what one does about it.

Jung's view of God, or of the creative source in nature, is that God contains some energies that are conducive to the welfare of humans and others that are not. This is the way reality functions, for Jung as well as for Navajos. Anybody could be invaded by the destructive aspects of his or her Shadow, leading to a need for healing. If a person's Shadow invasion leads to wrongdoing to others, then for Jung as for Navajos that person is responsible and accountable and has a social obligation to acknowledge and try to understand socially disruptive impulses as well as to find ways to heal them and redirect his or her energies more constructively. This is an acknowledgement of wrongdoing and an attempt to take responsibility for it without recourse to labels of "guilty" or "sinful."

Sander's interpretation of Coyote as exemplifying Jung's category of the Shadow side of personality and of society seems to me to be a better interpretation of *hochxo* than seeing *hochxo* either as a guilt-based moral category or as an aesthetic category. On a Jungian interpretation, *hochxo* is the Shadow side of *hozho*, where the possibility of disorders is built into the very nature of order as always excluding something. Jung thinks of much mental or emotional illness as the breakthrough of the Shadow side of oneself into one's personality, leading to inner conflict and a breakdown of the personality that no longer experiences itself as unified under familiar patterns of order in thought and action. To become well, one must find a way to deal with the Shadow side of the personality in a manner that is not self-destructive or other-destructive. *Hochxo* is not only disorder; it is illness in a Jungian perspective. *Hozho* is not only order; it is health in a Jungian perspective. And health can be understood both as individual health and the health of the body politic.

In conclusion, a Jungian can interpret *hozho* as health (i.e., as personal and social harmony, order, and well-being). Its opposite, *hochxo*, can be seen as ill health (i.e., as personal and social disharmony, disorder, or ill-being). *Hochxo* is exemplified by the archetypal figure Coyote, or one's Shadow; that is, the hitherto unconscious aspects of self that have been excluded from the self-concept and that can break into consciousness and disturb and cause conflict (*hochxo*) in one's personal and social harmony, well-being, and health. We will keep in mind that this restoration of unconflicted personal and/or social well-being and harmonious order, or health, may at times incorporate or at other times more firmly exclude the aspects of self that were previously excluded.

The Navajo Holy People can be seen as Jungian archetypes that mobilize and energize one's capacity for *hozho* or health. We need to add here that *hozho* is more than a state of harmony within oneself and between self and society, for it also includes the idea of being in harmony with nature's energies as represented by the Holy People. Justice would then be a procedure that restores an offender, a victim, and all concerned to emotional and social health, as well to a healthful or harmonious relationship with nature. The peacemaker court can thus be seen as having a preventive and educative function with respect to crime, or social ill health, in addition to resolving a particular dispute.

As presented above, a Jungian interpretation of the Navajo theory of justice does not rely on construing *hozho* or *hochxo* as concepts based on Western ideas of guilt and sin or as denoting aesthetic or epistemological categories, as previous interpretations have suggested. Instead, it uses the concepts of health and ill health in a way that does not label criminal offenders as guilty and yet holds them responsible and accountable for their conduct. This interpretation seems to me to be closer to and more accurate to the profundity of the Navajo Peacemaker Court's Healing and Justice Ceremony than are the alternative interpretations of *hozho* and *hochxo*.

NOTES

I appreciate my year of postdoctoral studies at the Carl Jung Institute in Switzerland in helping to deepen my understanding of Jung's theory. I also want to express my appreciation for the assistance of research librarians at the University of Florida and University of Florida Law School libraries in a search of many new computer networks for relevant material. Also, I want to thank Jeffrey Ian Ross and Larry A. Gould for helpful references and for editorial suggestions, and Thomas Alexander and other members of the Society for the Advancement of American Philosophers for helpful feedback on two excerpts of the present essay that I presented at two SAAP conferences.

1. In Yazzie (1997), there is mention on pp. 7 and 8 of the ways in which Peacemaker Courts identify the causes of the problems of offenders and attend to the prevention of violence in the future.

2. Also see Mischke (1981), which contains a discussion of the Navajo use of healing practices to deal with the Shadow side of the personality. A booklet called "Suggested Symposium Critiques for the Presentation of the Dine (Navajo) Cultural Knowledge," prepared by "Walk of the Warriors," P.O. Box 1775, Crownpoint, NM 87313, makes reference to Navajo archetypes.

3

Criminalizing Culture

An Anthropologist Looks at Native Americans and the U.S. Legal System

Dorothy H. Bracey

Although early anthropologists were frequently interested in issues of crime and deviance (e.g., Hoebel, 1954; Malinowski, 1926), contemporary scholars in the discipline have, with some exceptions (e.g., Hutchings, 1993), avoided these subjects. To the extent they have turned their attention to drugs, alcohol, delinquency, or crime prevention, they have tended to study these phenomena in urbanized Western societies, primarily the United States (Bourgois, 1989; Gibbs, 1988; Podolefsky, 1985; Singer, 1985).

Part of this trend may be due to difficulties in defining crime and deviance across cultures or to a reluctance to address apparently negative issues in small, marginalized, or oppressed communities. Scholars often have qualms about adding to already negative stereotypes and fear appearing to "blame the victim." Calling attention to violence, sexual assault, juvenile delinquency, or property crime has the potential to reflect badly on people whom we feel have already been victimized by colonialism, economic exploitation, or prejudice.

Alcoholism among Native Americans has been, since the 1960s, a partial exception to this observation (e.g., Grobsmith, 1989). Significantly, much of this literature uses a medical model of alcoholism while simultaneously pointing out that liquor was introduced to Native Americans by Europeans (see Chapter 6 of this book). It is interesting to note that work suggesting that flamboyant drinking is actually highly compatible with the practices, goals, and values of many tribes (e.g., Levy and Kunitz, 1974) has not received sustained attention.

The recorded rate of crime among Native Americans is higher than that for the general U.S. population and presents a major problem for individuals and communities (LaFree, 1995: 174; but see Silverman, 1996; see also Chapter 10 of this book). At the same time, Sidney Harring (1982: 100) points out that the rate varies from one reservation to another, that patterns of violent and nonviolent crime are inconsistent, and that the rates of violent crime among rural Native Americans approximate those of their urban counterparts.

This complex situation can be explained by standard criminological theories—control, strain, anomie, and disorganization—but only when the elements of these theories are interpreted in light of the particular cultural and historical circumstances of Native Americans. This is one of anthropology's contributions to criminology—the examination of the application of theory regarding the symbols, beliefs, and meanings of the groups to which the theory is applied.

This chapter is an attempt to do two interrelated things: (1) to identify several aspects of Native American culture that have the potential to promote conforming behavior; and (2) to point out how frequently these institutions and beliefs have come into conflict with the economic and political interests and values of the mainstream United States, how often those conflicts have been litigated in U.S. courts, and how often legal processes have undermined the status and power of those institutions that might have fostered law-abiding behavior. By denying the legitimacy of these institutions—by criminalizing important aspects of Native American culture—the U.S. legal system has weakened or eliminated those very cultural forces that might have controlled crime.

CULTURE AND SOCIAL CONTROL

One early study of deviance among Native Americans introduces the way in which the study of culture can complement criminology in explaining crime. T. D. Graves (1967: 306–321) analyzed causes of deviance (measured as high alcohol consumption, self-reports of problem behavior, and contacts with the criminal justice system) among Spanish and Indian residents of a single southwestern community. His data indicate that, within both groups, a combination of a high level of acculturation and high access to economic success produced a low rate of deviance, whereas high acculturation and low access were associated with high deviance.

But the similarity ended there. Among the less acculturated Spanish population, deviance was low regardless of the level of economic success. A different pattern appeared for Native Americans, where low acculturation resulted in a *high* rate of deviance, regardless of economic access.

Graves attempted to account for these differences by administering measures of alienation and deprivation. He found that (1) for acculturating members of both groups, these feelings were stronger for those with limited economic access than for those with good jobs and (2) the relatively unacculturated in both groups showed high levels of alienation and personal deprivation regardless of the nature of their jobs (1967: 314). Thus, for those who are assimilating in the direction of mainstream American culture, access to the economic rewards of that culture is an important variable in predicting their levels of mental health. This finding is in accord with R. Merton's theory of anomie (1938, 1957). Merton's theory does not, however, tell us why the unacculturated members of both minority groups have such a high level of negative feelings or why the different groups demonstrating the same psychological characteristics show dramatically different levels of behavioral deviance.

Turning to the anthropological literature provides a number of clues to the first part of the question. If alienation and personal deprivation result from a disjunction of means and ends, then it is important to recognize that cultural contact, colonialism, and economic exploitation can result in a breakdown of the ability to reach traditional ends as well as the new ones (Fisher, 1992; Stern, 1993). Traditional people may have little access to the means that lead to the new goals, but their historical objectives may themselves become unobtainable. Traditional Spanish goals such as the ownership of large tracts of agricultural or grazing land, the position of patron, and extravagant hospitality, as well as Indian goals of prowess in war and hunting or the attainment of widely respected leadership roles, are difficult or impossible to meet under present conditions. Since at least some Indians and Spanish Americans have been successful in pursuing mainstream American goals, it is possible to say that those group members who remain oriented toward traditional objectives may actually have a more difficult time attaining them than do members who are more acculturated.

This brings us to the second part of the question. If Graves's less acculturated Indian and Spanish respondents were equally alienated and despondent, why were their rates of crime and alcoholism so different? His work in this area is consistent with control theory (Hirschi, 1969), suggesting that even when there are psychological factors that would permit or promote deviant behavior, there may be forms of social control that militate against it. Those influences will differ from one culture to another. Thus, it was no surprise to find that unacculturated Spanish respondents were significantly more likely to be in intact marriages and involved in religious activities than were either their acculturated Spanish counterparts or the more traditional Indian respondents. The importance of the Catholic Church in Spanish American culture would lead to the prediction that traditionally oriented Hispanics would tend to enter and remain in marriages and take an active part in church activities. For many Indian tribes, however, the extended family of one's birth was more important and stable than the nuclear family, and traditional religious activities were often destroyed by the assimilation process. Consistent with this idea is the finding that it was acculturated Indians who were more likely to be in intact marriages and involved in formal religious institutions than those less acculturated. Family and religion are potent sources of social control; both tend to be highly conservative, using persuasion, peer pressure, and rewards and punishments to encourage conforming and law-abiding behavior from their members. Therefore, even if the less acculturated Spanish respondents felt frustrated and alienated, they found themselves enmeshed in institutions that discouraged the expression of those feelings in ways that would disgrace their families, meet with the disapproval of the religious congregation, or attract the attention of the criminal justice system. The less acculturated Native Americans, without the constrictions of these institutions, were more likely to act out those same feelings in ways that produced a high crime rate. Up to this point, the findings are consistent with classical criminological theories of social disorganization (Rose, 1954; Shaw and McKay, 1942).

I would like to take Graves's analysis of Native American deviance one step further. I suggest that unacculturated Native Americans have a low rate of participation in the institutions of family and religion because the traditional forms of those institutions have been deliberately undermined and weakened by the legal system of the majority American culture, and those institutions that survived economic and military opposition were and continue to be subverted in legislatures and courts. In the past, the destruction of Native American cultural institutions was an explicit part of the assimilationist policy of the United States. Although assimilationism is no longer the goal of the U.S. government, Native American institutions show the effects of hundreds of years of attempts to destroy them. Just as important, traditional beliefs and values continue to come into conflict with the beliefs and values of non-Indians, and these conflicts often come to state and federal courts and legislature. Individual laws and court decisions continue to weaken those institutions that have the potential to control crime and delinquency among those Indians who remain oriented toward traditional goals and values.

This is not to say that contemporary legislation has always undermined Native American institutions or that court decisions have always been decided against them; quite often, Indian culture has emerged victorious. But the very process of subjecting an institution to legislative debate and courtroom litigation calls into question the legitimacy of the institution. The process is an ongoing demonstration of the power of the majority's legal system over Native American culture.

In their drive to subdue and assimilate Indians, Euro-Americans strove to extinguish Indian culture. The legal system was an important tool in that drive. The very institutions that might have produced greater adherence to the law have been undermined by the law itself. Native American culture has been criminalized.

To illustrate this point, we can look at the contemporary history of the two institutions that criminologists have recognized and that Graves has identified as contributing to the control and direction of behavior—religion and family. These are institutions that elicit great respect in mainstream American culture. The First Amendment protects freedom of religion, and the family is continually extolled as the bedrock of the nation. The examples below are chosen to demonstrate that important aspects of these institutions have not only been under legal pressure in the past but continue to feel such pressure. The criminalization of culture is not something that has ended; it continues today.

RELIGION

Although the relationship between religion and crime is complex, recent scholarship has provided some clarification. C. R. Tittle and M. R. Welch (1983) report that, for adults, religiosity has its greatest effect on those who live in socially disorganized communities that do not consistently sanction deviant behavior. T. D. Evans et al. (1995: 210) found a strong negative relationship between involvement in religious activities and a wide variety of criminal behavior, a relationship that held regardless of denomination or context. This may be because such activities actually indicate a deeper commitment to religious beliefs and teachings, in that they regularly expose participants to "moral messages," or because participants receive "close monitoring and sanctioning of waywardness" from their fellows. Evans and colleagues suggest that, even for those who profess "hellfire beliefs or claim an internalized religious orientation in daily life, such religiosity is a less effective inhibitor for them than for those who regularly and directly account to a religious community" (210).

These findings have relevance for those interested in Native American crime, especially crime among more traditionally oriented Native Americans. Since so many Indian communities demonstrate all the indicators of social disorganization, residents of such places who participate in regular religious activities would be expected to demonstrate Evans's strong crime-inhibiting effects.

Although many Native Americans are Christians, others are more attracted to traditional beliefs, while still others have a syncretic belief system in which Christian, traditional, and contemporary ideas and institutions coexist. But whatever efficacy traditional and contemporary religious activities might have in inhibiting crime has been undermined by the hostile and unpredictable activities of courts and legislatures. This situation may shed light on Graves's finding that the rate of crime is particularly high among more traditional Native Americans and that this group is least likely to be involved in religious institutions.

Traditional beliefs (often called "spiritualism" by contemporary observers) differ from Christianity in that they pay less attention to the past and future than they do to the present. Although there are often stories of creation, they have no implication for the intrinsic good or evil nature of human beings and never refer to human domination of plants or animals. Even less attention is paid to the afterlife.

Native American religious beliefs and practices that do not resemble those of the dominant culture have been in danger for a long time. Missionaries considered adherence to them to be incompatible with conversion to Christianity, and legislators and criminal justice officials often found them to be immoral or threatening. From the 1880s to the 1930s, when assimilation was the official goal of the Bureau of Indian Affairs (BIA), the extermination of indigenous religious beliefs and conversion to Christianity were touchstones of government Indian policy. After the 1920s, with the beginnings of the policy of self-determination, Indian religious beliefs and activities were afforded legal protection. It has become clear, however, that when Native American religion clashed with values of the dominant society, even the First Amendment did not afford reliable protection.

Dancing

At the time of European contact, dancing was an integral part of the spiritual life of Native Americans throughout North America (e.g., Spradley, 1969). Dancing provided access to spiritual power and was a means of communicating with the supernatural world. Although there were always whites who appreciated both the aesthetic and religious aspects of Indian dancing, many others saw it as a waste of time, heathen, and unsettling. The Hopi Snake Dance, for example, was criticized for its supposed sexual excess (Fisher, 2001). Only after the establishment of reservations, however, did Indian agents see dancing as a threat to whatever marginal control they were able to exercise; agents often prohibited dancing, and punishing it was among the objectives of the courts of Indian offenses established after 1883 (Harring, 1994: 176.) The Sun Dance was officially banned in 1881.

This policy drew little attention until 1890, when Chief Sitting Bull was killed during an attempted arrest for violation of regulations designed under the assumption that "in order to protect and encourage the agricultural pursuits of the Sioux, it was necessary to smash the Ghost Dance and all vestiges of traditional society" (Harring, 1994: 185). The federal district court in Oregon (*United States v. Clapox,* 43 Fed. Rep. 575, 1888) had upheld the right of the Department of the Interior to promulgate such regulations; the court specifically mentioned the criminalization of several dances and "the usual practices of so-called medicine men" in its approval.

Judges, government officials, and law enforcement agents had an intuitive understanding of the role of religious activities in social control. They had no doubt that active participation in religion was associated with upholding the norms of other cultural aspects. But from their point of view, that was exactly the problem: as long as the religious activities involved were not those of the dominant culture, the norms being upheld were not those of the dominant culture either. The U.S. government joined with Christian churches in "the attempted destruction of traditional religions, the basis of tribal cultures. The federal government assisted in this objective by outlawing the practice of Indian religions" (O'Brien, 1988: 293).

In the early years of the twentieth century, the policy of assimilation began to coexist with a drive to preserve Indian art and culture and to protect Indian rights. By the 1920s, the Indian rights movement had officially replaced assimilation, but in fact, assimilation has never entirely disappeared. In the 1920s, the Office of Indian Affairs was still issuing circulars commenting that, on a number of reservations, "the native dance still has enough evil tendencies to furnish a retarding influence" (Fisher, 2001).

John Collier, who would become commissioner of the BIA under Franklin Roosevelt, provided leadership to a movement that would see Indian religious beliefs and practices come under administrative, legislative, and court protection. "Whereas the Bureau of Indian Affairs and the Indian Rights Association saw immorality and degradation in the ceremonies, Collier saw beauty and mystical experience" (Prucha, 1985: 61).

If that were the end of the story, there might be little more to say on the topic of Native American religion and crime. Surely in the last seventy years of constitutional protection, Indian beliefs and institutions would have revived in traditional or contemporary forms, providing religious freedom for those Native Americans not attracted to Christianity or secularism. The story is complicated, however, because a number of important Native American practices still conflict with values of the dominant society—values that have themselves been enshrined in law. Although a number of issues have been litigated repeatedly, I have selected three particularly important ones for examination: the sacramental use of peyote, the protection of sacred sites, and the right to acquire and possess eagle feathers for religious purposes.

Peyote

The constitutional protection of religious freedom has never been absolute. Courts have continuously stated that the free exercise clause of the First Amendment does not relieve citizens from the discharge of political responsibilities. In *Reynolds v. United States*, 98 U.S. 145 (1879), the Supreme Court found that laws outlawing polygamy applied to Mormons even though their religion commanded the practice. This decision first articulated the principle that laws could not interfere with religious beliefs but might interfere with religious practices. It is this tenet that has allowed the courts and legislatures to give ongoing scrutiny to the Native American Church's (NAC's) use of peyote as a sacrament.

Anthropologists date Native American use of peyote back 10,000 years. Early attempts by Europeans to eliminate the use of peyote began in 1620 with the use of Inquisition-type techniques and continued through the late 1800s in the courts of Indian offenses. These efforts did not stop the spread of the use; however, further unsuccessful attempts aimed at its abolition were made to include peyote in the Indian Prohibition Act (1897). They were followed by numerous state laws prohibiting its use; some of them did make exception for the religious use by Native Americans. BIA officials received federal funds to suppress its use on reservations until 1919.

The NAC filed papers of incorporation in 1918. Its struggles with federal attempts to suppress peyote use ended in 1965, when Congress passed the Drug Abuse Control Amendments with the intent to protect the sacramental use of peyote by Native Americans, although it actually left the issue to administrative regulations. In 1966, the Drug Enforcement Administration (DEA) adopted 21 CFR Sec. 1307.31, which provided that the listing of peyote as a controlled substance "does not apply to the use of peyote in the bona fide ceremonies of the Native American Church," although persons supplying peyote to the NAC are required to register and maintain records of purchase and distribution. Since this time, relations between the executive branch of the federal government and the NAC, in the context of peyote use, have been smooth (Peregoy, Echo-Hawk, and Botsford, 1995).

The state level, however, saw an increase in the number of antipeyote laws and prosecutions. What appeared to be a final resolution of the states' right to criminalize this Native American religious practice took place in 1964, when the Supreme Court of California considered *People v. Woody.* The California Court of Appeals had upheld the conviction of three Navajos accused of illegal peyote use. The state had argued that peyote use was harmful to Indians and that a religious exemption for Indians would have a negative impact on the enforcement of state drug laws. The California Supreme Court called these claims "untested assertions" and decided that the state had not met the well-established "compelling state interest" standard necessary to infringe on First Amendment rights. The Indians were freed, and a religious exemption to the California antidrug law was recognized. In the next few years, courts in Arizona, Oklahoma, and New York came to similar conclusions. But uncertainty remained since cases in other states, such as *State of Oregon v. Soto,* ruled that the First Amendment did not protect the Native American Church's use of state-proscribed substances.

Although twenty-eight states had provided some legal allowance for the sacramental use of peyote, none provided a full range of protection. In some, the legislation simply permitted defendants to assert religious use of peyote as an affirmative defense to a felony prosecution. Under such laws, NAC members could be arrested, fingerprinted, incarcerated, and left with a criminal record—even if their defense was successful. And twenty-two states provided no protection at all. People who obtained peyote legally in one state and wished to use it in another state in which it was also legal could presumably be arrested while traveling through a third state that offered no protection.

NAC members in any state that had not had its own test case had to fear that the practice of their religious beliefs would result in arrest and criminal conviction. In addition to this source of uncertainty, there was also some doubt about the extent of federal protection, since the NAC exemption from the narcotics legislation was based solely on DEA administrative regulation (Peregoy et al., 1995).

The U.S. Supreme Court surprised many First Amendment scholars with its 1990 ruling that the state of Oregon had the right to deny First Amendment protection to the Native American Church (*Employment Division of Oregon v. Smith,* 110 S.Ct. 1595). Not only did the court decide that the "compelling state interest" test placed too great a burden on the state, but it also exempted all state criminal law from the reach of the First Amendment. Oregon's fear that allowing the religious use of peyote would undermine its "war on drugs" did not even have to be "compelling"; the court held that as long as its criminalization of Indian culture was not specifically aimed at a religious practice, Oregon's action was protected by the Constitution.[1]

Justice Sandra Day O'Connor, who disagreed with the majority's abandonment of the "compelling state interest" test, nevertheless stated in her dissent that Oregon's criminalization of sacramental peyote met that test—in spite of the evidence that religiously prescribed use of peyote was not harmful in itself, that it did not open the floodgates to wider drug use, and that participation in the Native American Church combated alcoholism and other forms of deviance. The uncertainty and inconsistency surrounding the religious use of peyote was only settled in 1994, with Public Law 103–344. Technically an amendment to the American Indian Religious Freedom Act of 1978, the law protects the religious use of peyote by Native Americans.

A tiny number of NAC members found that the amended American Indian Religious Freedom Act still did not give complete protection to their worship. Not until 1997 did the Pentagon draft rules to allow Indian members of the armed forces to consume peyote at religious ceremonies. The rules forbade the presence of peyote on military vehicles, planes, vessels, or bases. Celebrants were to stop using peyote twenty-four hours before returning to duty and were to notify their commanders that they had taken the substance (Brooke, 1997). However, officials of the Strategic Air Command raised fears of hallucinogenic "flashbacks," and these fears delayed the formal implementation of the draft rules until 1999.

We find, therefore, that from 1883 to 1999, one of the most fundamental religious activities of nearly one out of ten Native Americans was either illegal, forbidden by government regulation, or labeled with inconsistent and uncertain legal status. Those Indians who found Christianity to be either unattractive or incomplete were barred by the law or fear of the law from partaking in this religious activity—one that was an integral part of their history for at least a century and was well integrated into the culture of at least fifty tribes.

Sacred Sites

The law has also denied other religious activities to Indians. In the last century, peyote was perceived to be a hindrance to assimilation; in this century, it ran afoul of American fear of drugs. But those who bothered to examine it could see analogies to Christian sacraments—it was consumed as part of a ceremony, in a sacred place, under the guidance of a spiritual leader, and in the company of fellow devotees.

The claim for protection of sacred sites, however, does not produce such structural similarities. Even those non-Indians who can relate to a sacred spring, cave, or mountaintop recognized the difficulty of granting sacred status to many square miles of ground. The problem is made even greater by the frequent claim that sacred spots cannot be identified to outsiders, so all the land surrounding them needs protection. Finally, the desire to protect land from the encroachment of outsiders runs into the dominant society's conviction that land should be used to extract the greatest economic benefit. When these culturally created assumptions about proper land use come into conflict, the government has tended to deny religious protection to sacred sites. Therefore, many Native Americans wishing to partake in religious activities on land that government has defined for other uses find that their activities have been criminalized.

In *Sequoyah v. TVA* (620 F.2d 1159, 6th Cir. 1980, *cert denied,* 449 U.S. 953), two bands of the Cherokee Nation asked for an injunction against the building of the Tellico Dam in Tennessee. The dam would create a reservoir that would flood the sacred birthplace and ancestral burial ground of the tribe. The Sixth Circuit held that the bands had not proven that worship at that place played a central role in their religious observance. The court suggested that the Cherokees' concern was based on cultural and historical reasoning rather than on religious values and that the First Amendment did not protect the former. In other cases, Indians have asked that logging, road building, tourist visits, and the expansion of ski areas be stopped in areas that had religious significance for them. In all cases, their requests were denied, usually on the grounds that privileging requests based on religious grounds over those based on economic grounds would be a violation of the establishment clause of the First Amendment.

Although Congress has periodically considered passing legislation that would protect Indian sacred sites, it has not done so. One problem faced both by Congress and the courts is that Western thought considers religion to be one of a number of institutions that, when taken together, make up culture. It is possible, therefore, to do as the court did in *Sequoyah*—to separate religious beliefs and practices from other beliefs and practices that are not religious. For Native Americans, as well as for many of the world's peoples, religion permeates and is inseparable from other aspects of culture. A legal system based on religion as a conceptually discrete institution is not equipped to deal with a pantheistic religion—one in which all aspects of culture and nature have spiritual associations.

Although Executive Order 61 FR 26771 (signed by President Bill Clinton on May 24, 1996), gives religious sites a level of protection they have not had before, political and administrative realities dictate an attitude of caution; rather than resolving the status of sacred sites, as the order was intended to do, it may simply establish another level of uncertainty. Indeed, the question of whether such special protection for Indian religious practices violates the establishment clause has already been raised. If this order is consistently and favorably enforced, however—and especially if it inspires congressional emulation—it may be an important step in strengthening the type of religious activities that would appear to be associated with the control of crime and deviance among traditionally oriented people.

Eagle Feathers

A third aspect of religion considered here involves the use of eagles in religious activities and artifacts. Eagles are symbols of divinity and play an important part in the spiritual lives of many tribes. According to native culture, the eagle is a messenger from the spirit world, and its feathers and body are vital for a number of ceremonies, particularly funerals and other rituals of the type that anthropologists call "rites of passage."

One of the most important cases, *United States v. Abeyta*, 632 F.Supp. 1301 (D.N.M. 1986), involved a decision that affirmed the free exercise right of an Isleta Pueblo man to shoot a golden eagle for use in religious ceremonies. The decision reads as if it finally affirms the right of Native Americans to kill eagles for religious use, but the actual situation is more ambiguous.

Congress passed the Eagle Protection Act in 1940 to protect the nearly extinct bald eagle. It contains a provision authorizing the secretary of the interior to permit the taking, possession, and transportation of eagles "for the religious purposes of Indian Tribes." In 1962, the golden eagle was brought under the protection of the act. The purpose of this legislation was clearly to protect a form of wildlife that was rapidly dropping in numbers due to hunting and the degradation of the environment.

A few months before *Abeyta*, the Supreme Court heard *United States v. Dion*, 476 U.S. 734 (1986), in which a member of the Yankton Sioux Tribe in South Dakota claimed that because of hunting rights granted by the U.S. government to the Yankton Sioux by an 1858 treaty, he was entitled to hunt eagles on reservation land. The court decided against him, finding that the Eagle Protection Act superseded the treaty rights. Although the court did not reach Dion's free exercise of religion claim, it implied that the legislation recognized the Indians' religious interests in hunting eagles and had made provision for such interests: "Congress thus considered the special cultural and religious interests of Indians, balanced those needs against the conservation purposes of the statute, and provided a specific, narrow exception that delineated the extent to which Indians would be permitted to hunt the bald and gold eagle."

A careful reading of this paragraph would lead to the impression that provisions exist to permit Indians to hunt bald and gold eagles for religious purposes. The impression would be wrong.

In the early 1970s, the government created the U.S. Fish and Wildlife Service National Eagle Repository to receive eagles that have died of natural causes or had been electrocuted, poisoned, or trapped and to then distribute them to Native Americans for religious purposes. As the superintendent of the repository admitted in an interview, "We try to send good feathers, and most people are satisfied.... You have to understand we don't get perfect carcasses in here. They've been in the field, they're dirty. Field personnel don't always know how to clean them. Sometimes they're worn; these feathers get worn" (Morris, 1996: 19).

The repository receives between 800 and 900 bodies per year and more than 1,000 requests. Over 3,000 Indians have filled out the three-page application and are on the waiting list; the waiting time for a whole bird is two years. These problems were recognized in 1994, when President Clinton issued a memorandum declaring that the administration would facilitate the collection and distribution of eagle feathers and parts for Native American religious purposes. He directed executive agencies to work cooperatively with tribal governments to accommodate religious needs (59 Fed.Reg.22, 593, 1994), but so far, the improvements have been minor.

Technically, there is an alternative. As the *Dion* decision suggests, the director of the U.S. Fish and Wildlife Service in Washington, D.C., has the right to issue a permit to a Native American to hunt eagles for the purposes of religious ceremonies. In fact, such a permit has never been issued.

Facts almost identical to these were cited in the *Abeyta* decision. In addition, the court heard evidence that the golden eagle was no longer in danger. For these reasons, the court decided that Abeyta's right to the free exercise of his religion was denied by the permit and repository system and that therefore his shooting of a golden eagle for religious purposes was not a crime.

On August 9, 1995, the U.S. Attorney's Office for the District of New Mexico filed three charges against Robert Gonzalez, a native of San Ildefonso Pueblo. No one contradicts Gonzalez's claim that he shot a bald eagle for religious purposes. The facts are similar to those in the *Abeyta* case. The main difference is that Gonzalez shot a bald eagle rather than a golden eagle. Although not as plentiful as the golden eagle, the bald eagle has been reclassified from "endangered" to "threatened" due to its population growth around the country, with New Mexico having one of the stronger populations. Nevertheless, Gonzalez was accused of a federal criminal offense for not having made use of the discredited repository system.

In January 1997, a U.S. district judge dismissed all charges against Gonzalez, but he did so on the narrowest possible grounds. Judge Parker observed that the form used for requesting eagle parts from the repository demands the name of the ceremony involved and the name of an approved religious leader. The judge noted accurately that most Native Americans consider their ceremonies sacred and secret and that many elders prefer that their religious identities not be known outside the tribe. The dismissal concluded that requiring this information placed an undue burden on Gonzalez's practice of his religion and was therefore unconstitutional. Presumably, therefore, if the U.S. Fish and Wildlife Service were to delete these two questions from the application, the repository system could continue unhindered. Unwilling to make even this compromise, the federal government promptly filed an appeal (Morris, 1997: 5).

The U.S. Court of Appeals for the Ninth Circuit contemplated and disapproved of *Abeyta* in 1997 when it heard *United States v. Frank and William Hugs* (109 F.3d 1375). The Hugs brothers acted as hunting guides on the Crow reservation in Montana and were observed shooting at bald and golden eagles. The trial court accepted their claim that they hunted eagles for religious purposes, but noted that the Bald and Golden Eagle Protection Act (BGEPA) contained no religious exception. Invited to follow the *Abeyta* decision and declare the BGEPA unconstitutional, the Ninth Circuit found itself willing to admit that the act imposed a substantial burden on the practice of Indian religions but also found that "the record establishes that a compelling government interest underlies the BGEPA, the permit system is the least restrictive means for effectuating that interest, and the defendants are precluded from challenging any deficiencies in the manner in which the permit system operates." The *Hugs* guilty verdict was affirmed.

Hugs makes it clear that, without federal legislation clearly permitting eagle hunting for Indian religious purposes, the right to participate in religious activities will continue to be surrounded by an uncertainty and tension between two cultural systems, an uncertainty and tension that currently undermine the legitimacy of both.

FAMILY

Graves points to the family as the other main source of social control for his traditionally oriented groups. His measure of family is an intact marriage. For Native Americans, this is a very minimal definition, since the nuclear family was traditionally embedded in an extended family, clan, band, village, or tribe. In many Indian cultures, marriage and the nuclear family it created had less importance than did the extended family of one's mother or father. Although some early court decisions recognized non-Western family structures (e.g., affirmation of Chippewa polygamy in *Kobogum v. Jackson Iron Co.*, 76 Mich. 498, 43 N.W. 602, 1889), there is a large body of statute and case law that damages the Indian family. In some cases there was a deliberate attempt to destroy native culture by destroying the family because of the nonconforming nature of the family structure. The assumption was that it would be easier to assimilate Native American children if they could be removed from Native American adults. In other cases, damage to the family is collateral, an unintended consequence of actions undertaken for another purpose.

One of the most important cases of the latter is the Dawes or General Allotment Act of 1887 (25 U.S.C. sec. 331). Although the professed aim of the act was to "break up the tribal mass" (O'Brien, 1988: 294) by allocating communal reservation lands to households or individuals, the result was the recognition and economic underpinning of nuclear families at the expense of other family types. No allowance was made for the more extended kinship units that were part of the traditional social control system.

Schools

Even worse for the family was the widespread institutionalization of boarding schools during the latter part of the nineteenth and the early part of the twentieth centuries. Whether on the reservations or at a considerable distance, these schools were designed to remove children from Indian culture and immerse them in that of the whites. The geographical and cultural differences between children and the adults of their families placed the boarding school students in a position in which neither Indian nor white proscriptions of deviant behavior appeared legitimate. They also undermined the power of family members over each other. Children subjected to the boarding school system were effectively removed from the control of the family, and no other institution took its place.

Adoption

But other government actions undermined the family even more permanently. A 1977 study reported that between one-fourth and one-third of all Indian children had been removed from their families, kinship groups, and culture to be placed in white foster and adoptive families (Task Force, 1976). White social workers, employed by state and Bureau of Indian Affairs programs, had been trying to protect Native American children from broken or otherwise seemingly unsatisfactory homes by placing them in white households. In separating children from their families and cultures, this practice echoed the boarding school experience.

Congressional hearings held in 1977 and 1978 focused on the harm done both to Indian culture and to the individuals adopted out. Congress recognized that the continuity of the tribe and its culture were seriously endangered by the loss of a large percentage of its children. Children adopted by white families described what it was like to be raised as a white child and then to find—usually in adolescence—that society did not consider them to be white. They were often totally unprepared for the racism they encountered. Although the hearings made no attempt to link these experiences to delinquency and crime, it is hard to believe that a link does not exist.

The hearings also revealed that white welfare workers often did not understand the concept of the extended family. Social workers perceived a child left with adults outside its nuclear family as being neglected or abandoned and would therefore proceed to terminate parental rights. Nor, in looking to place a child, did they consider that there might be scores of tribal members with valid claims of kinship to the child.

The result of these studies and hearings was the Indian Child Welfare Act of 1978 (25 U.S.C. sect. 1901 et. seq.). The act made several references to Indian culture and family structure and gave tribal courts custody over cases involving children residing or domiciled on a reservation. It also directed that in any adoptive placement under state law, preference must be given to placement with (1) a member of the child's extended family, (2) other members of the Indian child's tribe, or (3) other Indian families.

Section 1903 of the act directs that an "extended family member" shall be defined by the law or custom of the Indian child's tribe or, in the absence of such law or custom, shall be a person who has reached the age of eighteen and is the Indian child's grandparent, aunt or uncle, brother or sister, brother-in-law or sister-in-law, niece or nephew, first or second cousin, or stepparent.

This legislation, the provisions of which strengthen the Native American family and its ability to exert social control over its members, has not gone unassailed in the two decades since its passage. Its constitutionality has been questioned. It has been attacked as racist, and lines of cases have challenged tribal court claims of jurisdiction. In 1996, Congress came close to gutting its most important sections. Still unresolved is the question of jurisdiction in dissolution-based proceedings, that is, custody cases caused by divorce or separation. More than 70 percent of Indians marry outside their tribe, either to non-Indians or to members of other tribes. Tribal and state courts are still struggling over jurisdiction in such cases (Wexler, 2001: 1).

There remains, therefore, an uncertainty that reflects the tension between the group-oriented values of traditional Native American values and the individually oriented values reflected in the legal system of the United States. When combined, these complexities threaten to mount a set of permutations that builds the specter of repetitious litigation sure to drain the resources of tribes and individual Indians, the parties who must litigate against them, and the federal, state, and tribal courts that must hear the case.

> To put a poignant dynamic in cold legal terms, the question of whether a two-year-old Pueblo child will be allowed to retain her culture and traditions or be assimilated into the majority society can become moot during the pendancy of an average civil adoption case that is taken to the appellate courts. The same is true of the asserted right of an eighty-year-old medicine man to convey his sacred beliefs through the use of peyote or eagle feathers. (Wilkinson, 1987: 9)

CONCLUSION

From 1887 to 1934, there was a deliberate policy of assimilating Indians into mainstream American culture. The politicians and government officials of this period did not need anthropologists to explain to them that culture was vital to maintaining Indian identity and giving meaning to Indian life. It was because they understood this instinctively that they were so eager to abolish the culture of native America.

If the policy of assimilation ended with the passage of the Indian Reorganization Act in 1934, the criminalization of Indian culture did not. When the values and practices of Native Americans clash with those of other Americans, the dispute often winds up in the courts and legislatures controlled by those other Americans. Where many immigrant and ethnic groups have found their traditional life patterns despised and ignored in the United States, Indians are unique in that their traditions have been criminalized.

There is irony here. If there was instinctive understanding of anthropology, there was no similar understanding of criminology. Lawyers and legislators did not realize that the institutions they were outlawing were the institutions that prevented crime. By refusing recognition to non-Western forms of family or to religious practices that are inconsistent with the values of the majority, they raised the crime rate of Native Americans. An anthropologist looking at Indians in U.S.

courts and prisons may see racism but is most aware of legal ethnocentrism, of the certainty that only one design for life is deserving of legal protection.

NOTES

1. Largely because so many minority and mainstream religious organizations felt threatened by the *Smith* decision, Congress tried to reinstate the "compelling state interest" in 1993; ironically, the Religious Freedom Restoration Act (RFRA, 42 U.S.C. 200bb et seq) did not protect the religious use of peyote. This is actually irrelevant here, since the Supreme Court declared the RFRA unconstitutional in 1997 (*City of Boerne v. P. F. Flores*, 521 U.S.507).

4

Justice as Phoenix

Traditional Indigenous Law, Restorative Justice, and the Collapse of the State

James W. Zion

Justice is one of the most elusive terms in the English language. Without reviewing centuries of literature on the subject, let us say that justice is a feeling or affect. It is confidence in the integrity of processes, institutions, and actors who control and facilitate the resolution of conflict, and it is being able to live with the result because of that confidence. It is a feeling of satisfaction—or at least acceptance—of the process.

Justice is usually distinguished from *law,* another term that has been the subject of centuries of disagreement. We can say that law is about institutions that enforce norms (Bohannon, 1967: 45–50). It is a cognitive process in which actors in legal institutions justify their decisions using theories and terms familiar to them. As has often been noted, law may have very little to do with justice. Justice and law are not, in fact, the same thing. I think that it was an Alabama Supreme Court justice who once said (and I paraphrase), "If you want a legal decision, go to the courthouse, if you want justice, get a gun."

Two new justice movements have arisen in recent years: the traditional indigenous justice movement and the restorative justice movement. On one level, both trends deal with very concrete processes or techniques for handling disputes; particularly adult criminal and juvenile delinquency cases. On another, the two

51

movements, while working on procedures in institutions, are concerned with "justice" in the sense of confidence in the integrity of process and institutions that are nurtured by the direct participation of those who created a dispute or who are affected by it. Both movements use a discourse in which they set up a straw man of the weaknesses and shortcomings of adjudication and compare them with the values and virtues of the given new model.

L. Nader and C. Shugart (1980: 64) suggest that there has been too much emphasis on "microjustice," which is the handling of a particular case in the context of rules of law and of procedure. They urge us to address "macrojustice," which is identifying systemic problems and addressing common issues that arise from many individual cases. That idea has merit because if we are to understand the essentials of traditional and restorative justice, we need to think about what we are doing. Are these simply new adaptations of old techniques that are being applied to a new environment, or are they revolutionary approaches to resolving conflict?

We should also examine the context in which the two movements arise. Why did they start growing in recent years? What are the common forces that prompted their origin and increasing popularity? How are they alike and how are they dissimilar? What is the relationship between the two movements and what should it be?

Law is an aspect of culture (Grana and Ollenburger, 1999). One thing that all cultures share is myth, and one of the most important Western myths is that of the Phoenix—a bird that consumes itself by fire every 500 years and rises again from its ashes (Brewer, 1978: 972). Indigenous justice and restorative justice are the Phoenix because they arise from the ashes of the collapse of the state.

This chapter will examine the role of the collapse of the state in prompting the indigenous and restorative justice movements in the context of the nature of law, briefly describe the rise of the parallel movements, discuss their general thrust, highlight similarities and differences, and propose a relationship model. They are a Phoenix rising from the ashes of the state, and they both offer promise for effective participatory democracy; something that is missing from contemporary legal systems.

THE COLLAPSE OF THE STATE

The idea of the modern state, which "encompassed and transcended crown and land, prince and people," began with the Peace of Westphalia (1648) (Avalon Project, 1996; Wolf, 1951). The "signs" of the state are "the appearance of political units persisting in time and fixed in space; the development of permanent, impersonal institutions; the agreement on the need for an authority which can give final judgments, and the acceptance of the idea that this authority should receive the basic loyalty of its subjects" (Strayer, 1970: 10). However, a "state exists chiefly in the hearts and minds of its people; if they do not believe it is there, no logical exercise will bring it to life" (Strayer, 1970: 10).

The "permanent, impersonal institutions" that "give final judgments" are courts and other legal bodies. I think there are many forms of final judgment, depending on one's beliefs. In this context, the use of final judgment is fine. The hallmark of law is adjudication, and "adjudicatory decision making as opposed to mediatory activity is almost exclusively linked to the presence of central government. . . . Judges are creatures of the state" (Roberts, 1983: 5). The history of modern judicial systems shows that most conflicts in legal history were fought over who would control the judging and adjudication process and whether a centralized authority would make the rules (Berman, 1983).

One particularly important legal concept for indigenous peoples is that "law in the strict sense is found only where one group has conquered another and remains in the territory of the conquered as a dominant caste or class. The resulting social stratification is then rationalized. This is also a philosophy of the law relative power argument. The inferior group is subjected to punishment for any infringement of the interests of their superiors, and thus formal law comes into being" (Becker and Barnes, 1961: 30). Permanent, impersonal institutions are hierarchies that are the product of social stratification, which fosters tyranny, or "an abuse of hierarchy" (Sagan, 1995: 277). The relationship of hierarchal institutions with indigenous peoples is difficult because "political oppression is easier when there is a racial or cultural distinction between the masters and the oppressed. Tyranny will be harsher in a state established through conquest of one people by another than in a state where all share the same language, culture, and history" (Sagan, 1995: 277). This analysis begins with a general definition of the state in terms of its aspects or "signs" and focuses upon a particular definition of law as being the imposition of punishment and control upon an "inferior group." If we accept such a definition of law as being the relationship of the state with conquered peoples, how does that relate to the general population?

The essential dilemma of state institutions of dispute resolution is that they are hierarchal, and the key to understanding contemporary dissatisfaction with adjudication as a state institution is to identify the social stratification of adjudication as an impersonal institution and look at what such institutions do. Law and conquest are related. Following the discovery of Africa, the Americas, and the lands of the Pacific, there was a mass movement of conquering European state institutions that subjected indigenous peoples to their rule around the world (Fagan, 1984). Small groups of Europeans were able to conquer and occupy large land masses and populations by utilizing indigenous allies (Ferguson and Whitehead, 1992). The English developed their Indian policy through experiments on the Scots and Irish, who were still in a tribal state (MacLeod, 1967), and having subjugated them, the English used the Scots and Irish to capture and hold North America.[1] Too often, we forget that Europeans had tribal structures prior to the formation of the modern state, and the state used tribal peoples to overcome other tribal peoples, starting with the tribal peoples of Europe.[2]

One of the unique aspects of postcolonial states in which indigenous peoples are present is that when native peoples become the subjects of a new state, the indigenous form of government is not used (Mead, 1967).[3] Thus the indigenous peoples of the world live within the confines of the modern state in its various forms, and they are largely marginalized and excluded from membership in state institutions (Falk, 1992: 48). Given these definitions of state, adjudication, and tyranny, what are the primary characteristics of adjudication that influence the rise of the indigenous and restorative justice movements? Systems of social stratification vary from one state or jurisdiction to another; however, in those states with larger indigenous populations (the basis of this comparison), the hierarchy of power is more likely to be built upon race, wealth, and social status. The protection of resources, whether they be social, political, economic, or cultural, is more likely to receive greater emphasis by the dominant group where the minority group is viewed as a threat rather than as a quaint remnant of the past. Given historical patterns of settlement in many postcolonial countries (including the United States and Canada), the dominant population in numbers is "white" or "Anglo."[4] The U.S. legal hierarchy is dominated by the American Bar Association (ABA), and in most U.S. states, a person cannot become a lawyer or a judge of a court of record unless he or she has graduated from an ABA-approved law school.[5] Aside from the somewhat token efforts to recruit minorities, the bench and bar are dominated by Anglo middle-class lawyers, and the anti–affirmative action policies practiced in some states neutralize even sincere efforts to make the bench and bar look more like America.

State law is becoming more repressive, particularly in the United States. The most popular criminal justice policies and practices for those in political power include mandatory sentencing, "three strikes and you're out" criminal procedures, charging juveniles as adults, truth-in-sentencing, antigang strategies to attack identifiable minorities, drug courts, and a costly "drug war" that targets minorities and aliens (including indigenous groups in Latin America).

The United States has the highest imprisonment rate in the world (Wilson, 1997: 3–4), and U.S. minorities are swept up in an increasingly punitive criminal law. A great deal of it is prompted by politicians who have their eye on the first Tuesday in November (election day), and U.S. criminal law is actually "First Tuesday in November Justice Planning."

Advocates of indigenous and restorative justice have begun to recognize these aspects of state law. Despite recent indications of a decline in crime (National Institute of Justice, 1998), the indigenous justice movement recognizes that far too many of their members are in prison (Griffiths and Belleau, 1995; Grobsmith, 1996), and members of the restorative justice movement recognize the same thing. Both groups are attempting to get the state adjudication apparatus to adopt less punitive and more personal methods to address the needs of victims and to deal with offenders in a more humane way. That is actually macrojustice, where the focus is upon the individuals involved in the legal system and how we deal with them. The macrojustice reality is that indigenous justice and restorative justice are products of the collapse of the state.

As J. Strayer says, "A state exists chiefly in the hearts and minds of its people; if they do not believe it is there, no logical exercise will bring it to life" (1970, 5).

In recent years there have been many retrospectives on the 1960s, and many of the actors in the indigenous and restorative justice movements commenced their professional careers during that decade. In 1968, thousands of them took to the streets of the United States (and also in Paris and elsewhere) to protest the policies of their state. In the United States, antiwar protesters chanted, "Two, four, six, eight, organize and *smash* the state!"[6] There is an upcoming generation that asks, "What happened? Where have all the flowers gone? Is it all just fern bars and stock options, breast implants and cappuccino frappes from here till eternity? ... Well, it's kind of like your parents (whom, thankfully, you did *not* kill, despite Jerry Rubin's urgings) tried to tell you: If you weren't so damned self-absorbed, you might learn something" (R.U. Sirius, 1998, 89).

Instead, the new generation is organizing in a different way, outside authority structures, and "the focus of countercultural tribes is on evolving alternative identities" (R.U. Sirius, 1998). It is forming "tribes" in apolitical tribalism. What would happen if the two generations (the hippies and the new generation) were to join forces?

There are signs of the collapse of the state. Whether we use the thinking of the "smash the state" generation of the 1960s, or that of a new "tribal generation that is sometimes apolitical but is now coming to power, the point is the same: The state is collapsing with the rise of multinational economies and computer technologies, and alternatives to the state are being suggested by most fringe groups but sometimes mainstreamers too because it has become less important in the hearts and minds of many. It may be that actors in the indigenous and restorative justice movements want to temper authoritarianism and tyranny. They may want participatory democracy. Increasingly we recognize that law and adjudication are *not* the only game in town, and we do not have to play a dirty poker game because it *is* the only game in town. As R. Ellickson points out, only a minority of Americans "go to the law," and law may be irrelevant to social processes that utilize shared norms (1991).

THE TRADITIONAL INDIGENOUS AND RESTORATIVE JUSTICE MOVEMENTS

The leading traditional indigenous justice movements are centered in the United States and Canada, although significant movements exist in other parts of the world, including New Zealand (Pratt, 1996), and new indigenous justice movements may arise in countries such as Bolivia, which amended its constitution in 1994 to recognize indigenous customs and procedures (Zion and Yazzie, 1997: 56 n.4).

The indigenous justice movement in the United States is scattered and spontaneous. The courts of the Navajo Nation have been leaders in experiments to articulate traditional Navajo norms as law, develop a system of peacemaking using traditional justice bodies and procedures, and articulate what they are doing

(Valencia-Weber, 1994; Yazzie, 1994). In 1992, the Center for the Study of Law and Society at the University of California School of Law at Berkeley published a survey of the use of Indian customary law in American Indian nation courts and found that the use of customary law and practices is "pervasive" (Cooter and Fickinger, 1992). In 1993, *Mediation Quarterly,* one of the leading journals of mediation, published a special issue on Native American perspectives on peacemaking (LeResche, 1993). The subject of traditional Indian law is now popular at bar conferences, and some law schools are integrating it into their curricula. Four leading academics who are designing courses based upon traditional American Indian law are Carol E. Goldburg of the University of California at Los Angeles, Robert Porter of the University of Kansas School of Law, Peter d'Errico at the University of Massachusetts, and Gerald Gardner at the University of California at Berkeley.

The American indigenous law movement is not organized, and at this point, there are no national organizations or movements that advocate it. The Indian Tribal Justice Act of 1993 recognizes traditional Indian law, but that statutory provision was not the product of widespread lobbying; it was suggested by the courts of the Navajo Nation to make certain that Navajo common law would be recognized.[7]

The Canadian movement is more organized on a national level but less organized on the local level. The Royal Commission on Aboriginal Peoples of Canada was formed as a response to the 1990 Mohawk Indian uprising at Oka, Quebec. Given the platform of recognition of First Nations governmental authority, Canadian indigenous groups sought and obtained the right to form their own justice bodies (Royal Commission on Aboriginal Peoples, 1996). Unfortunately, while there is little time for Canadian indigenous groups to create their own justice institutions, they now have the established right to do so.

The literature of the restorative justice movement is now too large to review here (see McCold, 1997), but it dates from victim and offender reconciliation programs (VORPS), which started in Canada in the early 1970s (Hudson and Galaway, 1996: 1). New Zealand adopted a process called family group conferencing in 1985 (Jervis, 1996), and it is studying the possibility of expanding the process to adult crime (Ministry of Justice, 1995). Family group conferencing spread to Australia and other countries, and it is now becoming popular in the United States (*Real*Justice, 1998).

The movement has not yet reached a consensus on what to call itself—it is known as "restorative justice," "reparative justice," "peacemaking," or "conferencing," and perhaps other names will be articulated. There is no general agreement on a definition, but Tony Marshall provides the grounding for one: "Restorative justice is a process whereby all the parties with a stake in a particular offence come together to resolve collectively how to deal with the aftermath of the offence and its implications for the future" (Braithwaite, 1998: 8). Joe Hudson and Burt Galaway, who are also influential members of the movement, say that there are three fundamental elements of restorative justice definition and practice:

First, crime is viewed primarily as a conflict between individuals that results in injuries to victims, communities, and the offenders themselves, and only secondarily as a violation against the state. Second, the aim of the criminal justice process should be to create peace in communities by reconciling the parties and repairing the injuries caused by the dispute. Third, the criminal justice process should facilitate active participation by victims, offenders, and their communities in order to find solutions to the conflict. (Hudson and Galaway, 1996: 2)

The indigenous justice movement's elements are very similar, and it uses the same processes. However, one major difference is that indigenous justice relies upon group interaction and feelings. Indigenous justice utilizes feelings and spirituality to reach consensus when there is a dispute. In Navajo thinking, it is summed up by the term *hozho nahasdlii,* which speaks to right relations and the sense that the process has restored right relations and good relationships. Both movements share a desire for more personal and human ways to involve people in solving their own problems.

THE THRUST OF THE MOVEMENTS

There are several different camps within the two movements. The indigenous justice movement has its theorists and academics, but the initiatives now coming to light are largely spontaneous and community-based programs that are thus far from national focus.[8] The restorative justice movement has several distinct groups, including government programs, academics, nonprofits, and practitioners. Most of their attention is on process and technique within existing adjudication systems, but there are signs that restorative justice is also a social movement. The First North American Conference on Conferencing was held in Minneapolis, Minnesota in August 1998, sponsored by *Real*Justice, a nonprofit corporation (*Real*Justice, 1998), and although the program concentrated on the techniques and experiences of conferencing programs, the mood of the gathering was almost evangelistic.[9]

It is increasingly obvious that both the indigenous and restorative justice movements are reacting to abuses of authority, authoritarianism, and even tyranny. Both promote participatory democracy, although perhaps unconsciously. The republican form of government in parliamentary systems assumes that the electorate will select the wisest and most qualified of the people and allow them to make policy as a legislature or executive (law) and implement law as enforcers (police and prosecutors), adjudicators (courts), or disablers of crime (probation and corrections). The assumption is that elected officials will respond to the needs and the will of "the people," make wise decisions, and fairly administer the law. Liberal democracies use bills of rights to temper abuses, and (with the notable exception of the United States) a few attempt to entrench international human rights standards to promote checks on authoritarianism.

The problem lies in the very nature of the state, which includes hierarchical structure and class stratification backed up with force. The processes of indigenous and restorative justice seek to involve those who are directly affected by a dispute to make decisions, making state structures irrelevant or at least marginal. State institutions may be used to enforce decisions, but it is easy to see that indigenous and restorative justice attempt to avoid the state and its punitive processes.

SIMILARITIES AND DIFFERENCES

If it is true that the thrust of the two movements is to avoid the state or at least marginalize it and to use participatory democracy as a justice method, the question is, where do the two movements diverge?[10] They are similar in the processes they use. In fact, the lack of agreement on the name of the nonindigenous movement and its definition suggests something else: whatever we call it, it is in fact the prestate form of dispute resolution. To the extent either movement's decisions are accepted and comfortable for the participants, we may call the product "justice." Where do the differences lie?

One of the major differences between the two movements is that the indigenous justice movement is based on resistance to *political* repression, in addition to class and social stratification oppression. The indigenous justice movement is a form of nativism and revivalism or

> a conscious, deliberate, organized effort on the part of some members of a society to create a more satisfying culture. In revivalism, the aim of the movement is to return to a former era of happiness, to restore a golden age, to revive a previous condition of social virtue. In nativism, the aim of the movement is to purge the society of unwanted aliens, of cultural elements of foreign origin, or of both. (Wallace, 1968)

The rise of the indigenous justice movement corresponds with dissatisfaction at suppression, exclusion, and marginalization (with New Zealand, Australia, and Canada as leading examples) or with oppression (as in the United States, where Indian nation self-government is under strong attack) (Prygoski, 1995). The solution does not lie in direct confrontation with the state, because that will not work, given power imbalances and the general failure of guerrilla warfare (Laqueur, 1976).[11] Instead, indigenous groups can escape the state using traditional norms and practices.[12]

The focus of what is actually taking place in the indigenous justice movement is more specific than the restorative justice movement. Native peoples are fighting with or attempting to avoid the state as an oppressor that deals with them as disparate groups. In some countries, such as the United States and Canada, they have a political relationship with the state. In other countries, indigenous peoples are simply a minority (although they can be a majority in some states). Either way, indigenous groups demand political freedom *as* groups.

The personalities of the actors in the traditional indigenous justice movement are important (Hunt, 1967). In January 1996, the U.S. Justice Department became interested in restorative justice and held a national conference on the subject in Washington (Wallace, 1996). Chief Justice Robert Yazzie of the courts of the Navajo Nation was invited to participate to give an Indian point of view. Given its newfound zeal for restorative justice, the Justice Department conducted several regional restorative justice symposia and invited Indian nation representatives. One was held in Albuquerque, New Mexico, in October 1997 (U.S. Justice Department, 1997). The symposium involved Indian justice leaders of the American Southwest.[13] Some of the Indians in attendance expressed their dissatisfaction with the last-minute invitation given them, the lack of definition of their role in the symposium, and their marginalization as Indians. Others, primarily from New Mexico, were offended by the failure of the presenters to acknowledge that restorative justice actually has its roots in indigenous justice and by the use (some said "theft") of Indian concepts by non-Indian restorative justice practitioners. The Indian caucus then formed a working group to seek the revival of traditional justice in New Mexico. Indian cynicism about the intentions of the restorative justice movement is reinforced by the lack of mention of indigenous justice, although there is a growing literature in that field.[14]

If the traditional indigenous justice movement is in fact a nativist and revivalist movement, then there is one very important difference from the restorative justice movement: voice. If traditional indigenous justice is "a conscious, deliberate, and organized effort ... to create a more satisfying culture" and "to return to a former era of happiness, to restore a golden age, [and] to revive a previous condition of social virtue," voice will be an important issue. *Voice* simply means indigenous peoples setting their own agendas, controlling their own processes without interference, and having opportunities to tell outsiders what they are or are not doing on their own. One of the fundamental problems with state law in indigenous territories is that a police model of state law, commonly referred to as the crime control model, was imposed, suppressing traditional methods where people took care of their problems almost unconsciously. What we know as "restorative justice" or "peacemaking" was exercised in families as a common social practice, without the formality or structure we see in modern programs. That is what national governments destroyed when they imposed commissioners, village courts, tribal courts, and other instruments of control upon indigenous peoples.

The first attempts to establish a nontraditional legal regime for Indians was initiated by the Friends of the Indian, an elitist missionary group. Law was used to suppress Indian legal culture (Prucha, 1978: 295, 300), and the conquest continued with an insistence that Indian legal institutions and procedures must mirror those of the general society (e.g., National American Indian Court Judges Association, 1978). Modern tribal courts were authorized by section 16 of the Indian Reorganization Act of 1934, and a police model of justice was thrust upon them (Barsh and Henderson, 1978). These courts are colonial institutions that suffer from a lack of acceptance. In the end, they are an experiment in assimilation (Kickingbird, 1976).[15] Indian nations have been the subject of many failed experiments and the failed dreams of reformers who would try to turn Indians into what they are not.[16]

This situation creates dilemmas for Indian courts such as those of the Navajo Nation, which have a reputation for combining the best of state adjudication and traditional process. The Navajo Nation courts are following a parallel path with restorative justice and attempts to achieve similar goals, but with a difference: the Navajo courts are trying to survive attacks on their jurisdiction and competence while they seek to revive Navajo culture.

Traditional Indian justice offers a means to express indigenous voice. It may be the voice of justice leaders who have been a part of the dominant culture, its institutions, and its education systems. It may be the voice of articulate protraditionalists such as Navajo Supreme Court Chief Justice Robert Yazzie (Yazzie, 1994), Ada Pecos Melton (Jemez Pueblo) (Melton, 1995), William Bluehouse Johnson (Isleta Pueblo), or Carey Vicenti (Jicarilla Apache) (Vicenti, 1995). Traditional indigenous justice is also a platform for indigenous leaders who will never be known outside their communities but who will have an opportunity to express their voice and encourage indigenous voice in indigenous institutions.

The important lesson for the restorative justice movement is this: indigenous peoples suffer from centuries of mass posttraumatic stress disorder (Duran and Duran, 1995). They have come to recognize the injuries caused by law as conquest. They cannot rely upon the dominant world to clean up the messes it created, including high rates of interpersonal violence, family violence, child sex abuse, alcoholism, suicide, and the resulting anomie caused by failed attempts at assimilation. Many indigenous leaders trust and hope that a policy of going "back to the future" (Austin, 1993) will be the solution to those problems.

Indigenous leaders have been burned before, and some distrust the restorative justice model as another outside attempt to control their lives. The restorative justice movement must understand concepts of voice, self-determination, distancing from state authoritarianism, and a return to tradition without interference if it is to work with the indigenous justice movement successfully.

There is one other danger that the two movements share. When mediation was becoming popular, prominent figures in mediation were asked, "Where is mediation today? Where will it be in the year 2000?" Laura Nader gave us a very important warning. She said that mediation should be about "justice for the masses; the many" and not about status or money (Nader, 1985). That is a common problem. Another product of the 1960s is disillusionment. Many lawyers, judges, social workers, and activists want to get out of their fields and do something productive and relevant.

We cannot all become president, and there are many in the restorative justice movement (and many who are moving over from the mediation movement) who forget Nader's caution. They are in it for money and prestige and not to offer "justice for the masses; the many." As both indigenous and restorative justice develop, it will be important to keep something essential in our focus—that the new processes being offered are primarily a means to help people solve their own problems, improve their lives as individuals and as members of families and communities, and forge new societies, perhaps in the process becoming the apolitical "tribes" of the upcoming generation.

Another issue is whether indigenous processes can be replicated in Western systems. Carole Goldberg insists that the spiritual and cultural foundations of traditional justice are so particular to Indian cultures that there can be no borrowing (Goldberg, 1997). Van Ness developed a methodology to adapt indigenous peacemaking processes based upon a discussion of Palestinian *sulha* (Van Ness, 1998). Although Goldburg is correct that we cannot take an indigenous process and simply transfer it to another setting, it is possible to identify basic human dynamics in traditional processes to find lessons that can be used in all contexts (Braithwaite, 1998; Zion, 1998). There are opportunities for fruitful relationships among members of both movements, and taking advantage of them will increase our knowledge of prestate law in modern contexts.

WHAT IS THE FUTURE RELATIONSHIP?

The nonstate segment of the restorative justice movement offers the most hope, because if it can avoid dependence on state institutions and funding to the greatest extent possible, it has the best chance of getting away from impersonal institutions with the authority to render final judgments. Given its very personal inclusion models, it can foster genuinely popular justice. This would be essentially privatizing justice. Is that possible? The Navajo Nation judiciary is working on efforts to move peacemaking into local governments, called chapters, with an eye to restoring the Navajo tradition of handling problems within family and clan on a daily basis without the need for formal peacemaking institutions.

What should the relationship between indigenous and restorative justice be? That will be sorted out as the two recently developed movements grow. However, there are three issues that should be addressed now: (1) education and voice, (2) a challenge to indigenous justice, and (3) a challenge to restorative justice.

Margaret Mead recognized the education and voice issue when the problem of how to apply postcolonial policy arose in the instance of Papua New Guinea (Mead, 1967). She asked how an independent modern state could be formed in a former colony populated with large numbers of "primitive" (preindustrial) peoples. She recognized the role of education but wanted one that is relevant to the aspirations and voice of peoples who would be part of a modern state.

There are many academics in Indian studies, Indian law, and other programs who are addressing traditional legal education and promoting indigenous voice (e.g., Blanchard, 1997), but one outstanding example is Marianne O. Nielsen of the Criminal Justice Department of Northern Arizona University. She has developed justice curricula for the benefit of Indians of northern Arizona that incorporate their traditional and modern law and government, and Nielsen supplements them with worldwide indigenous points of view. She works with her students to give them tools to permit them to choose a career in a modern justice program or to return their own communities as a matter of choice. Nielsen also has an innovative approach to "voice." Why not gather the writings of Indian jurists and publish them for all to share? Nielsen's important text, *Native Americans and Criminal Justice* (1992) (with Robert A. Silverman of Queens University), may be the first book-length collection of articles by and about Indians with a focus upon traditional Indian law. The opportunity for voice must be expanded. There should be opportunities for Indian justice leaders to publish their views of traditional law, and there should be openings for indigenous people who otherwise might not publish to express their views (as with programs to work with traditionalists). For example, the Navajo Nation judicial branch initiated a "Navajo Law Project" based upon interviews with male and female "singers," or religious practitioners, in which Navajos are developing their own traditional law curricula, training materials, and policy documents. Those kinds of initiatives, which involve grassroots justice practitioners, should be supported.

John Braithwaite is one writer who actively considers the approaches and challenges offered by non-Western dispute resolution:

> 1. Helping indigenous community justice to learn from the virtues of liberal statism—procedural fairness, rights, protecting the vulnerable from domination.
> 2. Helping liberal state justice to learn from indigenous community justice—learning the restorative community alternatives to liberalism. (1998: 30)

Although much of this chapter is devoted to the implications of the collapse or irrelevance of the state, that does not mean that liberal statism has nothing to contribute to the debate. In fact, its ideas are designed to protect individuals from abuses by the state. Thus Braithwaite's challenge has merit. At present, many indigenous governments or justice bodies that exist in various places of the world are based upon an imposed state model (St. J. Hannigan, 1961). Most Indian nation governments of the United States follow a standard Indian Reorganization Act of 1934 model with councils and courts, and even Indian nations without such a constitution and bylaws (e.g., the Navajo Nation) use the same general model. Canada followed the same model for band councils under the Indian Act, but did not require court systems. For the most part, the councils look like a corporate body, with a board of directors. Many Indian governments of the United States do not have constitutionally entrenched courts or genuinely independent judicial systems with real authority to protect those they serve from their own government. Given that Western structures were imposed on Indian nations, they must develop an ethic and habit of procedural fairness, respect for rights, and protection for the vulnerable. The indigenous justice movement is in fact a challenge to modern indigenous institutions, because as with adjudication systems, ordinary people have been locked out. To the extent that indigenous peoples are the victims of imposed hierarchies, the virtues Braithwaite mentions in his first challenge are important.[17]

Braithwaite's second challenge is equally important. One of the struggles of the modern state is that with its emphasis on individualism, group and community values are excluded. State thinking seems to believe that individualism cannot be reconciled with the values of the group. Navajo Nation justice Raymond D. Austin responds to the second challenge with a very important concept, which he calls "freedom with responsibility" (Austin, 1993). In Navajo thinking, individualism is not only prized; it is basic. It is most often expressed in the Navajo maxim, "It's up to him." Navajos deplore coercion and see it in its extremes as witchcraft. On the other hand, freedom is exercised in the context of responsibility to one's family, clan, and community. Yes, a person is free to do what he or she wants, but there are consequences when the exercise of freedom injures another or endangers the welfare of the group.

There are many rights that lie outside the law. One of them is the right to insult a neighbor or show disrespect to someone in a public place. That is not against the law so long as we do not use "fighting words" to provoke a fight. We are free to express disgust about anyone, so long as we do not say something false that injures another, and we are almost absolutely free to vent bitter disgust against public officials.

People are free to try to impose our will on others, using the tactics of the argument from superior knowledge, position, or the ability to exercise some kind of leverage. If anyone wonders why indigenous people seem to distance themselves from people of contemporary Western culture, it is because the latter are pushy and domineering and use these tactics.[18]

One of the things indigenous justice can teach is respect for people when we deal with them. At end, the common bond between indigenous justice and restorative justice is a more human way of dealing with each other. On one level, the two systems offer methods to resolve disputes. On another, they can teach habits for everyday life as we form new "tribes" to escape the state or make it irrelevant. The beginning of that process is "freedom with responsibility," Justice Austin's alternative to individualism versus community.

CONCLUSION

The indigenous justice community has its own agenda, one that is quite different from the restorative justice agenda. E. Sagan (1995) picks up on a definition of law based upon conquest and describes political oppression in states established through conquest as "tyranny," and that is precisely the case. People who are comfortable with the modern state and its unified language, culture, and history may be content with a melting pot or even a cultural diversity within a unified culture model, but indigenous peoples want to keep their unique languages, cultures, histories, and ways of life. At present, they are stuck with a sovereignty model because that is the doctrinal justification for their separate governmental existence (d'Errico, 1997), but in the end, they want to be able to live their own lives as indigenous peoples according to their own norms.

Although the two movements have different agendas and voice is an extremely important aspect of traditional justice, they have many things in common. Whatever name is used for the movements or techniques, they are the prestate form of dispute resolution. They are based upon relationships and work best where there are continuing relationships (and the new generation recognizes that fact as they form small "tribes"). The challenge to the two movements is to make them not only the poststate or alternative to state method but also a way of life in the communities where each of us live.

The modern liberal state has become irrelevant because its foundations are based on an authoritarianism inherited from monarchy. Contemporary law courts are very close to their English parent, and they are still trapped by the concept that the "victim" of a crime is the state and not the actual victim. Deterrence is popular with the First Tuesday in November justice planners, but it does not work. Their programs are as ashes, and it is from those ashes that the new Phoenix will rise.

NOTES

1. Irish bitterness about the brutality of the English is expressed well in an aphorism (attributed to Tom Paine): "The sun never sets on the British Empire because God wouldn't trust 'em in the dark."

2. Kurt Mendelssohn suggests that the "secret" of Western domination was the possession of the skills of natural philosophy or science with a resulting technological superiority over other peoples. He says that now that Asians possess those skills, Asians may come to dominance in the future (1976). One important aspect of national policies toward indigenous peoples is that because of technology transfers: "It seems a real possibility that tribal peoples armed with modern weapons and using state military practices will pose a greater challenge to state armies in the future" (Ferguson and Whitehead, 1992: 26).

3. The process prompted Franz Fanon to write his important work, *The Wretched of the Earth* (1963), which warns of the dangers of simply substituting indigenous actors for colonial rulers. Mead's point on the importance of education programs that suit the aspirations of indigenous peoples was recognized by Paulo Freire in *Pedagogy of the Oppressed* (1997). Rosemary Blanchard applies the lessons of both in models of Indian education geared to indigenous leadership (Blanchard, 1997). In the end, the important processes of the two movements under discussion must be moved into educational systems, and educators must be prepared to internalize the value of treating students as people rather than cattle.

4. "Anglo" is a preferable term because it stresses ethnicity and culture rather than race. Although modern anthropology urges us to discard race because it is a meaningless and irrelevant term, racial discourse still dominates politics. On the matter of numbers, in 1997 the Anglo population of New Mexico became a "minority," dipping to 49.8 percent and declining, as compared to 39 percent Hispanic, 9 percent Indian, 2 percent black and 1 percent Asian (Roberts, 1997). This is the start of a national trend that will fuel anti-immigrant, anti-"minority" (in relation to Anglos), and other movements to keep the Anglo group in power (Bennett, 1988).

5. Jerome Auerbach points out that the American Bar Association was founded to entrench an elite in the legal system, and that it had conscious policies to limit the numbers of minority, immigrant, and other groups of "others" in the bench and bar (1976).

6. The first line was, "One, two, three, four—we don't want your fuckin' war!" The author was there.

7. The language in the act was suggested by the Honorable Tom Tso, chief justice of the Navajo Nation Supreme Court. The author participated in the lobbying effort.

8. The U.S. Justice Department has recognized the potential of traditional Indian law in restorative justice and "drug court" programs. That could be a blessing or a curse—a blessing because Indian nations might get (limited) resources to develop indigenous justice programs and a curse because the heavy hand of Washington may attempt to control what is done.

9. The author participated with the Honorable Robert Yazzie, chief justice of the Navajo Nation Supreme Court.

10. In the end, the definitions of restorative justice stated above are really about participatory democracy in perhaps its most pristine form. Unlike Greek city trials, where the polis voted on guilt or innocence, indigenous and restorative justice makes participants the polis.

11. There is a third option in indigenous guerrilla warfare: the Zapatista Liberation Army is utilizing sophisticated propaganda warfare using fax machines and computers. Subcommandante Marcos ("El Sub") is faxing press releases from the jungles of Chiapas. This is an example of how indigenous peoples and their allies can utilize technology for resistance.

12. Indigenous process is for members of the group who accept it and outsiders who submit to it. Indian nations should consider using their exclusion power to require that anyone who enters their territory, including businesses, should submit to the process in advance and in writing. Although it is true that "you can lead a horse to water, but you can't make him drink," the horses must be led to the water to see if they will drink.

13. The author was present.

14. To be fair, Howard Zehr and John Braithwaite conspicuously give credit where credit is due in their writings.

15. Many Indian nation judges and justice planners are quite aware of the impediments created by the colonial origins of their court systems and public dissatisfaction with "outside" methods. The problem is complicated by the fact that in contemporary reservation societies, there are "moderns," "caught-in-the-middles" (boarding school alumni), "traditionals," and rising numbers of children (in very large age cohorts) who have little knowledge of their nation's language or culture.

16. One of the more bizarre experiments was the force-marching of almost 10,000 Navajos to a small patch of green on the alkali-laden Pecos River in New Mexico. An army officer from New England devised a scheme to divide Navajos into villages, each with a "chief" (and a subchief for every 100 souls), who would act as a judge for minor offenses and sit as a juror for major ones. At the end of the day, each "chief" would report to the fort commandant, most likely giving a report of the day before lowering the colors (Bailey, 1998). It was a total disaster, but typical of the results of forcing an alien justice system on peoples who are not prepared to accept it. Navajos know that such generals still exist today.

17. The author, who is not indigenous but who has worked with many grassroots indigenous leaders in the United States and Canada, can support Braithwaite's conclusion because the author has heard the same thing from many indigenous people who must remain anonymous.

18. The Navajo word for "lawyer" is *'agha'dii't'aahii*. On one level of translation, it means "one who can never lose an argument." The actual translation is "one who pushes out with words"—someone who is bossy and demanding, not a very nice person at all.

5

The Link between Environmental Policy and the Colonization Process and Its Effects on American Indian Involvement in Crime, Law, and Society

Linda Robyn and Thom Alcoze

Present criminal justice literature does not recognize the connection between the environment and criminal justice issues as they pertain to American Indian people. This chapter is an essential piece that attempts to fill the void in understanding native issues relating to criminal justice, law, and society. For the most part, native peoples have been denied equal access to economic power in the past throughout the United States and Canada, particularly in the area of environmental resources management. This is particularly important given the historical and contemporary connectedness of indigenous people to the land. Indigenous peoples have been uniformly excluded or at least marginalized when it comes to the passage of laws or decision making concerning the environmental impact of corporate intrusion upon their lands. When laws are passed and decisions made that adversely affect native lands, resistance by native people occurs. In times past, native resistance to this intrusion has had violent consequences, including victimization through loss of land base, autonomy, and resulting poverty. When native people resist, oftentimes they are arrested and experience the odyssey of a journey through the criminal justice system.

As we begin to examine the relationship between American Indians and criminal justice, law, and order, it is important to note that from an American Indian standpoint, policies and decisions of the courts do not take into consideration the origins and historical context of American Indian culture, that is, that all things are connected to the environment in the form of rituals, music, teachings, and beliefs. Although it may seem out of place in the context of what we normally consider criminal justice, there is an American Indian environment–criminal justice connection. The connection is that American Indian social protocols and appropriate behavior are patterned after the way American Indians interpret observations from the environment, that is, natural law. And so, to make the connection between the criminal justice system, law and order, and American Indian people clear, it is important to incorporate this cultural perspective into a theoretical and policy-oriented examination of criminal justice and American Indians. In short, indigenous people take a holistic view of the world; thus, issues cannot be segregated as is done by Europeans.

To understand this connection, it is important to step outside current criminal justice issues examined in a linear way on a surface level and explore in a circular fashion the deeper issues. The racism toward native peoples that is rampant in our current criminal justice system is related to issues of power and control waged by the government and powerful multinational corporations against native peoples. When native people oppose a way of life forced upon them, when they resist further environmental destruction of their lands and therefore of their way of life both physically and spiritually, they are criminalized by the Anglo system of justice. There is a cause-effect relationship between corporate/U.S. government theft of native lands, the destruction of the environment, and crime. Before government intrusion, native life, culture, environment, relationship to the land, and justice systems (i.e., peacemaking) functioned as a whole to the social structure and enhanced survival in their environment. Many tribes, like the Navajo, still use the land to survive today, but in a way that includes a social relationship to the environment that is unlike that of European-based culture. All these variables move together in a circle and are part of a whole. To explain, the social structure of American Indian tribes is comprised of various subsystems. The subsystems interact and react to each other in a search for compatibility. Disequilibrium occurs when outside negative variables occur: in this case, colonialism and Western (referred to in other chapters as European-based) methods of justice. These outside variables result in changes in spiritual, environmental, and other subsystems that reverberate negatively backward through the whole of indigenous culture. When an entire culture and way of life is taken away from a group of people and is replaced with a new system, everything collapses.

The present condition of native peoples in the United States cannot, thus, be understood without including their connection to the environment. The concept of linear law and order with which most people are familiar does not recognize this tie to the land. To understand the involvement of native people in the U.S. criminal justice system, it is important to see that the spiritual connection with the natural world is sacred to most native people and that they believe in a balance of power between humans, animals, all of the environment, heaven, and earth. All these pieces tied together make up the whole. Natural law, spirituality, or "The Way," as it is called by the Anishinabe people, guides the balance.

In contrasting the value system of many native people with current laws based on the U.S. capitalist system, it is reciprocity or reciprocal relations that define responsibilities and ways of relating between humans and the world around them. According to American Indian author and activist Winona LaDuke,

> Simply stated, the resources of the ecosystem, whether corn, rocks, or deer, are viewed as animate and, as such, gifts from the Creator. Thus, one could not take life without reciprocal offering, usually tobacco, or saymah, as it is called in our language. Within this act of reciprocity is also an understanding that you take only what you need and leave the rest. Implicit in the understanding of Natural Law is also the understanding that most of what is natural is cyclical: whether our bodies, the moon, the tides, seasons, or life itself. Within this natural cycling is also a clear sense of birth and rebirth, knowledge that what one does today will affect us in the future, on the return.

> These tenets ... imply a continuous inhabiting of a place, an intimate understanding of the relationship between humans and the ecosystem, and the need to maintain the balance. For the most part, social and economic systems based on these values are decentralized, communal, self-reliant, and very closely based on the land of that ecosystem. This way of living has enabled indigenous communities to live for thousands of years upon their land, as quite frankly, the only examples of continuous sustainability which exist of Turtle Island (North America). (quoted in Gedicks, 1993: x–xi)

Based on the above, we see that when the federal government effectively eliminated native peoples' control over their own lands and their connection to that land, these groups were placed not only in legal but also in social and cultural jeopardy. The government replaced native control and sovereignty with European colonialism and control. When the government removed native peoples from their homelands, outlawed native religion, and separated children from their families by forcing them to attend boarding schools, native ways of dealing with crime within their society were eliminated. Native communities dealt with crime through peacemaking in a holistic manner that included all things within the environment (LaDuke, 1999; Whaley and Bresette, 1994). Marginalizing the native population and eliminating their connection to the environment and their livelihood have also resulted in widespread poverty in indigenous communities. As criminologists, we understand the connection between poverty and the crime that it brings. When we begin to understand the importance of the connection to the total environment (including plants, animals, water, and the relationship of all things in a circular fashion), it becomes clear that when these elements were removed, all of life became unbalanced for native peoples. We can also see the importance of the natural environment and the importance of sustaining the environment, as the Chippewa say, through the next seven generations.

Removal from their homelands, parents separated from young children forced to attend government boarding schools, young women of childbearing age sterilized without their consent, and being plunged into poverty through forced removal and loss of their economic systems has caused enormous psychological damage and imbalance to many native people. Still, we scratch our heads and wonder why some native people lead dysfunctional lives and end up in conflict with the criminal justice system. We are not connecting all the parts of the puzzle.

In examining theoretical and policy directions concerning American Indians and the criminal justice system, consideration can be given to the holistic influence of the environment on American Indian cultures and institutions like the criminal justice system. It is imperative to recognize the relationship between all native peoples, the environment, and how the use of traditional knowledge develops and maintains their social institutions.

Whether consciously or not, American courts criminalize traditional knowledge; thus, it is not uncommon that Indian people who have challenged multinational corporate giants and the government through political activism have been criminalized and arrested to silence their claims. Leaving traditional knowledge out of policy is environmental injustice because it injures native peoples socially, and in effect all people, not only in the United States but worldwide.

When writing about indigenous peoples, the exclusion of environmental issues establishes an injustice because it does not recognize the origins of social institutions and their interrelatedness to the environment. Native peoples today use their sophisticated traditional knowledge, combined with militant strategies in some cases, to effect change. They fight for traditional knowledge and beliefs on behalf of indigenous people and are criminalized for this behavior. Providing equitable justice for indigenous people that includes a holistic view will establish an important precedent that can put social institutions such as criminal justice in a context where the connection between society and the environment is recognized.

The native peoples of the Americas represent a wide variety of cultures and social organization strategies. The diversity of native cultures and kinds of social organization that developed through time represent a high degree of sociopolitical complexity and vary according to the demands and necessities of the environment. For example, American Indian nations organized at the band level of sociopolitical development used effective strategies to take advantage of marginal habitats where resources were limited, such as the Arctic and the deserts of the Americas.

Traditional life for native peoples worldwide has been described as simple or primitive in both the cultural and intellectual sense. However, when we examine the cultures or societies of native peoples in the Americas and other areas around the world, we find high levels of sophistication and complexity that were integral to their success as nations.

Native peoples throughout the world have been denied equal access to economic power today and in the past. Examples abound of exclusion of native peoples worldwide in formulating important environmental policy that directly affects all aspects of their lives and cultures. Indigenous peoples and the wealth of sustainable knowledge they possess have not been included in decision making concerning the environmental impacts of colonialism, capitalism, and modern-day corporate intrusion upon their lands. There are also abundant examples of resistance to this intrusion on all levels, which has caused some native peoples utilizing their traditional knowledge to be criminalized for not adhering to the Western notion of law and order.

Indigenous knowledge is defined as the unique, traditional, local knowledge existing within and developed around the specific conditions of women and men indigenous to a particular geographic area (Grenier, 1998). These types of knowledge systems represent generations of cumulative knowledge based on observations and experiences. The very survival of native peoples on all levels depended on their being able to use knowledge in balance with the natural environment.

> Indigenous knowledge is stored in people's memories and activities and is expressed in stories, songs, folklore, proverbs, dances, myths, cultural values, beliefs, rituals, community laws, local language and taxonomy, agricultural practices, equipment, materials, plant species, and animal breeds. Indigenous knowledge is shared and communicated orally, by specific example, and through culture. Indigenous forms of communication and organization are vital to local level decision making processes and to the preservation, development, and spread of indigenous knowledge. (Grenier, 1998: 2)

Until recently, those seeking to exploit indigenous lands never considered drawing upon the vast wealth of indigenous knowledge. Specifically within the United States, loss of power and autonomy through the process of colonialism has relegated indigenous peoples to a position on the lower end of the hierarchical scale in American society. The legacy of fifteenth-century European colonial domination relegated indigenous knowledge to the categories "primitive" and "simple," not knowledge but more like folklore, as described earlier. It comes as no surprise then, that through the process of colonization, indigenous knowledge and perspectives have been ignored and denigrated in the past by social, physical, and agricultural scientists, biologists, and government colonial powers seeking to exploit indigenous resources.

Colonization, a major factor in the dysfunction found in most tribal systems, is more than just an economic domination of one people by another. Colonization continues to undermine the political, military, social, psychocultural, value system, and law and order knowledge bases of the colonized while imposing the values and culture of the colonizer. For the sake of economic control, the main impetus behind any colonization, the colonizer must devise ever new means of oppressing the colonized (Tinker, 1993).

Once we begin to view the original peoples of the Americas as nations, it is easier to examine the impact of European contact. The focus on harvesting resources from the eastern shores of North America, fur trading, and other similar activities changed to a desire for the removal or, in some cases, extermination of the original inhabitants to promote European colonization. The colonization of native North America can be divided into four relatively distinct phases. The phases are not set in a particular chronology, because different areas and peoples were affected at different times, but the pattern remains the same.

The first phase, sovereignty initial contact, resulted in an immediate increase in the material prosperity of native people. Native nations were originally independent of European cultural, political, social, and economic values. In most cases, there was a voluntary acceptance of the material objects imported from Europe and, to some extent, the nonmaterial aspects of European cultures as well. Native nations accepted some European technology and made native technologies available to the European explorers and settlers. In fact, the success of early European communities was directly related to their association with the original people in areas such as agriculture, medicine, and survival strategies.

Native people greeted Europeans with hospitality. Native teachings are consistent throughout most of the Americas in their placing important values on sharing and developing positive relationships with others, including outsiders. Native nations were not aware of the policies of European sovereigns to detach native peoples from their land because within the worldview of native nations, ownership of land, water, and air was not a reasonable consideration. This initial phase of contact was relatively short in terms of generation time and set the stage for a second phase of longer duration.

The second phase was characterized by shifts in values and beliefs for the native nations with regard to self-determination. Native people were quickly drawn into the economy of Europe. Trade goods such as steel, brass, axes, knives, and other material objects represented significant advances in convenience and efficiency. Furs and the fur trade were important agents in this transition. More time began to be expended to obtain furs and the trade value they represented at the expense of traditional subsistence activities. The Micmac of eastern Canada represent a nation that experienced a dramatic change in their traditional activities as a direct result of contact and the fur trade. Prior to the fur trade, the Micmac people were oriented toward fishing for seal and sea mammal hunting, but they became dependent on the fur trade and harvesting fur-bearing animals for barter. The subsequent reduction in traditional economic pursuits reduced the food supply of the people and made them more susceptible to famine.

Native peoples began to develop a dependence on all types of fur trade goods, which weakened their political and military autonomy and resulted in greater reliance on European aid and assistance with regard to interactions with other native nations. Competition, a nontraditional mode of thought, began to play an important role in these interactions. Competition for furs and fur-trapping territories also became intense. As the fur trade continued to develop, European traders began to alter the nature of the trade with native people. One of the first actions of this type consisted of changing fur trade items from durable goods to consumable commodities, such as alcohol. Fewer material goods were available for trade, and great quantities of alcohol were substituted for these material items. This, of course, had a direct and detrimental impact on native communities that had come to rely on the fur trade.

Disease also played an important factor in this transition phase. Native people throughout the Americas used a wide variety of medicines for curing known illnesses, but they had no impact on the diseases brought by Europeans. Ailments such as pneumonia, tuberculosis, smallpox, and others had dramatic impacts on entire populations of native people. For example, whereas plague outbreaks in Europe affected 15 percent to 25 percent of the population, the same diseases decimated native populations in the Americas on the order of 50 percent to 75 percent. The loss of so great a number of native people had immediate consequences on the social, political, economic, and spiritual integrity of each native nation affected.

Religion and the immense pressure to convert Christianity also intensified during this phase of contact. Missionaries, with the help of the U.S. government, coerced native people into establishing permanent settlements and agrarian lifestyles. Concerted efforts were made to resettle agricultural peoples into communities where the largest part of the population were Christians. These communities were the forerunners of the first reservations in the Americas. As native nations and sovereignty began to erode during this phase, dependence on European ways of life became certain.

The third phase of contact can be labeled as the colonial period, or the time when native nations became dependent. Reservations and progressive settlements characterized the dependence native nations began to have on the new governments and societies that colonized the Americas. This colonial period is also identified as a time when native people became irrelevant. Europeans were not natives, and Indians were transformed into an ethnic group within their own homeland. Native people became colonized and began to be treated as a minority. Although native peoples viewed the Europeans as coercive and a superimposed majority, they also held the belief that the newcomers were not inheritors but usurpers of Indian land.

The associated destruction of Indian rights and heritage through political, economic, cultural, and religious change characterized the loss of control and sovereignty native nations experienced. Lifestyles and customs were no longer expressions of native choice but examples of how native people have been coerced into social and ideological change. Since Indian people were clearly not the same as they were during first contact, these newcomers assumed that Indian people could be fully assimilated and changed to meet the needs of the dominant culture.

The view that the original nations could be assimilated is often based on an underlying idea that native culture is static and incapable of change. This misconception also encouraged a tendency to interpret all change as evolution toward assimilation rather than as an adaptive strategy for incorporating new ideas and technologies into an existing and growing culture. During this third phase of contact, native nations were least sovereign and most dependent on the new governments and societies of the Americas, but native people and their societies also began to search for their own identity and heritage. In doing so in an organized way, it became apparent to native peoples that all the heritage and culture of the original nations had not disappeared, as hoped by the dominant culture. Native people began to express their own beliefs that their survival as a people was connected to and depended on their traditional values, customs, laws, and beliefs.

The fourth phase of contact can be labeled rebirth, or decolonization. During this phase, native people began to express their historical understanding and identity of themselves as nations, cultures, and societies with great value and sophistication. This is the phase that can be identified with the particular time period occurring directly after World War II. During the decades since World War II, there has been a sharp upturn in native populations throughout the Americas. Greater organizational activities among native organizations and new leaders have helped shift the tide of thinking away from assimilation and toward political, social, legal, economic, and cultural self-determination. Native organizations and avenues for protest have only recently begun to be expressed as a reevaluation of native concerns in the areas of treaty and land rights; natural resources; and the revival of traditional native values, philosophies, and beliefs. The preservation and practice of native customs, religion, and other aspects of native culture are experiencing a very strong revival throughout the Americas.

Colonialism continues today, but with different players (e.g., banks, corporations, speculators, governments, development agencies, the justice system, and foreign powers). As illustrated by the last phase of the cycle of colonialism, indigenous peoples stand on the frontline of contemporary colonial struggles. They are sitting on resources the rest of the world wants at the lowest possible cost. Their territories are still considered frontier lands, unowned, underutilized, and therefore open to exploitation. Because indigenous populations are small, politically weak, and physically isolated, their vast environmental knowledge base is, for the most part, denigrated by these new colonizers, making indigenous populations easy targets as resource colonies. Central to the concept of resource colonization is, as J. Bodley emphasized, that prior ownership rights and the interests of the aboriginal inhabitants are totally ignored as irrelevant by both the state and the invading individuals (1982: 24).

The incongruence in the values and understanding of progress of two different cultures has been a major factor in the loss and destruction of indigenous lands and knowledge and a great source of dysfunction and imbalance among some native peoples. One of the major factors contributing to this loss is the Western linear concept of capitalism, which directly conflicts with circular knowledge and its notions of reciprocity practiced by many indigenous peoples. To illustrate, S. Messner and R. Rosenfeld write that the basic tenets of capitalism consist of achievement, individualism, universalism, and the fetishism of money (1994: 24). In that system, personal values tend to be evaluated in terms of success and achievement. The cultural pressures to achieve at any cost are very intense. There is a "strong achievement orientation, at the level of basic cultural values, is highly conducive to the mentality that it's not how you play the game; it's whether you win or lose" (70).

The second value orientation discussed by Messner and Rosenfeld (1994) is individualism, a variable that is in direct cultural conflict with most indigenous societies. People in U.S. society "become competitors and rivals in the struggle to achieve social rewards and, ultimately, to validate personal worth" (70).

The third value, that of universalism, also incongruent with indigenous knowledge and values, encourages everyone to aspire to social ascent on the basis of individual achievements. According to Messner and Rosenfeld, universalism refers to the way all Americans, "regardless of social origins or social location, are encouraged to embrace the tenets of the dominant cultural ethos" (1994: 8). The drive to succeed, or to at least keep trying, is therefore universal to our culture. "This universalism of goals is in many respects a matter of pride for Americans. It reflects an underlying democratic ethos and a belief in a common entitlement for everyone in society" (1994: 8). However, in a stratified society such as ours, this universal application of the goal of monetary success creates serious problems because of the severe economic inequality between different groups within our society. Therefore, those who are economically unequal are then labeled as "unsuccessful" or "unequal" (1994: 8). Finally, Messner and Rosenfeld propose that money is a value in itself. They make the point that "the distinctive feature of American culture is the preeminent role of money as the metric of success. . . . Money, in this context, is a currency for measurement of achievement" (1994: 70–71).

Adhering to the values of capitalism, free enterprise, and individualism has brought regions and indigenous peoples into social conflict, which still occurs today. Indigenous cultures, spirituality, language, and knowledge were also at the mercy of colonizing societies. Even though cultures and knowledge have been worn away and some tribes have been totally eliminated through genocidal practices, the roots of many indigenous peoples have remained strong.

In retrospect, the historical relationship that evolved between colonizer and colonized lends insight into the reason why exploitation still occurs today. American Indian tribes, specifically, believe in a strong sense of balance. The trees, the earth, and the sense and sight of the environment itself influenced the thought processes of the Indians in creating the notion of balance. This precarious balance still exists, and the relationships between plants, animals, the elements, the air, water, wind, and the earth are all equally and evenly placed within the whole. For many American Indians even today, their way of life revolves around the environment. One does not, and indeed cannot, own the other if a healthy balance is to be maintained. Rather, only what is necessary to survive is taken from one another (Ramirez, 1992).

The incongruence in the values and in the understanding of progress between these very different cultures helps explain the lack of inclusion of indigenous knowledge in all areas, including criminal justice and laws of the dominant culture. The American Indian values discussed expressed the strong relationship between family members, kinship ties, the environment, and the knowledge of the unity of all these things. European values allowed land and environment to be viewed as commodities to be exploited, and Europeans imposed their will upon the land with little thought to the consequences. For example, the knowledge and values of the Indian people of the Great Lakes emerged from their woodland cultures and spirituality. There was a timeless value placed on all things.

European American values of power, materialism, economic efficiency, and immediacy have led to confusion and misunderstanding about other people and their ways. The views of many European Americans toward family and religion, for example, differ from the views of many American Indians. Even though not all European Americans were Christians, the knowledge contained in that religion is not connected to the earth or environment in the same was as the religion of "The Way" of American Indians. The most disturbing aspect of this cultural conflict is that both sides see their values and way of looking at life as the only correct way. In this context, the unequal balance and hierarchical social structure produced by the expansionary needs of capitalism is, to many American Indian people, highly destructive to their perception of the need for balance between the physical and spiritual worlds.

The sharp contrast between these two sets of cultural views is a major point of contention between dominating cultures and indigenous peoples today. These differences also describe changes beginning to take place in many indigenous communities. As project after project came about on some reservations with disastrous results, people in other targeted areas began to take notice. Indian people, extremely knowledgeable about the environmental stability of their homelands, decided mining was not worth the monetary gain. Richard Quinney writes that "without critical thought we are bound to the only form of social life we know: that which already exists. We are unable to choose a better life; our only activity is in further support of the system in which we are currently a part and which continues to exploit us" (1974: 401). By utilizing the type of critical thought Quinney writes about, indigenous peoples are calling for inclusion by challenging powerful multinational corporations and governmental institutions through a critical perspective on power and control.

As indigenous peoples continue to challenge the power structure of multinational corporations and the state and assert their sovereignty rights as First Nations to control the natural resources within their territories according to treaties, the question of power and control over resources is changing. In a society built upon hierarchical power such as the United States, the control of resources is governed by the interests of those most privileged by power. Scholars who examine American Indians as indigenous peoples from a critical perspective argue that Indian people have historically been stripped of their power, except for treaty rights. Indian resistance through the assertion of treaty rights to keep their land base and protect their resources threatens the privilege and control of powerful multinational corporations and the state. As an example, by utilizing their knowledge that posits that all parts of life and the earth are connected, the Chippewa have fiercely resisted the destruction of their environment and the nullification of treaty rights. When Indian people challenge established social power and hierarchies, the notion of business as usual is challenged, and efforts have been made by corporations and the state to neutralize and control this growing opposition standing in the way of profit maximization. Those less powerful who resist established order are often labeled as deviant and fall under the purview of the criminal justice system (see Bresette and Whaley 1994; Gedicks, 1993, 2001; LaDuke, 1999).

There are many stories of a small minority of relatively powerless people empowering themselves with knowledge of the environment and economy, added to their own knowledge base, to resist injury and harm they believe will be brought about by those in positions of economic and political power. American Indians who resist these environmentally destructive mining projects have also been denigrated in the media by corporations seeking to mobilize public opinion in favor of mining projects. Again we see the connection between the environmental issues of great importance to American Indian people and crime, law, and order.

From a critical criminological standpoint, the primary targets of social control are those who resist, disrupt, or otherwise threaten the existence of structured economic inequality (Pfohl, 1994: 196). Indian resistance is labeled as criminal and oftentimes as impeding progress. To understand the "criminality" of any individual or group requires a critical examination of interactive connections between individual experience and the historically specific character of material and social relations. In applying this notion to American Indians, the argument can be made that being Indian in America is not simply about perceived physical differences (and many times even physical differences are blurred) but is a set of social and material relations between American Indians and white Americans that extends back to the time the first treaties were made (Michalowski, 1990: 196). Indigenous peoples have existed within and adapted to a set of material and controlling social relations that provides others with greater access to wealth and therefore power than themselves.

Social control is always an exercise of power. Linear logic would argue that those less civilized (i.e., indigenous peoples who have different ways of utilizing knowledge) were unable to properly exploit the land and its resources; therefore, those deemed to be civilized (the colonizers) would determine how to use the land as well as the who and why would do so in making the laws concerning that land and the environment. As Ward Churchill and Winona LaDuke (1992) write,

> Land has always been the issue of greatest importance to politics and economics in this country. Those who control the land are those who control the resources

within and upon it. No matter what the resource issue at hand is, social control and all other aggregate components of power are fundamentally interrelated.

The many stories of resistance are not solely about Indian resistance but about an environmental social movement able to counteract corporate power as well. The assertion of native land rights takes place in the context of an environmental movement willing to accept other ways of knowing and understanding, appreciate the knowledge native people have about the environment, and welcome native leadership in environmental battles. Again, we see the connection to crime, law, and order, as native peoples continue to challenge the most powerful institutions of a large nation-state by using their capabilities to blend the assertion of treaty rights with innovative and sometimes militant forms of environmental activism.

The state and multinational corporations have used their hierarchical positions of power as a mechanism of social control, keeping Indian people powerless and in a position of relative disadvantage. It is clear that when the efforts of those privileged by power have been blocked by resistance based on treaty rights, they have dealt with the tribes in unethical ways, causing great injury and harm. Those in powerful positions have countered Indian resistance by using the force of racism.

Examining these situations from a critical perspective helps facilitate an understanding of the way in which those in power participate in creating an environmentally harmful atmosphere that maintains current hierarchical positions of power. The critical perspective offered here to examine the relationship among environmental issues, crime, and law and order can be applied to deconstruct the unequal relationship between the state and corporations and those less powerful and to begin to reconstruct a better form of balance.

As Indian tribes continue to use treaty rights as a defense in the U.S. justice system, new definitions of who they are and the role they play economically emerge. Circular ways of viewing profitable business in environmentally sustainable ways will assist in redefining the ways Indian people, corporations, and the state do business and will redefine the relationships among these actors. This redefinition will also affect the way Americans view our current justice system and law and order as they pertain to indigenous people. New and different ways to take what is needed from the environment without causing total environmental devastation and without criminalizing indigenous people who resist the destruction of their homes and culture must be reexamined in the future. Decreasing the environmental deterioration occurring today will require alternative approaches to economic security that include sustainable land use practices. Sharing the knowledge that American Indian people have in this area will place the focus on cooperation rather than hierarchical control. Rearranging this focus will have enormous impacts in the area of policy implication.

POLICY IMPLICATIONS

Policy is built on a variety of philosophical and epistemological arguments ultimately grounded in subjective choice and developed using political skills of strategy and persuasion. The central question is, what philosophical and epistemological frame of reference is best suited for a policy leading to environmental justice and power relations based on reciprocity, rather than hierarchical domination in which indigenous peoples are currently criminalized for resisting? The critical perspective used here stresses the significance of values in rethinking how environmental policy should be formulated and is tested by placing views about the environment into an American Indian way of life. In other words, there is a need to reconceptualize those values deemed to be authoritative. Societal decisions about resource allocation should be grounded in doctrines and principles stressing reciprocal power and a holistic way of viewing the environment.

For most of the twentieth century, positivist philosophies dominated social science, promoting the belief that questions and problems posed in the social world could be understood and solved using the same techniques as those applied to the physical world. Some have come to question the ability of positivist approaches to deal with complex social issues like those considered in U.S. public policy (Fischer and Forester, 1993). The basic problem with the positivist approach is its inability to provide a way to transcend political interest in order to obtain policy knowledge.

What is suggested here is how policy analysis might benefit from a methodology that acknowledges that scientific knowledge depends upon the normative assumptions and social meanings of the world it explores. Political scientist J. Dryzek (1993) suggests that policy analysis should address ethics and normative theory and the apparent normative basis of the status quo in the decision making process, that is, the values and interests represented in the existing regime and policy processes.

The critical perspective proposed here challenges policy analysts to place themselves within an environmental justice framework so as to uncover the underlying assumptions that may contribute to and produce unequal protection. A framework such as this addresses the ethical and political questions of who gets what, why, and how much (Bullard, 1994: 119). Addressing ethical and political questions such as these is important because one frame of reference by itself does not inform the whole of the problems associated with negative environmental impacts on people of color and low-income groups.

A critical perspective challenges the policy analyst to choose among social values, and because values underlie decisions, the policy analyst should recognize that the choice of a frame of reference is culturally bound and dependent, a point made by discussing the American Indian way of life.

A WAY OF LIFE

A critical perspective offers a new frame of reference for policymaking grounded in the doctrines and principles of American Indian views on the environment. The American Indian perspective demands critical thinking about the policies of the private and public sectors developed by those in power in response to environmental issues. The critical perspective questions the assumptions upon which current policies are based and examines traditional solutions, as well as advocating new ways of thinking about the environment, which do not include criminalizing those who resist current corporate/government practice. It allows for different realities and reciprocal relations of power based on mutual respect, which should be reflected in laws and policy made to include indigenous peoples.

Formulating environmental policies from a critical perspective includes taking into consideration questions about human responsibilities with regard to the environment and how these responsibilities ought to be reflected in policies adopted by the government and private companies, as well as in the habits of the population as a whole.

As Native people continue to view their history and future from a critical perspective, they will necessarily reinterpret the values and validity of our own traditions, teachings, and culture within a contemporary context. With this in mind, there is much to share with our global society. One of the most important of these, from a native as well as human perspective, is the reestablishment of a land ethic that is based upon the sound experience of our heritage. Some of these values may be transferable to the whole of society as we move into a new century. Native philosophies of the land demonstrate an ethic that represents the earth as vital because we are all born of the earth and require the resources of the earth for our very survival. Native traditions express our relationship with the earth as that of children to their mother, because all the two-leggeds, as well as the rest of creation, rely on the earth for all that is necessary for our survival. In this way, the earth and the land is our mother. Many American Indian tribes mean that quite literally. From this perspective it is also possible to see how the relationships that we form with nature are essential. This elemental teaching, which originates in native culture, expresses our relatedness to nature, creation, and each other. It is important to understand that we must begin, as a global society, to acknowledge this wholeness, or relatedness. To illustrate, for many Ojibwa people, the environment is not an issue. It is a way of life. As with other tribes, the Ojibwa consider themselves inseparable from the natural elements of their land.

Environmental sustainability is the ability of a community to use its natural, human, and technological resources to ensure that all members of present and future generations can attain a high degree of health and well-being, economic security, and a say in shaping their future while maintaining the integrity of the ecological systems upon which all life and production depends (Cortese et al., 1994). Included in environmental sustainability is economic security, ecological integrity, democracy, and community from which our notions of crime control, law, and order emerge.

The teachings of our ancestors tell us we are part of nature and must begin to express an idea of community rather than conquest. Native teachings can help us to understand our relationship with life and creation as well as expand our awareness of nature and natural cycles. We can begin to see that the earth is a source of all our needs, in fact, our only source. As human beings it becomes increasingly valuable for us to recognize this relationship so that we may benefit by using the gifts of creation effectively and efficiently. Such an awareness of life can have a profound effect on global society as a whole. As a community sharing life with the earth, we can see our dependence on, not independence from, nature, and realize that holistic indigenous knowledge concerning the environment is essential to our survival as a whole. The teachings that native peoples of the Americas present to our global society can be utilized in many ways, if other people give them the chance.

American Indian holistic views of the environment have come into conflict with the dominant capitalist nature of early European settlers and continue to do so today. Since the settlement of the area that is now the United States, control of the land and natural resources has been a source of conflict between Euro-American settlers and indigenous nations. Disputes over land use and ownership have defined the totality of government-Indian relationships from the first contact to the present day. The European perspective of exploitation of land and its resources will continue into the foreseeable future. Mining projects, development proposals, and get-rich-quick schemes have been inflicted upon tribes for years. Millions of dollars are at stake, with large multinational corporations and the federal government clamoring to do business on reservations.

The 562 federally recognized Indian tribes and 314 reservations, along with other restricted and trust lands within the United States from Florida to Wisconsin to Alaska, are among the most exploited and environmentally degraded lands anywhere in rural America (Wilkins, 2002: 30). With the consent of the Bureau of Indian Affairs, corporations and federal agencies have pressured, bribed, cajoled, and enticed their way onto reservations to mine for strategic minerals that would devastate the sacred rice beds of the Sokaogon Chippewa; to strip-mine coal, as on the Crow and Navajo reservations; to drill for oil, as on the Blackfeet reservation; and to site garbage dumps and medical waste incinerators, as on the Salt River and Gila River reservations. This historically created process of exploitation and expropriation goes on and on (Knox, 1993: 50).

This belief that natural law (all of life naturally moves in a circular fashion) is supreme law and should provide the guiding principles upon which societies and peoples function is what distinguishes the American Indian perspective on the environment from the dominant capitalist paradigm of Eurocentric environmental exploitation. The holistic view of sustainability of the Ojibwa people is that laws made by nations, states, and municipalities are inferior to natural law and should be treated in this manner (LaDuke, 1993).

Holistic environmental paradigms stand in sharp contrast to life in an industrial society. Natural law is preempted in industrial society as human domination over nature becomes a way of life. In contrast to the American Indian cyclical process of thinking, this linear concept of progress dominates industrial societies. Progress is defined in terms of economic growth and technological advancement and is key to the development of dominant civilized societies. From this perspective, the natural world is seen as something wild, in need of taming and cultivation. Those not part of this mentality are seen as primitive and in need of being civilized. Civilizing those not part of the dominant paradigm is the philosophical basis of colonialism, conquest, and the view of Western knowledge as the only legitimate way of knowing. American Indian philosophies, values, and knowledge are largely excluded in those policy decisions that benefit large corporations and serve the interests of the state.

There is a vast social distance between all involved that causes a breakdown in communication as well as misinterpretation of each other's actions. The late Walt Bresette, who was an activist and member of the Red Cliff band of Chippewa, argued that Indians and non-Indians alike are being victimized by large corporations that reduce economic options (Bresette, 1992). Along those same lines, activist and author Al Gedicks writes, "the sooner we stop labeling native issues as something separate and distinct from our own survival, the sooner we will appreciate the critical interconnections of the world's ecosystems and social systems" (1993).

CONCLUSION

Environmental protection or harm follows the path of least resistance. Environmental harm is connected to many things, such as the air we breathe, our food, water, lifestyles, social systems, and even legal decisions. Developing economically sustainable alternatives will depend on many variables such as research, effective organizing and lobbying, legal representation, effective use of the media, development of interactive skills involving native rights and environmental movements, and earnest inclusion of native beliefs and values concerning the environment.

Including these values singularly or in combination, depending on the context, into the political deliberative and allocative process can help bring about environmentally sound, long-term, sustainable economic alternatives, thus improving the state of poverty many Indian reservations currently experience. With the reduction in poverty will come a reduction in crime. With the inclusion of indigenous knowledge and values, socially harmful interaction between economic and political institutions can be decreased while at the same time helping restore the balance that is so important to many native peoples. Clearly, incorporating these kinds of values and beliefs into policy decisions challenges the harmful and wasteful projects of profit-maximizing corporations and growth-at-all-costs government policies.

In light of the history of hierarchical power discussed here, we can see that the powerful rituals that occur every day that give us our commonsense notions of business as usual are socially constructed. These rituals control our perceptions, evaluations, and interactions with others. From a critical perspective, it can be argued that the world American Indians experience has been artificially given to them by the material and symbolic power of ritual. Conversely, state-corporate actors and their interactions with American Indians are historically situated in colonial-style treaties. This situation has allowed the resistance of American Indians to the environmentally destructive forces proposed by multinational corporations to be seen as an action that challenges state-corporate senses of what things are and what they should be.

As a global society, it is possible to examine our relationship with the earth and realize that our future lies in our ability to sustain ourselves and the developments we choose to impose on the environment. Native traditions have incorporated many ways in which to harvest resources that will not destroy their future availability. We cannot return to a pristine existence, but we can make better or best use of what we now have. We have an opportunity as a society to integrate our ways of doing things to match the patterns and requirements of nature. Cooperation with the environment is one way to integrate native traditional values and mainstream concepts of development and future survival. With the assistance of native traditions and teachings, we as an American society can begin to identify patterns of nature that do work and present us with alternatives to ecological and global crises.

What appears to be natural in the way society currently lives, does business on a daily basis, and takes collective action to survive is not natural. The hierarchical structures that favor the control of some classes of people by others is not natural. Rather than being a matter of reciprocal struggles, social control has become a mode of domination for American Indian people, in all aspects of their lives.

Corporations and the state would have us believe there is no other way to survive economically. As J. Mander (1991) writes, the only group of people, so far, who are clear-minded on this point are native peoples, simply because they have kept their roots alive in an older, alternative, nature-based philosophy that has remained effective for tens of thousands of years and that has nurtured dimensions of knowledge and perceptions that seem outdated. It is crucial that Eurocentrism be reassessed for its impacts on the environment, tradition, and native peoples because native societies and their knowledge of the environment, not our own, hold the key to future survival.

Native nations in the Americas achieved an ecological balance with their environment. The great success that native people experienced using natural patterns and strategies for survival is available to us now. It may be time for us to begin to examine the alternatives they have used throughout history to achieve the survival of their societies. If we are going to make policy changes in some aspects of criminal justice, at some point we have to expand the vision in a way that includes holistic innovation. From an American Indian context it is important, once again, to recognize the influence of past history, cultural perspectives, and environmental relationships. The logic that led us into the problems our society faces today, in criminal justice and environmental conflict resolution, is not adequate to develop informed solutions to these contemporary concerns.

Traditional knowledge, in all forms, is connected to the environment from which American Indian societies emerged. To expand our perspective, we must understand the connection between American Indian criminal justice application and the relationship between that culture and the natural environment. The role of the environment in American Indian culture creates a holistic perspective that influences indigenous institutions such as criminal justice, education, religion, community and interpersonal relationships, resource use, harvest, and many other important aspects of people's lives.

Social cooperation, not competition, can become a driving force. It may be possible to see our relationship with nature and the earth as a community of people living in interdependent interaction with all communities and institutions of the earth. We can begin to become beings, persons, and societies that are part of nature once again, changing the shape of the way we deal with crime, law, and order.

III

Current Policy Issues
Affecting Native Americans
and Criminal Justice

6

Alcoholism, Colonialism, and Crime

Larry A. Gould

Today the rate of alcohol-related deaths for Native Americans in the United States is seven times that of the general population. For those Native American youths between the ages of fifteen and twenty-four, the alcohol-related death rate is more than twelve times that of the comparable general population, while for those Native Americans between the ages of twenty-five and thirty-four, the rate is thirteen times greater. It is not uncommon for Native communities to experience "cluster suicides" related to alcohol and other substance abuse. Substance abuse among Native Americans, the rate of which is twice that of the general population, is a leading contributor to health problems (Grim, 2002).

The consumption of alcohol and other drugs is not a new phenomenon among many Native Americans. Historically, however, usage was primarily limited to ceremonies and religious rituals in a closely controlled social setting (Snake, Hawkins, and La Boueff, 1976). River tribes of the Southwest believed that ritual drunkenness brought a purification of mind and heart that would produce much-needed rain for their crops. Part of their ceremony included the consumption of fermented saguaro cactus juice (Parry, 1967: 112).

In his review of ritualistic and nonritualistic consumption of intoxicants, Jack Waddell (1980) notes the controlled nature of intoxication among four groups of indigenous people in the southwestern United States. The Papagos had a long history of ceremonial intoxication and positive valuing of intoxication under controlled conditions embedded within their cultural context. In contrast, the inhabitants of Taos Pueblo rejected intoxication as a component of the system of rituals. The Diné (Navajo) maintained a unique ceremonial concern with personal health in which alcohol was served primarily to integrate social groups and cement social obligations to kinsmen. Then again, the Western Apache used alcohol as a means of binding locally meaningful social groups but did not incorporate it into rituals (Waddell, 1980: 227–228).

In this chapter I review the social, political, individual, cultural, criminological, and economic impact of alcohol on indigenous peoples. There is little doubt that the introduction of alcohol has had a long-term negative impact, but that effect is not limited to the social structures of indigenous peoples. I suggest that, to some extent, alcohol was used by Europeans not only as a means of profit making but also as a means of colonization and subjugation. I also argue here that some segments of the European-origin population continue to use alcohol as a tool to demoralize, demean, and disenfranchise indigenous peoples, as well as a way to enrich themselves.

The survival of indigenous peoples and their culture continues to be challenged by the abuse of alcohol and the attendant stereotyping attached to it. A variety of theoretical propositions, ranging from the biological (indigenous people are genetically different) to the psychological (indigenous people drink because of low self-esteem, anxiety, frustration, boredom, powerlessness, peer pressure, and isolation) to the sociocultural or environmental (deculturation, governmental paternalism, deprivation, persistence of traditional patterns, poverty, and recreation) are used to attempt to explain the rate of alcoholism and levels of individual consumption among indigenous peoples (Mall, 1984). Singly, none of these propositions can fully explain alcohol use among indigenous peoples and/or its impact on indigenous communities, nor should it; however, used in combination, the propositions can begin to explain the problems and their impact. The evaluation of this issue—and thus its potential solutions—must be studied as much as possible within the context of indigenous culture, as opposed to studying it from a European-based perspective.

All too often, the stereotypes of an indigenous person among both the uninformed and the bigoted in the United States were those of either the noble savage or the drunken Indian. Sadly, stereotypes have continued to promote the image that a greater percentage of indigenous people consume alcohol than actually do. It is important not to equate the consumption of alcohol in a particular population with the number of problem drinkers in that population. Most research suggests that about the same number of indigenous people (in the United States) drink alcohol as in the general population; however, this same body of literature indicates that those indigenous peoples who do drink are more likely to be binge drinkers and that indigenous peoples as a group have about twice the percentage of problem drinkers as the general population.

In a speech marking the 175th anniversary of the Bureau of Indian Affairs (BIA) in 2000, Kevin Gover (then head of the BIA) apologized for the past treatment of indigenous peoples, including a legacy of racism and inhumanity that extended to massacres, the forced relocation of tribes, and attempts to wipe out Indian language and cultures. Gover was quoted as saying:

> This agency participated in the ethnic cleansing that befell the Western tribes. It must be acknowledged that the deliberate spread of disease, the decimation of the mighty bison herds, the use of the poison alcohol to destroy mind and body, and the cowardly killing of women and children made for a tragedy on a scale so ghastly that it cannot be dismissed as merely the inevitable consequence of the clash of competing ways of life. ("BIA Head Apologizes for Legacy of Racism" *Great Falls Tribune,* September 9, 2000, p. 1)

There is little or no credible research that contradicts the substance of Gover's speech. Prior to their first significant and sustained contact with Europeans, the indigenous people had well-established cultures, flourishing economic systems, societal structures, and well-developed means of social control. Shortly after their first significant contact with Europeans—whether through deliberate design or as the result of unintentional behaviors—indigenous institutions were severely disrupted and, in some cases, completely destroyed (Nielsen, 1996). The strongest evidence supports the proposition that the destruction of indigenous culture was in fact, deliberate (Gibson, 1980) and that the distribution of alcohol played a significant role in the process.

The three most disruptive influences on indigenous culture and thus the most important issues involved in colonization were disease, technology (guns), and the introduction of alcohol (Diamond, 1997; Nielsen, 1996; Snipp, 1989: 6–11, 13; Snyder-Joy, 1996). Included in this mix was a belief in the superiority of the Europeans, fostered first by their religious tenets and later by the theory of social Darwinism that was (and is) commonly held by many of European heritage. Europeans, as the result of their religious beliefs, fledgling technology, and at times brute power and arrogance, felt that they were superior to all others. Social Darwinism was the belief that humans were the pinnacle of evolutionary change and that Europeans, in particular, were the pinnacle of human evolution (Trigger, 1985). Many Europeans believed that, as a result of their obvious superiority, they had the right to impose their culture, economy, laws, and religion on inferior peoples. In gratitude, indigenous people were expected to give up their land, economy, beliefs, and means of social control (Gibson, 1980; Nielsen, 1996) to accommodate Europeans' need for more resources, wealth, land, and space for an ever-expanding population.

European expansionism led to the conquest or subjugation of indigenous peoples, which typifies the process of colonialism. Regardless of the European nation involved, indigenous peoples have been relegated to a colonized status through acts of brutalization, exploitation, segregation, expulsion, and, for some, annihilation. Wittingly or unwittingly, the distribution of alcohol has contributed to both the process and the continuing effects of colonization. Alcohol was first used as a means of separating indigenous peoples from their land and other valuable goods and then as a means of dehumanizing and devaluing them (Backman, 1992; Mancall, 1996; and Saggers and Gray, 1998). In particular, the dehumanization has continuingly affected the view those of European heritage have held of indigenous peoples.

The view many Europeans have had of indigenous peoples has historically been based on either a lack of criminological theory, a misuse of criminological theory, and/or a misinterpretation of criminological theory (Nielsen, 1996). Rather than investigate crime and criminal justice policy in the context of indigenous communities, those of European heritage have been able, until recently, to dismiss these issues as having any importance. In part, European Americans have been dismissive of indigenous peoples as the result of the stereotypes that characterize them as nothing more than drunken Indians. This has, in all too many cases, allowed some to dismiss indigenous peoples as being culturally and socially inferior. It is interesting to note that many have profited considerably from the sale of alcohol to indigenous peoples while at the same time condemning them for drinking.

One of the more poignant comments on the relationship between whites and indigenous peoples is, "Behind every blackfella[1] gettin drunk, there's a whitefella gettin rich" (anonymous quote in Saggers and Gray, 1998). Substance abuse, particularly the abuse of alcohol, has been an issue of grave concern for indigenous peoples. Despite laws in the United States that, until 1953, prohibited the sale of alcohol to indigenous people, high rates of alcoholism have been the rule rather than the exception among many tribes (Beauvais, 1992). Despite some attempts by various governing bodies to control access to alcohol, these laws were never consistently enforced, allowing Europeans to use alcohol as one of the tools in the colonization process (Mancall, 1996).

The distribution and use of alcohol has led to an increased likelihood of social dysfunction or disorganization, cultural violence, economic deprivation, cultural conflict, and a perceived sense of powerlessness among indigenous peoples (Bachman, 1992). Arrell Gibson (1980) argues that these outcomes were actually intended by early European settlers and by at least one American president (Andrew Jackson). Benjamin Franklin is quoted as saying, "If it be the design of Providence to extirpate these savages in order to make room for cultivators of the earth, it seems not improbable that rum may be the appointed means" (Diamond, 1992: 1). Either directly or indirectly as the result of the aforementioned problems, alcohol abuse has also resulted in increased levels of homicide, health problems, crime, domestic violence, sexual assault, problems with children, and a lowered quality of life (Saggers and Gray, 1998). It could therefore be argued by those who wished to eliminate indigenous people from the scene that they were not fit for assimilation. The case is fairly similar in Canada, Australia, and New Zealand (Saggers and Gray, 1998). In short, alcoholism among indigenous peoples has been found to intensify social disorganization, anomie, and feelings of alienation (Bachman, 1992; Kahn, 1992; Kraus and Buffler, 1979) and has been associated with significant increases in violent behavior (Greenfeld and Smith, 1999; Reina, 2000).

Unfortunately, these relationships have been used by some to illustrate the uselessness of trying to understand the root of the problems or the interconnectedness of these issues. "This is what Indians do: They get drunk, fight, and kill each other. They were doing it a long time before whites got here and they will continue to do it regardless of our best efforts to train them. If you want a policy, then make a way to keep the damn Indians on the reservation where we (whites) don't have to keep cleaning up the mess they make of everything" (Winslow Intoxicated Street People Project, Gould, 1998a).

Although the crux of the argument made in this chapter is that the distribution of alcohol and the refusal of various governments to provide adequate treatment for substance abuse is part of an effort to continue the colonization process of indigenous people, local distributors' profits from the sale of alcohol cannot be ignored. There are many examples involving the sale of alcohol to indigenous peoples that defy common sense, such as Whiteclay, Nebraska; Luepp, Arizona; Gallup, New Mexico; and Tennant Creek in the Northwest Territories of Australia, to mention a few. In each of these cases, whites are making considerable profits by selling alcohol to indigenous people. The effects of the resulting abuse then have negative impacts on the very communities in which alcohol is sold, causing an outcry from the community members, usually whites.

BEFORE AND AFTER EUROPEAN ARRIVAL: A BRIEF HISTORY

A somewhat common explanation for the high levels of alcohol consumption among indigenous people is the claimed absence of alcohol in precontact societies (Saggers and Gray, 1998) and thus the lack of social control to regulate its use once it was introduced. In most indigenous cultures this was not entirely true and must continue to be refuted. Alcohol was used in precontact societies, but its use was generally limited to spiritual ceremonies, some rites of passage, and to a limited extent in some tribes in social settings. In this sense, it was highly controlled in its use, and the use was not widespread.

The early colonists on the North American continent believed indigenous peoples should either be fully integrated into the colonies or fully eliminated. The English, Spanish, and French all wanted the Indians to become their exclusive trading partners and consumers of trade goods produced by Europeans (Gibson, 1980; Mancall, 1996). The colonists wanted furs and skins, but the trade network could only function if the colonists provided a commodity that indigenous peoples wanted but could not or chose not to produce for themselves. Although many items such as guns, knives, trinkets, and seasonings were traded, the one item most often and most universally desired was alcohol (Mancall, 1996). Additionally, indigenous peoples were often plied with alcohol during trading negotiations so that the traders could get better deals for their goods (Gibson, 1980). It should be noted that alcohol, as opposed to guns, knives, and other implements, is quickly consumed; therefore it needs constant replenishment. The constant need for the replenishment of items that were either consumed or not easily replaced put the indigenous peoples at a clear disadvantage.

During his term in office, Andrew Jackson oversaw several treaties with the leaders of tribes in the areas that are now Alabama, Mississippi, and Tennessee. He coached his commissioners to use bribes to quench the cupidity of certain chiefs and authorized the use of public funds to purchase barrels of whiskey for entertaining indigenous representatives during council proceedings (Gibson, 1980: 49).

Reuben Snake, George Hawkins, and Steve La Boueff (1976: 3–4) note that although there were methods of social control for dealing with violent members of an indigenous community, there were no traditional means of coping with the actions of people under the influence of alcohol. Although not socially accepted, the intoxicated person was not considered to be in control of his or her actions, and existing means of social control did not provide for the administration of strong restrictions or the meting out of punishment to individuals who were drinking or intoxicated. There is strong evidence that, prior to the introduction of alcohol by Europeans to indigenous peoples, the level of family and *familia* violence was nowhere near the level it has reached today (Mancall, 1996; Maracle, 1993; Saggers and Gray, 1998).

THE IMPACT OF ALCOHOL ABUSE

Although diseases were traditionally the principal destroyers of indigenous populations, killing up to one-half of the members of virtually every tribe that came into direct contact with Europeans, alcohol also played a large role. Diseases destroyed physical health, whereas alcohol affected the vitality of indigenous populations through the disruption of traditional native lifestyles, poverty, dislocation, and degradation, all of which contributed to increased death rates (Devitt, 1999; Gibson, 1980; Grim, 2002).

Alcohol-related mortality among indigenous peoples is not uniformly the same among or even within tribal groups (Mall and Johnson, 1993). M. Dufour, D. Bertolucci, and H. Mailin (1985) found that more indigenous people in Oklahoma died from alcohol-related causes than did blacks or whites; however, further analysis suggests that Cheyenne-Arapaho tribal members had proportionately far more alcohol-related deaths than did Seminole tribal members. The Cherokee tribe had a slightly higher percentage than that of the Seminole and thus was similar to Oklahoma whites and blacks in the percentage of alcohol-related deaths (Mall and Johnson, 1993). Contrary to some of the stereotypes, in a comparative study of drinking habits, J. G. Bachman and colleagues (1991) found that the highest percentage of alcohol use in the twelve months preceding their study was reported by white males (88.3 percent), not indigenous males (82 percent).

The problem is that those indigenous males who do drink tend to consume more and are at greater risk of developing drinking-related problems. Similarly, more white females (88.6 percent) reported that they consumed alcohol in the last twelve months prior to the study than did indigenous females (81.3 percent). In a report prepared by the U.S. Department of Health and Human Services (1987), it was found that some tribal groups have proportionately fewer drinking adults than does the U.S. population as a whole (30 percent compared to 67 percent), whereas other tribes have more drinkers (69 to 80 percent).

The distribution and consumption of alcohol has been associated with the acculturation and thus the disruption of the culture and infrastructure of indigenous peoples. Louise Jilek-Aall (1981: 157) suggests that the alcohol-related problems of present-day indigenous peoples are the direct result of the use of alcohol by Europeans as a means of facilitating or forcing the acculturation of indigenous peoples to European lifestyles. Jerrold E. Levy and S. J. Kunitz (1974) note that attempts on the part of indigenous peoples at acculturation are correlated highly with the frequency and volume of drinking. In other words, "being like a white man means drinking like a white man" (121).

Although there is not a clear linear relationship between acculturation and alcohol use, some consistencies do exist (May 1982a, 1982b). Drug and alcohol use tends to be lowest for indigenous youths reporting the highest levels of acculturation, whereas those youths with middle-level acculturation were highest in stress and alcohol use (Longclaws, Barnes, Grieve, and Dumoff, 1980; May, 1982b). Indigenous youths adhering principally to traditional beliefs and ways of living tend to have the lowest level of alcohol related problems (Winfree, Griffiths, and Sellers, 1989).

Using a cross-sectional methodology in which different groups of youths (twelve to seventeen years of age) from the same tribe were studied five years apart, Larry Gould (1999b) found significant increases in alcohol consumption. The changes were found to be related to increases in social disorder/dysfunctionality, unemployment, and access to resources normally available to other youths. The social disorder was most often played out in terms of dysfunctional family situations, breakdowns in the infrastructure of the community, and a lack of appropriate role models. What is most interesting about the finding is the relationship between increased consumption of alcohol and suicide ideation and risk taking. In the first study, Gould (1999) found the prevalence of alcohol use in the male respondents to be similar to that of males in other comparable populations. However, it was noted that female respondents were more likely to be consumers of alcohol than were females in other similar populations. In the 1999 study, there appeared to be a significant increase since 1994 in the consumption of alcohol among Hualapai youth, and the level of consumption had increased at a far greater pace than it had for comparable populations. The proportion of males reporting the consumption of alcohol in 1994 was 59.1 percent (n = 13), but the 1999 data suggest that the proportion of males reporting alcohol consumption had risen to 88.9 percent (n = 15). The percentage of females having consumed alcohol in 1994 was 76.9

percent (n = 20), whereas in 1999 the proportion of females reporting alcohol consumption had risen to 92.6 percent (n = 21).

If, in fact, these figures are correct, it would make Hualapai youth some of the heaviest consumers of alcohol in the United States, regardless of age, gender, race, or other demographic variables. It is also noted that the proportion of respondents reporting the consumption of alcohol in the thirty days prior to the survey had increased from 1994 to 1999. In 1994, 36.4 percent (n = 8) of the males reported having had a drink in the last thirty days, whereas in 1999, 66.7 percent (n = 12) reported having had a drink in the last thirty days. In 1994, 61.5 percent (n = 16) of the females reported having had a drink in the last thirty days, but in 1999, 69.2 percent (n = 18) reported having had a drink in the last thirty days (Gould, 1999a,b).

The results of the 1999 survey suggested a dramatic increase in suicide ide-ation over that expressed in 1994. As was the case in 1994, females tended more often than males to have suicidal thoughts and actions. If the data collected in 1994 and again in 1999 are accurate, then this is the single strongest indicator of a serious problem among Hualapai youth. The level of suicide ideation not only exceeds the level reported in 1994 but also exceeds the level reported in other similar populations. In 1994, 5 percent of the males reported having considered suicide as an option; by 1999, 31.6 percent of the males were reporting that they had considered suicide. The increase for females was not quite as dramatic as it was for males, but there was an increase from 1994 (26.9 percent) to 1999 (35.7 percent). It is also noted that the number of males who actually attempted suicide increased from zero in 1994 to three (15.8 percent) in 1999. As noted previously, prior research suggests that an increase in thoughts of suicide, and most particu-larly a rise in attempted suicides, is a very strong indicator of an anomic state (the breakdown of organizational and cultural controls for individuals).

The result of increases in alcohol consumption such as that depicted among the Hualapai and other tribes is the creation of a generation of people who are unconnected to their own culture. Additionally, they are not connected to or, worse yet, are rejected by European-based culture. The loss of a generation of people means that important traditions, rituals, knowledge, and interconnected-ness among the tribe are lost. Failure to correct the problem leads to a continued cultural loss, to the point at which the tribe can no longer function.

Since the beginning of colonization by Europeans, the introduction and wide distribution of alcohol has been seen by many as contributing to criminal behavior (Cutter and Perkins, 1976). Some have noted that there may be fewer sober people in indigenous communities who can exercise control over intoxicated people. This is usually explained as part of the individuals' autonomous right to be their own boss. In such circumstances, the intervention of the police into situ-ations in which they might not normally intervene is often welcomed, particularly in cases involving violence (Brady and Palmer, 1984: 37). It is noted, however, that in some indigenous communities, the police find it very difficult to deal with intoxicated people. In particular, Navajo police officers tend not to believe that much can be done using either traditional or European methods of social control to alleviate the problem (see Chapters 8 and 9 of this book).

By stereotyping indigenous people as alcoholics and drunks, it becomes easier for some segments of the population, particularly those of European heritage, to dismiss them (Mihesuah, 1996). Drunkenness among upper- and middle-income people and even some lower-income groups in the United States and Canada is often less visible than that of lower-income groups, as they tend to drink in places subject to less scrutiny (Bachman, 1992; Gould, 1999). As a large proportion of indigenous people have lower incomes, they are often forced to frequent cheap bars and "dives" where they are more likely to become easy targets for public criticism and/or victims of routine crimes such as mugging, theft, and assault (Colorado, 1986; Gould, 1998b). Such is the case in Winslow, Arizona, where alcohol consumption results in ten to fifteen deaths a year as the result of hypothermia and alcohol toxicity (Gould, 1998). In Gallup, New Mexico, the extent of the problem is very similar (Colorado, 1986; Devitt, 1999). The "out-of-sight, out-of-mind" philosophy is so ingrained that excessive drinking only becomes an issue if it directly impinges on the daily lives of whites. In both cities, there seemed to be little concern that alcohol beverage outlets were making tremendous profits through the sale of alcohol to people with drinking problems or, worse yet, to people who were already visibly intoxicated. The preferred method of treatment by the police has been to move the intoxicated people along by making life as difficult for them as possible and harassing them when complaints were received (Devitt, 1999; Gould, 1998a). Another tactic has been to transport intoxicated Indians outside town limits, dropping them off on the side of the road to fend for themselves, regardless of the weather conditions or the state of intoxication.

One of the results of excessive alcohol consumption is an increase in levels of violent and nonviolent crime (Bachman, 1992; Devitt, 1999; Gould, 1999a). It is not uncommon to find that the very people who sell excessive amounts of alcohol to indigenous people and those who otherwise profit from these sales complain the loudest about the resulting increases in crime. The people who sell alcohol to indigenous people are often the very same people who want the police to exercise a lot of control over them. They want to sell their product, but as soon as the transaction is consummated, they want the Indians to move on until they need to buy alcohol again. Laurence French and Jim Hornbuckle (1982) found that in Nebraska, indigenous peoples constitute 1 percent of the population, but are arrested for 7 percent of all serious crimes and 25 percent of all public intoxication events, thus suggesting that there many repeat offenders. Alcoholism, alcohol-related accidents, suicides, homicides, and cirrhosis account for 35 percent of all indigenous deaths (French and Hornbuckle, 1982: 165; Lex, 1985: 154). Accidents account for about one-fourth of the deaths among indigenous people in the United States, and about 75 percent of those accidents are alcohol-related (Lex, 1985: 155). Suicide and homicide tend to occur most frequently in younger populations. The suicide rate for indigenous youths is almost double that of the overall population, and about 80 percent of the suicides appear to be alcohol-related (U.S. Department of Health and Human Services, 1987). Homicide rates among indigenous people in the United States are about three times that of the overall population, and about 90 percent of those deaths involve alcohol consumption (Greenfeld and Smith, 1999; Lex 1985: 155).

These statistics, startling as they are, are more problematic when the reactions of some European descendants who live near reservations are taken into consideration. One respondent to the Winslow Intoxicated Street People Project said, "This is what Indians do, they get drunk and either kill themselves or kill somebody else. It is their national past-time. Why should we be expected to deal with it? Let them take care of their own" (Gould, 1998a). Another person interviewed stated, "This is exactly why we don't want a treatment center for Indians in our town. It will do nothing more than draw more drunks into town where they will fight and kill each other. With that much killing going on, they could hurt a citizen" (Gould, 1998a). The attitude of these two respondents, although not representative of all people of European heritage or all people in Winslow, Arizona, does illustrate the view of a number of very vocal people. The underlying feeling is one of denial of any responsibility for or connection to the problem, as well as denial of any social responsibility for helping to alleviate the problem.

J. O. Whittaker's (1982) research on a Midwestern reservation suggests that alcohol-related problems directly or indirectly affect all aspects of life, both on and off reservations. He estimated that one of every three Indians over the age of fifteen drank to excess. Using the Centers for Disease Control's Youth Risk Behavior Survey, Gould (1999a) found that 88.9 percent of the reporting males and 92.6 percent of the reporting females on the Hualapai Reservation (Arizona) between the ages of twelve and eighteen consumed alcohol to the point of intoxication. This was a significant increase in reported consumption from the same survey conducted in 1994, in which 59.1 percent of the males and 76.9 percent of the females between ages twelve and eighteen reported similar behavior.

Charles Grim (2002) reports that alcoholism kills indigenous people at more than five times the rate of other Americans. Worse yet, it kills younger people, ages twenty-five to thirty-four, at ten times the rate of other young adults. In the same article, King notes that alcoholism usually begins early in the life of indigenous youth and strikes hard. Dale Walker, chairman of the Healthy Nations Advisory Council, a Cherokee and a University of Washington professor of psychiatry, reports that Indians do not have the access that others do to such vital basics as jobs, housing, education, and other practical life needs (Grim, 2002).

The relationship between alcohol consumption and violence is strong among many indigenous peoples (Devitt, 1999). Thus crimes such as rape, homicide, and suicide occur with much higher frequency in indigenous populations as compared to other populations, regardless of the geographic area. Alcohol is involved in 75 percent of all fatal accidents (three times as many for indigenous peoples as for other racial groups) (Kuttner and Lorinez, 1967), 80 percent of all suicides, and 90 percent of all homicides involving indigenous people (French and Hornbuckle, 1982).

Although in this chapter I focus on the North American continent, the extent of the issues can be illustrated by examples from as distant a place as Australia. Estimates in Australia suggest that 60 to 80 percent of violent crimes committed by Aborigines involve alcohol, and that in the more remote areas of Australia, the rate is between 80 and 90 percent (Western Australia Task Force on Aboriginal Social Justice, 1994: 452). These percentages compare to approximately 30 to 70 percent among non-Aboriginal populations in Australia (Alexander, 1990: 26). Compared to non-Aboriginal populations, Aboriginal people were much more likely to be held in custody for public drunkenness or in protective custody (27 percent compared to 57 percent, respectively) (Alexander, 1990). E. Hunter, W. Hall, and R. Sparge (1992) report that about half of the adult male indigenous population under age fifty had been in prison and that the risk of imprisonment increased with the frequency of alcohol consumption.

Substance abuse is inordinately harmful to the health of indigenous people (Grim, 2002; Moncher, Holden and Trimble, 1990). Native Americans lead all U.S. populations in rates of alcohol-related cirrhosis, diabetes, fetal abnormalities, accident fatalities, and homicide (Pedigo, 1983; Travis, 1983; Ward, 1984). There is a long-recognized connection between alcohol abuse and liver disease. Alcohol abuse resulting in or associated with malnutrition can lead to other disorders that, if not fatal, can significantly reduce the quality of life. Heavy consumption is also associated with anemia; pancreatic disease; diabetes; cardiac problems, including arrest; renal failure; and other disorders that reduce the quality of life and lead to long-term hospitalization and/or death. Deaths related to alcoholism are four times higher for indigenous people than for the general population, and 70 percent of all treatments provided by physicians at Indian Health Service clinics are for alcohol-related diseases or resulting trauma (Lamarine, 1998; Silk-Walker, 1998).

Maternal drinking leads to an increase in the incidence of neonatal problems and fetal alcohol syndrome (FAS) (Coulter, 1993; Godel 1992; Peterson, 1984), which in turn can result in behavioral problems and in contact with the justice system. Inebriated indigenous people in New Mexico and Arizona are often the victims of vehicle accidents as they walk along roads; they might also succumb to hypothermia after they lie down and pass out (Gallaher, 1992; Gould, 1998a). Children of parents who abuse alcohol are at an increased risk of injury from abuse and neglect (Berger and Kitzes, 1989; Lujan, 1989).

Another problem concerns the connection between the locations at which alcohol is sold and the impact on highway accidents resulting from drinking and driving. An unintended consequence of moving the sale of alcohol off a reservation is the creation of "death alleys." These occur when people drive off the reservation to the nearest alcohol beverage outlet, consume alcohol, and then try to drive back to the reservation. One example of this is a stretch of U.S. 97 in the Yakima Valley in Washington State. The Yakimas, as the result of federal legislation, forbid the sale of alcohol both on tribal land and on private land within the reservation, regardless of ownership. This includes private and public lands that are part of the checkerboard lands or continuous to them. Seventy-eight percent of the vehicle-related deaths on the Yakima reservation are alcohol-related, compared with 39 percent of the accidents throughout the rest of Washington. U.S. 97 has been the scene of the state's most gruesome drinking and driving accidents. Similar death alleys occur on U.S. 89 between Flagstaff, Arizona, and the Navajo Reservation; Arizona 66 (the old U.S. Route 66) between Truxton, Arizona, and the Hualapai Reservation; and between Whiteclay, Nebraska, and the Pine Ridge Reservation in South Dakota. Route 666 (the Devil's Highway), going north from Gallup, New Mexico, is also subject to a disproportionate number of alcohol-related fatalities.

POTENTIAL EXPLANATIONS FOR THE PROBLEM

As mentioned previously, many have presented the argument that the near absence of alcohol in precontact societies may have played a large role in postcolonial abuse of alcohol among indigenous people. This argument has relied on the assumption that, when alcohol was introduced, people drank in a largely unregulated way, which led to excess (Saggers and Gray, 1998). As a singular explanation, this approach has been refuted on two grounds: first, as previously noted, some indigenous groups did have access to psychoactive substances, including alcohol, prior to first contact. Second, this view supposes that indigenous cultures are somewhat static, a view contradicted by archaeological studies (Flood, 1995; Rowley, 1974). Other studies suggest that some indigenous people have incorporated the use of alcohol into their societies in regulated ways (Collman, 1979; Sansom, 1980).

There is no single explanation for alcohol abuse among indigenous peoples; however, one of the most prevalent theories is that the loss of or modifications in culture is a principle component of alcohol abuse. Another approach suggests that the introduction of alcohol resulted in changes that affected the culture. It was disruptive of existing social patterns and tribal hierarchy, while at the same time it was used as a tool in unfair trade practices (Gibson, 1980). To suggest that one approach is correct to such an extent that the other approach is incorrect ignores not only the problems but also the potential solutions. Saggers and Gray (1998), in their review of the indigenous people in Australia, Canada, and New Zealand, provide an excellent overview of the prevailing thoughts and of some alternative views.

Although many Europeans of varying classes and cultures immigrated, the culture of the colonist (United States, Canada, New Zealand, and Australia) was most often dominated by the political and economic elite. With some few exceptions, the culture, views, and values of the elite were held up as the goals toward which all members of the society, indigenous and otherwise, should strive. Homogeneity of the cultural values was intended to be the outcome. Groups not subscribing to the beliefs and values of the dominant group were viewed as anomalies that needed explanation (Levy and Kunitz, 1974: 9–24).

When European-based theories were applied to indigenous people, the usual outcome was that the latter lost their culture because they were deemed to be inferior. It was supposed that there were two aspects to this loss: indigenous people were feeling the impact of anomie[2] (or normlessness) or were in a state of stress as a consequence of difficulties acculturating (or assimilating) to the supposedly homogeneous wider society (Saggers and Gray, 1998). As a result of colonization, indigenous cultures were viewed as having been lost and having lost their traditional roles, thus having no social structure by which to guide their behavior or institutions that could provide social control over behaviors (Saggers and Gray, 1998). Those taking this stance suggest that the resulting breakdown of culture resulted in a psychological loss of individual autonomy, a feeling of alienation, and loss of identity and self-esteem.

Several researchers present the argument that the high levels of alcohol abuse reported among indigenous people result from an attempt to deal with the psychological problems associated with being in an anomic state or with the frustration of not being able to reach the goals set by the wider society (Albrecht, 1974; Eckermann 1977; Graves, 1967; Kamien, 1978). Alcohol is often used to relieve, through self-medication, feelings of anxiety and depression. The effects of alcohol as a medicinal aid for the treatment of anxiety and depression are short-lived and destructive. The level of tolerance is quickly reached; thus to alleviate the symptoms of anxiety and/or depression, considerably more alcohol is needed. The living conditions on most reservations and in nonreservation Indian communities is such that there are high levels of depression and anxiety. The lack of proper medical resources increases the likelihood that self-medication through the use of alcohol will be high.

The position illustrated above is not without its critics. Two propositions suggest that high levels of alcohol consumption among indigenous people cannot be explained by the anomic model. First, in their study of the Navajo, Levy and Kunitz (1971) found that the anomic explanation was not supported by the pattern of alcohol consumption among various subgroups of Navajo. They found "the highest intensity of involvement with drinking and the greatest use of alcohol was found among the most traditional and least acculturated group, while the lowest use and involvement was found in the most acculturated off-reservation group" (1971: 109).

The second criticism (Saggers and Gray, 1998: 75) suggests that contemporary indigenous people do not live in a cultural vacuum and that their cultures, like all cultures, are in a state of constant change as a result of the impact of broader social, political, and economic changes. The question is, how fast can a society adapt if it chooses to do so, and what are the relative costs of adapting versus not adapting? Neither Levy and Kunitz (1971) nor Saggers and Gray (1998) suggest this denies that indigenous people may feel pain and a sense of loss as a consequence of not being acquainted with their traditional culture. In fact, for some, the inability to connect with their traditional culture may be the impetus for increased alcohol abuse, and increased connection to traditional culture may decrease alcohol consumption.

Ronet Bachman (1992) reports that alcohol consumption is a strong intervening variable in a theoretical model for indigenous homicides. She argues that the powerlessness resulting from colonization is the result of social disorganization, a culture of violence, economic deprivation, cultural conflict, and perceived powerlessness, compounded by alcohol consumption. Bachman's proposition seems to fit neatly with the earlier works of Philip May (1982a), Lyle Longclaws, Gordon Barnes, Linda Grieve, and Ron Dumoff (1980), and L. Thomas Winfree, Curt Griffiths, and Christine Sellers (1989). Supporting Bachman's argument are the writings of R. Blauner (1972: 23):

> Colonization (subjugation and dehumanization) begins with a forced, involuntary entry. Second there is an impact on the culture and social organization of the colonized people which is more than just a result of such "natural" processes as contact and acculturation. The colonizing power carries out a policy which constrains, transforms, or destroys indigenous values, orientations, and ways of life.

Third, as noted earlier, alcohol was used as a trade item and as a means of beguiling indigenous leaders during treaty negotiations. A final fundamental ingredient of colonization is racism. Racism is a principle of social domination by which a group seen as inferior or different in terms of alleged biological characteristics is exploited, controlled, and oppressed socially and psychologically by a superordinate group (Blauner, 1972: 396).

Gould (1998a) reports a recurring theme among a small group of whites in which the general view suggests that "a drunk Indian does not possess political power" (quote from a respondent, bar owner number 1), or worse yet, "Give them all a bottle and a gun or knife, let them kill each other and then jail the last one standing" (quote from a respondent, packaged liquor store owner number 2). Although these statements are both racist and extreme, they express the feeling, to some degree or another, of the very people who profit from the sale of alcohol to indigenous people. That is in part because they know that there will be more standing in line. It was not uncommon for a store owner to have someone arrested in the morning and then sell to that person as soon as he or she bonded out.

CONCLUSION

The history of the introduction and continuing use of alcohol by Europeans and those of European heritage as a means of controlling, oppressing, and dehumanizing indigenous peoples, although circumstantial, still makes a strong case. In fact, if one were to use the weight of the circumstantial evidence to pronounce guilt, the finding would be guilty as charged. First, alcohol was used to steal indigenous goods and lands. Then it was used as part of an effort to demoralize and at the same time to create health problems; finally it was used to criminalize indigenous behavior.

It is interesting to note that the government has done little for indigenous people, compared to other social and cultural groups, to provide appropriate levels of funding for health and addiction problems. At the same time the government continues to criminalize some of the behavior, such as public intoxication and homelessness, that results from the abuse of alcohol. Although the thrust of the use of alcohol has changed over time, the outcome that is expected by some groups of Europeans remains the same today as it was 400 years ago: the destruction of indigenous peoples.

NOTES

1. The term "black-fella" is often used by Australian Aborigines to describe themselves.

2. The concept of *anomie* was developed by Durkheim (1952). Anomie refers to a pathological state of society in which consensus on social norms has broken down as a consequence of industrialization and increasing individuation. It is important to note that the term anomie has been extended to include the state of mind of an individual living in such a society (Merton, 1968: 215–217).

7

Examining the Interpretation and Application of the Indian Child Welfare Act of 1978

Tracey M. Bouvier

Congress enacted the Indian Child Welfare Act in 1978 in response to the gross inequities that Native Americans have endured since Europeans first arrived on this continent. The explicit purpose of this act was to establish minimum federal standards for the removal of Native American children from their families to protect the best interests of children and to promote the stability and security of Indian tribes and families (25 U.S.C. §1902).

Any meaningful discourse on the enactment and implementation of the Indian Child Welfare Act of 1978 (25 U.S.C. § 1901, et seq.) ("the act") must be preceded by a discussion of the impact of institutionalized assimilation efforts on Native American tribes and their people. Indeed, it was the deliberate, widespread breakup of Native American families through oppressive governmental policies that ultimately prompted the enactment of this federal remedial policy in an attempt to prevent the further destruction of Native American families, communities, and tribes.

THE HISTORICAL BASIS FOR THE CURRENT POLICY

As early as the mid-1600s, Native American families were being destroyed as European explorers abducted them and brought them back to Europe for "show and tell" (Joe, 1988: 1). In 1863, as part of a widespread governmental policy of "exile or extermination," Kit Carson and his soldiers burned Navajo cornfields, slaughtered sheep, confiscated horses and cattle, killed Navajo men, and enslaved Navajo women and children. In total, 8,354 Navajo people were removed from their homes and relocated them to eastern New Mexico (Joe, 1988; Sheridan, 1995).

Beginning in the 1880s, Indian children were sent to government boarding schools across the country (Hauswald, 1988; Kunesh, 1996). The Phoenix Indian School opened in 1891 with forty-two students; by 1907, enrollment was up to 750 Native American children, representing thirty different tribes (*The Native American,* 1916). L. Hauswald (1988: 44) observes the Navajo experience at these often harsh and brutal schools: "Children worked four or more hours a day at manual labor, were marched to and from classrooms and dormitories, were severely punished for the use of the Navajo language, often were not free to visit home."

Boarding schools, representing the epitome of governmental institutions in assimilation and cultural suppression, further destroyed Native American families. Some children never returned home (Joe, 1988; Kunesh, 1996). Hauswald (1988: 45) observes the damaging effects of these schools on Native American children and families: "The impact of boarding school on children is perhaps seen most clearly when they become parents themselves. Though these parents are often bilingual, they have internalized a negative self-image and are insecure in their role as parents." P. H. Kunesh (1996: 30) further discusses the consequences of these assimilation efforts: "Cultural disorientation results in acting out in socially aberrant behavior, delinquency, and estrangement from Indian family members."

A recent relocation effort has also greatly affected Navajo and Hopi families and communities in Arizona. In 1974, Hopi and Navajo lands were partitioned by the federal government (Public Law 93–531) in response to a long-standing land dispute between the two tribes (Joe, 1988). As J. R. Joe explains, Navajo tradition emphasizes a child's ties to the land, family, and custom, yet 6,000 to 8,000 Navajo people have been forced to leave ancestral lands. Others have been unable to build homes near their families because of the construction freeze imposed by the relocation policy.

Stock reduction was another mandated element of the relocation effort that began in the 1930s and 1940s (Joe, 1988). The outcome of this forced legislation on the lives of Navajo people, whose livelihood has depended almost solely upon their livestock, is not difficult to comprehend. Many Navajo people were left in poverty, and unemployment rose, as did the number of Navajo people on welfare (Joe, 1988). As Sheridan (1995: 22) articulates: "Seven decades of Arizona history are refracted through the lenses of people who began the century as proud and independent farmers and who ended it as impoverished wards of the state."

Ironically, the devastating poverty and dependence resulting from the government's oppressive social, cultural, and economic policies were used as grounds to remove Native American children from their homes, further severing Native American families (Kunesh, 1996). Kunesh discusses how the Bureau of Indian Affairs (BIA) and religious organizations advocated the removal of Native American children from their families on misguided charges of neglect. For example, it is reported that up to 2,000 Hopi and Navajo children were taken every year by the Latter Day Saints Placement Program, which then placed the children with Mormon families (Kunesh, 1996).

Four years prior to the act's implementation, Congress began to assess the impact of government assimilation policies that resulted in the "wholesale removal of Indian children from their homes, ... the most tragic aspect of Indian life today" (*Mississippi Band of Choctaw Indians v. Holyfield,* 490 U.S. 30, at 32). Oversight hearings in 1974 resulted in the following additional findings: "The adoption rate of Indian children was eight times that of non-Indian children. Approximately 90 percent of the Indian placements were in non-Indian homes" (*Holyfield,* 490 at 33). "Many of the individuals who decide the fate of our children are at best ignorant of our cultural values, and at worst contemptful of the Indian way and convinced that removal, usually to a non-Indian household or institution, can only benefit the Indian child" (Chief Calvin Isaac, quoted in Metteer, 1998: 424).

INDIAN CHILD WELFARE ACT OF 1978: MINIMUM STANDARDS

Congressional Declaration of Policy

The Indian Child Welfare Act was adopted by Congress in 1978 with the following declaration of policy:

> The Congress hereby declares that it is the policy of this Nation to *protect the best interests of Indian Children and to promote the stability and security of Indian tribes and families* by the establishment of minimum Federal standards for the removal of Indian children from their families and the placement of such children in foster or adoptive homes which will reflect the unique values of Indian culture, and by providing for assistance to Indian tribes in the operation of child and family service programs. (25 U.S.C. § 1902; emphasis added)

Policy Standards for the Protection of Native American Children

Three conditions are necessary for application of the act: the initiation of a child custody proceeding involving an "Indian child" within the meaning of the act who is not a resident of, or domiciled on, his or her tribe's reservation. In these situations, state courts are provided concurrent jurisdiction with tribal courts. The pertinent provisions of the act are discussed in the following section.

Definitions

For the purposes of the act, "Indian child" is defined as any unmarried person under the age of eighteen who is either a member of, or eligible for membership in, an Indian tribe and is the biological child of a member of an Indian tribe. "Indian custodian" is defined as an Indian person who has legal custody of an Indian child. "Parent" is defined as a biological parent or parents of an Indian child, or an Indian person who is the lawful adoptive parent of an Indian child.

Jurisdiction

If an Indian child is domiciled or resides off of the reservation, the state court, in a foster care placement or termination of parental rights, shall, "in the absence of good cause to the contrary," transfer the matter to the tribe upon petition of either parent, Indian custodian, or the tribe, absent objections by either parent. The tribal court may decline jurisdiction. The act further allows for tribal court intervention at "any point in the proceeding."

Court Proceedings

In an involuntary proceeding for foster care placement or termination of parental rights in a state court, if the court knows or believes that an Indian child is involved, the party seeking the action must notify the child's parent or Indian custodian and the child's tribe of their right of intervention.

A court order for foster care placement must be supported by "clear and convincing evidence" that the child's return to a parent or Indian custodian "is likely to result in serious emotional or physical damage to the child" and may include expert witness testimony.

The evidence necessary to effect a termination of parental rights requires the highest standard of proof, "beyond a reasonable doubt," that returning the child to the parent or Indian custodian "is likely to result in serious emotional or physical damage to the child."

Parental Rights

In a voluntary termination or foster care placement, written consent, at least ten days after the birth of the child, is required. Consent to a foster care placement may be withdrawn at any time. Consent to the termination of parental rights or to an adoptive placement may be withdrawn at any time, for any reason, prior to the entry of a final decree.

Placement

The following preferences shall, absent "good cause to the contrary," be given in any adoptive placement of an Indian child under state law: (1) an extended family member, (2) other members of the child's tribe, or (3) other Indian families.

In any foster care or preadoptive placement, the Indian child shall be placed in a setting that "most approximates" a family and best meets any special needs. Absent "good cause to the contrary," the following preferences shall be given: (1) an extended family member, (2) a foster home approved by the child's tribe, (3) an Indian foster home approved by an authorized, licensed non-Indian authority, or (4) an institution approved by an Indian tribe.

Improper Removal

If an Indian child has been improperly removed from the custody of a parent or Indian custodian or improperly retained, the child shall be returned unless the child would be subject to "substantial and immediate danger or threat of such danger."

BUREAU OF INDIAN AFFAIRS (BIA) GUIDELINES

Although guidelines were adopted by the BIA in 1979 to provide further direction in Indian child custody proceedings (44 Fed. Reg. 67,584, 1979), they are expressly intended as such and are not binding, unless specifically provided. Therefore, the guidelines will only be discussed in the context of their reference in guiding court decisions.

State courts are initially vested with jurisdiction in child custody proceedings involving Native American children who reside off the reservation. Therefore, state courts are charged with the application of the act's provisions. Although Congress clearly intended a uniform set of standards in the removal of Native American children from their homes, courts have inappropriately applied state law to the interpretation of numerous definitions and provisions of the act (see, for example, *Mississippi Band of Choctaw Indians v. Holyfield*, 490 U.S. 30, 1989). Consequently, variations in state laws have resulted in a different construction of the act throughout the country.

Although a comprehensive overview of the multitude of factors affecting the act's compliance throughout the United States is not feasible, an examination of Arizona court cases may provide valuable insight. For one thing, it is estimated that in 1998, the Native American population in the state of Arizona totaled 256,183, representing the third-largest Native American population in the country (U.S. Census Bureau, 1999). Furthermore, it is estimated that in 1998, the Native American population of Arizona represented 5.5 percent of the total Arizona population, ranking Arizona the sixth highest among the states in the percentage of Native American population (U.S. Census Bureau, 1999).

Additionally, although some states have implemented guidelines specific to Indian child welfare issues, most states, including Arizona, rely on case law interpretations of the act. As such, it is not uncommon for Arizona courts to cite cases in other jurisdictions to support their decisions.

ARIZONA COURT INTERPRETATION AND APPLICATION

On numerous occasions the Arizona Court of Appeals has reviewed challenges to trial court decisions involving the interpretation and application of the act. The majority of these cases are examined below within the context of the act's procedural and substantive provisions.

Matter of Appeal in Pima County Juvenile Action No. S-903, 130 Ariz. 202, 635 P.2d 187 (Ariz.App. 1981)

In this case, the Arizona Court of Appeals addressed the issue of whether "good cause" existed for the state court to retain jurisdiction in the child custody proceeding. The child's natural mother voluntarily relinquished her parental rights upon the birth of her child but revoked custody seven months later. Shortly after this time, the mother requested the tribe to intervene, and the tribe filed the necessary petition for intervention. However, at the final hearing, the lower court denied the transfer of the proceeding to a tribal court and failed to recognize the mother's revocation, citing abandonment as cause for severing the mother's parental rights. Moreover, the court held that the removal of the child from his adoptive parents would result in "serious emotional or physical damage to him" (635 P.2d at 190).

The Court of Appeals vacated the severance order and returned the child to the natural mother. The court's decision was based on three arguments: First, the tribe had exclusive jurisdiction because the court found that the child's domicile was the mother's reservation until a new one was legally acquired. Second, absent this argument for exclusive jurisdiction, the court determined that the case should have been transferred to tribal court since the relinquishment was found to be timely and properly filed and no reason was necessary for withdrawing consent. Third, the court argued that the termination of the mother's parental rights was not supported with evidence "beyond a reasonable doubt."

Matter of Appeal in Maricopa County Juvenile Action No. A-25525, 136 Ariz. 528, 667 P.2d 228 (Ariz.App. 1983)

This case also addresses "good cause" exceptions concerning the transfer of a case to tribal court upon petition. In this case, a nonnative mother consented to the adoption of her child around May 1979. The child was placed in a nonnative foster home and the putative father, a Pima Indian and member of the community, although notified, did not acknowledge paternity at that time. A petition to adopt the child was filed in February 1980, and several months later, an order terminating the rights of the putative father was filed. In November 1981, the tribal community was granted an order to intervene in the proceeding. In December 1982, the adoptive parents divorced. In approximately July 1982, the community asserted that the child was an "Indian child" and therefore subject to the act but did not offer evidence in support of this contention. Shortly thereafter, the putative father acknowledged paternity. However, one month later, the adoption was granted when the court determined that it was in the "best interests" of the child to remain in her placement with the adoptive parent.

The community appealed, arguing that the original placement was not in compliance with the act and that "good cause" was never established to avoid placement preferences mandated by the act. However, the court of appeals affirmed the lower court's decision, holding that the act was not applicable until the father established paternity, at which time removal of the child from its nonnative adoptive family would cause "psychological damage."

Matter of Appeal in Maricopa County Juvenile Action No. JS-8287, 171 Ariz. 104, 828 P.2d 1245 (Ariz. App. 1991)

The Arizona appellate court in this case also addressed the issue of whether the best interests of the child constitute "good cause" to deny the transfer of a case to tribal court. In this case, the pueblo did not file a petition for the transfer of the case to tribal court until more than two years after notification of the dependency proceedings. The court held that good cause existed for denying the transfer to tribal court "because the child had resided with foster adoptive parents since she was five months old and she had formed a bond with the only parental figures she had known." The court further held that "transfer to an out-of-state tribal court would be disruptive to her and *not in her best interest*" (828 P.2d at 1251, emphasis added). The Arizona Court of Appeals upheld this decision.

Matter of Appeal in Coconino County Juvenile Action No. J-10175, 153 Ariz. 346, 736 P.2d 829 (Ariz. App. 1987)

Another controversial issue in the interpretation of the act is the lower court's assertion of a "good cause" exception to the placement of Native American children with Native American families. In this case, the placement of a Native American child with a nonnative foster family was challenged by the child's father. The child's father was a member of the Navajo tribe, and the child's mother was nonnative.

It was never disputed by the trial court that the proceeding was a child custody proceeding. Furthermore, the trial court established that the child was an "Indian child" within the meaning of the act. However, the court acknowledged that the child had spent only "a few hours" on the Navajo reservation and had only "minimum contacts" with Native American relatives.

Therefore, although the requisite conditions clearly existed for the application of the act in this case, the trial judge attempted to apply a "good cause" exception to the child's placement with a Native American foster family on the grounds that removing the child from a nonnative home to a native home would result in "culture shock."

In this case, the trial court's attempt to circumvent the act through the use of an "existing Indian family" exception did not withstand the scrutiny of the Arizona appeals court. The Arizona Court of Appeals vacated the lower court's decision, holding that "the fact that a child may have been living in a non-Indian home is no reason, standing alone, to dispense with the provisions of the act. . . .

When the act is read as a whole, it is clear that Congress has made a very strong policy choice that Indian children, including those who have a non-Indian parent, belong in an Indian home" (736 P.2d at 832).

Matter of Appeal in Maricopa County, Juvenile Action No. JD-6982, 186 Ariz. 354, 922 P.2d 319 (Ariz. App. Div. 1 1996)

This appeal involves the issue of whether the transfer of jurisdiction to tribal court is appropriate over the objection of a parent. In this case, the father of the child was an enrolled member of the Tohono O'odham Nation, and the mother was not Native American. The trial court had appointed an attorney and a guardian ad litem to represent the mother. The child was placed in the custody of the child's paternal grandmother, who resided within the nation. Although the mother did not object to the placement, she did object to the transfer of the custody proceeding to the nation. The guardian ad litem, however, failed to object, believing it was in the mother's best interests to transfer the proceeding. Although the mother had been diagnosed as a schizophrenic, the court held that she was not determined to be incompetent for the purpose of objecting to the transfer of jurisdiction.

The guardian ad litem appealed the lower court's decision, arguing that although the absence of an objection mandates the transfer of a case to tribal court, the existence of an objection does not bind the court to deny a transfer of jurisdiction. The Arizona Court of Appeals affirmed the lower court's decision, holding that the mother's objection was valid and further that it is not within the court's discretion to transfer jurisdiction of a child custody proceeding to tribal court over the objection of a parent. Thus, although the absolute power of parental objection to deny transfer of jurisdiction to tribal court under the act was disputed, the decision in this case follows the court's holding in *Maricopa Juvenile Action No. JS-7359* (159 Ariz. 232, 766 P.2d 105, Ariz.App. 1989) that the objection of a parent "*mandate[s]* the retention of jurisdiction by the Arizona court" (922 P.2d at 321, emphasis added).

A COMMON THREAD

These cases demonstrate a discretionary interpretation of the act by the state's lower courts, clearly departing from the obvious intent of Congress. In some cases, these lower court decisions passed examination by the Arizona Court of Appeals, resulting in the retention of state court jurisdiction and nonnative placements. It is important to note that Arizona's treatment of the act is not unique but illustrates the disparity of state court interpretations throughout the United States (Dale, 1991; Gallagher, 1994; Jones, 1997; Metteer, 1998; Stiffarm, 1995). Although Congress intended to achieve nationwide consistency in applying the act, B. J. Jones (1997: 396) eloquently observes: "This objective has proven to be illusory and the goal of uniformity a farce. Many state courts have created exceptions to the application of ICWA and have interpreted the statute in such a manner as to render many of its provisions superfluous."

Although specific provisions of this Indian child welfare policy are often broad and ambiguous, its intent is to provide "minimum" standards for protecting Indian children and their families and tribes. In *Mississippi Band of Choctaw Indians v. Holyfield* (490 U.S. 30, 1989), the only Indian Child Welfare Act case to be reviewed by the U.S. Supreme Court, the court acknowledged that the purpose of the act was "in part, to make clear that in certain situations the state courts did *not* have jurisdiction over child custody proceedings. Indeed, the congressional findings that are a part of the statute demonstrate that Congress perceived the States and their courts as partly responsible for the problem it intended to correct" (490 U.S. at 45).

It is clear from a review of Arizona cases that the state's courts have devised numerous strategies throughout the course of child custody proceedings to avoid application of the act. For example, in one case, three deficient grounds were used by the lower court to avoid the application of the act: (1) a deficient definition of "domicile," (2) failure to acknowledge the mother's relinquishment of her consent to adoption, and (3) the "best interest of the child" test (*Pima County Juvenile Action, No. S-903*, 130 Ariz. 202, 635 P.2d 187, Ariz. App. 1981).

In another case, the court placed the burden for establishing paternity upon a Native American father, thus avoiding transfer to the tribal court, even when the tribe petitioned for intervention (*Maricopa County Juvenile Action No. A-25525*, 136 Ariz. 528, 667 P.2d 228, Ariz. App. 1983). Then, once paternity was established, the nonnative adoptive placement was held to be in the "best interests of the child" because of the length of time that had elapsed.

Moreover, although the Arizona Court of Appeals determined in *Maricopa County Juvenile Action No. JD-6982* (186 Ariz. 354, 922 P.2d 319, Ariz. App. Div.1 1996) that it is *mandatory* for the state to retain jurisdiction where a parent objects to the transfer of jurisdiction to tribal court, this interpretation appears to be discretionary. Although some researchers would agree that retention is "mandatory" in this situation (Snyder, 1995), others would disagree, asserting that upon parental objection to a transfer of jurisdiction, state courts "may" retain jurisdiction (Stiffarm, 1995). The act clearly allows for "good cause" exceptions to the act in issues related to jurisdiction and placement. Absolutely, good cause exceptions should prevail in certain situations. Disturbing, however, is the widespread abuse of discretion, developed under the guise of "good cause" exceptions, to sidestep the spirit and intent of this federal remedial policy.

"Good Cause" Exceptions

As M. J. Dale (1991: 386) observes, "Good cause is by its nature a subjective standard." The act does not establish a standard of proof for "good cause" exceptions to jurisdictional and placement issues (Aamot-Snapp, 1995). Although the guidelines developed by the BIA attempt to narrow the field of "good cause" exceptions to the act, state courts have expanded this term beyond the scope of the guidelines to include such exceptions as the "existing Indian family" exception. That was used to avoid placement of a Native American child with a Native American foster or adoptive family by the lower court when the child had spent little time on the reservation or with native family members (*Coconino County Action No. J-10175,* 153 Ariz. 346, 736 P.2d 829, Ariz. App. 1987). Although the "existing Indian family" exception was denied by the Arizona Court of Appeals in *Coconino County Action No. J-10175* (153 Ariz. 346, 736 P.2d 829, Ariz. App. 1987), and later denied by the U.S. Supreme Court in *Holyfield* (490 U.S. 30, 1989), courts in several states have continued to rely on variations to this exception (Jones, 1997).

Another "good cause" exception that has been widely employed in avoiding the application of the act is one that places a mainstream standard of "the best interests of the child" above a "best interests of the Indian child" test. Indeed, the Arizona Court of Appeals determined in *Maricopa County Juvenile Action No. A-25525* (136 Ariz. 528, 667 P.2d 228, Ariz. App. 1983) and *Maricopa County Juvenile Action No. JS-8287* (171 Ariz. 104, 828 P.2d 1245, Ariz. App. 1991) that the traditional "best interests of the child" standard constituted "good cause" to avoid transferring jurisdiction to tribal court.

As one researcher observes, "The best interest of the child doctrine is deeply ingrained in American jurisprudence" (Dale, 1991: 365). Dale explains that the act, however, rejects an "Anglo best interest of the child test," which is based on "Anglo middle-class" standards (1991: 370). The U.S. Supreme Court in *Holyfield* quoted the Pima County court (635 P.2d at 189), concluding that: "The act is based on the fundamental assumption that it is in the Indian child's best interest that its relationship to the tribe be protected" (490 U.S. at 50). The Pima County court further expressed anguish over the attempted use of a traditional "best interest of the child" test. It concluded that the "evil which Congress sought to remedy by the act was exacerbated by the conduct here under the guise of 'the best interests of the child'" (635 P.2d at 193).

One of the issues that contributes to the use of a mainstream "best interest of the child" standard by state courts is the courts' consideration of "psychological" or "emotional" damage in removing a Native American child from a current nonnative placement. This argument is made on the basis of the attachment of a Native American child to a nonnative family, which is often the situation after protracted court proceedings. However, this issue was addressed in *Holyfield,* wherein the U.S. Supreme Court rejected this argument.

The act clearly mandates placement preference, "absent good cause to the contrary," with (1) members of the Indian child's extended family, (2) other members of the Indian child's tribe, or (3) other Native American families. The U.S. Supreme Court in *Holyfield* acknowledged this provision as the "most important substantive requirement imposed on state courts" (490 U.S. at 36) and further recognized that this placement preference extends beyond the wishes of parents who consent to an adoption. Therefore, even in cases where a tribe does not accept jurisdiction (*Maricopa County Juvenile Action No. JS-8287,* 171 Ariz.

104, 828 P.2d 1245, Ariz. App. 1991), if the child meets the act's definition of an "Indian child," the act nevertheless applies, and placement preferences pursuant to the act are thus mandated. In this case, if the act's placement preferences had been followed from the onset of the dependency proceedings, a traditional "best interest of the child" test would not have been necessary.

TRENDS IN PLACEMENTS SINCE THE INCEPTION OF THE ACT

As the foregoing review illustrates, state courts have disparately interpreted the act and, at times, successfully impeded its intended purpose. Although the Arizona Court of Appeals has attempted to rectify some of the abuses by lower courts (*Pima County Juvenile Action No. S-903,* 130 Ariz. 202, 635 P.2d 187, Ariz.App. 1981; *Coconino County Juvenile Action No. J-10175,* 153 Ariz. 346, 736 P.2d 829, Ariz. App. 1987), it has not always taken a hard line on these issues. In some cases, the Arizona appellate court has allowed lower courts to avoid the transfer of jurisdiction on the basis of a traditional "best interest of the child" test that considers the emotional damage in removing the child from the nonnative family (*Maricopa County Juvenile Action No. JS-8287,* 171 Ariz. 104, 828 P.2d 1245, Ariz. App. 1991; *Maricopa County Juvenile Action No. A-25525,* 136 Ariz. 528, 667 P.2d 228, Ariz. App. 1983). In another case, the transfer of jurisdiction to a tribal court was avoided on the basis of the court's interpretation of parental objection as absolute power against such transfer (*Maricopa County Juvenile Action No. JD-6982,* 186 Ariz. 354, 922 P.2d 319, Ariz. App. Div. 1 1996). Thus, the overall impact of this legislation in Arizona is not clear.

One method of measuring compliance with the act's provisions is to analyze changes in adoptive and foster care placements since the act's inception. A quantitative study conducted by A. E. MacEachron and colleagues (1996) analyzes changes in the rates of foster care placements and adoptive placements of Native American children based on data from 1975 and 1986. This research demonstrates a 42 percent decrease in the rates of foster care placements in Arizona from 1975 to 1986. Furthermore, the rate of adoptive placements decreased by 98 percent in Arizona over the same period of time.

Although these statistics are impressive in addressing overall rates of change since before the inception of federal Indian child welfare policy, it is important to note that this study is not without limitations. The authors concede problems in reconciling variations in the data sources. Moreover, there is an inherent failure of a quantitative analysis to address the issue of Native American children who never come to the attention of tribal authorities.

Although this study would suggest that the act has been successful in reducing foster care and adoptive placements of Native American children, other researchers would argue that the act has been only "partially successful," since Indian children are still "greatly overrepresented" in substitute care. The number of Indian children nationwide in such care actually increased in population from

7,200 in 1980 to 9,005 in 1986 (Kunesh, 1996: 26). Therefore, although these statistics would indicate a trend toward Native American self-determination in child welfare issues, various limitations in this study prevent a clear understanding of the act's compliance.

Upon a review of the act's legislative history, its provisions, the U.S. Supreme Court's discussion of this legislation, and Arizona court interpretations, what does become apparent is that the act has been inconsistently interpreted by state courts. That has not infrequently resulted in the retention of state court jurisdiction and nonnative placements.

THE IMPACT OF ARIZONA COURT INTERPRETATION AND APPLICATION OF THE ACT ON NATIVE AMERICAN CHILDREN, FAMILIES, COMMUNITIES, AND TRIBES

Undoubtedly, the act is a monumental step in the direction of Native American sovereignty and self-determination and in recognizing the best interests of Native American children. A quantitative analysis reflects positive trends in the placements of Native American children since the act's inception.

Yet, as previously discussed, some courts rely on a majority culture "best interests of the child" standard, resulting in the placement of Native American children outside their culture. This standard for Native American children is refuted upon a review of the research examining the effects of a nonnative placement on a Native American child. Testimony from the U.S. Senate oversight hearings in 1974 revealed: "They were raised with a white cultural and social identity... . Then during adolescence, they found that society was not to grant them the white identity that they had" (*Holyfield,* 490 U.S. at 33). A 1984 report by the American Indian Tribal Court Judges Association further describes the plight of Native American children raised with nonnative families:

> Indian children placed in non-Indian homes often feel rootless. In adolescence and/or when they leave the non-Indian family, many find that they are neither Indian [nor] non-Indian. These rootless (anomic) feelings often lead to acute hopeless and powerless feelings closely associated with abandonment and stressful loss. The result is a suicide rate among non-Indian adopted Native American adolescents that is twice that found on any reservation. (quoted in McCarthy, 1993: 871)

Furthermore, when a Native American child is placed with a nonnative family, the child is often denied exposure to his or her own cultural heritage. R. M. Underhill (1979: 89) discusses the ties that a Papago child has to its extended family and community: "The Papago child was born not into a single family but into a group. All decisions were made, all actions undertaken, with the advice and help of these relatives who were, one old man told me, 'the other end of his navel cord.'"

The child's removal from his or her native culture also has long-term effects on the child's tribe, which depends upon its children for survival: "When the power [to grant an adoption] is used to remove an Indian child from the surrounding most likely to connect that child with his or her cultural heritage, that decision unintentionally continues the gradual genocide of the Indians in America" (Justice Fadeley, quoted in Aamot-Snapp, 1995: 1167).

Tribal sovereignty and self-determination are further threatened by the courts' discretionary construction of the act. Kunesh (1996: 17) defines "tribal sovereignty" as "the force that binds a community together and represents the will of a people to act together as a single political entity." Even though federal policy in Indian child welfare is believed to be "one of the singularly most important pieces of federal legislation recognizing tribes' sovereign rights to protect the interests of their communities and their children" (Kunesh, 1996: 34), these efforts toward tribal sovereignty continue to be threatened by the disparate treatment of the act by state courts. As the *Holyfield* court observes, "Probably in no area is it more important that tribal sovereignty be respected than in an area as socially and culturally determinative as family relationships" (490 U.S. at 34).

It is clear from this discussion that the interests of Native American children, families, communities, and tribes are inextricably connected and, moreover, that the act's noncompliance deeply affects all these entities. Therefore, it is crucial to Native American children, families, communities, and tribes that Arizona courts be held to a higher standard in rejecting federal policy mandates concerning the removal and placement of Native American children. This opinion is widely held among advocates of this policy, as well as among the members of the U.S. Supreme Court. Thus, several alternative strategies have been either proposed or implemented for attempting to increase the overall impact of federal Indian child welfare policy.

IMPLICATIONS FOR POLICY AND RESEARCH

Some advocates would argue that the best way to ensure a higher level of compliance with the act is to limit state court discretion by requiring adherence to BIA guidelines (Stiffarm, 1995). Others argue for a complete eradication of "good cause" exceptions to the transfer of proceedings and placement preferences listed in the act, arguing that "nationwide uniformity" of the act—as called for by the *Holyfield* court—necessitates such reconstruction of the act (Metteer, 1998). Similarly, but more liberally, Aamot-Snapp (1995: 1,194) argues for "several specific exceptions" to the act's provisions. Others call for the exercise of greater authority by federal courts as provided by Congress (Jones, 1997). Jones provides a strong argument for federal courts to intercede where state courts attempt to bypass the act. Indeed, in the absence of some form of accountability, compliance with the terms of the act will always be questionable. Although this solution would appear to provide much-needed accountability in state court interpretations of Indian child welfare policy, there is little assurance that oversight by federal courts will take place.

One policy that appears to be fulfilling this accountability role is a child welfare services agreement between the Navajo Nation and the Arizona Department of Economic Security. According to Dolores Gray Eyes (personal communication, April 26, 1999), the agreement was signed in 1987 for the purpose of improving the coordination of services in Native American child custody proceedings, both on and off the reservation. For example, with regard to child custody cases that fall under the provisions of the act, the agreement provides for state child welfare agency recognition of the Navajo tribe's licensing of foster care and adoptive placements. The agreement is supported by an intergovernmental agency (IGA), including staff from the Navajo Nation and the Arizona Department of Economic Security. The IGA is notified of all Arizona child custody proceedings that potentially involve Navajo children and provides services pursuant to the agreement. Furthermore, the IGA meets on a quarterly basis to staff cases and receive administrative training. The need for this type of interagency collaboration is clearly implicated in this review of Arizona cases, and, according to Gray Eyes, appears to be successful in returning Navajo children to the reservation.

CONCLUSION

The Indian Child Welfare Act of 1978 clearly represents a vital step in federal legislation toward enhancing Native American sovereignty and self-determination and simultaneously toward protecting the best interests of Native American children. This important federal legislation has potentially positive consequences for Native American children and their families and tribes, but those consequences have so far eluded researchers. Although a statistical analysis shows a positive trend in placements since the act's inception, Arizona courts have at times successfully circumvented the true spirit of the act. Obviously, more research is necessary to shed greater light on these issues.

Furthermore, the establishment of interagency coalitions represents a crucial step toward protecting the best interests of Native American children. It also helps to promote the stability and security of Native American tribes and families in the interpretation and application of federal Indian child welfare policy. This type of interagency collaboration has the potential to provide the necessary accountability to ensure that the spirit and intent of the act are followed throughout the course of child custody proceedings. However, although such a collaborative effort is promising, further research is necessary to determine the impact of this coalition on the outcome of Native American child custody proceedings.

In the meantime, Arizona courts continue to construct discretionary interpretations of the act, applying their own far-reaching exceptions to the policy's provisions. The result is continued assimilation and cultural suppression, as well as threats to Native American sovereignty and self-determination. The recognition of these consequences by Arizona courts is imperative. As Congress explicitly stated when it enacted this federal remedial legislation (25 U.S.C. § 1901): "[T]here is no resource that is more vital to the continued existence and integrity of Indian tribes than their children."

8

Law Enforcement and the American Indian

Challenges and Obstacles to Effective Law Enforcement

Eileen Luna-Firebaugh and Samuel Walker

What does it mean to be a tribal police officer? What are the intricacies of this role? How do the tribal community and the tribal police department interact and solve the problems facing Indian Country? These questions and others frame the challenges facing American Indian tribal governments as they seek to advance tribal self-determination and sovereignty in the United States today.

A 1999 study by Lawrence A. Greenfeld and Steven K. Smith for the Bureau of Justice Statistics (BJS) painted a bleak picture of the American Indian community. This research found that American Indians experience per capita rates of violence that are more than double those of the U.S. population in general, and Indian young adults—those between the ages of eighteen and twenty-four—were the victims of violence at the highest rate of any racial group considered by age, about one violent crime for every four persons of this age.

The study found that American Indian women are the victims of crime at a rate that is nearly 50 percent higher than that reported by black males. Yet another startling fact is that American Indians are usually criminally victimized by someone of another race. At least 70 percent of the crime experienced by American Indians is interracial, with the criminal perpetrator being white in 60 percent of the cases.

The incarceration rate for American Indians, reflected in the Greenfeld and Smith study, is similarly startling. American Indians were held in local jails at the highest rate of any racial group. Further, on a per capita basis, American Indians were incarcerated in prisons at a rate that was 38 percent higher than the national rate.

The predominant factor in the BJS study was the effect of alcohol consumption. Almost half (46 percent) of all convicted American Indians in local jails were under the influence of alcohol when they committed the offense for which they were convicted. This percentage rises to 70 percent when only violent crimes are considered. These percentages contrast starkly with all other racial groups, where only a third or less were reported to be under the influence of alcohol during the commission of nonviolent crimes and 41 percent for violent crimes.

The effect of these statistics and the environment they create in Indian Country is a problem for both tribal governments and tribal law enforcement agencies. The decisions that must be made, the policies and protocols that must be developed, and the staff that must be recruited and trained are challenges that must be overcome if crime and criminality are to ease in Indian Country.

CULTURAL CONFLICT

The interaction between law enforcement and American Indians has historically entailed one of the most challenging sets of negotiations facing Indian Country and its peoples since colonization.[1] Law enforcement, in the way it is most commonly conducted in the United States, is a foreign concept to most Native American communities. The concept of "professionalized" policing, with its emphasis on technology, specialized police activities, and restricted use of police discretion, does not conform with the style of peacekeeping most commonly used in traditional or rural communities.

This Western style of law enforcement was imposed on Indian peoples by the U.S. government, through the use of the plenary power doctrine. This doctrine, invented by the U.S. Supreme Court in the early 1800s, with the rulings in the Marshall trilogy (*Johnson v. McIntosh,* 21 U.S. [8 Wheat.] 543, 5 L.Ed. 681 [1823]; *Cherokee Nation v. Georgia,* 30 U.S. [5 Pet.] 1 [1831], and *Worcester v. Georgia,* 31 U.S. [6 Pet] 515 [1832]), and furthered by the ruling in *Lone Wolf v. Hitchcock* (187 U.S. 553, 23 S.Ct. 216, 47 L.Ed. 299 [1903]), maintains that the U.S. government has absolute power over Indian tribes and peoples, irrespective of tribal sovereignty, treaty rights, or even covenants of international human rights. External law enforcement, relying as it does on the control of behavior by outside forces rather than by self-discipline or the action of family, clan, or tribe, does not fit Indian traditions.

Given the overlay of the imposed structure over the traditional systems, the relationship between Indian peoples and law enforcement, even Indian police, has been difficult. The example of the 1890 killing of Sitting Bull, the greatest maker of medicine of the Great Sioux Nation, by Indian police employees of the U.S. government, still remains one of the examples given when Indian peoples discuss law enforcement on reservations. This killing, which occurred after Sitting Bull had voluntarily turned himself in for embracing the Ghost Dance religion, is often cited as evidence to support Indian contentions that police and the policing of Indian communities are suspect and not in the best interest of Indian peoples. Unfortunately, Sitting Bull's death is not the only example of bad policing that can be cited when discussing the policing of Indian communities.

THE PROBLEMS WITH PROFESSIONALIZED POLICING IN INDIAN COUNTRY

The concept of "professionalization" dominates policing in the United States. The development of standardized codes and protocols and the standardization of training and structures of administration are widely perceived as worthy goals. However, many problems arise with a "professionalized" policing approach as it is attempted in Indian Country. Professionalized policing is based within an adversarial context, with the police officers holding the "thin blue line" against wrongdoers for the benefit of an uninvolved community. It is based on quick response to calls for service and on a hierarchical system of management and decisionmaking. This structure and these emphases, by their nature, are difficult to apply in Indian Country (Luna, 1997).

Much of Indian Country is rural. The populations can be widely dispersed, often reached by unpaved and unmarked roads. According to a recently conducted national survey of American Indian tribal police, most tribal police agencies have ten or fewer sworn officers, and only half have 911 emergency response systems.[2] Thus a conventional service response approach to policing can be remarkably ineffective.

The situation facing American Indian tribal police is particularly difficult. The 1997 *Report of the Executive Committee for Indian Country Law Enforcement Improvements* authored by Kevin V. Di Gregory, deputy assistant attorney general, and Hilda A. Manuel, deputy commissioner of Indian affairs to the U.S. attorney general and the secretary of the interior (Washington, October 1997), found that tribal law enforcement was "fragmented," with "poor coordination" and a "lack of adequate resources." It concluded: "There is a public safety crisis in Indian Country."

In addition to the coordination problems, there are networks of reciprocity and responsibility within Indian communities that can unite when faced with the imposition of a law about which they may know little and that, in any case, they may not support. Couple these factors with an historical distrust of police, be they Indian or non-Indian, and you have a situation that may not be best policed with conventional methods.

THE INTERRELATIONSHIP BETWEEN TRIBAL SOVEREIGNTY AND COMMUNITY EMPOWERMENT

However difficult the establishment and implementation of tribal law enforcement agencies may be in Indian Country, the benefits that may accrue to tribal communities are significant. American Indian tribal sovereignty has been under attack by the Congress and the U.S. Supreme Court during recent years. Court decisions such as that of *Seminole Tribe of Florida v. Florida* (517 U.S. 44 [1996]) have been setbacks for the assertion of tribal rights to self-determination. Legislation such as that proposed in the 106th Congress by Senator Slade Gorton (R-Washington), which attempts to restrict tribal sovereignty, threatens tribal governments and chills the movement toward tribal community empowerment.[3]

The development and promulgation of a strategy to further tribal sovereignty, self-determination, and community empowerment in this hostile environment is critical if Indian Country is to survive and prosper. However, the question arises as to how this strategy can best develop. One way is the pursuit of "de facto" sovereignty. It arises naturally from the undertaking of the competent provision of essential governmental services, whether or not explicitly permitted under existing state or national laws. Although de jure tribal sovereignty, that which flows from legislation and court decisions, is under attack, the concept of de facto sovereignty has become more accepted and is heightened by the movement of tribal governments to provide law enforcement services to their members.

THE FRAGMENTATION OF INDIAN LAW ENFORCEMENT

Complicated legal issues face tribal, state, and local law enforcement in Indian Country or in areas geographically adjacent to reservations. In states other than those in which Public Law 280 applies (discussed below), subject matter jurisdiction over criminal conduct is usually determined on the basis of three issues: (1) whether the parties involved in the incident are Indians, (2) whether the incidents giving rise to the complaint took place in Indian Country, and (3) the nature of the offense. For the purpose of this chapter, "Indian" is defined as a person of Indian blood who is recognized as a member of a federally recognized tribe. Indian Country includes (1) all land within the limits of any federal Indian reservation, (2) all dependent Indian communities, and (3) all Indian allotments.

The Major Crimes Act

The Major Crimes Act (18 U.S.C. sec. 1153 [1988]) gives the federal government jurisdiction over thirteen violent felonies[4] when those criminal acts are alleged to have been committed by an American Indian. The Assimilative Crimes Act (18 U.S.C. Sect 1162) and the Organized Crime Control Act have also been held to apply to Indian Country. These laws restrict the activities of tribal law enforcement.

For those felonies covered by the act, there is the necessary involvement, at some level, of federal law enforcement agencies.

Criminal Jurisdiction under Public Law 280

Under general principles of federal Indian law, states do not have direct jurisdiction over reservation Indians. However, Congress has the power to vest federal authority with the states, which it did with the 1953 passage of PL 83–280 (18 U.S.C. Sect 1162). Public Law 280 expressly grants concurrent jurisdiction over Indians within Indian Country to six mandatory states[5] and allows other states to take jurisdiction voluntarily,[6] with the consent of the tribal governments. Congress has allowed PL 280 states to retrocede the assertion of jurisdiction on a piecemeal basis, so even where it is the law, PL 280 does not apply with every tribe within a given state.[7]

Congress did not grant the states regulatory jurisdiction over Indian Country under PL 280. Language in Public Law 280 specifically precludes the states from taxing the reservations for services, such as law enforcement and access to state courts, rendered pursuant to such jurisdiction;[8] from infringing on water rights (28 U.S.C. Sec 1360 [b]); or from interfering with, controlling, or regulating any rights or privileges related to hunting, fishing, or trapping afforded under federal treaty, agreement, or statute.[9]

Public Law 280 remains a significant factor in Indian Country today. The states in which the act is a factor include those with extremely high proportions of Indian peoples.[10] The tribes in these states often have police departments, even though the states, under PL 280, are required to provide law enforcement services. In these instances and in others, tribal and state powers are concurrent, even though some states, particularly California, have denied that such tribal jurisdiction exists (Goldberg-Ambrose 1994).

VARIETIES OF INDIAN LAW ENFORCEMENT

Approximately 170 reservations have law enforcement departments. This number reflects a period of significant growth during the 1990s.[11] It is this growth that necessitates a careful look at how the departments are being planned and implemented and what approach is being taken to the development of appropriate protocols and procedures. To this end a national study of American Indian tribal police was conducted during 1996–1998. This chapter is based on the results of this survey.

Tribal Law Enforcement Structures

The law enforcement agencies operating within Indian Country consist of five distinct types. These forms are not mutually exclusive and often operate simultaneously within the boundaries of a given reservation. Two types involve the Bureau of

Indian Affairs (BIA-LES and PL 638), which traditionally had responsibility for all law enforcement on Indian reservations. Although in the past states had no responsibility for law enforcement on Indian lands, that changed with the 1953 passage of PL 280 (18 U.S.C. Sec. 1162). For a number of years, the result of this exercise of federal plenary power was that few, if any, Indian nations in PL 280 states developed police departments. This situation has changed, however, and now throughout the United States, even where PL 280 exists, many Indian nations have their own tribal police that they fund and control.

Tribal police departments often operate on reservations covered by other forms of law enforcement, including BIA, PL 638, and/or self-governance–funded law enforcement programs. All this, of course, creates problems of overlapping jurisdiction and conflicts of law.

BIA-LES

On sixty-four reservations the police are BIA personnel, funded and directed by the bureau, with little or no accountability to the tribal councils or tribal governments resident on a given reservation. Bureau policies are controlling, and any concerns regarding law enforcement conduct or procedures must be addressed through BIA administration.

Public Law 93–638

Approximately ninety tribes have exercised their rights under PL 93–638 and have taken over law enforcement functions, in whole or in part, from the BIA. Through this act, the tribe must enter into an agreement with the bureau and sign a contract that mandates certain law enforcement activities. The tribe agrees to provide those mandated services in exchange for federal funding through the bureau. There is no control mechanism, however, to ensure that the services are, in fact, provided, nor are there any external standards against which the services provided are routinely measured.

Tribally Funded Police

An ever growing number of reservations, now approximately sixty, have tribally funded police. These police departments are controlled by and accountable to the tribal governments directly. The reservations are free to conduct their law enforcement activities as they see fit, which has resulted in significantly different training and qualifications of personnel. The codes, policies, and police protocols, where they are in place, vary widely.

Self-Governance

Under the Indian Self-Determination Act of 1994 (H.R. 4842), twenty-five tribes direct their own law enforcement activities. This act empowers the secretary of the interior, upon the request of a tribe, to grant funds for the purpose of "the strengthening or improvement of tribal government," including the provision of law enforcement services, the nature of which is determined by the tribe. Although a reporting requirement exists within the act, the nature and contents of the report are not delineated.

State Law Enforcement Pursuant to Public Law 280

A number of reservations (thirty-nine) and 106 rancherias (small, rural, Indian areas, many of which are not federally recognized) are situated within those states that were delegated law enforcement authority pursuant to PL 280. The Bureau of Indian Affairs has no authority to act in these areas. Often, whether because of the relatively remote locations of the Indian areas or negligence or unwillingness, the local sheriff does not provide adequate law enforcement services to the tribes. This neglect has forced a number of tribes to try to fend for themselves or to do without.[12]

RESOURCES AND STAFFING PROBLEMS

The challenges for the adequate provision of law enforcement services that face American Indian tribal police departments are significant. Budgetary constraints, a shortage of personnel, and widespread rural jurisdictions create problems. The commitment to tribal sovereignty can negatively affect the willingness of the tribal government to enter into cooperative agreements with non-Indian police agencies.

Personnel

The national study of American Indian tribal police departments revealed that more than half (54.8 percent) of those that responded to the survey have ten or fewer sworn officers. Only 13 percent have twenty-one or more sworn officers (see Figure 8.1). The relatively small size of most of these departments is comparable to most police departments in rural areas throughout the United States.

It is difficult for a tribal police department of this size to have specialized units. Instead, the officers are generalists. They must meet the needs of tribal members across a sometimes wide geographic area. Almost half of all tribal police agencies (46.6 percent) have operating budgets of $500,000 or less (see Figure 8.2). Most agencies (41.4 percent) report that the Bureau of Indian Affairs (BIA) provides 100 percent of the operating budget. Only 17.2 percent indicate that they receive none of their budget from the BIA.

The high percentage of tribes that receive all or a significant level of law enforcement services from the BIA raises the issue of accountability. The BIA is not accountable to the tribes for which it provides services. Where, as with law

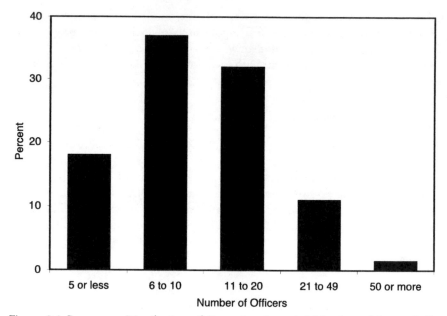

Figure 8.1 Percentage Distribution of Reporting Agencies' Number of Sworn Police Officers

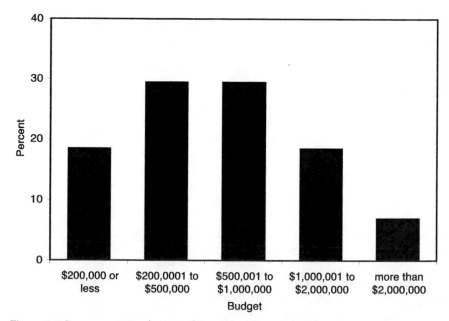

Figure 8.2 Percentage Distribution of Reporting Agencies' Budgets

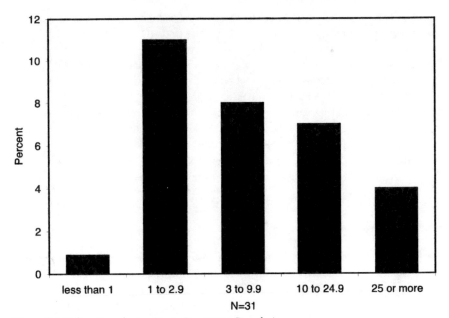

Figure 8.3 Police-Population Ratio Per 1,000 Population

enforcement, the services provided are critical and the manner in which they are provided can be such a point of community contention, the fact that an unaccountable agency is so heavily invested can be extremely problematic. Half of the responding agencies (thirty-one) provided usable data on reservation populations that permitted calculation of police population ratios (see Figure 8.3). Extreme variations exist in these ratios.

About a third of the reservations (eleven out of thirty-one) have police to population ratios in the range of 1 to 3 per 1,000, which is roughly comparable to most cities and counties in the United States. About one-fourth (eight out of thirty-one) have relatively high ratios (3 to 10 per 1,000). Another third, however, have extremely high police to population ratios. Seven reservations have ratios in the range of 11 to 25 per 1,000, and four have ratios in excess of 25 per 1,000. One tribe reported a police to population ration of 140 per 1,000, and another reported a ratio of 240 per 1,000. Only one tribe reported a ratio of less than 1 per 1,000.

The "Report of the Executive Committee for Indian Country Law Enforcement Improvements" found a "chronic shortage of personnel" in tribal law enforcement agencies.[13] It estimated that the overall police population ratio was one-half of the equivalent ratio for non-Indian communities when, according to the 1996–1998 study, about two-thirds of all reservations have police to population ratios that are either higher or extremely higher than equivalent non-Indian communities.

Given these police to population ratios, it is hard to explain the findings of the report. Perhaps part of the explanation is that the report was based on aggregate data, not on data from individual tribes or agencies. Another factor could be that the "chronic shortage" may not be a result of a lack of personnel per se, but either a lack of adequate personnel relative to the geographic size of the community and/or a lack of resources (e.g., lack of 911 systems, insufficient number of vehicles, etc.) that prevents effective service to the community.

Given the reported inadequacy of police services in Indian Country, it is unfortunate that only half (50 percent) of the tribal police departments reported participating in a 911 emergency telephone system. The possible problem of inadequate numbers of police per square mile is undoubtedly compounded by the lack of such a system.

Personnel Policies

A significant percentage of the tribal law enforcement responding to the study (41.1 percent) pay their patrol officers $10 per hour or less (see Figure 8.4).

It is difficult to assess the adequacy of this pay rate, however. Although this rate would be extremely low for non-Indian agencies, it must be measured against the levels of poverty and unemployment faced by those living in tribal areas. A comparison with these figures indicates that tribal police may be among the privileged few to have adequately paid employment.[14]

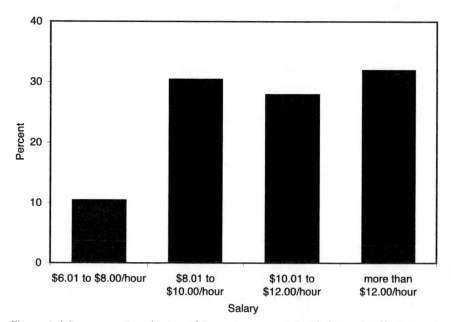

Figure 8.4 Percentage Distribution of Reporting Agencies' Tribal Patrol Officer Average Hourly Salary

Although the pay levels may be low, the tribal police departments do provide benefits that are common to law enforcement in the non-Indian community. Ninety percent of all agencies provide sworn officers with life insurance, 65 percent provide retirement benefits, and 92 percent of officers receive annual leave.

Although the educational level on many reservations is very low, the tribal law enforcement agencies uniformly require at least a high school degree or a GED for employment.[15] Only one tribe reported not requiring a high school diploma. This educational requirement is consistent with the majority of rural and even urban police departments in the United States. An additional factor for American Indian tribal police departments is the obvious preference for hiring Indian people into sworn positions. Although only 10 percent of the agencies reported requiring tribal membership for new employees, the vast majority (85.5 percent) reported having a Native American preference for new employees.

The issue arises as to the legal propriety of a Native American hiring preference instituted by tribal governments. The Indian Civil Rights Act (25 U.S.C. Sec. 1301–1303 as amended) states in part 1302. "No Indian tribe in exercising powers of self-government shall (8) deny to any person within its jurisdiction the equal protection of its laws or deprive any person of liberty or property without due process of law," but this wording has not interfered with the right of a tribal government to establish a Native American preference for hiring.

Operational Policies

American Indian tribal police departments and those local law enforcement agencies that abut reservations have significant jurisdictional issues to overcome if they hope to provide quality service to Indian peoples. With rural and tribal law enforcement strained because of wide geographic dispersal and limitations on 911 service, the ability to provide adequate service and to enhance officer safety can depend upon good working relationships between local and tribal law enforcement. Unfortunately, these good relationships do not always exist.

Cross-Deputization

Cross-deputization of law enforcement personnel is a common measure by law enforcement agencies to maximize police services. Although it would seem to be a logical choice to enhance service provision where tribal and state lands are contiguous and intermingled, it is not a simple question for tribal governments. With cross-deputization, tribal police are given deputy status by state authorities, and state police are given deputy status by tribal officials. Thus, both the tribal police and state law enforcement have the power to arrest wrongdoers, whether or not they are Indian and whether or not they are on the reservation.

Almost half (42.6 percent) of the responding tribes cross-deputize their officers with county sheriffs' departments. Only 13 percent reported that their officers are cross-deputized with other tribal law enforcement agencies, only 11.5 percent cross-deputize with city police departments, and only 6.6 percent cross-deputize with state law enforcement agencies.

Although cross-deputization may seem like a good idea, cooperation between the tribal, state, and local agencies has not been good. One stumbling block is that sometimes only one agency wants to cross-deputize. Another is that often state agencies refuse to recognize the training received by tribal police officers, allowing only those who have graduated from state police academies to be state-certified.

The issue of state concerns regarding law enforcement training prior to cross-deputization is a critical one for tribal governments. Tribal sovereignty and the issue of culturally appropriate law enforcement practices cause many tribes to prefer to have their sworn officers trained by the tribe, rather than by a state academy. The BIA Indian police academy, widely seen by tribes as an acceptable alternative, has become a limited option because of restrictions on the available training opportunities and the significant cost to the tribes.

Co-investigation and Mutual Aid Agreements

Local and state law enforcement agencies and tribal governments also fail to exercise joint jurisdiction in co-investigation of criminal incidents and mutual aid agreements. Such hesitation to use programs standard in the field of law enforcement generally results from issues of tribal sovereignty and cultural compatibility of police training. Approximately one-half of the responding tribal law enforcement agencies (45.9 percent) have a formal mutual aid agreement with the county sheriff. Only 26.2 percent have a mutual aid agreement with city police, however.

Most tribal law enforcement agencies co-investigate criminal incidents with other agencies. Almost half (49.2 percent) co-investigate with the county sheriff, and 42.6 percent do so with state law enforcement agencies. The vast majority of tribal police departments (88.5 percent) co-investigate with the Federal Bureau of Investigation (FBI). This high number is probably a function of the Major Crimes Act and the resultant federal jurisdiction over the act's enumerated felonies.

Written Policies and Procedures

Given the recent establishment of most tribal police departments and the informality with which many operate, the development of written, comprehensive bodies of policies and procedures is critical. Most tribal police departments have written, formalized procedures, although some have collections of standing orders that serve as protocols. Most of the responding tribal police departments (93.4 percent) have a written policy on the use of deadly force by their officers. Only slightly more than half (55.7 percent) of those policies represent a "defense of life" standard. This rule, first adopted by the New York City Police Department in 1972, and now the norm in mainstream policing, limits police shootings to situations that pose a threat to the life of an officer or another officer. This policy also bans warning shots, shots to wound, and shots at or from moving vehicles. Officers are required to write a report each time they discharge their weapon. Most agencies (82.3 percent) have a written policy on handling domestic violence incidents. Two-thirds (66.1 percent) of those policies represent a "mandatory arrest" standard.

Accountability Systems

Almost all agencies (93.5 percent) have a formal procedure for handling community complaints against their officers. One-fifth (21.3 percent) have a community review board for handling complaints. Only 13 percent, however, have a brochure explaining the complaint process.

These systems vary from tribe to tribe, but all fall within the general structures common in the non-Indian community. The tribal accountability systems generally rely on investigations of misconduct done by the police departments themselves. The findings of these investigations are then reviewed by boards of tribal community members who may comment on the adequacy of the findings and in some cases may hold their own hearings on the allegations of wrongdoing (see Table 8.1).

Tribal Jails

The BJS Study (Greenfeld and Smith 1999) found that there are fifty-six jails run by tribal governments in Indian Country (see Table 8.2). The jails are located in twenty different states, some of them under the jurisdiction of Public Law 280. Four of the jails are jointly run by tribal consortiums, whereas a number of the others receive inmates from other tribes on a contract basis. BIA data reported in the study indicated that tribal jails employed 659 persons and had an authorized inmate capacity of approximately 2,000 adults and juveniles.

Indian people have had many adverse experiences in jails and prisons run by federal, state, and local governments. Thus, although the development and staffing of tribal jails can be both a financial and operational burden for tribes, it can also bring significant benefits for tribal people. Tribal jails allow tribal members to be housed within or close to their home tribal community, thus increasing the possibility of family and cultural contacts while also holding miscreants directly accountable to the Indian nations themselves. This can be a significant step forward for law and order in Indian Country.

CONCLUSION

The pursuit of tribal sovereignty and self-government necessitates the development of democratic institutions within tribal governments that are both adequate and accountable.[16] Where these institutions of government are not accountable or do not meet the needs of tribal members, they can do more harm than good. Tribal

Table 8.1 The Structure of Tribal Police Oversight Boards

	State	Composition of Board	Officers on Board	Authority	Policy	Public Meetings	Confidentiality of Records
Santa Ana	N.M.	Tribal Council (TC)	Yes	Mandatory	Yes	Yes	Unknown
Rocky Boy's	MT	TC/Law Enf. Committee	No	Advisory	Yes	Yes	Unknown
Pine Ridge	S.D.	Independent	No	Advisory	Yes	Yes	Yes
Lac du Flambeau	WI	Independent	No	Mandatory	Yes	Yes	Yes
Spirit Lake	N.D.	Independent	Yes	Advisory	Yes	Yes	Yes
Menominee	WI	Independent	No	Advisory	Yes	Yes	Yes
White River	AZ	Independent	Yes- half officer/half Community	Advisory	Yes	Yes	
San Carlos	AZ	TC/Law Enf.Committee	No	Advisory	Yes	Yes	Unknown
Muckleshoot	WA	Independent	No	Mandatory	Yes	Yes	Yes
Fort Hall	ID	Independent	Yes	Advisory	Yes	Yes	Yes
Kickapoo	KA	Independent	Yes-half officer/half Community	Mandatory	No	Yes	
Cheyenne Arapaho	OK	Independent/elected	Yes	Mandatory	No	No	
St. Regis	NY	Independent	No	Advisory	No	Yes - upon request	Yes
Creek	OK	Independent/elected	No	Advisory	Yes	Yes	
Navajo	AZ	TC	Yes	Advisory	Yes	Yes	Yes
Rosebud	S.D.	Independent/appointed	Yes	Advisory	No	Yes	
Lummi	WA	Independent/appointed	Yes	Advisory	Yes	Yes	
Mohegan	CT	Ombudsman	Yes	Advisory	Yes	Yes	Yes
Hannahville	MI	Independent/TC	No	Advisory	Yes	No	No
Fort Peck	MT	Independent	Yes	Advisory	No	No	Yes
Omaha	NE	Ombudsman	Yes	Advisory	Yes	Yes	Yes
Cheyenne River	S.D.	Independent/TC	Yes	Advisory	Yes	Yes	Yes

Table 8.2 Tribal Jail Capacity and Jail Staff, by State and Tribe, 1998

State	Tribe	Adult Cap.	Juvenile Cap.	Staff
Alaska	Metlakatla Indian Community	8	0	4
Arizona	Navajo Nation	208	36	96
	Colorado River Indian Tribes	30	8	12
	Fort Mohave Indian Tribe	1	1	4
	White Mountain Apache Tribe	31	17	22
	Hopi Tribe	68	28	8
	Tohono O'odham Nation	33	16	31
	Gila River Indian Community	73	32	40
	Salt River Pima-Maricopa Indian Community	70	33	18
	San Carlos Apache Tribe			
	Hualapai, Havasupai, Prescott Apache, and Tonto	38	0	14
	Apache Supai Tribe	36	8	7
	Pascua Yaqui Tribe	1	1	6
California	Chehalis Indian Tribe	2	0	1
Colorado	Southern Ute Tribe	4	0	5
	Ute Mountain Ute Tribe	4	0	5
Idaho	Shoshone-Bannock Tribe	24	6	4
Michigan	Saginaw Chippewa Tribe	2	6	9
Minnesota	Boise Forte Tribe	8	1	0
	Red Lake Chippewa Tribe	18	4	13
Mississippi	Mississippi Band of Choctaw Indians	32	8	17
Montana	Blackfeet Tribe	34	8	12
	Crow Tribe	34	34	5
	Gros Ventre and Assinboine Tribe	8	2	5
	Assinboine and Sioux Tribe	21	0	19
	Northern Cheyenne Tribe	10	21	3
	Chippewa Cree Tribe	22	3	3
	Confederated Tribes of Salish and Kootenai	16	4	11
Nebraska	Omaha Tribe	20	12	9
Nevada	Battle Mountain, Duckwater, Ely, Goshute, South	20	12	9
	Fork, Elko Band, and Wells Band	28	0	5
New Mexico	Jicarilla Apache Tribe	0	8	0
	Laguna Pueblo Tribe	12	4	5
	Mescalero Apache Tribe	24	0	7
	Taos Pueblo	8	0	5
	Ramah Navajo	10	0	5
	Isleta Pueblo	6	0	6
	Zuni Pueblo	22	12	13
	Navajo Nation	41	14	21
North Dakota	Spirit Lake Sioux Tribe	25	8	5
	Standing Rock Sioux Tribe	42	8	8
	Turtle Mountain Chippewa Tribe	22	8	8
	Three Affiliated Tribes	8	0	6
Oklahoma	Sac and Fox Nation	0	69	23

Table 8.2 *(continued)*

State	Tribe	Adult Cap.	Juvenile Cap.	Staff
Oregon	Confederated Tribes of Warm Springs	32	12	13
South Dakota	Cheyenne River Sioux Tribe	53	10	24
	Crow Creek Sioux Tribe	10	4	2
	Lower Brule Sioux Tribe	14	2	4
	Oglala Sioux Tribe	52	32	31
	Rosebud Sioux Tribe	48	16	12
	Sisseton-Wahpeton Sioux Tribe	16	4	5
Utah	Uintah and Ouray Tribe	24	0	5
Washington	Olympic Peninsula Tribes	14	4	8
	Puget Sound Tribes	7	1	7
	Kalispel and Spokane Tribe	8	0	4
	Confederated Tribes of Yakama Nation	30	17	10
Wisconsin	Menominee Tribe	32	10	16
Wyoming	Shoshone and Arapaho Tribe	26	4	6

This chart was originally published in Greenfeld and Smith (1999).

police departments, given their importance in the maintenance of law and order and the protection of tribal members, cannot be allowed to fit into the latter category. They must be both culturally compatible and effective in reducing crime and in providing law enforcement services to a largely underserved population. The question becomes how it can best be done.

To truly meet the needs of Indian people, tribal police departments must be carefully planned and implemented to fit each community and the challenges it faces.[17] They must be accountable to the tribal government to ensure that any defects in the original design, staffing, or operations can be corrected as they become apparent.

The concept of community policing, an approach that is beginning to take hold in the non-Indian community, is easily applicable to Indian Country. This approach to policing is based on the concepts of restorative justice and the enhancement of community cohesion and action, ideas that fit well within Indian Country.

The community policing approach of proactive peacekeeping rather than arrests and crime control after an incident also fits well, as does an emphasis on responsibility and accountability of law enforcement to the community, rather than only to the department's chain of command. The devolution of power to and community consultation with a broad-based circle of responsible leaders is a common approach to decisionmaking in many Indian communities. This element alone could greatly enhance the work of police in Indian communities.

However, one criticism often levied against community policing systems, with their emphasis on devolution of authority and decisionmaking from the top of the hierarchy to lower-level officers, is that the resultant reduction in centralized control can also lead to a lack of appropriate accountability. In order to overcome this danger, tribal police departments should develop clear rules and protocols for officers to follow, thus alleviating the tendency to make up rules as questions arise.

Tribal police departments are perfectly positioned to reflect the best in American policing. They are close to their communities, generally reflect the diversity of those communities, and are in the early stages of development. The importance of this early stage of development cannot be overstated, as bad habits and tolerance of misconduct have not yet had the opportunity to become deeply rooted in the departments. Tribal police departments are thus at a critical stage in their development. Making the correct decisions now will be of great significance for the development of tribal police programs in the future, as well as for the enhancement of tribal sovereignty and self-governance.

NOTES

1. Portions of this article were originally published in Luna, *The Growth and Development of Tribal Police* (1998).

2. Research conducted by the authors, 1997–1999. Information obtained from this study serves as the basis for the data to be found throughout this chapter.

3. The American Indian Civil Rights Enforcement Act (S.2298); the American Indian Contract Enforcement Act (S.2299); the State Excise Sales and Transactions Enforcement Act of 1998 (S.2300); the Tribal Environmental Accountability Act (S. 2301); and the American Indian Tort Liability Insurance Act (S.2302) all require the waiver of tribal sovereign immunity as necessary to enforce the acts.

4. Murder, manslaughter, kidnapping, maiming, a felony under chapter 109 A, incest, assault with intent to commit murder, assault with a dangerous weapon, assault resulting in serious bodily injury, arson, burglary, robbery and a felony under section 661 of this title within Indian Country.

5. Alaska, California, Minnesota, Nebraska, Oregon, and Wisconsin.

6. Florida, Idaho, Iowa, Montana, and Washington. The state of Nevada asserted jurisdiction and then retroceded it.

7. Carole Goldberg-Ambrose, *Planting Tail Feathers: Tribal Survival and Public Law 280* (American Indian Studies Center, 1997).

8. Ibid., pp. 86–89.

9. Ibid., pp. 45–124.

10. PL 280 states at present are the following: "mandatory": Alaska, California, Minnesota (except Red Lake), Nebraska, Oregon (except Warm Springs), and Wisconsin. "Optional" states, which assumed full or partial jurisdiction, are Arizona, Florida, Idaho, Iowa, Montana, Nevada, North Dakota, South Dakota, Utah, and Washington.

11. This study conducted by the authors found that the number of tribal police departments had grown from 114 tribes in 1995 to 170 as of fall 1996.

12. For more on the subject of Public Law 280, see Goldberg-Ambrose, *Planting Tail Feathers.*

13. See the comment on a "chronic shortage of personnel" in Indian Country law enforcement agencies, ibid., p. 6.

14. The 1980 U.S. Census figures revealed that the percentage of reservation-based American Indians over the age of sixteen who were employed was slightly higher (65 percent) than the percentage of the general population (62 percent); the income levels were significantly lower. The median family income in 1980 for reservation-based American Indians was $9,920, and 45 percent were living below the poverty threshold of $7,412. These numbers compare negatively to the general population median income of $19,920 and to the only 12 percent of the general population who were living below the poverty threshold in 1980.

15. The 1980 U.S. Census figures revealed that only 43 percent of American Indians over the age of twenty-five who resided on reservations were high school graduates, as compared with 67 percent of all Americans.

16. For more on this subject, see Stephen Cornell and Joseph P. Kalt, "Reloading the Dice," in *What Can Tribes Do?* (American Indian Studies Center, 1992).

17. The Federal Community Oriented Policing Services (COPS) program contends that there are five elements necessary for law enforcement to become culturally competent: (1) valuing diversity, (2) having the capacity for cultural self-assessment, (3) being conscious of dynamics inherent when cultures interact, (4) gaining cultural knowledge, and (5) adapting to diversity. These elements are provided to law enforcement agencies as part of the COPS information kit.

9

Policing Native Americans Off the Rez

Jeffrey Ian Ross

In many U.S. cities, particularly those in the western United States, among the homeless and downtrodden are a sizable number of Native Americans. The more visible can be found sitting on park benches, hanging out on "skid row," drinking alcohol from paper bags, sprawled out on sidewalks sleeping, or hidden in doorways at night (e.g., Kuttner and Lorincz, 1970). They have typically made their way to an urban location from the reservation and are either finding it difficult to go back or do not want to return. Alternatively, these individuals may have lost their marginal jobs and are now caught in a downward economic spiral.

Eventually, they may be picked up by police and will appear in front of a commissioner or judge, usually much more frequently than members of comparable groups of "down and out" individuals. Typically they are charged with petty crimes or misdemeanors such as driving without a license, driving with an expired license, public intoxication, or possession of small amounts of street drugs. For the police, conducting these types of arrests is relatively routine and easy. Offenders are typically well known to the officers, court personnel, and people who work in the local lockup; they are often repeat offenders, day in and day out (Hagan, 1966; Harring, 1982).

Unfortunately, little scholarly research has been conducted on the relationship between Native Americans and municipal police in border towns or metropolitan areas with moderate to large populations of indigenous peoples. In this chapter I attempt to redress this shortcoming by outlining the problem, reviewing the research, and presenting some potential areas for future investigation. Although in some parts of the United States, native reservations abut municipalities (including big city jurisdictions) (Fogelson, 1977) and natives are just as likely to have contact with park or housing police, the focus of this chapter is on municipal policing in large urban centers. Understandably, policing Native Americans may be more of a problem for small town police forces (e.g., Galliher, Donovan, and Adams, 1975; Royster and Fausett, 1988), the focus of the chapter is on the big city environment.

THE PROBLEM

In order to convey the importance of the problem, I examine the number of Native Americans living in major metropolitan areas, the statistics on Native American crime and arrests, and finally the possibility of recruitment of Native Americans onto large municipal police forces.

The Distribution of Native Americans in Cities

Perhaps demographics have an impact on the importance of Native Americans in cities? In order to determine the distribution of natives in the United States, I looked at the most recent national census (2000). Although this type of analysis does not uncouple the categories of American Indian and Alaska Native, it gives us a reasonable guide to those locations (other than reservations) where Native Americans live. And even though cities are major focal points since the suburbanization of the United States, a considerable number of native people live in the neighboring suburbs or counties. According to the 2000 census, three counties are identified as having the largest number of Native Americans or Alaska Natives: Los Angeles County, California (138,700); Maricopa County, Arizona (75,900); and McKinley County, New Mexico (57,100). These locations should come as no surprise, because each is relatively close to native reservations.

Alternatively, narrowing the focus to cities, New York City, Los Angeles, and Phoenix have the highest populations of native peoples: New York perhaps because it is the largest city in the United States and Los Angeles and Phoenix because they are close to nearby reservations. For example, just south of Phoenix is the Gila River Indian Community, a reservation consisting of the Pima and Maricopa tribes. Phoenix is also the location of more than one Indian school and is bordered on the south by the Gila and on the east by various Apache reservations. It also attracts Navajo, Yavapai, White Mountain Apache, some (but not many) Hopi, Pima, Tohono O'odham and other tribes because of the demand for unskilled labor. Once again using census figures and understanding that people are quite often multiracial or multiethnic, I can further break down the categories into two types: those individuals reporting that they are Native American and Alaska Native alone or in combination with one or more other races and those individuals who claim to be American Indian and Alaska Native alone. The figures are as follows: New York City: 87,200/41,300; Los Angeles: 53,100/29,400; and Phoenix: 35,100/26,700.

Although these numbers may seem high, when you calculate the numbers as a percentage of the total population living in these cities to provide a proxy measure of the importance, you get a very different picture. They are, respectively using American Indian and Alaska Native figures combined: New York City (0.01 percent), Los Angeles (0.02 percent), and Phoenix (0.04 percent).

More specifically, based on 1997 data from the Bureau of Justice Statistics, collected through the Law Enforcement Management and Administrative Statistics (LEMAS) study, which every four years compiles information on almost all police departments in the United States, the following communities have the largest number of sworn native officers: Modesto, California (10 percent); Tulsa, Oklahoma (6 percent); Long Beach, California (5 percent); Duluth, Minnesota (4 percent); and Lawrence, Kansas (4 percent) (Reaves and Goldberg, 1999). But these statistics should be treated cautiously, as will be demonstrated further in the chapter (see Table 9.1).

The Thorny Issue of Crime and Arrest Rates

Perhaps if we had a sense of the arrest rates or criminality among Native Americans, then we could get a handle on how much of an issue Native American crime is for local law enforcement. Although the paucity of this kind of analysis has been identified by others (Young, 1990), Native American arrest rates have ranged from a low of 1,699 per 100,000 in 1935 to a high of 15,123 in 1960. Since then, the rate has declined. Following this peak, American Indian arrest rates show a more gradual decrease, with the most recently published studies (based on 1985 data) indicating an American Indian arrest rate of between 7,859.2 and 8171.5 per 100,000, depending on whether the census figures were used to calculate the rate and whether they included Alaska Natives as well (Green, 1999: 184). Despite this statistical data, it has been noted that native criminality is higher on the reservation than off. And since the figures presented above do not disaggregate between Indian Country and cities, it is difficult to know with much confidence how much criminality there is by urban natives.

Table 9.1 Top Five Local Police Departments with High Number of Native Americans, as Identified by LEMAS, 1997

Police Dept.	# Sworn Officers	% of Native Officers	# of Native Officers
Tulsa, OK	800	6.0	48
Long Beach, CA	838	5.0	42
Modesto, CA	248	10.0	25
Duluth, MN	141	4.0	4
Lawrence, KS	110	4.0	4

Recruitment of Native Americans on Police Forces

By logical extension, it would stand to reason that in jurisdictions with the highest number of Native Americans, there would be a greater proportional number either of native police officers or of police, divisions, or units charged with providing policing services to Native Americans.

One way to understand this issue, once again, is through the LEMAS database. An examination of the numbers of Native Americans in police departments immediately shows their relative absence. For example, in the 2000 LEMAS survey of 17,784 police agencies (Hickman and Reaves, 2002: table 7), Asians, Native Hawaiians, or other Pacific Islanders, American Indians, and Alaska Natives comprised only 2.7 percent of the total. This figure contrasts sharply with the numbers of Black/African Americans, and Hispanic/Latinos in police departments. Despite their numbers in the general population, Native Americans are rarely hired and trained to work for municipal police forces. That may be because of a shortage of appropriate applicants in the local labor market, or it may reflect a natural and historical antipathy between Native Americans and the dominant white police departments. It may also be that suitable trainees go somewhere else, like federal law enforcement, where they are paid better and possibly receive more prestige. Quite often, there are a limited number of Native American candidates in the pool of those interested in being police officers, and many of them work on reservations, leaving a very small number available for employment in urban areas.

In order to determine the contextual issues of native police officers on forces, I made several inquiries through the offices of chiefs of police and/or the chief information officer at several cities (including those previously mentioned) and in police departments where incidents of police insensitivity to Native Americans have been reported in the media or documented by investigative bodies (i.e., Seattle, Minnesota, and Oklahoma City). These inquiries were generally ignored, but I performed a series of follow-up contacts, and a handful of forces provided me with relevant information. (See chapter appendix for questionnaire and Table 9.2.)

Results from the Questionnaire

What became immediately clear was that there are noticeable differences between the statistics reported in the 1997 LEMAS survey and those that I gathered. For

Table 9.2 Response to Native Americans in Municipal Policing Questionnaire, 2003

Police Dept.	# Sworn Officers	% of Native Officers	# of Native Officers
Tulsa, OK	766	9.0	67
Long Beach, CA	950	0.8	8
Modesto, CA	264	0.4	1
Duluth, MN	143	2.0	5
Lawrence, KS	138	10.0	14

Administered September 11, 2003, and completed November 5, 2003 many departments, the number of Native American police officers differs radically from those reported in 1997. This may be simply a result of the six-year time lag.

Although most departments reported a low number of Native American police officers as a percentage of the total, one agency claimed to have one captain, four sergeants, and five corporals, all of whom are Native American. Another police force estimated the total number of native officers and then qualified the statement by saying, "but not all of those officers claim Native American affiliation."

Most of the departments said that there were no special efforts to recruit Native Americans on their police department. Two suggested that they actively recruit all minorities. Another said: "The chief of police teaches a course at a university at the local reservation. They also participate in career fairs at the university/college on the reservation."

Although most departments reported that calls for service and/or crimes by or against Native Americans were negligible problems for their department, one representative said that, "We don't keep statistics on race of victims, so I can only say we have frequent contacts with Native American victims and suspects."

Most of the police forces report that there are no special case workers in the department or community that can serve as a liaison to the department. One department qualified this answer by outlining the partnership they had with a local hospital through what they called Mental-Health Evaluation Teams (MET). "For example, if they were dealing with a Native American person, they might call on one of our sworn officers who is also Native American in an attempt to gain a better understanding of that person's needs. Unlike the patrol officers, the MET Team has the time, resources, and experience to offer the quality service that is often required by people with special needs."

And finally, most respondents said that no contact was made with other large metropolitan police departments with respect to recruiting Native American police officers or sharing in expertise. Only one police force mentioned that it maintained contact with a Native American colleague who had moved on to another police department, but the quality of this relationship was not followed up on.

REVIEWING THE RESEARCH

To better understand this subject matter, I briefly review the research on Native Americans and policing. In the main, references to policing Indian peoples can be found in policing texts or in a number of tertiary subject areas.

Little scholarly research exists on the role of indigenous people in the criminal justice system. That should come as no surprise to most criminologists, as the absence of minorities' perspectives in criminal justice sources, including introductory texts, has been previously noted (Mann, 1993; Walker and Brown, 1995). There is, however, sporadic research by federal government departments that is relatively useful in providing insights into the plight of native policing, conducted by researchers who have been contracted by the government to review policing practices or by commissions of inquiry into some aspect of policing involving Native American peoples in the United States. Unfortunately for my purposes, the majority of research on the relationship between Native Americans and the criminal justice system looks at this subject matter in the context of Indian Country (e.g., Deloria and Lytle, 1983; MacLeod, 1937; Wachtel, 1982). Why? It only makes sense. The lion's share of natives live on reservations carved out for them some two centuries ago by the federal government.

In recent years, largely through the financial sponsorship of the U.S. Department of Justice (National Institute of Justice or Office of Community-Oriented Policing), there has been increased professional (e.g., Etheridge, 1977) and scholarly interest on the plight of policing in Indian Country (e.g., Barker, 1998; Feinman, 1986; Luna, 1997, 1999; Wakeling, Jorgensen, and Michaelson, 2001; Chapter 8 in this volume). This research, focusing particularly on native police officers and their work, has been conducted by a handful of academics and researchers working at universities. True research has been produced on the role of police officers in Alaskan villages, in particular the Village Safety Police Officers (VSOP) program (e.g., Angell, 1981; Marenin, 1992a, 1992b, 1994; Marenin and Copus, 1991; Rennin, Marenin, and Corpus, 1991), but it generally ignores large cities like Anchorage or Juneau, Alaska. Missing from this mix, however, is an extended discussion of the relationship between Native Americans and police in cities.

The Policing Texts

Several introductory texts on policing in the United States have been published. Since most are directed to municipal policing and natives are generally underrepresented in these contexts, rarely is there any mention of policing this subgroup of the dominant population. When they do mention policing of Native American communities or Native American police officers, it is usually in the context of policing in Indian Country.

If the subject matter of policing is not found in the dominant policing texts, then perhaps it will be included in the numerous edited books, readers, or anthologies that are frequently used in upper-division policing classes? The answer is a resounding "no."

Tertiary Subject Areas

Some of the research and writing concerning Native Americans and policing can be found in the literature that deals with U.S. police and minority relations (Shusta et al., 1995). Although some of this information is present in Canadian texts (e.g., Fleras, Desroches, and Cryderman, 1986; Jayewardene and Talbot, 1990; Lee, 1981; Ungerleider and McGregor, 1991), U.S. textbooks seem to ignore this topic. Here too, however, Native Americans are treated in passing, or the geographical focus is on Indian Country.

CURRENT AND DEVELOPING POLICY AREAS

Prompted by periodic instances of insensitivity in police-native relations throughout the country, the U.S. public, policymakers, and police personnel realize that better solutions must be found to avert potential crises.

Four policy issues most relevant to the policing of Native Americans can be identified. These areas are, in increasing importance: the recruitment of Native Americans onto police forces, the attitudes of Indians toward police and vice versa, violence against Indians by police, and the delivery of police services to Native Americans.

First, in former settler states (e.g., Canada, the United States, and Australia), there has been a movement toward indigenizing the police. During the last decade of the twentieth century, many justice officials believed that the policing of Indian peoples would be improved if it was done by natives themselves. It has been assumed that Native American police officers would be particularly sensitive to the needs of fellow Native Americans and Indian police would commit less violence toward Indian peoples. Unfortunately, there is considerable simplistic thinking concerning natives policing themselves. Scholars have simultaneously been cautious enough to point out that "Changing who wears the uniform without simultaneously reducing risk, or providing alternative resources to deal with it, does nothing to change the ability of any type of policing service to meet the security needs of the community" (Landau, 1994: p. 26; Landau, 1996).

Hiring appropriate Native Americans to join municipal police forces has been difficult. According to several police personnel whom I have interviewed, one of the largest problems with recruiting natives onto police forces is that since they are in such high demand, those who are relatively capable end up getting hired away from the forces from which they first started, lured by better pay, benefits, and working conditions.

Second, like many African Americans and Hispanics in the United States, Native Americans have a considerable amount of distrust and antipathy toward the police (Skoog, Roberts, and Boldt, 1980; Williams, Chadwick, and Barr, 1979). Missing is how the dominant settler communities feel about police-native relations, Native Americans as perpetrators of crime, and so on. This sort of information is necessary to convince the dominant white population, which ultimately holds the purse strings, that native-police relations need more resources. With occasional exceptions (Parnell, 1979), little is known about how the police feel toward Native Americans.

Third, although anecdotal information exists, little systematic research has been conducted on the problem of violence (and abuse) against Native Americans, partly because this subject matter is rarely a cause of study. When studies are produced, they are usually in the context of governmental inquiries examining some sort of real or alleged abuse. Fourth, by far the greatest area of importance is the research and scholarship examining the provision of policing services to native communities, including such issues as response time and the ability to properly intervene when there is a case of domestic violence or intoxication.

Conclusion

Rigorous analysis is a necessary step in remedying unresolved difficulties in the understanding of social control in this subject and policy area. Two issues, however, are of particular concern. Perhaps one of the reasons why the recruitment, selection, and training of Native American police is so difficult is because law enforcement in the United States is still heavily immersed in the European means of social control and values that do not work well or conflict with those of Native Americans.

Additionally, by far the dominant research has been on policing on the reservation or in Indian Country (e.g., Carter, 1976). This is true despite the fact that a considerable amount of research on the role of and difficulties faced by Native Americans in municipal contexts exists (e.g., Dosman, 1974). Meanwhile, the majority of research on policing in the United States concentrates on urban contexts. What is clearly missing is research on policing native peoples who live in the cities (Griffiths, 1994: 125). Hopefully this research will lead to well-informed policies and practices that are properly implemented. It would also mean that more Indian people would be trained and recruited by municipal forces and given a wide range of roles and responsibilities, instead of simply just working in their own communities.

Appendix: Native Americans in Municipal Policing Questionnaire

1. What is the total number of sworn officers in your department?
2. How many Native American police officers do you currently employ?
3. Are there special efforts to recruit Native Americans onto the department?
4. To what extent are Native American calls for service and/or crime by or against Native Americans a problem for the department?
5. Are there special case workers that the department uses in sections of the town or city that deal with the Native American community?
6. Do you have any contacts in other large metropolitan police departments that deal with similar issues with their Native American officers and community?

Notes

Special thanks to Natasha J. Cabrera, Larry Gould, Matthew J. Hickman, and Catherine Leidemer for comments. I also want to extend my appreciation to Kim Pressley and Mark Sherwood, Tulsa Police Department; Mike Patrick, Lawrence Police Department; W. Paul LeBaron, Long Beach Police Department; the Modesto Police Department; Cyndi Montgomeri, Minneapolis Police Department; and Jim Wright, Duluth Police Department, for responding to my questionnaire.

Imprisonment and American Indian Medicine Ways

A Comparative Analysis of Conflicting Cultural Beliefs, Values, and Practices

William G. Archambeault

Although each Native American culture was unique and the healing traditions of each were geographically different, *all* of these systems were *holistic;* they treated the body, the mind, and the spirit or soul together. Modern medicine is often criticized because of its failure to address the holistic nature of the human, despite the fact that spiritual and psychological systems of beliefs have long been recognized as being associated with patient recovery.

SURVIVING SEVEN CENTURIES OF ETHNIC CLEANSING AND CULTURAL GENOCIDE

A great deal of indigenous healing knowledge was destroyed by the actions of white European and U.S. political powers. An understanding of this history places in context the struggles of native peoples for their rights today. These actions included the U.S. policies of stealing the lands and later the natural resources on reservation lands through executive and congressional acts and policies, such as the Dawes Commission (1887–1912) and the 1950s termination of reservations; and U.S. policies aimed at destroying Indian religions and healing. The reality for American Indian peoples was that they were not made citizens of the United States until 1924 and were banned from citizenship in some states until the 1970s.

The Rising Phoenix

As late as the 1950s, some traditional ceremonies were banned on Indian reservations, such as the Sun Dance, sweat lodges, and even certain forms of traditional dancing. Despite centuries of discrimination, ceremonial and healing knowledge and traditions had been preserved, and this knowledge was rekindled among some tribal peoples. The political militancy of organizations such as the American Indian Movement (AIM) in the 1970s, the legal advocacy of organizations such as the Native American Rights Fund, and militant actions such as the seizure of Alcatraz Island and the siege at Wounded Knee II combined with public awareness to bring about many long-overdue changes in U.S. and state policies toward Native Americans. American Indian study programs were established at some universities, and many reservations founded community colleges. There was also a growing "pan-Indianism" that united Indian peoples from many different tribes into coalitions of politically active groups aimed at bringing about more change. However, the centuries of damage to Indian cultures and healing traditions could not be healed quickly.

Two successes of united Indian political efforts were the American Indian Religious Act (AIRA) of 1978 and the 1993 Religious Freedom Restoration Act (RFRA). AIRA made it possible for many previously banned ceremonies and medicine healing ways to be conducted both on and off reservations, but the legislation did not guarantee to American Indians the same First Amendment protections enjoyed by Christian, Jewish, Islamic, and other religious groups. For example, it is acceptable for Christian or other denominational services to use wine or other forms of alcohol in religious services, despite legal prohibitions against alcohol sale and consumption on reservations. By contrast, members of the Native American Church and others who used sacred ceremonial substances, such as peyote or eagle feathers, still could not do so. Further, the law did little to guarantee that Indians who were confined in correctional facilities had access to traditional healing ceremonies or sacred locations.

These weaknesses were overcome in 1993 by RFRA. In 1994, however, the U.S. Supreme Court ruled RFRA to be unconstitutional. So, in the practice of their traditional religions, American Indian peoples today do not enjoy the same protections and First Amendment rights as do those of other groups. The vestiges of centuries of bias and discrimination remain.

According to the 2000 U.S. Census, 4.1 million people identify themselves as "American Indian." Approximately two out of three live in suburban or urban areas, with the remainder living in rural or reservation areas. Many native peoples today are isolated from the traditional homelands and their tribal cultures. It is said of many native peoples today what many Indians said of whites who invaded their lands: "They have lost their spiritual center, harmony, and balance." Evidence of this fact is seen in many ways, especially when examining criminogenic and social disorganization factors.

Criminogenic and Social Disorganization Factors

Criminological and criminal justice knowledge about Native Americans is limited. Until after 1995, federal funding policies on minority research and traditional academic criminological research generally ignored crime and justice issues among American Indians.[1] What is known and recently reported is surprising to many who are not familiar with the historical treatment of Native Americans in the United States. For example, American Indians have the highest victimization rate for crimes of violence—including rape, sexual assault, robbery, and aggravated assault—of any minority in the United States (Greenfield and Smith, 1999; Rennison, 2001). Victimization is twice that of African Americans and four times that of Asians. This rate is the highest in all settings—rural, urban, and suburban—and for both genders. Further, although for all other racial groups the perpetrator of violence, including murder, is most likely the same ethnicity as the victim, the perpetrator of violence against an American Indian is most often white. The bias against American Indians also shows in the fact that between 1973 and 1997, of the 139 people sentenced to death, 52, or more than 37 percent, were Native Americans, although Indian populations accounted for only about 1 percent of the population at the time.

Crimes related to alcoholism, drug abuse, family violence, assault, and other acts of violence are prevalent on many reservations and communities. Self-degradation, suicides, alienation, and despair are also common. The rate of reported child sex abuse is significantly higher on Indian reservations than among the general population (National Indian Justice Center, 1995). Suicide rates are more than 100 percent greater, and homicide rates are over 170 percent higher on Indian reservations than among the general public, yet medical resources are significantly lower (Young, 1991; Young and French, 1997). Given these facts, it follows that disproportionate numbers of Native Americans are found in the populations of jails, prisons, and other forms of correctional control. Lawrence Greenfeld and Steven Smith (1999), for example, found that the number of Indians (per 100,000 population) under some form of correctional control was more than twice that of the general population. They also reported that the number of Indians held in jails was the highest for any minority group. Even these numbers are misleading and underestimate the number of native peoples held under some form of correctional control for at least two reasons: (1) mainstream criminology and criminal justice journals and federally funded minority crime-related studies continue to discriminate against Native Americans by ignoring American Indian justice issues or simply ignoring the existence of Indian populations in minority studies; and (2) Indian peoples in some U.S prisons continue to experience cultural genocide because of imposition of ethnic labeling policies as a means of denying many native peoples access to traditional healing ceremonies. This matter is further explained in the next section.

PRISON MANAGEMENT AND TRADITIONAL NATIVE AMERICAN HEALING: A COMPARISON OF BELIEFS AND VALUES

The rise of Indian political activism in the late 1960s and the 1970s led to an increased awareness of native heritage and the wrongs that had been done against native peoples over the centuries. One effect of these changes was the emergence of Native American cultural, medicine, and mentoring programs in a few U.S prisons. States with large native populations, such as Minnesota and California, as well as the Federal Bureau of Prisons (FBOP), began programs for Native Americans. Some of them even included sweat lodge ceremonies, which in some prisons involved the actual building of a physical structure. However, the spread of Native American cultural programs has not been uniform. Today, there are prison systems in many areas of the United States that do not even count Native Americans as a separate ethnic category, let alone provide special programs for native prisoners.[2]

Labeling, Cultural Genocide, and Prison Reform

The effects of legal labeling of American Indian peoples are discussed in detail elsewhere (Archambeault, 2003b: 290–292). However, it is important at this juncture to understand that an individual's "legal label," as recognized by a prison, dictates whether an individual offender has the right to access Native American healing. There are three different legal labels or statuses that apply: (1) Indians enrolled in a federally recognized tribe, (2) Indians enrolled in a state-only certified tribe, and (3) Indians without status. Only persons from a federally recognized tribe have a clear claim to access tribal healing ways, and then only if to do so is not a threat to prison security. Generally, members of most state-only certified tribes can also claim access, but it is often at the discretion of prison authorities. Indian people without legal status in a recognized tribe are often denied their First Amendment freedom of religion if their choice of religion is tribal or even "generic Indian" in many prisons. In short, if a person is not a "card-carrying Indian," the inmate often is denied access to traditional American Indian healing ways.

Furthermore, in some states, such as Louisiana, inmate intake sheets do not even have a racial or ethnic block to check "American Indian" or "Native American," although other minorities, such as African American, Hispanic, and Asian, are included. Intake officials are forced to check either one of the other minority designations or "other race." State prison systems ignore Native Americans in classification so that they can avoid civil rights and Equal Employment Opportunity violations. If a prison system does not have a "sufficient mass" of Indian prisoners, then it is not obligated to provide access to Native American healing ceremonies or counselors. So, if it counts "other races" instead of "American Indian," the prison system avoids having to deal with the issue. Cultural genocide, in the form of religious discrimination against American Indians, is alive and well in many U.S. prisons today.

Prisons in the United States today are subject to continuous legal accountability (court intervention, litigation, and legal reform) in addition to public and political scrutiny. Yet, the dominant prison management style of the nineteenth century maintains its preeminence into the twenty-first century. The typical prison of today can best be described as an authority-centered, politically sensitive, paramilitary, formal rule–driven, and highly impersonal organization for both inmates and employees.[3] These are essentially totalitarian institutions whose highest goals are to prevent escape, protect the life and property of staff and inmates, ensure security, and avoid disruption of routine operations. Prison security concerns, as well as compliance with various health and safety laws, restrict the exercise of all forms of religious expression to varying degrees. However, Native American religions and healing ceremonies are restricted in many ways that do not negatively affect most other religions. Since prison management practices and procedures are derived from Western concepts of law and justice, it is necessary first to understand how they conflict with Native American values and beliefs.

UNDERSTANDING CULTURAL CONFLICTS IN PRISON

Conflict between Native Americans and prison authorities often exists even in those prisons in which traditional healing and mentoring programs are provided. Under the best of circumstances, there is often an uneasy truce between the prison administration and the Native American communities, both inside and outside the prison. Periodically, this fragile truce is broken, the points of conflict coming from many sides. Sometimes it arises from differences in tribal customs and cultures among the inmates themselves.[4] More often, however, the conflict arises from a clash of the values and laws of the dominant society with the diverse traditions and cultures of Native American peoples. Even within those prisons with high levels of cooperation between native communities and prison authorities, there is often a mutual lack of understanding about the critical cultural values of each respective group as they apply to a wide range of issues and concerns. This lack of mutual understanding is evident in the interactions of prison religious programs and native medicine people who come into prisons to provide traditional healing ceremonies for Native American inmates. Below I present an analytical conceptual schema, derived from my own field research with Native American medicine people, that compares the values of correctional prison management with those of traditional native healing and mentoring. Examined next are the concepts of justice and legalism, time, location, movement, and learning.

Concepts of Justice and Legalism: Effects on Traditional Native Healing

Native American concepts of *justice* are fundamentally different from the concepts of justice that derive from the U.S. Constitution and related legal, political, and social systems. Western concepts emphasize authority, protection of individual property rights, hierarchical social relations, maintenance of order through written laws and formal enforcement of proscribed law, individualized competition, and individual acquisition of material goods. By contrast, Native American concepts of justice emphasize tribal sharing and tribal ownership of material possessions, spiritual bonding and balance with nature, living in harmony with each other, respect for diverse individual behavior, the natural equality of all peoples and all living things, adherence to the natural laws of nature, and compliance with tribal customs, beliefs, and ceremonies. Whereas Western justice concepts emphasize the legalistic protection of individual rights and the formalized punishment of wrong-doing by legal proscription, Native American concepts of justice place emphasis on restoring balance and harmony among the tribe members through mediation and mutual agreement between victim and wrongdoer. The use of traditional methods of healing and mentoring, including the use of sweat lodges, pipe ceremonies, and smudging, among others, are the key to restoring balance and harmony within many tribes (Armstrong, Guilfoyle, and Melton, 1996b; Dickson-Gilmore, 1996; Dumont, 1996b). These differences are summarized in Table 10.1.

Many Native Americans view prisons as continuations of nineteenth-century boarding school policies and practices that attempted cultural genocide. Prisons by their very nature are totalitarian institutions, rigidly regulating every aspect of life and moment of linear time. By contrast, the Native American healing ways and values that medicine people bring into the prison are traditions handed down

Table 10.1 Comparison of Prison Management and Native American Values on Justice

Native American Values	Prison Management Values
Emphasize: • Tribal sharing and ownership of material possessions • Spiritual bonding and balance with nature and each other • Respect for diverse individual behavior, natural equality for all peoples and living things • Restoring balance and harmony among the tribe through mediation and mutual agreement between victim and wrongdoer • Use of traditional methods of healing and mentoring are the key to restoring balance and harmony	Emphasize: • Authority, protection of individual property rights, order maintenance through written laws and formal enforcement of law • Legalistic protection of individual rights and formalized punishment of wrong-doing by legal proscription • Prison policies developed to ensure health and safety of staff and inmates and to prevent escapes

from their ancestors. Native American healing traditions and religious practices were often ignored or condemned as pagan, and native prisoners were routinely denied access to healing ceremonies in many prisons and jails until the passage of the American Indian Religious Act of 1978 and subsequent changes to this act that "legitimized" such practices.[5]

After AIRA, traditional ceremonies could not be automatically forbidden by institutional policy, and sacred objects could not be arbitrarily labeled as "contraband" and seized. However, although AIRA was a significant step forward for Native American prisoners' rights, it did not provide the full protections that many had hoped. Prison officials in many jurisdictions continued to limit traditional ceremonies and to define sacred objects as "contraband," but when challenged in court, prison officials had the burden of proof of showing that objects such as pipes or feathers posed a significant safety or health risk. Some prison systems were able to work out meaningful compromises with native communities, both inside and outside prison, but other prison systems continue to arbitrarily deny native prisoners access to traditional ceremonies.

The mechanism used was simple: fail to count Native Americans as a separate ethnic category within the prison population and avoid the obligation of providing for such services. With the passage of the Religious Freedom Restoration Act (RFRA), hopes rose that discrimination against imprisoned Native Americans would end. As previously mentioned, however, these hopes were dashed with the June 25, 1997, U.S. Supreme Court ruling declaring that RFRA was unconstitutional. As a consequence, the practice of ignoring Native American minorities and their traditional spiritual needs in prison populations continues today in the District of Columbia and in the states of Louisiana, New Hampshire, New Jersey, Ohio, and Vermont, among others.

On the positive side, the FBOP and the prison systems of many states have gone to great efforts both to develop cultural awareness programs for Native Americans and to provide for their unique spiritual and healing needs. Often Native American culture teachers, healers, and medicine people are paid staff or consultants who bring ancient knowledge and wisdom into prisons from the outside. Although some of these programs are of recent origin, others have existed since the 1960s. These programs, however, are subject to changing political and legal trends.

Often, changes in the values and laws of the dominant society result in unintended and disruptive changes within the prison systems that adversely affect Native Americans. For example, the Minnesota Department of Corrections (DOC) has one of the oldest continuous Native American education and healing programs in the United States. In June 1998, the DOC—in response to changing public health laws and policies concerning the harmful effects of smoking—implemented a "no smoking and no tobacco" policy in its prisons. Tobacco, smudging materials, and other objects used in Native ceremonies were redefined as "contraband" and removed from the cells of all inmates, including Native American prisoners. This change in policy and prison operating rules created much tension within the

Minnesota prisons between officials and Native American prisoners. It also created conflict with native communities outside the prisons as well, resulting in class action lawsuits brought on behalf of native prisoners confined in the facilities. Thus, even when correctional officials and prison personnel have good intentions with respect to Native American rights, changes in law force them to take actions that contradict the interests of native prisoners and disturb the peace and harmony of long-standing programs.

Linear Time versus Natural Cycles of Time, Events, and Location

Most prisoners belonging to the dominant U.S. religions (i.e., Christian, Jewish, Muslim) have adapted themselves to these restrictions. Religious services begin at specific times and end at specific times in specific controlled locations within the prison. Additionally, most of the religions normally conduct their services within rooms or buildings. Consequently, these dominant religions can provide services in prison under conditions that, although far from ideal, resemble those in which services are conducted outside the prison. By contrast, when a medicine person conducts ceremonies in prison, he or she does so in a totally alien environment. Consequently, friction and often conflict develops between medicine people and correctional personnel, including chaplains and religious coordinators. To understand the essence of this conflict is to understand key differences in the concepts of time, events, and location between the Western and native worlds (see Table 10.2).

Linear versus Natural Cycles of Time

Concepts of *linear time* provide the context within which prison operations and activities are regulated by a twenty-four-hour clock. Linear time conceptualizes all human historical and present activities as moving through space toward some unknown or future ultimate goal or purpose. Along the way, time is organized into conceptually manageable and operationally measurable units, such as hours, minutes, days, weeks, months, and years. Western culture assumes that these units of time are real and that people living within this culture must structure their lives to conform to these units. Consequently, prisons regulate every minute of every inmate/resident's day.

Linear time contrasts sharply with native concepts of natural *cycles of time* and events. Cycles of time conceptualize time as continuous and repeating cycles of natural events that are dictated by the forces of nature as planned by the Creator. Different tribal cultures view time in their own unique ways. From the view of many Native American cultures, linear time is artificial or out of balance with nature. Although the seasons and the moons have specific meanings within cycles of nature, smaller units of time (i.e., days, hours, minutes) often do not.

Event-Oriented Time

Among most native cultures, time is event oriented, meaning that the human activity is ready to begin when all the people and all the objects needed for the

Table 10.2 Comparison of Prison Management and Native American Values on Time and Freedom of Movement

Native American Values	Prison Management Values
Natural cycles of time: • Time as continuous and repeating cycles of nature • Recognize cycles of the sun and moon as real. Do not recognize small units of linear time as being real.	Linear time: • Conceptualize all human historical and present activities as moving through space toward some unknown or future ultimate goal or purpose. • Time is organized into conceptually manageable and and operationally measurable units. • Assume that these abstract units of time are real and that people must structure their lives to conform to them.
Event: • An event is ready to begin when all people and objects are assembled. An event ends when the natural cycle of time has elapsed.	Activity: • Prisons organize inmate activities according to small units of linear time. Each activity has a rigid beginning and stopping point.
Location: • Native healing involves natural processes and most ceremonies occur in natural surroundings. Some require specific locations in nature.	Assigned location: • Prisons assign ceremonies to designated, secured locations within the prison.
Freedom of movement: • Healing in nature requires freedom of movement as the individual experiences the healing energies of Mother Earth.	Restricted movement: • The movement of all prisoners within an institution must be tightly controlled, supervised, and restricted by physical barriers.

event come together or arrive. Events occur in their own time and begin and end in their own time. This is especially true where healing ceremonies are concerned. In terms of time, healing ceremonies last as long as needed, and the spirits will tell the medicine person or mentor who is conducting the ceremony when it is finished. Linear time has absolutely no meaning in relation to healing ceremonies.

Location of Ceremony and Freedom of Movement

Finally, related issues crop up regarding location and freedom of movement. Many native healing ceremonies historically took place in nature, out-of-doors in specific locations upon Mother Earth. According to some traditions, the healing energies for many ceremonies can only be conducted in certain geographical locations. Others were held in lodges built on Mother Earth. There is a specific context and terminology to the usage that is attractive to many readers in this area. It is not just about building outside; it is about significant connectedness to one's beginning. To accommodate modern life in urban settings, traditional ceremonies are sometimes conducted in rooms of houses or apartments, especially during winter. However, even these indoor ceremonies usually require that participants be free to move about; to burn sage, cedar, or sweet grass; or to go outside for brief periods of time, perhaps to make tobacco offerings or to face a particular direction.

Prisons have the legal responsibility to control their inmate populations and their movements. Freedom of movement and choice of location for ceremonies are restricted by policy and physical plant design. In prisons that allow outdoor ceremonies such as sweat lodges, certain areas of recreation yards or campus areas are set aside for this purpose. During scheduled periods of time, inmates have limited freedom of movement within these designated areas.

Conflict between Western and Native Religious Values in Prison

Within prisons, frictions sometimes emerge between Native American medicine people and religious service coordinators or chaplains over the issues of linear time versus natural cycles of time, event-oriented time, location, and freedom of movement. Although much of this tension is unavoidable, most of it is manageable. On one side of the issue, chaplains and religious coordinators within prison often bend rules to accommodate the needs of native peoples and medicine ceremonies but are often viewed by the very people they are trying to help as instruments of the natives' repression. Prison staff often have great difficulty understanding why a healing ceremony cannot be conducted within a particular time frame and location. Prison staff also do not understand the resentment that some native medicine people feel when they have to ask prison staff for basic ceremonial items.

Interviews with medicine people who were brought into prisons revealed deep and long-standing frustrations.[6] They are often made to feel as if they are children when they enter a prison to provide services. They must ask a Western religious coordinator for essential items such as tobacco, matches, and smudging materials. Pipes and other sacred objects are often locked in cabinets under the coordinator or chaplain's control. Full-time chaplains and religious coordinators supervise native inmates who maintain sweat lodges and surrounding grounds. Permission must be obtained for everything connected with ceremonies.

The perceptions held by prison officials of medicine people differ markedly from those held by chaplains and religious coordinators who try to bend every rule possible in favor of medicine people. Often the cooperation that these chaplains receive and the lack of complaint from medicine people are perceived to be tacit approval for conditions under which traditional healing programs are administered.

Table 10.3 Frequently Cited Frustrations among Medicine People Working with Prison Inmates

- Being made to feel regulated, second-class individuals by chaplains of other Western religions
- Being pressured to conduct ceremonies in fixed time periods, as do chaplains of other denominations
- Having some prison staff treat sacred objects with disrespect, such a flushing an eagle feather down a toilet
- Having prison staff change the rules on what can and cannot be done from one shift to another
- Having sacred objects important to individual prisons taken from them, such as tobacco and smudging materials

According to prison rules and policies, medicine people are often allowed to give sacred objects (such as eagle wings, crystals, tobacco, or small medicine bags) to inmates with whom they are working. Medicine people resent these items being taken away from individual inmates just because one group of correctional officers interprets the rules differently than do guards on another shift. Naturally, medicine people resent these items being confiscated by guards and disposed of without respect (e.g., being flushed down a commode).

SACRED OBJECTS AND PRACTICES VERSUS HEALTH AND SAFETY RISKS

The traditional native person in prison considers certain objects and prayer forms to be sacred, whereas prison officials consider the same objects or actions to be health or safety risks (tobacco and smoking, eagle feathers, medicine bags, pipes, sage, sweat lodges, Sun Dances). Also contributing to a lack of understanding between Indian people and corrections officials are differences in learning styles and differences between tribal-specific healing ceremonies. These differences are discussed below (see Table 10.4).

Smoking Tobacco

Tobacco use and tobacco smoking of any form have become national health issues since the 1980s, as the health risks to the general public have been recognized in medical and legal circles. Laws prohibit smoking tobacco products in many public buildings, restaurants, and the workplace, among other locations. Under these laws, prisons are viewed as public institutions subject to the same regulations. Consequently, prisons in many states and those operated by the FBOP have imposed regulations that prohibit tobacco smoking or the possession of tobacco products.

To Native Americans, tobacco is a sacred herb used in many different ceremonies and by itself. Its possession and use in the form of smoking or simply as

Table 10.4 Comparison of Prison Management and Native American Values on
Sacred Objects, Ceremonies, and Human Learning

Native American Values	Prison Management Values
Sacred objects (unregulated): <ul><li>eagle feathers</li><li>tobacco, cedar, sage (smudging)</li><li>the pipe: smoking tobacco or knickknack</li><li>animal parts</li><li>medicine bags</li><li>crystals and stones</li><li>herbal medicines</li></ul>	Health and safety concerns (regulated): <ul><li>eagle feathers</li><li>tobacco, cedar, sage (smudging)</li><li>the pipe: smoking tobacco or knickknack</li><li>animal parts</li><li>medicine bags</li><li>crystals and stones</li><li>herbal medicines</li></ul>
Sweat lodge ceremonies: <ul><li>Purification of mind, body, and spirit</li></ul>	Sweat lodge ceremonies: <ul><li>Prison safety and health issue; where permitted must be tightly regulated</li></ul>
Learning through experience: <ul><li>Humans must be allowed to follow the path of their life unrestricted and without interference from others</li><li>Human beings must be allowed to experience life, make decisions, and live with the consequences of those decisions without interference from others</li></ul>	Compliance to external rules and controls: <ul><li>Prisoners must always be closely supervised and actions controlled by correctional personnel and by the physical design of the prison</li><li>Emphasis on external control and compliance to prison rules reinforced by punishment</li></ul>

an offering made to Mother Earth is a form of religious expression; tobacco and its many uses is a form of prayer.

The use of tobacco and the smoking of tobacco products is widespread among Native Americans, especially on reservations. In some locations, it is not uncommon to see children as young as nine or ten years old chain-smoking cigarettes along with their parents. On some reservations, 95–100 percent of tribal members smoke tobacco products unless specific medical conditions prohibit the activity.

Many Native Americans believe that because tobacco is viewed as a sacred herb, they are immune from the negative medical effects from smoking. Ironically, medical literature does not refute these beliefs. Native Americans on reservations disproportionately suffer from other kinds of cancers, but smoking-related cancers appear to be rare.

Although tobacco and its usage have sacred meanings within Native American culture, it is regulated by prison safety rules. In prison, tobacco and smoking may be contraband and highly regulated or a forbidden practice. The prison, as a publicly operated institution, must comply with all reasonable health standards in efforts to protect its inmate population. As the risks of both primary and secondary smoke on human health have become known in medical circles many prisons have taken steps to comply with standards. As the same time, efforts to regulate tobacco usage in prisons conflicts directly with the religious rights of Native American prisoners to have and use tobacco.

Eagle Feathers, Pipes, Medicine Bags, and Other Objects

For Native Americans, tribal traditions and culture define many different objects as being sacred. Yet to prisons and the values of the dominant society, these same objects often present health and safety issues. It is the first priority of any prison to protect the lives and safety of inmates and staff. Because of legal and moral liability, prisons are obligated to protect human life from all forms of potential risk.

From the prisons' perspective, any feathers, furs, and animal parts may contain harmful bacteria or harbor hidden diseases. Some objects may also be used as weapons and must be treated as contraband, such as eagle claws, animal teeth, crystals, bones, and stones. Likewise, objects such as pipes may be very valuable and may set off conflicts between groups of inmates who want to steal or deface the pipe and those who want to protect it. Medicine bags are also sometimes viewed as potential threats to prison safety because they are worn around the neck; the leather around the neck may allow another inmate to choke the wearer, and the contents of the bag are not immediately discernable by prison staff and may contain contraband items.

Both the prison and the inmate population have compelling constitutional legal foundations. Native peoples have a constitutional right to practice their religious beliefs, and prisons have the obligation to protect life and safety of inmates and staff. Consequently, each prison system—and, to some degree, each prison—must craft its own operational policies that balance these divergent sets of rights and protections.

Learning through Experience versus Compliance with Prison Rules

Native American traditions teach that each individual must be allowed to find his or her own path. To do this, the person must be allowed to experience life on its own terms. In accepting responsibility for his or her own decisions, the individual must also accept the consequences of the actions taken. Individuals must always be allowed to seek advice, knowledge, and guidance from elders and mentors. However, any form of intervention on the part of anyone else is seen as interference with that person's journey and must be avoided.

Although personal responsibility and loyalty to the family, clan, or tribe were always stressed and compliance with traditions and customs was always regulated within every native culture, individuality in terms of following one's own spiritual path was also stressed. In some cases, spiritual insights gained from vision quests or other ceremonial activities superceded compliance with tribal customs, even if the individual's path deviated from tribal traditions.

By contrast, the nature of prison organizations regulate every aspect of an inmate's daily life. He or she is told when to wake, when to eat, how to dress, and how to behave; failure to conform to these rules and regulations result in negative sanctions in the form of punishment. Prisons and prison staff attempt to regulate inmate behavior and activities through external means of control.

The means of control used by prison staff and the physical design of the prison itself are contrary to the values of traditional Native American cultures. Depending on the individual, prison means of control are also contrary to many individual inmates' life experiences (see Table 10.4). Medicine people brought in to conduct traditional healing ceremonies from outside the prison can help to mediate these inmate-staff conflicts. However, where the tribal traditions of the inmate population are significantly different than those of the outside medicine person, then such conflicts may actually be intensified.

Sweat Lodges and Purification Ceremonies

Perhaps one of the most controversial types of ceremonies, found in a few prisons but prohibited in many others, are sweat lodge ceremonies, also called purification lodges. Their construction and rituals vary widely among different tribal cultures, and they are used for different purposes. However, in general, sweat lodges are used as places of prayer, self-cleansing, and self-sacrifice. Sometimes they are used as a means of healing; sometimes they are used simply to prepare the person for the next ceremony to follow.

During most "sweats," someone leads the prayers and rituals, usually conducted in a tribal language but also frequently in English or French. The drum is often used, and chanting takes place. Sweats get their name from the fact that red-hot rocks, or "grandfathers," are brought into the lodge, water is poured upon the rocks, and the small, cramped space of the lodge is heated by steam to very high temperatures. Some ceremonies require each participant to pray, and water is poured on the rocks each time. Some sweats become acts of physical endurance as participants pray—each in his or her own way. Every sweat is different, and the experience of each participant is highly individualized.

To prison security, however, sweat lodges represent serious risks. For example, six- to nine-inch-diameter rocks are heated to glowing hot by a huge fire. These hot rocks must be carried the few feet from the fire pit to the lodge pit by a participant who must use a shovel or pitchfork. Then the outer cover is closed, and security is denied visual observation of the activities that take place within the lodge. Security is concerned about the fact that the rocks and the shovel or fork could be used as weapons. A red-hot rock thrown on a person could seriously burn or maim them. Many kinds of acts between inmates could take place in the darkness of the lodge.

The safety of the lodge in any prison is directly dependent on the qualifications of the outside consultant medicine person who is running it. In general, medicine people are screened and selected to fill these critical roles. In turn, they tend to be strict about selecting inmates to participate. Potential troublemakers are automatically eliminated. If the person running the lodge views the ceremony as a religious ceremony and is serious about protecting its sacred nature, the medicine person will be very careful about who is allowed to participate. Under such conditions, security violations and injuries are virtually unheard of.

Conflict between Different Tribal Customs and Cultures

One problem that frequently confronts and sometimes baffles correctional officials is intertribal conflict among inmates as to how ceremonies are supposed to be conducted and who is qualified to conduct those ceremonies. Sweat lodge and pipe ceremonies, for example, are similar in many aspects for the Sioux (Lakota, Dakota, Nakota) and for Ojibwa/Chippewa (Anishinabe) cultures. However, important differences exist in rituals, formula, the wording of prayers, the arrangement of sacred items, and language. Native peoples from one culture often object to native peoples of other cultures conducting these similar ceremonies.

The practice of Native American medicine or healing today is highly individualistic—an aspect that has probably not changed for thousands of years. There are practitioners who have been guided by tribal culture or by the traditions of a medicine society and who have received proper instruction from elders. There are also some who have not received any special training or guidance. According to native tradition, each healer or mentor acquires his or her individual medicine power by learning to harness the healing powers within the individual as given and guided by the Creator. Each healer combines these individual energies with those of the physical and spiritual worlds around him or her. Tribal culture and mentoring by other medicine people assist the individual in cultivating his or her own abilities and knowledge. Customs and ceremonies, such as the vision quest, fasting, praying, and mentoring, all lead each individual to find his or her own path to spiritual power and healing knowledge.

Commonalties among Different Tribal Traditions

Despite these differences, native medicine and mentoring traditions do share some commonalties, which are summarized in Table 10.5. Sometimes correctional staff are able to "build bridges" between individual inmates of different cultures by focusing on some of these commonalties.

UNDERSTANDING WHAT IS ALLOWED
AND WHAT CANNOT BE PERMITTED

For safety and health reasons, not all forms of Native American healing can be allowed within the confines of a prison—even a progressive one. This distinction is discussed below.

Table 10.5 Common Beliefs and Traditions in Native American Healing Traditions

- The Creator placed each tribe of native people in a particular place on mother earth[1].
- It is the duty of each group of native peoples to live in balance with all of creation and to protect the creator's gift to them[2].
- The Creator would never place a disease upon mother earth without also placing a cure for it[3].
- The Creator taught native peoples which animals and plants (herbs, grass, bark) could heal illness or wounds and restore holistic balance[4].
- Native peoples acquired knowledge about healing by observing the animals[5].
- The grandfathers and grandmothers taught the native peoples how the human spirit could be helped on its journey and how it could be used to aid in the healing process[6].
- Practitioners of Native American healing are referred to by a variety of titles[7].
- Native peoples formed medicine families, clans, and medicine societies through which later generations could be mentored in the healing arts[8].
- Native peoples recorded sacred teaching about healing onto birch bark scrolls, bison hides, rocks, building blocks, and other forms of sacred carvings[9].
- Traditions and stories are orally communicated.

[1.] The belief that the Creator had placed each tribe of native people in a particular place on Mother Earth. For each tribe, living where the Creator had placed them was living in Eden. In the place that the Creator had assigned to the people, the Creator had placed all the animal, fish, bird and plant life necessary to sustain life and to cure all illnesses. Living in the geographical location assigned to a native people by the Creator is essential to understanding the medicine or healing powers of a particular tribe's medicine culture.

[2.] The belief that it was the duty of each group of Native Peoples to live in balance with all of creation and to protect the Creator's gift to them. Living in balance with each other and with all living things on Mother Earth were critical to maintaining good health. Most forms of healing aimed at restoring this balance.

[3.] The belief that the Creator would never place a disease upon Mother Earth without also placing a cure for it. Finding a cure, however, assumed that the Native people lived where the Creator has placed them and lived in balance with all other life.

[4.] The Creator taught Native Peoples which animals and plants (herbs, grass, bark) could heal illness or wounds and restore holistic balance. This knowledge, however, was often limited to the particular geographical location that the people believed had been given them by the Creator.

[5.] Native Peoples acquired knowledge about healing by observing the animals. They saw what the animals did, especially the deer, when they were sick or wounded and followed the animals example. They ate what the animals ate when they became sick and rubbed herbs, plants or bark mixtures onto wounds as they had observed the animals doing. In the oral traditions of almost every tribe, animal spirits themselves taught the people cures for different illnesses or injuries.

[6.] The grandfathers and grandmothers taught the Native Peoples how the human spirit could be helped on its journey and how it could be used to aid in the healing process.

[7.] Practitioners of Native American healing are referred to by a variety of titles. Most commonly they are called mentors, medicine people, and healers, among other names. Each tribe or culture applies a slightly different term to these men and women. Here we shall use the generic terms *medicine person* or *healer*.

[8.] The Native Peoples formed medicine families, clans, and medicine societies through which later generations could be mentored in the healing arts. The individuals who were members of these groups were recognized as mentors, healers, shamans, or medicine people. [It should be noted, however, that generally medicine people do not call themselves *healers*. Rather, this is a term applied to them by others. Most medicine people see themselves as conduits through which the healing powers of the Creator are channeled.

[9.] The native people recorded sacred teaching about healing onto birch bark scrolls, bison hides, rocks, building blocks of buildings and other forms of sacred carvings. In today's world we can call these mnemonic devices because, in reality, that is exactly their purpose.

Native Healing Ways Sometimes Permitted in Prisons

It should not be surprising that only some types of ceremonies are allowed in prisons under very regulated conditions. Where allowed, the most common ceremonies in prisons are smudging, pipe ceremonies, tobacco offerings, drumming and dancing, crystals, medicine bags, dream catchers, spiritual counseling and mentoring, sand painting or writing on tree bark, and medicine sticks, among others. In a few prisons, sweat lodges are permitted under very tightly regulated conditions. There are many other forms of healing and ceremonies that have not been mentioned here. Some are specific to particular tribes in select locations; some are allowed in some prison settings, but not in others. Other ceremonies are shared among many different tribes in a region. Some are individual to the healer or medicine person. Some forms have been lost to human memory.

Native Healing Ways Never Permitted in Prisons

Practices such as the Sun Dance, self-imposed blood-letting sacrifices, herbal medicines, vision quests, and many other types of traditional healing ceremonies are generally not allowed in any prison. However, in some prison systems, American Indians with good conduct records are allowed to travel and participate in these ceremonies.

CONCLUSION

During the 1960s, many prison officials viewed Islam and black Muslims as threats to institutional security. Today, many prison wardens and security chiefs view Islamic leaders, as well as leaders of other faiths, as people who can bring understanding and hope and reduce tensions among inmate populations. In a few instances in which prison officials have come to understand American Indian traditions, similar results have occurred. In all these situations, understanding is a two-way street. Prison officials have come to understand and accept the religious beliefs of different people. Likewise, religious leaders understand that the one way they can help the people in prison is to accept the limitations of and work with prison security to maintain order and safety. Often, this requires compromise on both sides as well as goodwill and understanding.

Even under the best of circumstances, however, the totalitarian nature of prisons and the rigid rule orientation of prison management directly conflicts with the cultural values of traditional Native American healing ways, as well as with the values of medicine people who bring these traditions into prisons. Consequently, traditional healing methods that are found in only a few prison systems around the United States operate in a totally alien environment from that of the ancestors. Even more fundamentally, a great many prison wardens and security personnel must overcome their own religious biases against Native American healing and religious practices. Many prisons must overcome the vestiges of ethnic genocide aimed at eradicating Indian cultures and values. Discriminatory ethnic labeling and screening of people for eligibility to participate in Native American ceremonies must stop. All prison inmates who operate within the framework and limitations of reason-based security concerns should be allowed to participate in native healing ceremonies, just as they can participate in the faith-based activities of other religions. It should be left up to the medicine people who come into the prison to conduct healing ceremonies to screen inmates for participation.

Correctional officials must come to understand Native American values and beliefs and impart this understanding to subordinate employees. Native American people need to recognize the difficulties of operating any prison. Correctional officials need to have a basic understanding of some traditional healing ways, although they will vary with the types of tribal people incarcerated. Native peoples should accept that not all forms of traditional ceremony are possible within the confines of prison.

NOTES

This chapter is based on a paper presented at the forty-first annual meeting of the Western Social Science Association Conference, Fort Worth, Texas, April 22, 1999.

1. See Archambeault (2003) for a more detailed discussion of this issue. Approximately 95 percent (or more) of "minority focused" federally funded research and articles published in mainstream criminology and criminal justice publications ignore Native American issues and peoples, except for grants that focus on American Indian populations. Prior to 1994, biases of mainstream criminology and criminal justice led American Indian justice and crime issues to be ignored in approximately 99 percent of these publications.

2. These states include Louisiana, New Hampshire, New Jersey, Ohio, and Vermont, as well as the District of Columbia.

3. Although no prison is really typical of any other, these conditions exist to varying degrees in all prisons. The higher the security rating of a prison (e.g., maximum security) the more totalitarian prison operations and life become for both employees and inmates.

4. Conflicts sometimes arise between different native groups over who should be allowed to conduct traditional ceremonies, how (rites, rituals) the ceremonies are to be conducted, how lodges are to be constructed, or even what language is to be used during a ceremony. These issues are intensified by historical tribal conflicts such as those between the Navajo and Hopi or the Chippewa/Ojibwa and the Sioux.

5. Referenced here are changes made to Title 42, the Public Health and Welfare Act, Chapter 21, Civil Rights, Sub-Chapter I, "The American Indian Religious Freedom Act of 1978." Section 1996 states: "it shall be the policy of the United States to protect and preserve for American Indians their inherent right of freedom to believe, express, and exercise the traditional religions of the American Indian, Eskimo, Aleut, and Native Hawaiian, including but not limited to access to sites, use and possession of sacred objects, and freedom to worship through ceremonials and traditional rites."

6. Interviews took place during September 1998 on the Red Lake, Cass Lake, and Leech Lake Chippewa Reservations in Minnesota. The Minnesota example illustrates the fact that even in well-intentioned and well-run Native American healing programs in prisons, conflicts continue to arise.

Criminalization of the Treaty Right to Fish

Response of the Great Lakes Chippewa

Linda Robyn

Lands ceded to the U.S. government by the Chippewa in the Treaties of 1837 and 1842 guaranteed the continued privilege of hunting, fishing, and gathering wild rice upon the lands, rivers, and lakes included in the territory area. Over time the government used the legal system to remove resources ceded to Indians while simultaneously attempting to use the legal system to criminalize long-standing behavior that was also guaranteed by treaties. As the government exercised its power over the Chippewa, treaty rights that promised the continuance of fishing, hunting, and gathering were severely eroded, thus criminalizing behavior that was previously protected by precedent. The political assault against Indian treaties began in 1973 when two Chippewa men were arrested for ice fishing on off-reservation waters. With this arrest, the knowledge and methods of hunting and fishing passed down from elders through the ages became criminalized, and the Chippewa were punished for continuing their traditions. This chapter outlines the *Voigt* decision reaffirming Chippewa treaty rights and the ensuing intense racial hostilities that pitted whites against Indians both in court and at the boat landings with the beginning of each new fishing season every spring.

WISCONSIN'S *Voigt* DECISION

In the vast cession of land that occurred in 1837 and 1842, the Ojibwa people, also known as Chippewa or Anishinabe, in the upper Great Lakes region kept the right to hunt, fish, and gather on lands they sold to the U.S. government. Treaty rights were never sold by the Chippewa, nor were they granted or given by the federal government (Great Lakes Indian Fish and Wildlife Commission, 1993). The Chippewa kept the right to obtain food and other necessities on ceded lands to ensure future generations would always have a source of food and survival. Never were these practices to be criminalized and sanctions applied to the Chippewa as they exercised their treaty rights.

The long-forgotten issue of treatied hunting and fishing rights reappeared with the *Voigt* case that began in the U.S. District Court, Western District of Wisconsin, in 1973 (U.S. Department of Interior, 1993). From that case emerged intense racial hostilities that pitted whites against Indians in fierce confrontations in court, and in violent confrontations at the boat landings each spring. There were misunderstandings and confusion about promises contained in the treaties regarding the rights of the Chippewa to hunt and fish on ceded lands. The media virtually ignored the economic and political context of the issue. As is usually the case with media, reporters chose to focus on the sensational aspects of the racial conflict instead. Ignored by the media was another variable in the equation: that because of their unique holistic relationship with the environment, the Chippewa adhere to strict environmental practices ensuring that fish and game would not be depleted but would remain numerous and strong.

The political assault against Indian treaties in the Midwest began with the *Voigt* case after two Chippewa men were arrested for ice fishing on off-reservation waters and for using a fishing shanty that had no name or address attached by the Department of Natural Resources. In response to this arrest, the Lac Courte Oreilles filed suit against the state for violating the Treaties of 1837 and 1842, which granted them fishing rights off the reservation (*Lac Court Oreilles v. Voigt*, 700 F. 2d [7 Cir. 1983]). The tribe claimed state laws interfered with tribal hunting, fishing, and gathering activities guaranteed in the Treaties of 1837 and 1842 (Great Lakes Indian Fish and Wildlife Commission, 1993).

In 1978, the federal district court granted summary judgment in favor of the state of Wisconsin and dismissed the action (Great Lakes Indian Fish and Wildlife Commission, 1993). The basis for the court's decision was that all rights under the Treaty of 1854, which had established permanent reservations for the Chippewa in Wisconsin, Michigan, and Minnesota, had been revoked (Great Lakes Indian Fish and Wildlife Commission, 1993). In 1983, the Seventh Circuit Court of Appeals in its *Voigt* decision reversed the district court ruling, finding that "the Indian band's usufructuary rights established by the 1837 and 1842 treaties were neither terminated nor released by the 1854 treaty" (Great Lakes Indian Fish and Wildlife Commission, 1993). Therefore, the appellate court reaffirmed the rights of six Chippewa bands to hunt, fish, trap, and gather wild rice on nonreservation lands in Wisconsin, and sent the case back to the district court for further proceedings to determine the scope of the treaty rights, the extent to which the state might regulate the exercise of these rights, and what damages, if any, the tribes might recover as a result of the state's infringement of the treaty rights (Great Lakes Indian Fish and Wildlife Commission, 1993). In 1983, the U.S. Supreme Court refused to hear the state of Wisconsin's petition to appeal the *Voigt* decision reaffirming Chippewa treaty rights.

After the decision of the Seventh Circuit Court of Appeals, the five other Chippewa bands in Wisconsin joined in the lawsuit (Bad River, Lac du Flambeau, Mole Lake, Red Cliff, and St. Croix), and the six plaintiff tribes proceeded with the case in district court (Great Lakes Indian Fish and Wildlife Commission, 1993). The proceedings were divided into three phases by the district court:

Phase I: Declaratory Phase—determination of the nature and scope of the treaty rights;

Phase II: Regulatory Phase—determination of the permissible scope of state regulation;

Phase III: Damages Phase—amount of damages, if any, to which the tribes were entitled for infringement on treaty rights (Great Lakes Indian Fish and Wildlife Commission, 1993).

Phase I proceedings to determine the nature and scope of the treaty rights were held in December 1985 before Judge James Doyle. Judge Doyle ruled that all resources in the ceded territory could be harvested by tribal members using all modern methods of harvest. Doyle further ruled that the resources could be personally consumed, traded, or sold in the modern-day market economy. Finally, the judge ruled that tribes are entitled to as many of the resources as will ensure their members a modest living (Great Lakes Indian Fish and Wildlife Commission, 1993). Judge Doyle died of cancer in 1987, and the case was transferred to Judge Barbara Crabb. The state of Wisconsin wanted to appeal Judge Doyle's ruling, but Judge Crabb denied the request and proceeded with the case in district court.

On August 21, 1987, Judge Crabb reaffirmed the standard principles found in other treaty rights throughout the country. Crabb further asserted that the state may regulate in the interests of conservation as long as such regulations are reasonable and necessary for the conservation of a species or resource, do not discriminate against Indians, and are the least restrictive alternative available (Great Lakes Indian Fish and Wildlife Commission, 1993). Judge Crabb also ruled that the state may impose such regulations as are reasonable and necessary to protect public health and safety. However, she held that the tribes possess the authority to regulate their members and that effective tribal self-regulation precludes state regulation (U.S. Department of Interior, 1993).

To determine what the permissible scope of state regulation should be, the tribes, court, and the state agreed to break Phase II down into smaller subphases intended to address regulatory questions about specific resources. These October 1988 proceedings dealt specifically with walleye and muskellunge harvests, and many issues regarding these resources that otherwise would have gone to separate trials were mutually resolved in dealing with this subphase (U.S. Department of Interior, 1993). On March 3, 1989, Judge Crabb came to a decision on the subphase portion addressing regulatory questions on these particular resources by issuing a ruling that as long as the tribes adhere to regulations incorporating the biologically necessary conditions set by the state at trial, the tribes are self-regulating as to walleye and muskellunge. Crabb ordered the state not to interfere with the tribes' regulation of the treaty walleye and muskellunge harvest, except as the tribes have otherwise agreed (U.S. Department of Interior, 1993). In other words, the state of Wisconsin could no longer run roughshod over the tribes' regulations in matters concerning the harvesting of fish.

Then, in May 1990, Crabb issued a decision in keeping with various issues presented for resolution. Consistent with Crabb's decision on walleye and muskellunge harvests, she enjoined the enforcement of state law, provided that the tribes enact a system of regulations consistent with her decision, and the tribes have done so (Great Lakes Indian Fish and Wildlife Commission, 1993). However, in spite of these rulings and even though the U.S. Constitution states that treaties are the "supreme law of the land," the state administration of Governor Tommy Thompson criticized the Chippewa for exercising their treaty rights. Indeed, as one report noted, "the state of Wisconsin has acted as if its problem in northern Wisconsin is the result of Chippewa behavior" (Strickland, cited in Midwest Treaty Network, n.d.).

FISHING RIGHTS STRUGGLES IN CONTEXT

Since the 1950s, battles fought by indigenous people in North America have involved preservation or restoration of their historical traditional economies. One of the most critical battles in the past several decades involves treaty-guaranteed fishing rights in the Pacific Northwest and the state of Wisconsin. Indians in the Northwest began being arrested for fishing on their own federally supervised lands in 1913 (Jaimes, 1992). The struggles of the Chippewa of the Great Lakes in Wisconsin are almost identical to those of the northwestern tribes; however, the fishing controversy in northern Wisconsin did not begin until two Chippewa men were arrested in 1973 by state game wardens for attempting to spearfish in an area outside their reservation (Fixico, 1987).

Despite clear treaty language permanently ensuring the right to fish, indigenous peoples of the Northwest have, for more than a century, suffered systematic deprivation of their rights to fish. The negative consequences to their economy from the criminalization of behavior and social and cultural practices have been profound. When the northwestern tribes finally began to assert their treaty rights to fish in the 1950s, they encountered increasingly severe clashes with federal and local authorities and non-Indian commercial and sport fishers. It would be just the same for the Chippewa thirty years later. Lengthy court cases ensued, challenging the denial of native fishing rights, especially in the state of Washington. As a result of these court cases, a pattern of bilateral negotiations emerged by which some of the most extravagant abuses of Indian rights have been ended. The issues associated with northwestern Indian fishing rights are by no means entirely resolved, but terms like comanagement and cooperative resource management are now in place when discussions of the fishing industry occur between state planners and representatives of native nations in Washington, Oregon, and Idaho (Fixico, 1987).

The process the indigenous peoples of the Northwest have endured since the 1950s may provide a basis upon which to resolve the crisis in Wisconsin. If so, then perhaps the de facto negotiation of modern treaties developed with regard to fishing rights can serve as a model by which to address other Indian reserved rights, such as those pertaining to hunting and the gathering of wild rice in the years ahead (Fixico, 1987).

The nature of the fishing rights struggles in Wisconsin that began in the 1980s has to do with the Ojibwa (or Chippewa) people and their relationship with the environment of the Great Lakes (see Chapter 5 for more information on the holistic view of nature). Clan laws among the Chippewa and other woodland peoples must be obeyed by all members of the community in order to achieve peace and harmony within the community. Most woodland peoples like the Chippewa who have clanship systems and clan laws believe these laws must be obeyed to avoid disrupting natural relationships with the environment. Not adhering to these laws will result in human controversy, and natural calamity will result. Like the other essential elements of native society—person or self, extended family, community, and nation—clan or society has a fundamental role in constituting the internal nature of Native Americans (Fixico, 1998).

Despite claims made by the anti-Indian movement (the same group of people who wish to criminalize long-standing Indian behavior) in Wisconsin, treaties allowing the Chippewa to spearfish are not old, outdated documents. As will be illustrated further, treaties do not allow the Chippewa to deplete the resources, as anti-Indian groups would have us believe, but rather protect the land and all the creatures upon it. There is an underlying agenda at the heart of the fishing rights controversy in Wisconsin, which is the strong desire to open up the northern part of the state to mining. While inadvertently assisting the anti-Indian movement in Wisconsin by narrowly focusing public attention and discussion on sensational aspects of the treaty controversy, the media have ignored the economic and political context of the fishing rights issue (Gedicks, 1991).

INTRODUCTION TO THE CONTROVERSY IN WISCONSIN

Northern Wisconsin communities have been bitterly divided over the issue of Chippewa spearfishing rights. Since the 1983 court decision reaffirming Chippewa off-reservation treaty rights, Wisconsin Chippewa have been confronted by angry crowds of white protestors at boat landings as they try to exercise their legal right to fish outside reservation boundaries. Intense racial conflict has been expressed by protestors hurling rocks, yelling racial slurs like "timber nigger" and "welfare warrior" at Chippewa spearfishers. Posters advertising the "First Annual Indian Shoot" have been placed in northern Wisconsin bars (Metz, 1990).

Treaties signed in 1837 and 1842 in which the Chippewa ceded land to the federal government allowed the Chippewa to retain their rights to hunt, fish, and gather on all lands within that ceded territory, which includes roughly one-third of northern Wisconsin. The U.S. Constitution states that treaties are the "Supreme Law of the Land, but Governor Tommy Thompson's administration has criticized the Chippewa for exercising their treaty rights" (Gedicks, 1991: 163). This criticism has gone so far as to blame the Chippewa for economic problems in northern Wisconsin (Strickland, Herzberg, and Owens, 1992). A. Gedicks writes that as early as 1984, an ad hoc commission on racism in Wisconsin emphasized the larger significance of the attack on treaty rights: under challenge is the continued existence of Indian governments with the power to make their own laws to govern the conduct of their members and to control their territory (Strickland, Hertzberg, and Owens, 1992: 7). Factors that contribute to this racial conflict include the public's lack of knowledge about treaty rights and the scapegoating of the Chippewa for the depressed economy of northern Wisconsin (Great Lakes Indian Fish and Wildlife Commission, 1993). A deliberate attempt to mislead the public about the issues is not uncommon when one group, usually the more powerful group, tries to portray another group as being deviant. If that group is successful in portraying the less powerful group's behavior as deviant, the next step is to criminalize the behavior, thus further moving the behavior beyond that which is generally accepted.

Another crucial factor is the desire of the state of Wisconsin to open up northern Wisconsin to mineral resource exploitation by some of the world's largest and most powerful mining corporations. According to the U.S. Civil Rights Commission as cited in the *Milwaukee Sentinel* (1986), rather than viewing the white backlash to the assertion of Indian treaty rights as a product of the excessive political and material demands by Indians, this interpretation argues that the non-Indian interests, both government and private, that have been unfairly profiting at Indian expense have found their individual advantages disrupted by Indian legal and political victories and have organized to recapture their preferential position. When viewed from the perspective of those people controlling resources, it is possible to see the convergence between the anti-Indian movement, represented by groups like Protect Americans' Rights and Resources (PARR) and Stop Treaty Abuse (STA), and the pro-mining policy of the Thompson administration in Wisconsin (U.S. Commission on Civil Rights, 1981). To understand the controversy surrounding Anishinabe (Chippewa/Ojibwa) fishing rights that have been at issue in northern Wisconsin, it is important to begin by examining this issue as it relates to treaties entered into during the 1800s between the Chippewa and the U.S. government, guaranteeing the right of the Chippewa to continue their hunting, fishing, and gathering economy.

In the U.S. Constitution, Indian tribes are recognized as distinct political and legal entities bound by numerous federal laws and executive orders and by the federal judiciary. Before the arrival of Europeans in North America, all tribes were independent and sovereign nations in their own right. The relationship between Europeans and Indian nations at first contact was in most cases one of one government to another under principles of international law that endure today. Historically, tribes possessed all the rights and powers inherent in any sovereign nation. In times past, tribes enjoyed the complete right of self-government, to make their own rules and laws and to be governed by them, in all areas of life (U.S. Department of the Interior, 1991). When the Northwest Territories of 1787 were established, the area now known as Wisconsin became part of the United States. Wisconsin became a separate territory in 1836 and became a state in 1848.

Formal relations between the U.S. government and the Anishinabe were established in the late 1700s, but the controversy surrounding fishing rights centers around treaties agreed to in the mid-1800s. The treaty of 1837 was agreed to with the understanding that "the privilege of hunting, fishing, and gathering the wild rice, upon the lands, the rivers, and lakes included in the territory area, is guaranteed to the Indians during the pleasure of the President of the United States" (Strickland, Hertzberg, and Owens, 1992: 20). The treaty of 1842, in accordance with the treaty of 1837, states that the Indians stipulate for the right of hunting on the ceded territory, with the other usual privileges of occupancy, until required to move by the president of the United States (Strickland, Hertzberg, and Owens, 1992).

In 1850, President Millard Fillmore signed a removal order that sought to expel the Chippewa from these territories under the federal policy of western resettlement of Native Americans. "However, at the urging of the Wisconsin State Legislature and Wisconsin citizens, President Fillmore rescinded the removal order and allowed the formation of reservations in the ceded territories of Wisconsin" (Strickland, Hertzberg, and Owens, 1992: 20). After the removal order was rescinded, the exercise of treaty rights by the Chippewa was increasingly restricted until about 1908, when the state of Wisconsin began to strictly and systematically enforce game laws against the Chippewa (i.e., criminalize behavior that was previously sanctioned by treaty). The removal order rescinded by the president reminded the Chippewa how vulnerable they were to the whims of the government. The formation of reservations resulted in the creation of checkerboard land ownership patterns. Non-Indians could move into territory that was previously home to the Chippewa. With non-Indians now residing on ceded land, it became increasingly easier to restrict the hunting and fishing rights of the Chippewa. Treaty rights that promised the continuance of fishing, hunting, and gathering were eroded as the government exercised its paternalistic powers. Knowledge and methods of hunting and fishing passed down from elders through the ages became criminalized, and the Chippewa were punished for continuing their traditions.

Not long after the 1850 removal order came the federal government's General Allotment Act of 1887 (or Dawes Act), which helped establish the anti-Indian movement. As the communally held reservations were divided into individual parcels, or allotments, to be conveyed to individual Indians, the remaining surplus land was made available to white settlers. The jurisdictional complications that followed between tribal, federal, and state governments provided fertile ground for the growth of the anti-Indian movement, as resident and absentee non-Indian landowners and businesses objected to the growing exercise of general governmental powers by tribal governments. This was particularly true in the areas of taxation, zoning, construction, and land use (i.e., hunting and fishing rights) ordinances. The discovery of valuable minerals on certain lands left little doubt that these lands would be closed to Indian selection and left open to non-Indian business owners. Not only did Euro-Americans have their eyes on the vast amount of wealth that lay on the surface of the Chippewa's woodland home, but they were also interested in the vast amount of wealth contained in the minerals buried beneath the soil. In particular, the copper deposits on Isle Royale became an issue: "As a result of this concern, Isle Royale was the only island of the Great Lakes specifically mentioned in the Treaty of Paris in 1783" (Gedicks, 1993: 50).

In 1826, Henry Schoolcraft had confirmed that there were indeed deposits of rich copper along the Lake Superior shoreline, exceeding all other copper deposits anywhere in the United States. Schoolcraft discussed this part of the country as being an important area in which to exploit mineral discoveries. He knew that the copper, iron, and lead would be important to the rapidly expanding country. Schoolcraft was a superintendent with the Office of Indian Affairs and actively promoted mineral development (Gedicks, 1991). The next twenty-eight years brought about a series of four treaties between the United States and the Chippewa in which they were removed from the mineral districts, thus opening up this land to white miners. The United States gained the mining rights to all of Chippewa country in the 1826 Treaty at Fond du Lac. The Winnebago, Potawatomi, and Chippewa were dispossessed of their lead mines with the Treaty of Green Bay in 1828. The treaty of 1837 proved the most legally important treaty in terms of establishing Chippewa hunting and fishing rights in Wisconsin. Article 5 of this agreement guaranteed "the privilege of hunting, fishing, and gathering the wild rice upon the lands, the rivers, and the lakes included in the territory ceded" (Fixico, 1998: 109).

The Chippewa living in the Keeweenaw copper districts were dispossessed of their minerals with the Miners Treaty of 1842. The provisions of the 1842 Miners Treaty stated that unless the Chippewa agreed to cede their mineral rights to the U.S. government, they would be moved from their home in the upper Great Lakes region to Oklahoma (Gedicks, 1991). The western boundary of this treaty was originally set at the Montreal River on the Michigan-Wisconsin border. When Robert Stuart, Michigan's Indian superintendent at the time, learned that the minerals extended even further west, he recommended the government include all unalienated Chippewa land along Lake Superior. According to Stuart, the main importance of Wisconsin territory lay in its great mineral productiveness. Not only were fishing and hunting rights eroded, but the Chippewa were now dispossessed of the further iron wealth of northern Minnesota with the Treaty of 1854 (Gedicks, 1991).

In these four treaty negotiations the federal government, state governments, and Indian tribes understood the stakes. In each instance, the tribes resisted, and the white man triumphed (Gedicks, 1991). The stakes were high in these transactions, with the government securing a definite capitalist advantage. The tribes endured immense suffering because of the unequal nature of this relationship, as evidenced by the Treaty of 1854. With this treaty, the government was able to secure, for its monetary gains, the northern shore mineral resources as well as valuable pine timberland. The natives who lived along the shores of Lake Superior were not removed, allowing lumbering firms, shipping companies, miners, and railroad construction companies to exploit them as a cheap labor resource (Danziger, 1990).

Because of the exploitation exercised by the government, the Chippewa became impoverished, while several generations of East Coast copper- and iron-mining families, including the Agassizs and the Rockefellers, were enriched. Also set in motion were the great mining and lumber booms that could not be translated into other economically successful ventures, leaving large portions of the Lake Superior region in severe economic depression that still continues to this day (Gedicks, 1991).

One example of Indian exploitation by a giant multinational corporation occurred with Exxon in Crandon, Wisconsin, in 1976. At that time Exxon discovered one of the world's largest deposits of zinc-copper near Crandon. Merely one-half mile away from the discovery site is the Sokaogon Chippewa reservation. Gathering wild rice is a practice that has been carried on for centuries in that area. Not only is it a cash crop, but it is also used to feed the tribe and as part of this particular band's religious ceremonies (Gough, 1980). Not understanding the importance of wild rice to Chippewa culture, Exxon's environmental impact report stated that "the means of subsistence on the reservation may be rendered less than effective, and the wild rice growing on the lake was mistakenly identified by an Exxon biologist as being a bunch of weeds" (Exxon, 1983).

Treaty rights guaranteeing hunting, fishing, and gathering rights established by the federal government and the Chippewa mattered little in the equation of mining and thus were conveniently ignored by Exxon. Gedicks writes that this attitude goes right to the core of the resource colonization process, what R. Davis and M. Zannis have referred to as the expendability of native peoples: "Simply stated, the difference between the economics of the old colonialism with reliance on territorial conquest and manpower and the new colonialism, with its reliance on technologically oriented resource extraction and transportation to the metropolitan centers, is the expendable relationship of the subject peoples to multinational corporations" (Davis and Zannis, 1973).

Thus it becomes clear why the state of Wisconsin and Exxon wanted to remove the obstacle of treaty rights. Millions of dollars to be gained from the Crandon mining project were at stake for both the state of Wisconsin and Exxon.

Tony Earl, governor of Wisconsin at the time (1982–1986), ardently supported the mining project, but the Chippewa treaties were a strong legal defense against the potential environmental damage that was highly likely to occur if that mine went forward. J. Mayers and R. Seely (1990) suggest that the implications of that mine on the Wolf River and the people who live downstream were among the most serious questions raised about that mine, because of the treaties (Mayers and Seeley, 1990). All the conflict with grassroots organizing efforts by influential environmental organizations and tribal resistance based on the authority given in the treaties resulted in Exxon's withdrawal from the Crandon mining project in 1986.

The Chippewa people were not alone in exercising tribal authority at this time, nor were organized reactions to the exercise of tribal authority limited to Indians in Wisconsin. Precursors to the anti-Indian organizations that formed in Wisconsin after Chippewa treaty rights were affirmed in 1983 with the *Voigt* decision. Groups such as the Quiault Property Owners Association in Washington State, Montanans Opposed to Discrimination, and Wyoming Citizens for Equality in Government were only three of many groups that came together in 1976 in the Interstate Congress for Equal Rights and Responsibilities (ICERR) (Gedicks, 1991). These groups formed a highly organized anti-Indian network that linked on-reservation non-Indian landowner opposition to tribal governments with off-reservation non-Indian sport and commercial fishers opposed to treaty-protected fishing rights (Ryser, 1991).

The issue of off-reservation treaty rights began to fade from public attention in early 1970s and reappeared only in the mid-1970s after members of the Lac Courte Oreilles (LCO) of the Lake Superior Chippewa challenged the state's right to limit treaty-recognized hunting and fishing rights in the ceded territories both on and off the reservation. Some of the anti-Indian groups that formed in reaction to the famous *Voigt* decision included Wisconsin Alliance for Rights and Resources (WARR), Equal Rights for Everyone (ERFE), STA, and PARR.

The resource politics of these anti-Indian groups began in reaction to the 1974 *Boldt* decision, reaffirming the off-reservation fishing rights of many Washington State Indian tribes. Tribes in the Northwest, like Indian tribes of the Great Lakes, have very clear language in their treaties ensuring the right to an indigenous economy. Even so, tribes of the Northwest were deprived of their legal treaty right to fish for over a century. Also at stake are the social and cultural practices of tribes in the Northwest as well as in Wisconsin (Jaimes, 1992).

Gedicks (1991) writes that according to Lowman (1978),

> the *Boldt* decision was part of a larger conspiracy involving the federal government and big oil companies to secure greater federal control over the nation's energy resources. Lowman based this conclusion in 1969 when Alaska natives blocked construction on the oil pipeline by claiming aboriginal title to Alaska by becoming allies with the oil companies. As allies of the oil companies, natives then lobbied Congress for a settlement paid for by the U.S. taxpayer.

On the surface, it seems as though Lowman's perspective is a criticism of government and corporations conspiring together with Indians as victims caught in the middle. But, as noted by Gedicks, Lowman's complaint is that many of these energy resources are off-limits to energy companies; that tribes are refusing to do business with energy companies, and when tribes have done business with the large companies, it has been at exorbitant prices. Lowman blames the situation on the Council of Energy Resource Tribes (CERT), which represents "some 23 energy-rich Indian tribes in the western United States" (Lowman, cited by Gedicks, 1991: 19).

The implicit environmental rights of treaty Indians to protect fishing habitats, addressed in Phase II of the *Voight* decision, form another obstacle to energy companies' access to Indian resources (Cohen, 1986). Lowman perceives this as a special right for Indians effecting environmental controls over issues such as land use planning, zoning, power plant locations, logging practices, and dam building (Lowman, cited by Gedicks, 1991: 19). Lowman writes that "for the federal government to nurture the concept that one small racial minority should be designated as having the unique status to sue all others in America for all the environmental changes which have occurred since 1776 is just too much" (ibid.: 20). If this is not convincing enough to abrogate Indian treaties, Lowman raises the red flag of national security: when the internal security of this country is endangered, is the game worth the price of the candle? When Lowman's rhetoric is reduced to its essentials, it is revealed as a corporate critique of tribal sovereignty (Gedicks, 1991). With Indian tribes in the western United States battling state and corporate attempts to neutralize their treaty rights to fish, the negative reaction to the *Voigt* decision reaffirming off-reservation fishing rights in Wisconsin comes as no surprise.

THE PRO-MINING AND ANTITREATY BACKLASH

The *Voigt* case has been the focus of sustained public controversy in recent years. This case forms the legal framework for the current practice of Chippewa spearfishing, which has been the focus of much negative attention. Each spring tribal declarations to invoke the right to spearfish receive heavy media coverage. Unfortunately, little insight is provided into how these declarations are completed and into the intensive efforts by tribes to balance tribal needs with those of other user groups (Great Lakes Indian Fish and Wildlife Commission, 1993). The public response to court decisions and to the practice of spearfishing during the spring season has ranged from outright hostility from antitreaty sport fishing groups to demonstrations of support for the Chippewa.[1]

After the *Voigt* decision in 1983, antitreaty groups in Wisconsin, such as the Wisconsin Alliance for Rights and Resources , Equal Rights for Everyone, Protect Americans' Rights and Resources, and Stop Treaty Abuse, have tried to convince the public that the Chippewa were out to "rape the resources, overharvest deer and fish, and exercise their treaty rights without limitations, which would destroy the entire tourist economy of northern Wisconsin" (Gedicks, 1991). D. Fixico (1998) writes that "tourists in northern Wisconsin generated seventy cents of every dollar in the region's economy. As many as 1.2 million sports fishermen visited each year, and the many hunters who arrived annually did not understand the treaty rights guaranteed for the Chippewa" (Gedicks, 1991).

As stated earlier, Wisconsin's media did little to dispel the fears and racism of sport fishers, hunters, and people in the tourist business. What escaped media attention is the fact that the Voigt Intertribal Task Force (VITTF), comprising representatives from Chippewa tribes that signed the 1837 and 1842 Treaties, first meets and reviews printouts prepared by Great Lakes Indian Fish and Wildlife Commission biologists. The information gathered details walleye recruitment classifications, acreage, type of population estimate, and safe harvest levels. Once the information is gathered, tribal representatives work together to divide the resources among the tribes so that the combined harvest of individual tribes does not exceed the safe harvest level for any ceded territory lake (Great Lakes Indian Fish and Wildlife Commission, 1993).

Contrary to the claim made by sport fishing groups that the "deviant" Chippewa are out to "rape the resources," a strict spearfishing permitting system and harvest monitoring system are in place (Great Lakes Indian Fish and Wildlife Commission, 1993: 10). The Chippewa bands, through this commission, have developed a permitting system to allocate fishing opportunities among tribal members and to prevent tribal harvests from exceeding harvest quotas. This publication states that permits are issued at tribal offices and at some designated boat landings by clerks and wardens from the commission. The daily permit identifies the lake, the day, and the daily bag limit. The number of permits that can be issued is determined daily by dividing the remaining tribal quota for a lake by the bag limit selected for that lake. When fishing is completed, tribal members are required to bring their harvest to a designated monitoring area where a Great Lakes Indian Fish and Wildlife Commission (GLIFWC) creel clerk/warden team counts and records the amount of fish taken, as well as the length, sex, and species of the fish on a catch report form. This information is then summarized by GLIFWC biologists and made available through computer data to tribes, Wisconsin Department of Natural Resources (WDNR) staff, and the public (Great Lakes Indian Fish and Wildlife Commission, 1993). In addition to this extensive monitoring of walleye harvest, GLIFWC conservation wardens work in cooperation with WDNR wardens to patrol spearing landings and lakes. If a Chippewa spearer is found to be violating tribal off-reservation conservation codes (i.e., tribal laws), that person is issued a citation and adjudicated in tribal court. Also important is that tribes restrict the harvest of large walleye, which protects females filled with eggs and ensures that they are not the majority of the spearing harvest, as antitreaty organizations claim. To further counter the inappropriate accusations of antitreaty groups, several tribes collect and successfully rear eggs taken from speared fish for restocking (Great Lakes Indian Fish and Wildlife Commission, 1993).

What sport fishers and antitreaty/anti-Indian groups refuse to recognize is the importance of the natural environment to the Chippewa culture. The fishing regulations outlined above are practiced by the tribes but not taken into consideration by most of the general public. These regulations ensure that the ancient relationship with the environment of the Great Lakes based on the natural law of the universe will continue for future generations of all people.

The Chippewa relationship to the environment is based on the peace and harmony associated with the concept of natural law, which follows the path of sustainability and conservation of all resources. As Winona LaDuke (1993) writes, laws made by nations and states are inferior to this supreme law and should be treated as such. Many Chippewa believe that natural law holds the key for societies and people to successfully function in a sustainable way. Viewed from this perspective, the importance of balance becomes easier to understand.

LaDuke writes that within this context, Anishinabe (Chippewa) have developed a code of ethics and a value system that guides their behavior in accordance with natural law: *mino bimaatisiiwin,* which means "the good life or continuous rebirth." This principle guides them in how they should behave toward others and toward animals, plants, and the ecosystem, and it is based on tenets of reciprocity and cyclical thinking (LaDuke, 1993). Reciprocity for many Chippewa defines the responsible way for humans to relate to the ecosystem. The resources of the earth are viewed as gifts from the Creator and are not taken without a reciprocal offering, usually tobacco, or *saymah,* as it is referred to in the Ojibwa language. Also understood as part of reciprocity is the notion that only what is needed is taken, and the rest is left alone because what one does today will return to affect everyone in the future (LaDuke, 1993). Therefore, to deplete fish, game, or wild rice resources would amount to cultural doom for the Chippewa of northern Wisconsin.

This type of living stands in sharp contrast to that of industrial society. In industrial society, human dominion over nature has preempted the perception of natural law as central. From this perception of progress as an essential component of societal development (defined as economic growth and technological advancement) comes the perception of the natural world as wilderness in need of cultivation, or taming, and of some peoples as being primitive while others are civilized. This, of course, is the philosophical underpinning of colonialism and conquest (LaDuke, 1993).

Misunderstandings about the differences in the lives of many Chippewa and about Chippewa hunting and fishing rights led to strained Indian-white relations in northern Wisconsin, which intensified each time fishing season came around. Hunters and sport fishers who opposed treaty rights confronted Indian fishers at the lakes. Racial slurs and derogatory terms were shouted back and forth by both whites and Indians. The racism fueled by the spearfishing controversy became so intense that Indian and white children could not attend the same schools, nor could their parents eat at the same restaurants. These confrontations became so heated that the state of Wisconsin and the Indians entered into negotiations that resulted in state officials and Chippewa leaders reaching twenty-three interim agreements and a settlement to end all the legal and racial controversy (Fixico, 1998).

Even though Governor Tommy Thompson tried to deny the relationship between racism and spearfishing, the two were clearly related, and the racist behavior did not end in spite of agreements and settlements designed to deter this type of behavior. Sentiment against the Indians continued to grow and resulted in "outright ridicule, and Treaty Beer was introduced during the summer with proceeds used to support the abrogation of Indian treaty rights" (Fixico, 1998: 112). Even though production of the beer ended due to boycotts of the product, 700,000 cans were brewed by Hiberna Brewery (Fixico, 1998).

Negotiations continued between the state and the Chippewa. Both sides wanted to reach a final solution, but the Chippewa did not want to compromise their treaty rights (Fixico, 1998). No amount of compromise had any positive effect in ending racial harassment, which included:

- A plot uncovered by a Milwaukee newspaper to pool $30,000 to hire a hit man to assassinate tribal leaders.

- Signs bearing such legends as "Save a Walleye, Spear a Pregnant Squaw."

- Effigies of Injun Joe hanging in the woods at landings and Indian heads impaled on spears, like horror movie props.

- Patrol car tires slashed, rocks thrown through truck radiators, organized attempts to force tribal vehicles off the road, and police officers hurt in melees with protestors.

- Pipe bombs found at landings with makings for more discovered in a nearby home.

- Shouts of Timber nigger! "The only good Indian is a dead Indian!"

- "Rape our women, not our walleye!" "Kill em!" "Scalp em!" coupled with a thesaurus of obscenities (Native Prisoners' Rights Committee News, 1989).

Even though little in the way of recourse for racial hostilities was found in the courts, there was, at least, some measure of due process for the Chippewa. In the Northwest, tribes responded in a different manner to their crises in the total absence of any modicum of due process. A series of fish-ins were initiated in western Washington and along the Columbia River when Makah elders asked for participation from fifty indigenous nations (more than forty came). In defiance of regulations that abridged their rights, they fished at times and places forbidden by state law (but guaranteed under provision of the treaties). The outcome included repeated arrests, jail, confiscation of gear, and frequent physical violence (Jaimes, 1992). In the instance of the Washington tribes, the response of the state was violent.

It was in this context of violence and racism that the first fishing rights cases went to the U.S. Supreme Court, beginning with the tribes in Washington and then continuing with the Chippewa of Wisconsin. All of the protests and attempts to coerce the Chippewa into giving up their treaty rights could not erase the fact that the Chippewa were indeed granted the right to harvest and sell hunting, fishing, and gathering products and to exercise these rights on private land to produce and harvest a quantity sufficient to enjoy a modest living. When the court placed limits on the amount of game and forest products (excluding commercial timber) that the Chippewa could take, neither the state nor the Chippewa appealed the ruling. The Lac Courte Oreilles announced the tribes' acceptance of the court ruling by releasing a statement: "The ... Lake Superior Chippewa ... have preserved [their hunting, fishing, and gathering] rights for generations to come [and they] have this day foregone their right to further appeal.... They do this as a gesture of peace and friendship towards the people of Wisconsin, in a spirit they hope may be reciprocated on the part of the general citizenry and officials of this state" (Satz, 1991).

Historically, the Chippewa have had to submit to a paternalistic government, coercive threats of removal from their homelands, and a confusing mix of Indian-white relationships affecting them culturally, politically, and socially. The Chippewa people are aware of all that has been taken from them over the past 300 years, and now look at their rights as a tribe and as individuals. The revitalization of tribal councils from the 1950s through the 1980s led to a departure from the previously submissive posture of the Chippewa and the hold of Euro-American domination over their lives. The Chippewa are empowered and able to stand against those who would abrogate treaty rights with the stroke of a pen for purely capitalist gains.

CONCLUSION: IMPLICATIONS OF THE *Voigt* DECISION FOR WISCONSIN'S ECONOMY

Chippewa resistance to attempts to erode and dissolve treaties has risen from the past history of Indian-white relationships involving exploitation, racism, broken promises, discrimination, and victimization. The relationship has been unequal in the past in that the Chippewa had very little influence on decisions made by white people. With the media focus on the sensational aspects of the spearfishing controversy, not much light has been shed on the issue of how treaty rights and environmental protection work together for the benefit of all. Contrary to claims by anti-Indian groups, all studies done on the impact of spearfishing have failed to find any evidence that the Chippewa are a threat to this resource (Gedicks, 1991).

Hysteria has been constructed by anti-Indian groups surrounding what they consider outdated Indian treaties and misuse of resources. However, the state of Wisconsin has also played a part. The Strickland report noted that the state appears to be trying to regulate the Chippewa indirectly, through the manipulation of public opinion (Strickland, Hertzberg, and Owens, 1992). The hysteria generated by the fishing controversy is reminiscent of the panic experienced by settlers in the 1800s over rumors of Indian uprisings. Angry protestors, sport fishers, those in the tourist industry, the state of Wisconsin, and the multinational corporate giants would like to see the dissolution of treaties without realizing the benefit treaties have for all people. The executive branch of the state of Wisconsin has skillfully used the hysteria generated by the fishing controversy as a tool to actively promote mining in ceded territory of the Wisconsin Chippewa, which potentially will cause serious long-term damage to the resource and economic base of northern Wisconsin. The effects of such environmental damage on the tourist industry of northern Wisconsin are not addressed by anti-Indian, anti-treaty groups, yet they remain certain that tribal sovereignty is a threat to the resource base (Gedicks, 1991). The anti-Indian groups fail to realize that treaties that protect hunting, fishing, and gathering also protect the environment. What good is the treaty right to spearfish, if the waters and fish are forever poisoned by the environmentally destructive process of mining? If mining districts are established and the waters and fish are poisoned, no one will be able to consume the fish, which will have devastating economic effects on the tourist industry of northern Wisconsin. The bottom line is that treaties protect the land and resources of everyone.

However, natural law and sustainability have usually taken a backseat to the economics of capitalism in U.S. industrial society, and the anti-Indian movement has historically been linked to the economic expansionary needs of U.S. capitalism (Gedicks, 1993: 5). When the dominant European American society needed land and raw materials for expansion, Indians were defined as a problem or a threat, and their lands and resources were taken. Now, it turns out that some of the last remaining energy and mineral resources are located on Indian lands or on off-reservation lands in the ceded territory of Wisconsin. The hysteria generated by anti-Indian groups and the state is apparent in the state's handling of the spearfishing issue, as well as the mining issue. "The Chippewa have been portrayed as the culprits on the spearfishing issue and totally ignored for their leadership role in trying to protect the resources for both Indian and non-Indian populations in the ceded territory of Wisconsin" (Gedicks, 1991: 4).

The economic potential of mining in Wisconsin is enormous. The public has become more aware of serious environmental damage that could result from mining, and the anti-Indian groups have become more politically sophisticated and influential in mainstream politics at state and national levels (Gedicks, 1991). Focusing on sensational aspects of the treaty issue have clouded the underlying economic and political context of this issue, which is most important to keep in mind.

With the Chippewa portrayed in such a negative way and the scenarios played out over these past years at the boat landings, misunderstandings of cultural differences between non-Indians and Indians create the likelihood of societal reaction. White culture and traditional Chippewa culture, with its belief in natural law, lie at opposite ends of the spectrum. This vast expanse of social distance between

Indians and non-Indians involved in the fishing controversy and fueled by mis-interpretation of each other's actions may cause breakdowns in communication between all involved. Protestors would not be at the boat landings if they did not fear their lifestyles were in danger. Threads of exploitation and misconceptions on both sides are woven throughout this scenario. Perhaps the fishing controversy has more to do with being out of balance than with anything else.

Through the *Voigt* decision, the court has decided that the rights agreed to in the treaties between the Chippewa and the U.S. government will be honored. The imbalance of racial hostilities that came about during the fishing rights controversy and decision will take time to resolve itself. Balance is necessary to sort out bad and evil as well as to realize our limits. It is important to remember the underlying economic and political context of this issue in order to regain a sense of balance. As we take what is out of balance, such as rage and anger over the fishing controversy and attempted abrogation of the treaties for capital gain, and turn this sentiment around to be used strategically, the racial imbalance and resulting hostilities experienced on all sides will have a chance to heal. In their place, balance with all of creation and revitalization of tradition will begin to flourish for the benefit of everyone.

NOTES

1. Per Carol Edgerton of the Native American Center in Madison, Wisconsin, the beginning of the spring spearfishing season depends on when the ice melts, usually around April 15. The season usually runs from the last two weeks in April into the first two weeks of May. Spearfishing starts in the western part of the state where the ice first melts and spreads to the eastern part of the state. The St. Croix, Bad River, and Red Cliff bands are usually the first to begin spearing, followed by the Lac Courte Oreilles, Lac du Flambeau, and Mole Lake bands. Cited by Linda Robyn, "State Corporate Crime and the Issue of Chippewa Treaty Rights," unpublished paper, 1992.

Indian Gaming and the American Indian Criminal Justice System

Nicholas C. Peroff

The criminal justice system in Indian Country includes everything from criminal behavior that may lead to an individual's entry into the criminal justice system; to police, prosecution, and pretrial services; to the courts and corrections; and eventually to the exit of individuals from the system. Although there has been limited interest in the relationship between Indian gaming and the American Indian criminal justice system in general, one exception is a growing amount of research that has sought to explore possible relationships between Indian gaming casinos and criminal behavior, both on Indian reservations and in adjacent non-Indian communities. In this chapter I review the available literature on the relationship between Indian gaming and the criminal justice system, offer insight into what American Indians themselves think about possible linkages between casinos and crime within their communities, and conclude with a consideration of the mixed positive and negative impacts of Indian gaming and their connection to criminal justice in Indian Country.

THE INDIAN GAMING INDUSTRY

The Indian gaming industry in the United States is a recent phenomenon (see Anderson, 1999; Bloom, 1993; Eadington and Cornelius, 1998; Mason, 2000;

Mullis and Kamper, 2000; Peroff, 2001). The earliest stages in the development of Indian tribal gaming began in the late 1970s and early 1980s, when tribes in Florida, Connecticut, Wisconsin, and California first opened low-stakes bingo halls on their reservations and then gradually expanded their gaming enterprises. By 1988, when the U.S. Congress passed the Indian Gaming Regulatory Act to provide a common statutory basis for the industry, Indian gaming was a $500 million business. Today, gross annual revenues exceed $14 billion.

Of the 562 federally recognized tribes in the United States, about one-third, or 201 tribes, ran 330 gaming operations in twenty-nine states in 2002 (National Indian Gaming Association, 2003; National Indian Gaming Commission, 2003). Gaming revenues vary tremendously from tribe to tribe. Although Indian casinos average $44 million in revenue per year, the top forty-one casinos average $230,000,000 and the bottom ninety casinos average $775,000 (National Indian Gaming Commission, 2003). About one-fourth of all Indian casinos are in California and a little less than half of all revenues earned in Indian gaming are earned by tribes in California (Hostetter and Olvera, 2003). Indian gaming revenues represent less than 10 percent of total revenues earned annually for the entire gaming industry in the United States (National Indian Gaming Association, 2003).

INDIAN GAMING AND ORGANIZED CRIME

Only limited research exists on a direct relationship between Indian gaming and criminal justice systems on Indian reservations. What does exist tends to focus on gaming as a new and much-needed source of revenue for system-related services. Some tribes appear to fund several components of the criminal justice system (Apesanahkwat, 1999: 3). Others tend to focus available resources on one area of public safety, such as police protection (e.g., De La Torre, 2003; Henry, 1999; Hill, 2000; Northern Plains Indian Law Center, 2003). Still other tribes use gaming revenues to contract out for police and other public safety services from surrounding non-Indian communities (Gorman, 1998; MAGNA Management Consulting, 2000).

Limited attention has also focused on various claims of a relationship between Indian gaming and organized crime. For example, *Fortune* magazine and the *Wall Street Journal* published articles that argue, in turn, that organized crime on Indian reservations is rampant and that the corruption of Indian gaming by criminal interests is a scandal waiting to happen ("Big Chief Pataki," 2002; "Indian Casinos Today," 2002; Useem, 2000). The forms of alleged corruption range from criminal efforts to control investments in or the management of Indian casinos to money laundering and include allegations that organized crime has infiltrated casino equipment vendors and other suppliers to tribal gaming operations ("Native American Gaming," 2002; Rezendes, 2000). Asian-based organized crime is also linked to loan sharking and other forms of exploitation of Asian customers at the Mohegan Sun and Foxwoods Casinos in Connecticut (Burgard and Green, 2002).

Those who see the potential for an infiltration of Indian casinos by organized crime base their concerns on the observation that Indian casinos are largely self-regulated and that oversight by the National Indian Gaming Commission, Internal Revenue Service, and other federal agencies is inadequate because of chronic underfunding, understaffing, and constraints on federal regulators who must respect Indian tribal sovereignty (Rezendez, 2000). Nevertheless, although it is true that there have been isolated incidents (e.g., profit skimming at a casino operated by the Rincon Indian Band in California is the most publicized case of infiltration to date), there is no evidence of a systematic penetration of the Indian gaming industry by elements of organized crime (Buffalo, 2002; Fine, 2001; Ohr, 2001).

OPPONENTS AND PROPONENTS OF INDIAN GAMING

Critics of Indian gaming have written books (Benedict, 2000, Eisler, 2001), established anti–Indian gaming websites (Tribal Nation, 2003), and formed interest groups to oppose both Indian and non-Indian casinos (Reno, 1999). Perhaps the most vehement opponent of Indian gaming is a group called Tribal Nation, which has specifically targeted the Foxwoods and Mohegan Sun Casinos in Connecticut. The group's website states that its members "want to inform everyone of the crime statistics associated with casinos and more importantly the criminal records of 'Indians' who own these casinos" (Tribal Nation, 2003: 1). To that end, the group publishes a multiyear compilation of local and state crime statistics connected to the operation of the two casinos and a lengthy list of the individual arrest records of tribal members who are identified by name on the website.

In nearly all cases, opposition to Indian gaming has two characteristics: a non-Indian origin and an assertion, usually stated without supporting evidence, that there is a linkage between Indian casinos and criminal behavior. Although it is certainly true that Native American support for gaming is not unanimous, even within tribes that operate casinos today, the Navajo Nation receives the most publicity for its opposition to gaming, which is based in part on religious grounds and in part on a fear that gambling addiction and increased crime will follow casino gaming on their reservation (Henderson and Russell, 1997).

Gaming opponents tend to believe that casinos are generally magnets for crime (Fairbanks, 2003; McCue, 2003; Morita, 2002; Murphy, 2002; "No Slots for Tracks," 2002; Podger, 2003; Rosenbaum, 2002; Solomon, 2002; "State Doesn't Need New Casino," 1999; Vaillancourt and Sargent, 1999; Wichner, 2002), or worry about increases in specific crimes such as burglary, robbery, and prostitution (North Carolina Criminal Justice Analysis Center, 1999; Peele, 2001). They also worry about increased police, court, and jail costs—especially in adjacent non-Indian communities (Muir, 2003; "Rising Crime," 2000; Sutherly, 2003)—or are concerned about increases in crimes indirectly related to gambling addiction, such as burglary, theft, and embezzlement (Hughes, 2003).

The proponents of Indian gaming dispute or downplay linkages between casinos and increased criminal behavior and emphasize the alternative view that Indian casinos contribute to declining crime rates in reservation communities. Some Native Americans argue that tribes are sovereign Indian nations and therefore should not have to worry about such externalities as increased crime in adjacent non-Indian communities (Lorber, 1998). More commonly, proponents of Indian gaming ignore or downplay alleged relationships between gaming and increased criminal behavior and instead cite unconfirmed statements or observations that crime rates decline with the establishment of Indian casinos (Axtman, 2002; Wichner, 2002).

National proponents of Indian gaming, such as the National Indian Gaming Association and state organizations such as the California Nations Indian Gaming Association, argue that gaming generally improves the situation of Indians and non-Indians who live in and around Indian casinos (e.g., California Nations Indian Gaming Association, 2003; National Indian Gaming Association, 2003). Typical of the claim that Indian gaming leads to less crime is the engaging but unsupported statement of the chair of the Wampanoag Indian Tribal Council (Massachusetts) who urges people "to consider the overwhelming body of evidence that has shown Native American Indian gaming produces good-paying jobs, improves household incomes, and reduces social ills, such as crime in the areas surrounding most Native American Indian gaming and entertainment centers" (Paulson, 2001: 1).

ANALYTICAL PERSPECTIVES

Efforts to examine positive and negative linkages between Indian gaming and criminal behavior have been met with mixed results. There have been some reasonably thorough journalistic investigations of Indian gaming and crime (Francis, 2003; Randazzo, 2003; Roberts, 2001). A survey of state and tribal criminal justice agencies in North Carolina revealed two equal and opposing groups of opinion about the likelihood of increased crime if Indian casinos were permitted in the state (North Carolina Criminal Justice Analysis Center, 1999). The reported results of federally sponsored research have also tended to be inconsistent and inconclusive (General Accounting Office, 2000; National Gambling Impact Study Commission, 1999).

Many obstacles face anyone attempting to obtain an independent and objective perspective on the relationship between Indian gaming and crime. Although there is considerable research on the relationship between gambling and crime in general, Indian casinos are often not specifically targeted or identified and may not even be included within the scope of the reported research. Much of the research on gambling and crime is vulnerable to the charge that it is "agenda-driven" because it is sponsored by the gaming industry in general or by gaming tribes (Walker, 2001) or law enforcement agencies (Wheeler, 1999) in particular. Another problematic issue is that state and local non-Indian governments sponsoring the research seem most interested in finding support for their efforts to pass along the costs of alleged gaming-related crime to tribes operating Indian casinos (e.g., Thompson, Gazel, and Rickman, 1996).

Much of the available research to date suffers from methodological problems and inconsistencies, weak correlations, and questionable statistical analysis (Walker, 2001). Indian gaming is a relatively recent phenomenon, so either data are simply unavailable or relationships between gaming and crime have not, as yet, materialized. Moreover, Indian casino earnings and other gaming-related data are difficult to obtain because the information is proprietary. And although associations between Indian gaming and crime may spill over beyond reservation boundaries into adjacent non-Indian communities, most go unexplored because local governments are reluctant to do research outside of their immediate jurisdictions.

Guided by the assumption that Indian casinos may be directly or indirectly related to many forms of criminal behavior, research on casinos and crime has gone in many directions. Some observers have suggested that casinos may increase crime because they concentrate cash and people in one area where criminals, mostly non-Indians, can easily prey upon their victims (North Carolina Criminal Justice Analysis Center, 1999). Research is exploring what many believe is a strong relationship between casinos and gambling addiction that, in turn, leads to the commission of embezzlement, fraud, forgery, and other illegal acts to finance pathological gambling behavior (Committee on the Social and Economic Impact of Pathological Gambling, 1999; French, 2000; Lesieur, 1998; Wellford, 2001). Criminal behavior may also take the form of profit skimming and other white-collar crimes committed by casino management and the corruption of tribal political leaders (Barlett and Steele, 2002a; 2002b; Barsamian, 2000; "FBI Agent," 2000).

Few doubt that Indian casinos have a significant impact on local reservation economies. It is a common assumption that casinos reduce crime because increases in local wages reduce crime. If casinos provide more jobs to low-skilled workers, the rate of crime should decrease. Casinos should also reduce crime indirectly by stimulating economic development (Grinols and Mustard, 2001: 10–11; Mollison, 2003a, 2003b). However, Indian gaming may harm economic development and raise the rate of crime by undermining the local business climate because casinos may attract an unsavory clientele and encourage prostitution, drug trafficking, and other illegal activities. And although a casino may improve local economies overall, the large increase in pawnshops that accompany new casinos suggests that the economic well-being of everyone within surrounding communities may be uneven at best (Grinols and Mustard, 2001: 11).

THE RELATIONSHIP BETWEEN INDIAN GAMBLING AND CRIME

The understanding of the association between tribal casinos, crime, and criminal justice in Indian Country remains incomplete, but it is improving with the help of recent research on the relationship between Indian casinos and criminal behavior. Only a few years ago, published research suggested that the relationship between legalized casino gambling and crime rates is statistically insignificant and that there is probably no relationship whatsoever between legal casino gambling in general and total crime rates (Horn, 1997). And early studies that looked specifically at the impact of Indian casinos on surrounding non-Indian communities found that, when Indian casinos opened, there was actually a net decline in certain crimes such as auto theft and robbery (Taylor, Krepps, and Wang, 2000).

A somewhat clearer picture emerged when research began to suggest that the impacts of new casinos on communities differed and that not all communities experienced the same "casino effect" on the incidence of crime (Stitt, 2000). And, for the first time, research suggested that the rate of crime in a community can increase after a casino opens (Evans and Topoleski, 2002: 40). In 2001, a study used local county crime data from 1977 to 1996 to examine the impact of non-Indian and tribal-owned casinos on crime rates and found a clear and distinct increase in most crimes after the introduction of casinos (Grinols and Mustard, 2001).

As of this writing, the most recent research available offers some important new insights into the relationship between Indian gaming and crime in counties with or near an Indian casino but does not look at the relationship between gaming and crime specifically on Indian reservations. Perhaps the most significant finding in this research is the existence of an important delay between the startup of a tribally owned casino and a large increase in crime and problem gambling in counties with or near an Indian casino (Evans and Topoleski, 2002). Although the counties experience an immediate increase in employment and a significant decline in mortality, presumably due to better socioeconomic conditions brought about by the casino's stimulation of the local economy, the benefits come at a cost. Auto thefts, larceny, violent crime, and bankruptcies all increase by about 10 percent four or more years after an Indian casino opens in a county. A greater concentration of people into small geographic areas generated by the casino opening is the most likely reason for the increase in property crime. The slow buildup of criminal activity for larceny and auto thefts over the first four years a casino is open is also consistent with the belief that casinos encourage pathological gambling and that the afflicted people eventually turn to crime to support their addiction (Evans and Topoleski, 2002: 45–46).

WHAT DO AMERICANS THINK ABOUT CASINOS AND CRIME?

There are statistically significant relationships between casinos and crime, and recent research suggests that Indian gaming contributes to increased crime in counties that house or are adjacent to Indian casinos. However, the issue of whether or not there is a relationship between casinos and crime on Indian reservations has not been adequately addressed to date. Moreover, little attention has been given to the broader issue of the effect gaming has had on American Indian criminal justice systems in general.

There are several reasons for this omission in literature, and many—such as the proprietary nature of much of the relevant data—have already been identified. Perhaps the biggest underlying reason for the absence of comprehensive research on the relationship between casinos and crime on reservations is that Indian tribes are sovereign nations and, for good reason, are very reluctant to approve research by nontribal members on their reservations. They assume, correctly, that individuals and organizations who oppose Indian gaming will use any suggestion of a harmful linkage between casinos and crime to support their campaigns against the Indian gaming industry.

Any systematic exploration of the relationship between Indian gaming and crime in Indian Country is well beyond the scope of this chapter, but some insight into the topic can be drawn from research now being conducted by the author on the Menominee Indian Reservation in Wisconsin. The research, now in its third year, is a follow-up study to an earlier project on the termination and subsequent restoration of federal recognition of the tribe in the 1960s and 1970s (Peroff, 1982). To date, nearly eighty semistructured, open-ended interviews have been conducted on the reservation and provide a basis for the following discussion.

Today, the Menominee Nation is working to build a basis of long-term economic and political strength to support the growth of greater tribal self-determination now and in the future. About half of the more than 8,200 enrolled Menominee tribal members live on the reservation. Although their forest remains central to the uniqueness of the tribe, the reservation economy is also supported by the establishment of a gaming casino in 1987. Although it is not large (less than $3 million in annual revenues), the casino is the largest employer on the reservation. Proceeds from gaming provide support for police, tribal courts, and other services related to public safety, as well as a broad range of health, education and welfare services, economic development programs, and many other forms of community investment.

One question used in all of the interviews asked respondents to identify the most significant changes that have accompanied the establishment of the Menominee Casino on their reservation. Although individuals identified several positive and negative impacts of gaming on the reservation, they only made direct connections between the tribe's casino and crime on the reservation about 15 percent of the time. The most common concern expressed by respondents involved observations of an increased incidence of gambling addiction among Menominees, especially the elderly. An association between the casino and substance abuse was mentioned with about the same frequency but was often qualified with the observation that alcohol has long been a problem on the reservation. One respondent wryly observed that since people now have more money in their pockets because of better employment opportunities in the casino, there is now a "better quality of drugs" (more cocaine and heroin) available on the reservation.

A chronic problem with gangs and juvenile delinquency is also linked to Indian gaming because parents (especially single parents) work long hours at the casino, often from 5 or 6 p.m. to 2 or 3 a.m. Their children, left unsupervised, are free to get into one form or another of delinquent misbehavior. Although youth gangs existed before the casino was built, lately gang members seem to be better organized, perhaps by kids returning to the reservation while their parents seek work at the casino.

Interviews, especially with Menominees employed at the casino, suggest that theft, fraud, bogus credit card use, prostitution, and drug trafficking have at one time or another all been observed in or around the casino. However, the incidence of such behavior seems to be very infrequent. Certainly a conclusion that the Menominee Casino is a "magnet for crime" is not supported by the available data. Some respondents did say, though, that they only began to feel that it was necessary to lock their doors after the casino appeared on the reservation. As for any relationship between the Menominee Casino and incidents off the reservation, the only relevant comment is an observation by a local newspaper reporter who said that more people in the adjacent city of Shawano, Wisconsin, were embezzling from local businesses to play at the casino.

CONCLUSION

Research completed to date on Indian gaming, crime, and criminal justice in Indian Country suggests that there is a statistically significant relationship between casinos and crime and also suggests that Indian gaming contributes to increased crime in counties that house or are adjacent to Indian casinos. The specific relationship between casinos and crime on Indian reservations remains a topic for future research, but it is safe to assume that most individual Native Americans on reservations probably respond to the presence of casinos in much the same way as people do everywhere.

Indian casinos provide new options for tribal members, for good and for ill. Some observers emphasize the former and point to new jobs, better services, improved public safety, and more economic development opportunities. Others stress the latter and call attention to increased gambling addiction, drug use, property crime, and the other ills that seem to accompany the gambling industry wherever it is situated. Whatever the negatives associated with gaming on Indian reservations, it brings new opportunities to places where opportunities have been scarce for a very long time. What, in turn, that means for criminal justice in Indian Country remains to be seen.

Research on Juvenile Delinquency in Indian Communities

Resisting Generalization

Lisa Bond-Maupin, Taka X. GoodTracks, and James R. Maupin

Early research conducted by non-Indian researchers of crime among Indian peoples concluded, based primarily on national arrest statistics, that Indian people are disproportionately "criminal" (Bachman, 1992; Leubben, 1964; McCone, 1966; Reasons, 1972; Stewart, 1964). Many analysts interpreted limited data in whatever way supported O. Stewart's (1964) contention that American Indians are the most "criminal" ethnic group in American society. Most recently, this theme has been reproduced in the popular media as a result of the release of a recent Bureau of Justice Statistics (BJS) report focusing on violent crime.

On the cover of this report entitled *American Indians and Crime* (Greenfeld and Smith, 1999) is a graph depicting American Indians over twelve years of age as twice as likely to be victims of violent crime than are members of all other racial and ethnic categories combined. This statistic has been widely cited in newspaper stories throughout the country as evidence that crime among Indians is "out of control." These reports of rampant crime among Indians are not limited to outlets such as the *New York Times, Albuquerque Journal,* or *Phoenix Republic. Indian Country Today,* the American Indian–written and –published newspaper providing national coverage of issues of significance to Indian peoples, also reported "jarring" increases in juvenile crime based largely on this report (Hill, 1999: A1).

These summaries do not mention several other findings in that BJS report. For example, the rates of arrests for violence among American Indian youth are the same as those for white youths, and the rates of murder of Indian peoples have remained steady for the last twenty years (with some decline in the last ten years). Also, when American Indians are the victims of violent crime, it is most often non-Indians who are the perpetrators, and the highest rates of violence are in urban settings (Greenfeld and Smith, 1999: vii–19).

The issues raised in the document are very important to Indian peoples. Yet, the BJS report is limited as a source of information about their experiences as victims, given that about two-thirds of American Indians live on or adjacent to largely rural reservations—candidates for the small population subgroups that the federal surveys used for this report likely did not measure. According to the BJS report,

> Most federal surveys utilize nationally representative samples of persons or households, thus limiting the capability to describe small population subgroups in detail.... In addition, sampling procedures relying upon selection of respondents within clustered geographical sampling units may by chance miss those areas where concentrations of residences of small subgroups (such as American Indians) may be located. (Greenfield and Smith, 1999: 34)

Even though the report is entitled *American Indians and Crime,* it is also profoundly limited as a source of information about delinquency and crime on the part of American Indians, given that it focuses on Indian victimization off reservations and provides data primarily on those crimes under federal jurisdiction. In addition, although the median age for American Indians is eight years younger than the average age for the U.S. population in general and this younger population lives mostly on reservations, little information is presented on youths' involvement in crime within Indian communities.

In this chapter, we review the small body of literature on delinquency in Indian communities and discuss the limitations of using the Uniform Crime Reports (UCR), Bureau of Indian Affairs (BIA), and off-reservation data to make generalizations about the experience of Indian peoples with crime across the nation. We conclude with an analysis of eleven years of tribal arrest/booking data from one American Indian community not previously studied and discuss the implications of this research for future study.

REVIEW OF THE LITERATURE

There are two published studies of delinquency and American Indians using reservation arrest data in addition to federal arrest data (Minnis, 1963; Peak and

Spencer, 1987). M. S. Minnis (1963) examined arrest rates from 1934 to 1960 using tribal law enforcement data to supplement the UCR. Comparing the UCR with tribal data, the author found lower rates of arrest among Indian people for all but three categories of offense: "personal demoralization (drunkenness, vagrancy, disorderly conduct, etc.), offenses related to the operation of a motor vehicle (driving while drunk, traffic, etc.)," and juvenile status offenses ("truancy, juvenile mischief, incorrigible") (Minnis, 1963: 401).

K. Peak and L. Spencer (1987) examined both UCR data from 1976 to 1985 and BIA arrest figures for 207 reservations in 1983. Using the UCR, they noted a rise in illegal activity among Indian juveniles off the reservation from 1976 to 1980 and a decline from 1980 to 1985. Although the authors blur adult and juvenile statistics in their discussion of on-reservation findings, their study is one of the most recent and extensive examinations of arrests on reservations. They found that "69 percent of the actual offenses that were investigated in 1982 involved the use of alcohol or drugs," with public intoxication accounting for almost one-third of all arrests (Peak and Spencer, 1987: 401). Arrests for disorderly conduct were the most frequent (45 percent), followed by drunkenness.

Some of the research of Indian delinquency utilizes self-report or survey data from youths living on reservations. M. A. Forslund and V. A. Cranston (1975) collected self-report data on delinquency from Indian and "Anglo" high school students on the Wind River Reservation in Wyoming. This self-report study was a follow-up to M. A. Forslund and R. Meyers' 1974 article in which the authors concluded that "the officially recorded delinquency rate of Indian youth from [this reservation] is relatively high compared to that of the general American population" (Forslund and Cranston, 1975: 193). In their self-report study, "delinquency" included twenty-nine acts—primarily status, minor, and property offenses—and were mostly school-related. In comparing self-reported delinquency among Indian and Anglo youths, they found that school-based offenses (truancy, theft from desks or lockers, fighting) and drug use were most common among Indian youths and that Indian girls were more likely to have run away from home or committed minor theft or vandalism than were Anglo girls. A higher proportion of Anglo males reported drinking alcohol and making anonymous telephone calls. Forslund and Cranston (1975) noted that Indian youths were concentrated in the lower class and significantly underrepresented in the middle class. When the authors controlled for social class, the number of race-based differences declined.

In a ten-year study involving more than fifty Indian reservations, E. R. Oetting and F. Beauvais (1985) surveyed all seventh through twelfth graders in reservation schools regarding their use of alcohol and drugs. Comparing the prevalence of use data on Indian youth with results from a "moderate-sized, Western non-Indian community," the authors found that "a greater percentage of Indian than non-Indian youth are getting drunk" and reporting having blacked out on three or more occasions (Oetting and Beauvais, 1985: 5, 13). They found that "for nearly every category of drug, Indian youth have higher use rates" (Oetting and Beauvais, 1985: 17).

In her study of three Seminole reservation communities, S. Robbins (1985) found that self-reported delinquency was least common on the most rural or isolated reservation. Robbins used a measure of delinquency that included mostly property offenses, ranging from theft of something worth less than $5 to taking someone's car without permission. She also included "physically hurting someone on purpose." Although she does not delineate in which acts youths were involved, Robbins reports that an average of 21 percent of respondents had done one of these things and 52 percent had done more than one of these things. She concluded that these reservations had "high rates" of delinquency and that on all three very few do not engage in criminality.

In some of the only published research on delinquency using tribal arrest and detention data, L. Bond-Maupin, C. Lujan, and M. A. Bortner (1995) examined the arrest and detention of youths by law enforcement in one southwestern reservation community. They found that although all youths arrested were jailed prior to a hearing, the pervasive use of detention did not reflect the severity of offenses for which they were charged. In this community, "74 percent of the charges for which youths were arrested and jailed were minor delinquency and status offenses" (Bond-Maupin, Lujan, and Bortner, 1995: 7). In this community, "less than 11 percent of the charges ... involved serious felonies [sexual conduct with a minor was the most serious charge] ... and close to one-third of the 'offenses' ... were nondelinquency charges" (Bond-Maupin, Lujan, and Bortner, 1995: 7).

In a second study, Bond-Maupin (1996) analyzed the rates of arrest and detention in the same community after the tribal government assumed control of the detention center under the provisions of the Indian Self-Determination and Education Assistance Act. Forslund and Cranston (1975) found that even though the tribe had initiated juvenile justice system reform, all charged youths were detained regardless of the severity of their charges. During this study period, serious felonies accounted for about 10 percent of the arrests (sexual assault was the most serious charge), whereas almost half of the detained youths were charged with status offenses.

Although the body of research on delinquency in Indian communities does not support the popular notion of a serious juvenile crime wave among Indian youths, profound differences among Indian peoples and a very small body of research limit any generalizations about Indian delinquency. T. L. Armstrong, M. H. Guilfoyle, and A. P. Melton, in their 1992 report to the Office of Juvenile Justice and Delinquency Prevention, note this "relative lack of general information and specific research findings on the causes, nature, and extent of ... delinquency among Native Americans" (1992: 2). That does not prevent them from coming to the conclusion that "the disproportionate extent to which Indian adolescents are involved in criminal and delinquent activities" is a serious problem in Indian communities, but they acknowledge that the diversity of language, culture, customs, traditions, and relationship to state and local governments make generalizations difficult (Armstrong, Guilfoyle and Melton, 1992: 2). M. S. Zatz, C. C. Lujan, and Z. Snyder-Joy also make this point in their chapter on the complexities of studying crime in Indian communities. Not only are intertribal comparisons difficult, but "research on a specific Indian population cannot be generalized to members of other tribes" (Zatz, Lujan, and Snyder-Joy, 1991: 111).

The 562 federally recognized tribes vary profoundly in the extent to which they rely on traditional systems of social control. Traditional forms of conflict resolution and responses to deviance vary greatly across Indian cultures. Reliance on traditional forms of dispute or conflict resolution is more common among isolated groups on larger reservations but takes varying forms (Zatz, Lujan, and Snyder-Joy, 1991: 102). In addition, not all Indian peoples view formal, Western law and ways as just or relevant. The extent to which members of Indian communities relate to law enforcement and the courts as "foreign" will also affect reliance on these mechanisms of control reflected in varying rates of reporting crime (Zatz, Lujan, and Snyder-Joy, 1991: 104).

Additional factors that make generalizations very difficult include the size of the reservation, the extent to which Indian youths are subject to multiple jurisdictions and police forces, the economic stability of a tribe and its relative resources, and the proximity of the Indian community to an urban area. I. F. Donnermeyer, R. W. Edwards, E. L. Chavez, and F. Beauvais (1996) found that Indian youths in contact with non-Indian youths are more likely to report gang involvement. Bond-Maupin (1996) discussed variations in police surveillance resulting in differences in arrest rates based on the concentration of very few BIA officers in the most densely populated areas of a large reservation. In addition, depending on their proximity to nonreservation communities and their relationship with the state and federal governments, some reservation residents are subject to surveillance by tribal, federal, city, and state law enforcement, whereas others are subject only to tribal and federal law enforcement. Indian communities also vary in the operation of bingo and casino establishments and revenues from settlements in disputes with states and the federal government over land and other natural resources.

There are also problems in the methods used to collect the national crime data sets maintained in the UCR, BIA, and the National Crime Victimization Survey data that call into question the reliability and validity of the claims made in reports using those data sources to make generalizations about crime among American Indians. The data used to "count" crime among American Indians are frequently incomplete, tend to overcount crime, and do not adequately represent the experience of crime in the small rural communities in which the majority of Indian peoples reside.

First, information recorded by individual tribes does not always include ethnic data or tribal affiliation of the offender(s). An erroneous assumption is made that all crime committed on reservations is committed by American Indians. Second, additional overcounting of crime may occur because of multiple law enforcement jurisdictions existing nearby and on reservations. A cross-deputized officer must submit a separate crime report for each appropriate jurisdiction, resulting in multiple counting and reporting of a single incident. Third, crime rates are based on U.S. Census population figures that tend to undercount the number of American Indian residents, the population figures used to calculate crime rates per 100,000 population. The result is an overestimate of the actual crime rate for American Indians.

There are additional problems. In the UCR, only one crime per incident—the most serious—is reported. Repeat offenders are not accounted for, potentially resulting in an overestimate of the actual number of individuals who commit crimes within Indian communities. Furthermore, information provided to the Federal Bureau of Investigation (FBI) for inclusion into the UCR is voluntary and tends to overrepresent suburban and urban areas and underrepresent rural areas (where most reservations are located). BIA crime data contain differences in the classification and recording of crime incidents across tribal law enforcement jurisdictions. BIA crime data also overcount crime because all offenses committed during a crime incident are recorded and counted as separate events. As discussed earlier, the National Crime Victimization Survey (NCVS) uses a sampling procedure to gather information from victims of crime that overrepresents suburban and urban areas and underrepresents rural populations, in which most American Indian reservations are located.

AN ANALYSIS OF JUVENILE CRIME ON
ONE AMERICAN INDIAN RESERVATION

In an effort to overcome the methodological problems of commonly used sources of crime data for American Indians and to continue the accumulation of studies that examine tribal data in community context, we analyze eleven years (1988–1998) of juvenile arrest records from one American Indian nation located in the western United States. The reservation of this American Indian Nation covers approximately 350,000 acres. The place is rurally situated, with the largest city of approximately 20,000 located about twenty-five miles away. There is considerable checkerboarding across this reservation; this mixed pattern of tribal, private, municipal, county, and state-owned land results in an exterior reservation boundary that includes nearly four times the land base actually possessed by the tribe.

The tribal population of roughly 1,400 increased by approximately 25 percent during the years analyzed. About 75 percent of tribal members reside on the reservation. In addition, nearly 1,500 nontribal Indian people reside on the land. Roughly 35 percent of the tribal population is aged seventeen or under, and approximately 65 percent of these youths (around 342 young people) live on the reservation.

The geographical characteristics of this reservation result in a complex law enforcement jurisdictional arrangement. Ten officers from seven distinct law enforcement agencies are on duty at any given time during the day. Two of the agencies and five of the officers are tribal. The others are a combination of local municipality, county, state, BIA, and FBI. Consequently, there is one law enforcement officer for every 150 tribal reservation residents and one law enforcement officer for every 300 individuals residing on the reservation on duty during any twenty-four-hour period.

This matrix of jurisdictions can lead to considerable jurisdictional confusion when responding to calls, investigating offenses, and making arrests; however, in this community, the agencies' work is well coordinated. All tribal and nontribal adults and juveniles arrested by any officer are typically booked through the tribal jail and are documented on the jail arrest log.

The tribal council provided us with the jail arrest log maintained by the tribal police for the eleven-year period between January 1988 and December 1998. Tribal officials assisted us in the interpretation of the log codes and information. The data in the arrest log include date of arrest, court of jurisdiction, sex, age, tribal status, and charges. Each of these items is included in the description of juvenile arrests and detention in this community.

In eleven years, there were 4,956 bookings of adults and juveniles. Five hundred and thirty bookings (10.7 percent of the total) were for juvenile-related issues. Many of the bookings for both adults and juveniles were for noncharge-able/noncriminal events such as protective custody, emergency commitment, and so on (GoodTracks, 1999: 41–55). Of the 4,956 total bookings, 2,550 were for chargeable/criminal events. Of those 2,550 bookings, 263 (10.31 percent) were of juveniles. Those 263 bookings represent 364 separate, recorded offense charges, or an average of 1.39 charges per booking. The average number of priors per booking was 0.92.

The charges for which youths were arrested over the eleven-year period are depicted in Table 13.1. The single largest category of charges was for illegal possession or consumption of alcohol (32.97 percent). Runaway and other status offenses accounted for 14.29 percent of the charges. Conduct offenses accounted for 7.97 percent, and minor property offenses represented 3.85 percent of the charges. Assault and battery accounted for 5.49 percent, and resisting arrest or escaping represented 3.30 percent of the charges. Slightly more than 4 percent of the charges were for driving under the influence. Only one charge (0.27 percent) was for drug abuse. The rest of the arrests were for court holds, prior warrants, failure to appear, moving violations, or other minor offenses.

More than half (66.2 percent) of the bookings were of males. Females accounted for 33.8 percent of the arrests. The single-largest percentage of bookings (27.6 percent) was of seventeen-year-old youths. Youths ages fifteen and sixteen combined accounted for nearly half the bookings (49.3 percent). The remaining bookings (23.0 percent) were of youths ages eleven to fourteen. Most (67.9 percent) of the bookings were of youths affiliated with the study tribe, but 28.8 percent had other tribal affiliations. Non-Indians accounted for 3.3 percent of the bookings. Most (96 percent) of the arrests were charged through tribal court.

Data used to count incidents of crime among American Indians rarely use the juvenile as the unit of analysis. The UCR is based on information that is inconsistent with regard to the identification of American Indians and uses the hierarchy rule to count only the most serious crimes, without distinguishing the actual number of individuals committing those crimes. BIA crime data record all offenses committed during a single incident, and each offense tally is counted as

Table 13.1

Charge Categories for All Offenses, 1988 -1998		
N = 364 offenses		
% of		
Charge Category	*Number*	*All Charges*
Illegal Possession/Consumption of		
Alcohol	120	32.97%
Drug Abuse	1	00.27%
Warrant, Failure to Appear,		
Court Hold	51	14.01%
Runaway and Other Status Offenses	52	14.29%
Conduct Offenses	29	7.97%
Minor Property Offenses	14	3.85%
Theft/Breaking and Entering	8	2.20%
Driving Under the Influence	15	4.12%
Assault, Assault and Battery	20	5.49%
Resisting Arrest/Escape	12	3.30%
Disobedience of Court Order/Contempt	17	4.67%
Traffic Offenses	20	5.49%
Other	5	1.37%
Total	364	100.00%

an arrest (GoodTracks, 1999: 42–45). We are able to overcome these problems with this case study because of our ability to analyze the actual jail arrest log of the tribal police.

The 263 bookings were of 143 individual juveniles. The number of juveniles arrested each year ranged from a low of eight in 1991 to a high of twenty-five in 1993, for a mean of eighteen juveniles each year. Table 13.2 depicts the distribution of the frequency of bookings and the number of juveniles by year. The mean number of priors for each juvenile was 0.85, and the mean number of total offenses with which each juvenile was charged was 2.56. The average number of years in which a juvenile was booked was 1.38, with 26.6 percent of the juveniles booked in two or more years. Males accounted for 59.4 percent of the juveniles booked, and females accounted for 40.6 percent. Tribal members accounted for 66.9 percent of the juveniles booked. Non tribal Indians accounted for 26.8 percent, and non-Indians accounted for 6.3 percent of the juveniles booked.

Discussion

Of the just more than 300 youths living in this reservation community, fewer than 6 percent are arrested each year. Even in this close-knit, relatively small community with high levels of surveillance from multiple police forces, arrest rates are very low. Those youths taken into custody are often arrested multiple times. These repeat arrests among the same individuals are not accounted for in aggregate custody statistics, in which the arrest and not the juvenile is the unit of analysis.

Table 13.2

Number of Bookings and Juveniles by Year—1988–1998
N = 263

Year	# of Bookings	Percent Change	# of Juveniles
1988	22		16
1989	22	0%	18
1990	27	+23%	22
1991	12	-56%	8
1992	20	+67%	1
1993	38	+90%	25
1994	20	-47%	16
1995	30	+50%	22
1996	27	-10%	23
1997	21	-22%	11
1998	24	+14%	19

The number of arrests each year has decreased as often as it has increased over the years. There is not a steady increase in juvenile crime reflected in the arrest figures for this community. We acknowledge that arrest records are limited as sources of information about actual delinquency, given that they reflect the decision making of law enforcement officials and measure delinquency that may not become official through adjudication. Unlike prior self-report data, arrest records allow for analysis of the full range of illegal activities in which youths may be involved. When this full range of activities is assessed, the relative severity of offenses becomes clearer. In addition, we are able to conclude that violence is rare among youths in this community.

This initial analysis of data from this community scratches the surface of the information needed in order to understand delinquency in this reservation. An in-depth case study would explore the ways in which changes in arrest practices and juvenile justice policies and resources have affected arrest rates. In addition, self-report and survey data would allow for more information about the kinds of illegal activity most common in this community and perceptions of youths and other community members about the correlates and causes of delinquency. In-depth interviews and historical analysis would allow for an understanding of the extent to which less formal, culturally derived methods of dealing with delinquency and social control exist in this community as alternatives to arrest.

CONCLUSION

The use of aggregate statistics to represent the experience of a population distributed across a vast geographical region is always difficult, if not impossible. The practice contributes to the notoriety of the ecological fallacy of inappropriately applying conclusions drawn from aggregate data to individual experiences. The media extrapolations using the information presented in the BJS report (Greenfeld and Smith, 1999) reflect that tendency. But there are other problems directly associated with this BJS report and prior research that has utilized aggregate data gathered from federal surveys to generalize about the incidence of crime among American Indians.

Robert Silverman raises several important considerations regarding the use of aggregate data acquired from federal surveys to typify the average experience of crime among American Indians. His primary contention is that the numerator and especially the denominator used to calculate arrest rates are inaccurately calculated and will produce greatly exaggerated estimates. The use of statistics based upon these flawed components produce statistics that incorrectly portray American Indians "as the most criminal population in the United States" and does not "reflect the best available information on the subject" (1996: 73). The BJS report (Greenfeld and Smith, 1999: 34) alludes to this problem in its conclusion by acknowledging that the "sampling procedures [of federal surveys], relying upon selection of respondents within clustered geographical sampling units, may by chance miss those areas where concentrations of residences of small subgroups (such as American Indians) may be located." The report also acknowledges that "UCR coverage of those arrests by tribal or BIA law enforcement agencies is not known, and the extent to which they are included in the national estimates" of arrests is not systematically described" (36).

There are other problems with using aggregated data, both in terms of methodology and for use in policymaking, apart from the probable inaccuracy of the information itself. As discussed above, considerable social and cultural variation exists across American Indian communities that results in different patterns of decision making, especially with regard to juveniles. Aggregate data do not reflect those differences. In addition, many reservation communities have relatively small populations. Combining what little accurate information is available from these sparsely populated communities with that from larger reservation constituencies tends to result in a portrayal of those smaller communities that is heavily influenced by the data available from the larger communities.

These weaknesses of aggregated data analysis are demonstrated in our analysis of the eleven years of arrest records for one tribe on an American Indian reservation. The data used for analysis in this case study make it possible to use two levels of analysis, aggregate as well as individual juveniles. The picture that emerges from this analysis is one of a community in which juvenile crime, both violent and nonviolent, is far below the estimates provided in the BJS report (Greenfeld and Smith, 1999). In addition, we were able to reveal that the juvenile crime in this community is the result of a small subset of the juvenile population.

It is our contention that policymakers must resist the urge to design and implement policy in individual communities based solely upon results derived from analysis of the aggregate data provided by the UCR or BIA. Juvenile crime is experienced within individual communities with unique characteristics. Each community is as likely to have as many differences as similarities in that experience. Policy designed to ameliorate juvenile crime within these communities will be most successful when based upon information acquired within the individual communities.

Recent Trends in Community-Based Strategies for Dealing with Juvenile Crime in the Navajo Nation

Marianne O. Nielsen, Dorothy Fulton, and Ivan Tsosie

Although juvenile crime in the rest of the country has been dropping, crimes by juveniles have been rising steadily in many Native American communities (LeClaire, 1999). Unfortunately, the Navajo Nation is no exception. Data on Native American delinquency are notoriously hard to collect (Armstrong, Guilfoyle, and Melton, 1996). Based on preliminary data collected from the files of the Navajo Nation Departments of Criminal Investigation and Law Enforcement, this chapter provides an overview of juvenile crime by Navajo Nation young people and describes some of the innovative strategies that have been developed to prevent crime and recidivism. These strategies focus on providing culturally knowledgeable and sensitive services to youth, their families, and the community.

BACKGROUND

The Navajo Nation is the second largest American Indian nation in the United States, with approximately 225,000 members. About 170,000 people, of whom

93 percent are Navajo, live on the reservation. This is likely a serious undercount, and it is anticipated that the next census will find a much larger population. The Navajo Nation covers about 25,300 square miles, encompassing parts of three states—Arizona, New Mexico, and Utah. About 51 percent of Navajo Nation members are age nineteen or under (Navajo Nation, 1995).

According to the Bureau of Justice Statistics (1999: 24),[1] 17 percent of American Indians arrested for Part 1 violent offenses in 1996 were under the age of eighteen.[2] (Part 1 offenses are the eight index offenses in the Uniform Crime Reports (murder and nonnegligent manslaughter, forcible rape, robbery, aggravated assault, burglary, larceny theft, motor vehicle theft, and arson). This is below the national average for the percentage of all juvenile arrests for Part 1 violent crimes. American Indian juveniles were arrested somewhat more often than were Asian and white juveniles but still fell below the average. The rate of arrests for black juveniles were far above the average. American Indian juveniles were as likely as American Indian adults to be arrested for Part 1 violent crimes. In other words, American Indian juveniles, at least according to the data gathered by local law enforcement agencies, are not unusual subjects for violent crime arrests (see Figure 14.1). In general, Native American juveniles had lower arrest rates for murder, rape, aggravated assault, and especially robbery than did juveniles of other racial groups. The categories in which they had much higher rates than other juveniles were property offenses and alcohol violations. Their rates resembled those of American Indians of all ages for rape and were much higher for liquor law violations (see Table 14.1) (BJS, 1999).

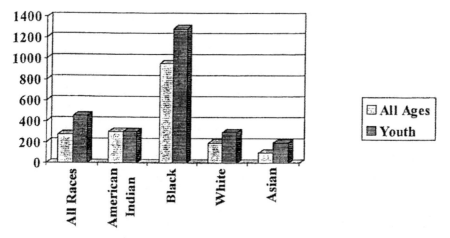

Figure 14.1
Violent Crime Arrest Rates by Race for All Ages and Youth (Number of arrestees for Part I violent crimes per 100,000 populations)
Note: Arrest for youth were based on the estimated number of arrests of persons under the age of 18 and calculated on the number of residents age 10–17.
Sources: FBI, Crime in the United States, 1996 as found in BJS 1999

Table 14.1   Arrest Rate Comparison for American Indian and All Other Racial Group by Youth and All Ages

| | Number of arrests per 100,000 population | | | |
| | All Ages | | Youth | |
	All Races	American Indian	All Races	American Indian
Total Violent	275	291	445	294
Murder	7	7	9	5
Rape	13	16	19	14
Robbery	59	37	165	67
Aggravated Assault	197	231	252	208
Total Property	1039	1369	2783	3026
Total Alcohol Violations	1079	2545	649	1341
DUI	553	1069	61	98
Liquor laws	255	727	510	1108
Drunkenness	271	749	78	135

Source: BJS 1999

Note: Arrest rate is the number of arrests per 100,000 resident population. Arrest rates for youth were based upon the estimated number of arrests of persons under the age of 18. The youth arrest rate was calculated on the number of residents age 10–17.

Fred Beauvais (1992) found that trends in overall drug use among American Indian and non–American Indian juveniles have followed very similar patterns in terms of dropping steadily since the early 1980s for the most-used drugs (marijuana, inhalants, and stimulants). The rates for cocaine and hallucinogens increased until 1990 and then began to decline as well. However, American Indian juveniles living on reservations consistently had higher rates of drug use during this whole period than did non–American Indian juveniles. American Indian juveniles as represented in the national statistics, therefore, are arrested primarily for substance abuse–related offenses, and their arrest rates seem to be following the same declining patterns as non–American Indian arrest rates.

In terms of victimization, the picture for American Indian youth is somewhat grim. American Indians are more likely to be victims of violent crime than are all other races in all age categories, including youths. This included men and women (BJS, 1999: 4). In contrast to other racial groups, American Indian youths ages twelve to seventeen were the least likely of all categories in that age group to be victimized; however, American Indian youths aged eighteen to twenty-four were the most likely of all racial groups in that category (BJS, 1999: 5). Despite the relatively positive picture for the twelve- to seventeen-year-old group, these two categories together account for 52 percent of all violent crime committed against American Indians (BJS, 1999: 5). Although no trend data were available for the general victimization of American Indian youth, they were available for murder victimization. The number of murder victimizations per 100,000 for Native American young people dropped from 5.0 in 1991 to 4.0 in 1996 for ages seventeen or younger, and from 9.7 in 1991 to 9.1 in 1996 for ages eighteen to twenty-four

(BJS, 1999: 20). These small changes are not likely to be statistically significant, but they may indicate a dropping trend in victimization.

The overrepresentation of American Indian juveniles in arrest statistics for certain categories of crime is magnified when it comes to incarceration. Indian and Alaska Native juveniles made up 1 percent of the population in all public long-term facilities in 1990–1991. The number of American Indian and Alaska Native juveniles in institutional facilities dropped 6 percent between 1983 and 1991, but the number of American Indian and Alaska Native juveniles increased 44 percent in open facilities (where they have access to the community) during the same time period. This last statistic reflects the general and severe increase in the number of all minority juveniles incarcerated (Snyder and Sickmund, 1995). Native American juveniles are the single largest category of juveniles incarcerated under federal jurisdiction—they comprised about 60 percent, or 75 of the 124 juvenile delinquents confined federally in 1994 (BJS, 1999: 30). Thomas LeClaire (1999: 5) states that the number of American Indian juveniles in Federal Bureau of Prisons custody "has increased by 50 percent since 1994" and that 68 percent of the 270 juveniles in custody were American Indian. This rise in incarceration of American Indians nationally has been an important part of the impetus for developing preventative and noncustodial programs based in Native American cultural values and procedures.

A number of possible explanations for these patterns of Native American juvenile crime have been suggested. Like indigenous peoples in other colonized countries around the world, Native Americans were marginalized from the dominant society. As Marianne Nielsen, James Zion, and Julie Hailer (1998: 143) describe in reference to Native American juvenile gangs:

> Native Americans have endured a century and more of government policies that ranged from genocidal to assimilative to supportive of limited sovereignty. The assimilative policies in general were, and still are (to the extent that they can still be found in American Indian law), important contributors to the development of social and economic conditions conducive to the development of Native American gangs.

T. L. Armstrong, M. H. Guilfoyle, and A. P. Melton (1996) suggest that numerous social and economic factors contribute to juvenile crimes, including substance abuse by both parents and youth brought on by social disorganization, demographics, economic deprivation, poor housing, poor education accompanied by high unemployment, a high dropout rate, a high percentage of women living under the poverty level, and youth maltreatment such as child abuse and neglect. These contributing factors could be quite relevant to Navajo Nation youth. According to Howard Snyder and Melissa Sickmund (1995: 9), 53 percent of Native American juveniles under the age of eighteen in the state of Arizona live in poverty, which is the condition in which the majority of Navajo live. This is followed by New Mexico, where 50 percent of the Native American youth live in poverty, and Utah, where the figure is 47 percent. These percentages compare to total youth poverty rates of 22 percent in Arizona, 28 percent in New Mexico, and 13 percent in Utah. The dropout rate for Native American youth in Arizona was 19 percent, for New Mexico, 14 percent, and for Utah, 16 percent. These rates compare to total dropout rates of 13 percent in Arizona, 11 percent in New Mexico, and 8 percent in Utah (Snyder and Sickmund, 1995: 16). Nationally, American Indian youth age fourteen or younger were also the victims of child abuse and neglect at an increasing rate. They were overrepresented twofold as victims of abuse. The rate went up 18 percent between 1992 and 1995 (BJS, 1999: 15); however, numbers from the Navajo Nation Department of Criminal Investigations (2000) indicate that reports of child abuse seem to be negligible, with zero to two cases being reported each year from 1997 to 1999. Sexual abuse victimization reports seem to be a great deal more frequent, but this rate is dropping rapidly for females (1997 = 161, 1998 = 135, 1999 = 117) and less rapidly for males (1997 = 68, 1998 = 53, 1999 = 53).

Explanations also focus on the lack of resources for law enforcement organizations. LeClaire (1999: 3) states that

> tribal and BIA law enforcement are underfunded. Tribal and BIA law enforcement agencies have insufficient staffing among uniformed police, criminal investigators, and detention staff and lack law enforcement, judicial, and detention facilities as well as basic communications and intelligence gathering technology. Although advanced technology is becoming increasingly available to state, local, and federal jurisdictions, many tribal and BIA law enforcement agencies lack even rudimentary crime reporting hardware and software.

In other words, there are a great many socioeconomic conditions in American Indian communities that could contribute to juvenile delinquency, and unfortunately, Native American criminal justice organizations have too few resources to do effective crime prevention work with American Indian juveniles, which is very likely also contributing to the increase in juvenile crime.

The Navajo Nation is no different. In general, total crime numbers for both adults and juveniles on the reservation have shown a somewhat bumpy pattern over the last ten years. Raw data were collected from the police districts of the Navajo Nation.[3] These data should be treated with caution because of problems of inconsistent reporting by districts and individual officers over time.[4] This means that these numbers are very likely an undercount, as well as being too inaccurate to use for the calculation of crime rates. Calculating crimes rates is also inadvisable because of the inaccuracy of Navajo Nation census counts. They are the only data available, however, and they will be used as rough indicators of trends on the reservation.

Based on these counts and as seen in Figure 14.2, it seems that the number of crimes dropped significantly after a high of 523 for Part 1 offenses in 1996 and a high of 476 for Part 2 offenses in 1997, but that both began to increase again

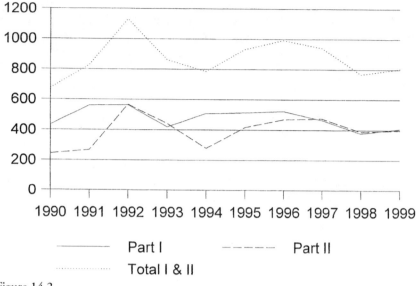

Figure 14.2
Navajo Nation Reported Crimes, 1990–1998

thereafter (Navajo Nation, 2000). Somewhat along the same line, the rate of juvenile crime also seemed to have been increasing steadily from 1997 to 2000. These trends, if valid, suggest that Navajo Nation juvenile crime trends are inconsistent with national statistical patterns for American Indian juvenile crime.

In the three categories of felony, misdemeanor, and drug-/alcohol-related offenses, the Navajo Nation trends for 1997 to 1999 seems to show a steady rise in arrests for both male and female juveniles (see Figures 14.3 and 14.4). When the arrest statistics are broken down into violent and property crime, the trend seems to remain upwards for male juveniles, though the numbers are too few to make any conclusions about females (see Tables 14.2 and 14.3).

Gang-related crimes also are an issue on the Navajo Nation. The Navajo Nation Family Court, for example, reported that 58 percent, or 621 of the total number of delinquency cases it handled in 1991–1992, were gang-related, with the largest categories being assault and battery (22.5 percent), property damage (16.7 percent), disorderly conduct (15.8 percent), and theft (14.2 percent). Other offenses included burglary, resisting arrest, trespassing, weapons charges, threatening, and criminal nuisance (Nielsen et al., 1998: 151).

The victimization numbers for juveniles on the Navajo Nation seem to contrast the steadily rising crime numbers. The number of juvenile victims seemed to have been dropping from 1997 to 2000. The most common victims of crime, as reported to the Navajo police, seem to be young women who are the victims of a felony offense, and the second most common are young men who are the victims of a felony offense. There seem to be relatively few victims of misdemeanor crimes, with the numbers being virtually equal for male and female juveniles (see

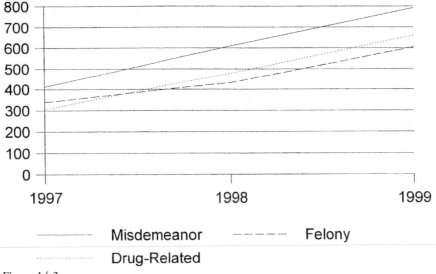

Figure 14.3
Navajo Nation Crime Statistics, Juvenile Males, 1997–1999

Figure 14.5). The high numbers of juvenile victims of felony crimes seem to be accounted for mainly by child sexual abuse victims. The low number of misdemeanor juvenile victims may result from juveniles choosing adult victims or committing nonpersonal offenses or may be a data collection artifact.

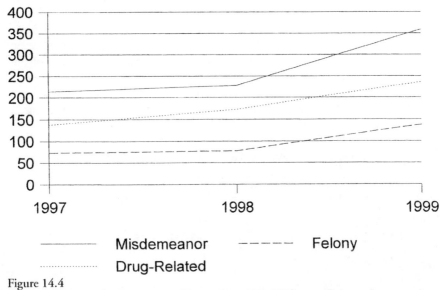

Figure 14.4
Navajo Nation Crime Rates, Juvenile Females, 1997–1999

Table 14.2   Navajo Nation Violent & Property Offences

| | For Juvenile Males | | |
	1997	1998	1999
Total Violent	4	7	17
Homicide	2	4	5
Sexual Assault	0	1	10
Robbery	2	2	2
Aggravated Assault	15	16	23
Total Property	159	205	283

There are a number of possible contributing factors to these crime patterns, which, to a great extent, reflect those found in the literature for Native American juvenile crime in general. The sheer number of young people in the prime at-risk category for crime may be one of the factors. Navajo Nation justice and social services practitioners, as well as gang research specific to the reservation, suggest a number of additional factors. The Navajo Nation Department of Law Enforcement (1995) mentions poor parenting skills; the publicity given by the media to gangs; lack of regulations that deter young people from, for example, staying out late; being exposed to undesirable influences such as violent and sexually explicit videos; and the ineffectiveness of arrest and detention as social control strategies (see also Nielsen, Zion, and Hailer, 1998: 151). Members of the Navajo Nation Judicial Branch took a slightly different approach, focusing on youth losing their traditional bearings (Nielsen, Zion, and Hailer, 1998). The Youth Coalition that designed the Hozhojhi Youth Diversion Project (described later) focused on the impact of family abuse; substance abuse; the lack of family communication skills; youths' gang involvement; and youth who do not complete their education, understand or practice their culture, or achieve their full potential (Navajo Nation, n.d.). The lack of social and recreational activities, especially in the evening, may also be a contributing factor (Donovan, 1997), as could the impact of high-density housing, which is the antithesis of traditional residence patterns (Mendenhall and Armstrong, 1997). The Navajo Nation criminal justice system also has few resources to dedicate to crime prevention, so intervention cannot occur with at-risk youth or with young people who commit misdemeanor offenses and are on the path to more serious crimes (Navajo Nation, n.d.).

Table 14.3   Navajo Nation Violent & Property Offences

| | For Juvenile Females | | |
	1997	1998	1999
Total Violent	1	1	1
Homicide	1	0	0
Sexual Assault	0	1	0
Robbery	0	0	0
Aggravated Assault	0	0	1
Total Property	26	33	50

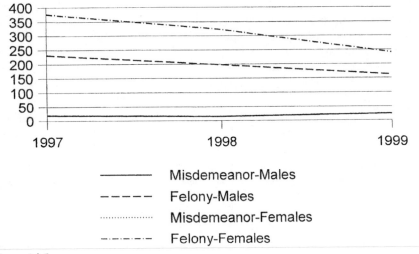

Figure 14.5
Navajo Nation Victims of Crime, Numbers of Male and Female Juveniles

These explanations of juvenile crime focus on the same factors that much of the literature on juvenile delinquency cites as being relevant to any ethnic group. The difference is found in the emphasis on the impact of colonialism and, most important, the loss of culture. The majority of the social conditions listed above arise out of marginalization resulting from colonial policies such as boarding schools (lack of parenting and communication skills), the reservation system (poverty, high-density housing, lack of employment opportunities, poor schooling, lack of social and recreational activities), legal restrictions on sovereignty (lack of resources and mandate for effective social control), and legal restrictions on the reproduction of culture (lack of self-esteem, loss of identity, search for identity through gang life). Substance abuse arises from these same conditions and acts as a catalyst for more social ills that affect young people, such as family violence, suicide, and child abuse and neglect. This explanatory emphasis leads very logically to a different and, from the non-Navajo point of view, innovative ideology and operational approach to preventing and dealing with juvenile crime.

STRATEGIES

Native American communities across the country have been looking for effective strategies to prevent juvenile crime and juvenile recidivism. LeClaire (1999: 7) recommended that tribes should have a wider range of sanctions available to them, including detention for serious offenders, drug courts, and "other alterative sentencing consistent with tribal traditions for lesser offenders." He also mentioned programs such as the Boys' and Girls' Clubs as being anticrime efforts. Federal funding appropriated for fiscal year 1999 to improve law enforcement in Indian Country focused primarily on (in order of funding dollars) policing via Community Oriented Policing Services (COPS) grants, detention, tribal youth programs, tribal courts, and the Federal Bureau of Investigation (FBI). Ten million dollars were requested to be distributed through the Office of Juvenile Justice and Delinquency Prevention for "comprehensive tribal juvenile delinquency prevention, control and juvenile justice system improvement for tribal youth" (LeClaire, 1999: 8). This request included funding for intervention programs for court-involved youth and for juvenile alcohol and substance abuse programs, as well as funding for improving the justice system. LeClaire (1999: 9) stressed that the Department of Justice would "work to ensure that our programs have the flexibility to accommodate tribal traditions and meet the unique circumstances of Indian country." The fiscal year 2000 budget also included increased funding for tribal youth programs, though again most of the funding was aimed at more "Western"-based control strategies such as policing, detention, courts, drug courts, and state attorneys (LeClaire, 1999).

Like other Native American communities, the Navajo Nation has been searching for innovative strategies to deal with juvenile crime in an effort to complement the services provided by the normal components of the juvenile justice system (police, courts, and corrections). Former President Kelsey A. Begay of the Navajo Nation (1998–2002) was elected on the platform of consolidating the direct services that the Navajo Nation provides to youth into one division and placing that unit under his administration. The communication, cooperation, coordination, and collaboration of direct services provided to youths became the nation's justice philosophy. These direct services covered a wide array of service domains and strategies that can be roughly divided into two categories, based on their foundation in a "European" model or a Navajo cultural model. The first category includes the majority of programs offered through law enforcement, the courts, and corrections. The second one contains programs that are structured differently and offer very different services, although the programs might still fall under the supervision of some component of the criminal justice system.

"European" Model Programs

The Navajo Nation Department of Law Enforcement developed a range of gang-related initiatives that could also be of service to youths who were not involved in gangs but who were at risk of becoming offenders. There were police officers in each command district who devoted themselves to gang activities, and the Fort Defiance District established a three-member gang unit. Its objectives were "the identification of high activity areas, the conduct of investigations, and the instilling of community awareness and support for deterrence initiatives" (Nielsen, Zion, and Hailer, 1998: 153). Operation "Safe Trails," based on the federal "Safe Streets" initiative, was developed in response to the increase in crime on the Navajo Nation. It targeted juvenile gang-related activity as one of its objectives.

The Multidisciplinary Gang Team was formed to target specific Navajo organized street gangs that committed violence offenses. The team used the Racketeer Influenced and Corrupt Organizations Act (RICO) criminal statutes to suppress gang activities and comprised members of law enforcement, criminal investigation, the U.S. attorney's office, the Navajo Nation prosecutor's office, and the U.S. Department of Housing and Urban Development.

The Students' Police Academies, begun in about 1998 in the Shiprock and Crownpoint Districts, provided high school students an opportunity to learn about law enforcement and the life of law enforcement personnel. Students attended the academy once a week for a semester to learn about laws, weapons usage, vehicle operation, and other aspects of law enforcement. An average of twenty students attended at a time.

Navajo Nation law enforcement agencies were also involved in a number of other efforts aimed at preventing crimes by and against Navajo Nation juveniles. The Navajo Nation Department of Criminal Investigations, for example, was a member of the Arizona Child Fatality Team, which was responsible for developing strategies for preventing injuries to children from all kinds of trauma, including child abuse and violence. The department was also a member of the Southwest Full Faith and Credit Task Force, which was working to prevent violence in schools and in the home by distributing educational documents and making presentations. Patrol officers from the Department of Law Enforcement were involved in providing educational presentations on youth and violence; acting as school resource officers; taking part in graffiti cleanup programs; taking part in car, truck, and bicycle shows; and setting up events in "Youth Jam Zones." The Piñon School, for example, reported that in 2000, there was a 20 percent decrease in crime and school disciplinary matters, partly in response to the presence of a school-based police officer.

The Youth Law Project was established in 1993 to help DNA–People's Legal Services "to take on cases and issues that have the possibility of helping many children." Funded primarily by private foundations, it provided legal assistance, legal representation, and information on a wide variety of topics, including child abuse and neglect, school discipline and student rights, welfare reform, some aspects of adoption, and other matters concerning children (DNA, n.d.). The program operated within the Navajo Nation but had jurisdiction in three states and in many other American Indian nations.

Juvenile misdemeanor offenses were dealt with in the family courts of the Navajo Nation. Youth adjudicated of a crime often were referred to the probation or parole services of the courts. They might also be assessed a fine. There was a formal diversion program for first offenders offered by the Navajo Nation Department of Youth and Community Services. Participants were referred into the program by the prosecutor's office. Minor first-time offenders and their parents had to attend a one-day presentation on juvenile law enforcement and prosecution in exchange for the nonprosecution of the charges brought against the juvenile. An analysis of the 513 juvenile first offenders charged in the Fort Defiance Agency between April

1994 and April 1996 revealed little reduction in recidivism; in fact, the recidivism rate was higher for those going through the program (17.5 percent) than for those not going through the program (15.8 percent) (Navajo Nation, n.d.).

In 2000, there was one juvenile detention center in operation in Tuba City, which had a capacity of thirty-six juveniles, and a second one was nearing completion in Chinle. The Chinle center was designed to hold fifty-two juveniles. The Tuba City center, operated by the Western Navajo Juvenile Service Coordinating Council, had insufficient funding to operate at full capacity. It housed juveniles in only two of its three wings. The third unit, intended for females, was unused. There was a strong possibility that the center might receive additional funding in 2001. Due to the lack of institutional capacity, juveniles were still shipped off the reservation. The Chinle facility might do a great deal to keep these juveniles at least on the reservation, if still far from home. Despite being a European-based model institution, the Tuba City facility operated from a culturally knowledgeable perspective as much as possible; for example, the center explained prevention as "an active culturally competent process of creating conditions and fostering personal attributes that promote the well-being of people" and used language from the Beauty Way to conceptualize the process (Western Navajo Juvenile Services, n.d.).

The Division of Diné Education also implemented programs in schools from kindergarten to high school aimed at preventing juvenile crime. A survey of Navajo Nation schools indicated that schools offered a variety of counseling programs. Career counseling programs were the most common, at 24 percent of counseling programs, but substance abuse counseling was second at 23 percent. Career, family, and mental health counseling were also offered. The substance abuse counseling programs were offered in fifty-two elementary schools, twenty-two elementary/middle schools, thirteen junior high schools, twelve high schools, seven combined junior and high schools, six K–12 schools, and one preschool. The most common substance abuse programs named by the schools were Drug Awareness Resistance Education (DARE), Basic Alcohol and Addiction Basic Education Studies (BABES), Gang Resistance Education and Training (GREAT), and the Beauty Way. A number of schools also offered before- and after-school programs, mainly academic tutoring and counseling programs. The greatest numbers of these programs were offered at the elementary school level (thirty-seven after-school and twenty-four before-school programs), followed by elementary/middle schools (twenty-one after-school and ten before-school programs). It is interesting that there were more programs at this level than at the junior and high school levels, where young people are at the age most at risk of committing crimes. Junior high schools offered a total of twenty-two programs, high schools offered a total of twenty-five, and combined junior/high schools offered nine total (Navajo Nation, 1999). Navajo Nation schools also received funding under a COPS grant to cost-share with the Navajo Nation police the cost of placing police officers in schools. Although some school programs, such as the Diné Beauty Way (now offered only on request), contained elements of Navajo culture, most of the others, such as the law enforcement–related GREAT and DARE programs, did not.

NAVAJO CULTURAL MODEL PROGRAMS

In an effort to develop new strategies, the Navajo Nation set up the Navajo Youth Crime Prevention Coalition, made up of representatives of the Navajo Nation Office of Criminal Investigations; Navajo Department of Law Enforcement; Navajo Department of Youth Community Services; Navajo Housing Authority and Navajo Housing Authority Drug Elimination Program; Rio Puerco Acres Housing Development; Navajo Nation Employee Assistance Program; several offices of DNA–People's Legal Services; several offices of the prosecutor (Navajo Nation); Youth for Youth (a private youth program); Navajo Nation Probation Office; Arizona Department of Education; Navajo Division of Health; Navajo Department of Behavioral Health; K'e Project (a private corporation); Navajo Recreational Center; Navajo Division of Social Services; Window Rock High School; Navajo Nation Fire and Rescue; Northwest New Mexico Fighting Back (a private corporation); Office of the Peacemaker; Window Rock District Court; Office of the Navajo Nation President and Vice President; and community representatives from Window Rock, Ganado, and St. Michaels. The coalition was established in November 1997 as a strategy for organizations to work together to promote spiritually, mentally, physically, and socially healthy families. Its vision statement was "Children and Families Walking in Beauty." The coalition's goals were to increase the involvement of parents, communities, and schools as partners in addressing youth issues; to educate the community on factors contributing to youth crime; to develop an appropriate database regarding youth crime; to establish an early crime prevention protocol (a referral system); and to maintain collaboration with resources in an effort to develop youth programs. The coalition's areas of focus were education, spirituality and traditions, public relations, funding, and recreation. In addition to serving as the steering committee for a pilot project called the Navajo Nation Hozhojhi Youth Diversion Project, the coalition became involved in the following activities: arranging a Major Beauty Way Ceremony for Navajo youth in Piñon, Arizona; sponsoring the Shi' Ke'—Shi' Diné Conference for Navajo youth and families in Window Rock, Arizona; making a presentation on youth crime issues to the Navajo Nation Council Joint Subcommittee; establishing a network of service providers; and recommending changes to the Children's Code of the Navajo Nation. The coalition also published a free magazine called *Native Youth*, designed to highlight and promote positive lifestyles for youth. At the time of this writing, future coalition plans included the development of Boys' and Girls' Clubs.

In the Window Rock and Shiprock districts, the formal diversion program operated by the Department of Community and Youth Services was taken over by the Navajo Nation Hozhojhi Youth Diversion Project, which was in the final stages of implementation at the time of this writing. Funded by the Office of Juvenile Justice and Delinquency Prevention, this program was designed to provide recidivism prevention services to youth under the age of eighteen charged with less serious offenses and living in the Window Rock, Fort Defiance, and Shiprock agencies of the Navajo Nation. Young people were referred to the program by the Office of the Prosecutor and Probation Services, and the program was under the direct supervision of the chief prosecutor. The program's objective was to reduce recidivism by providing court-involved youth with an intensive diversion project. It hoped to "catalyze healing in our community by giving youth and families the tools necessary to choose and follow a crime-free lifestyle" (Navajo Nation, n.d.).

The project offered three-week intensive programs for youth and their families. During a session, they attended educational presentations on family abuse, discipline and communication, drug and alcohol abuse, juvenile crimes and legal consequences, the impact of crime on victims and the community, and the Navajo view of offenses against the community. The young people and their families participated—together and separately—in traditional sweat lodges and talking circle/group therapy sessions. Upon entering the program, the young people were given alcohol and drug assessment screening and were referred to appropriate programs as needed. The program was also designed to provide aftercare so that the youths and their families would have access to continued informal counseling and referrals after they graduated. The youth were also encouraged to attend support groups for graduates, to hold additional sweats and talking circles, and to develop their own initiatives using the resources of the project.

The Yaa Da' Ya Program ("upward moving away" in Navajo), which ran from 1993 to 1997 under the sponsorship of the Office of the Peacemaker, Navajo Nation Judicial Branch, was another initiative that operated from a culturally knowledgeable and sensitive perspective. Funded by the (federal) Office of Juvenile Justice and Delinquency Prevention, the program operated in the community of Chinle and addressed delinquency cases. According to Jon'a Meyer (1999: 2), as originally envisioned, the project would take juvenile delinquents facing lengthy jail sentences and "redirect their lives in a positive manner by helping them develop lifelong plans." It used the same principles employed by peacemakers throughout the Navajo Nation and was based on two important processes: *hozhooji naat'aah,* or planning for good relations, peace, and harmony; and *hozhoji naat'aanii,* or talking things out so that good relations can be restored. The processes involved the young offender, family members, and members of support agencies and the community and occurred under the supervision of a *naat'aanii,* or peacemaker (Nielsen, Zion, and Hailer, 1998).

There were three staff members working on the project: a program coordinator, a family counselor, and a family peacemaker liaison. The peacemakers did not work for the project, but for the parties in dispute, and were approached as needed. The total number of participating youth by the end of the project was 110. This relatively low number was likely due to the impact of staff turnover on services. The project ended due to the uncertainty of continued funding. An evaluation done by Meyer (n.d.: 32) found that

> the Yaa Da'Ya program was beneficial to those who participated fully. Those who attended the peacemaking sessions and whose parents cooperated with the

program were significantly more likely to better their lives by discontinuing their criminal activities, eschewing their bad acquaintances, dealing with their dependence on alcohol and drugs, enhancing their scholastic records, and/or improving their general attitudes toward life and their families.

Factors correlated with this lack of success included participants not attending all of the peacemaking sessions, parents who would not cooperate, parents who could not afford the peacemaker's (modest) fee, and participants being sentenced to a period of probation too short to finish the process. The evaluator particularly emphasized the traditional aspects of the project as contributing to participant success.

Building on the model established by the Yaa Da'Ya program, the Piñon School on the Navajo Nation received funding from the U.S. Department of Education to implement a peacemaking process within the school and expand it into the community.

In addition to offering the formal diversion program, the Navajo Nation Department of Youth and Community Services also offered a wide variety of social and recreational programs aimed at preventing juvenile crime. The goal of these programs was to integrate youth into the community. Despite having limited funding, the department offered activities such as baseball and basketball leagues, football camps, the U.S. Marines Devil Pups Program (which chooses a qualified group of youngsters to attend boot camp), math camps, science camps, and many more programs. Because of the emphasis put on community reintegration by traditional Navajo justice practices, this strategy was placed in the culturally based category.

A number of efforts related to preventing or decreasing gang activities in high-density housing on the Navajo Nation were also implemented. These programs varied from European model–based to distinctly Navajo. According to research by Barbara Mendenhall and Troy Armstrong (1997), these strategies ranged from unfunded small-scale projects to larger programs funded by the Drug Elimination Program (DEP) of the U.S. Department of Housing and Urban Development through the Navajo Housing Authority. The small-scale programs included aggressive eviction policies based on tenant lease agreements; a 1995 youth curfew law; stringent enforcement of drug and alcohol violations on the Navajo Nation; the hiring and vocational training of local gang members to do community cleanup and fix-up work; a Neighborhood Watch program whose members patrol the community; the establishment of a Neighborhood Network Education Center funded by the U.S. Department of Education, which offers a reading challenge program for children, a video center for adult education and community entertainment, and a computer learning center; and a Youth for Youth program set up by gang members that provided community services for residents such as hauling wood, shoveling driveways, fixing roofs, and organizing community events. Two communities received large DEP grants. DEP grants focused specifically on drug and alcohol abuse but also on "poverty, crime, juvenile delinquency, inadequate housing, dysfunctional families, lack of positive role models, and poor education" (Mendenhall and Armstrong, 1997: 26).

By developing collaborations among community social service, criminal justice, and education providers, the DEP projects tried to enhance security in housing developments and provided prevention through direct counseling service and youth recreation programs, in-depth screening of housing applicants, and the development of resident organizations. One of the strategies used to enhance security was the encouragement of Navajo Nation police officers to move into the housing developments. Counseling services included direct and individual counseling and education in the areas of domestic violence, drug and alcohol abuse prevention and awareness, parenting skills, self-esteem, and anger and stress management. Recreational strategies included scouting, sports, ropes training, talking circles, Boys' and Girls' clubs, a bookmobile, sweat lodges, horsemanship, and cultural exchange visits to other Native American DEP projects (Mendenhall and Armstrong, 1997).

The Navajo Nation received funding to set up a drug court program under the supervision of the Navajo Nation Judicial Branch. The initiative was designed to be located in at least three major centers (Crownpoint, Tuba City, and Chinle) and to also serve their surrounding smaller communities. Unlike the drug court model usually funded by the Department of Justice, which focuses on intensive judicial supervision, sanctions, incentives, and treatment to help offenders stop using drugs (LeClaire, 1999), the Navajo Nation program was designed to integrate peacemaking into the process.

Many of these strategies do not fit neatly into our two categories of European-based and Native American–based models of deterrence. It is important to think of them in terms of their ideological differences, however, because of the varying responses these two kinds of strategies may receive from their constituents, as discussed below.

DISCUSSION

According to Lisa Bond-Maupin (1998) in a study of another southwestern American Indian juvenile justice system, Native American justice services modeled on the nonindigenous criminal justice system seldom meet the needs of juveniles and their families (see Chapter 13 in this volume). The programs were financially underresourced and had inadequately trained personnel, an absence of specialized services, insufficient staff, and ineffective services. Other issues raised in her study included cultural conflict, a lack of clear direction from tribal or federal governments about juvenile justice, the complexity of the experiences and needs of American Indian juveniles, and overlapping legal jurisdictions. She points out: "The development of a juvenile justice system in the image of those found in non-Indian communities contributes to the emergence of the same conflicts and contradictions existing off of the reservations" (1998: 39). Navajo Nation agencies working to prevent juvenile delinquency have run into many of these same problems, but that has not prevented them from developing new strategies or modifying older ones to fit a justice ideology based on Navajo cultural processes and values.

Although the Navajo Nation has the right to develop its own criminal justice system under the BIA Law and Order Code (1934) and the Indian Tribal Justice Act (1993), these pieces of legislation do not override earlier legislation such as the Major Crimes Act (1885), which limits the types of crimes the Navajo Nation can prosecute and hence its jurisdiction over some juvenile offenders. There are also problems of legitimacy; that is, aside from legal jurisdiction, there is also the question of how far the Navajo Nation can go in formalizing its traditional practices before resistance appears among important decision makers who control resources needed by the Navajo Nation in general and the juvenile programs specifically.

This legacy of limited sovereignty continues today. The majority of the programs offered through the "normal" components of the Navajo criminal justice system (and education system)—the gang unit, the DARE program, the GREAT program, the first offenders program, the family court—put very little emphasis on culturally appropriate content or approaches. They work from a "European" model—that is, a non–Native American paradigm. Exceptions are the Tuba City juvenile detention center, which has brought a number of important cultural concepts into its treatment approaches, and at least one of the school programs. The European-model programs are "indigenized," as Paul Havemann (1988) notes; that is, they have the image of being indigenous programs but are not completely indigenous-controlled. This means that because of a variety of constraints on the programs, these initiatives cannot stray too far from the dominant society model of justice.

Navajo Nation programs depend on a number of constituents. They rely on their funders since they have few alternative sources of funding. If funders are not comfortable or familiar with traditional cultural approaches to crime prevention (that is, they do not see them as legitimate), it is unlikely that such programs will be funded on a long-term basis. The programs also depend on other organizations within the criminal justice system to refer clients to them, to cooperate with and support them, and to give them their legal mandate to operate. In the case of the Navajo Nation programs, they must develop good relations not only with other Navajo Nation criminal justice organizations but also federal and state organizations. Federal law still requires that many funding grants written by American Indian nations must be "passed through" state governments. If the Navajo Nation, for example, applied for and received a grant from the Department of Justice for a new juvenile program, the funding would go first to the state and from there be disbursed to the nation, with many added delays and costs. This means maintaining good relationships with the state as well as with the federal government.

Juvenile programs also rely on the members of the Navajo Nation, who must be willing to be clients, to work for the programs, to provide them with information about community resources and issues, and to give them local political support. These dependencies place constraints on the programs. If the programs alienate any of their constituents, they will lose essential resources. This situation limits not only the autonomy of the programs but also the sovereignty of the Navajo Nation.

The more control the Navajo Nation has over the content and structure of its programs, the more leeway these programs have to incorporate aspects of Navajo culture. The most innovative programs described above all feature traditional aspects, including holism; family involvement; the incorporation of traditional spirituality, including ceremonies; and community involvement.

Previous research (Nielsen, 1998) found that new, culturally based programs may be resisted by important constituents in their environment—notably by members of the criminal justice system, community members, and political leaders—all for their own reasons. Members of the criminal justice system may resist because of concerns about introducing new culturally based interventions and management techniques and because of the uncertainty about their relationship to the new program. Community members may balk because they have been sufficiently assimilated into the European-model system to doubt the viability of traditional approaches. Political leaders are likely to be resistant because of concerns about their lack of control over an innovative and relatively autonomous program.

There are a number of factors working in favor of new programs based in cultural traditions, however. According to Marianne Nielsen (1998), they include the recent popularity of restorative justice models, which are perceived to resemble many American Indian culturally based programs, though the programs may have some significant differences (Meyer, 1998; Nielsen; 1998, Chapter 4 in this volume); the support of non–American Indian organizations who see the European-based justice system as ineffective in dealing with Native Americans; the supervision of well-established justice organizations; and the potential impact of these programs on reestablishing American Indian sovereignty.

In addition, the innovative programs have many of the ideal characteristics of Native American youth crime–prevention programs as defined by American Indian nations around the country. At a recent roundtable discussion on policy issues and recommendations concerning Indian youth gangs, violence, and suicide in Indian Country, tribal, federal, and state governments from around the nation discussed the importance of empowering families and communities; integrating culture and spirituality into programs; using holistic approaches that include multiple organizations, multiple service areas, and the community; continuing care; developing strategies that attack multiple problems including alcohol/substance abuse; developing culturally sensitive assessment tools; involving the community; and integrating reservation efforts with urban Indian programs (Roundtable, 1999).[5] By incorporating traditional features, the new juvenile strategies have won the support of a wide array of Navajo Nation organizations.

By staying within the legal jurisdiction of the Navajo Nation, however, the new juvenile strategies will likely excite little resistance from state and federal organizations—in fact, they have found funding from several federal agencies. This does not negate the possibility of resistance from criminal justice personnel and community members who prefer the European-based justice model to the new, more culturally oriented programs. The fact that the programs fall under the supervision of European-based services such as the prosecutor's office, the Judicial Branch, and the Navajo Nation Office of Criminal Investigations has likely alleviated some of these concerns.

The future for the new culturally based programs being implemented by the Navajo Nation is therefore, quite positive. Unless variables over which the Navajo Nation has little control—such as the cessation of funding—intervene, the new culturally based programs are likely to succeed and perhaps will become role models for new programs outside the Navajo Nation.

NOTES

Grateful acknowledgments go to Leah Phillips of the Office of Criminal Investigations for her assistance in collecting Navajo Nation data and to Dr. Larry Gould for helping to format it. A previous version of this paper was presented at the Academy of Criminal Justice Sciences annual meeting, New Orleans, Louisiana, March 21–25, 2000.

1. It should be noted that national statistics may be inaccurate because of inconsistencies in reporting, underreporting (for a wide variety of reasons), nonreporting, and inaccurate census counts (BJS, 2000: 34–36; Silverman, 1996).

2. For an overview of previous studies of Native American delinquency, see Armstrong, Guilfoyle, and Melton (1996).

3. Unless stated otherwise, all Navajo Nation statistics were provided by the Navajo Nation Department of Criminal Investigation.

4. Jurisdictional constraints also mean that young people committing offenses off the reservation are not counted; they would be included within the statistics for the relevant state. They would also be getting services outside the Navajo Nation; we thought it best not to report crime rates.

5. It should be noted that the importance of increasing funding, improving access to funding, and making funding more flexible were also important topics.

Scattered Like the Reindeer

Alaska Natives and the Loss of Autonomy

Nella Lee

We are very concerned and are sympathetic to our children because they are like orphans without parents and they are scattered like the reindeer without herders. (Toksook Bay Traditional Council, 1988, cited in Fienup-Riordan, 1990: 225)

SOCIAL STATISTICS

Alaska Natives have reached a point of substantive social and cultural breakdown after resisting the intrusions of nonnatives for more than 100 years. The reasons for the current state of affairs for Alaska Natives are complex, but the social conditions that shape economic and political conditions for most natives are far from ideal.

In 1990 there were 86,000 Alaska Natives living within the state (566,000 square miles). From 1980 to 1990, the native population increased by 21,595 persons, an increase of nearly 30 percent. Birthrates for natives were 124 percent to 155 percent higher than the state average of 24.4 per 1,000. Although birthrates are high, Alaska Natives constitute only 15.6 percent of the total population (Alaska Natives Commission, 1998; vol. 1: 112).

Death rates for natives in 1990 were 134 to 175 percent higher than the state average of 4.1 per 1,000. Forty percent of the native population was under the age of eighteen, making the dependency burden of working-age natives for nonworking natives a staggering 83.3 percent. In other words, approximately 17 percent of natives are economically responsible for more than 80 percent of the population. The annual average income of natives in 1990 was a mere $9,140, with 21.5 percent of natives living in poverty. The average unemployment rate for natives ranged from 11 percent to 29 percent, depending on the census area. Many bush villages lack sanitation and water systems, so that most native housing in rural areas does not have plumbing (Alaska Natives Commission, 1994; vol. 1: 112–115).

The Yup'ik populations of western Alaska have suicide and homicide rates that are four times the national rate, an accidental death rate five times higher, a tuberculosis mortality rate twenty-three times that of the nation, an infant respiratory disease mortality rate ten to fourteen times the national rate, a fetal alcohol syndrome rate twice as high as the rest of the nation, and an infant pneumococcal meningitis rate thirty-six times the national rate (Alaska Federation of Natives, 1989: 8).

Natives' rates of incarceration in Alaskan state prisons are disproportionate to their numbers in the general population. In 1985, of 2,124 incarcerated inmates, 34 percent were natives. Half of them were Yup'ik, who comprise only 3.5 percent of the total state population (Prisoner Profile Data, Department of Corrections, 1985). From 1980 to 1990, approximately 25 percent of all persons arrested, 25 percent of all persons convicted of felonies, and 34 percent of all persons incarcerated were natives. More than 55 percent of inmates doing time for violent crimes are natives; in 1990, 50 percent of all second-degree murder convictions were handed down to natives; the murder rate among Native Americans is four times the national average. Additionally, natives comprise 43 percent of Alaska's misdemeanor inmates and 41 percent of offenders on probation or parole. In 1992, 27 percent of all native males ages fourteen to seventeen were referred to the state juvenile intake system (Alaska Natives Commission, 1994: 9).

Natives comprise 38 percent of convictions for sex-related offenses, and first-degree sexual assault was the most common conviction for natives in 1987 (Alaska Federation of Natives, 1989: 13). The rate of child sexual assault has increased dramatically, from 185 cases reported in 1980 to 1,400 reported in 1986 (Alaska Federation of Natives, 1989: 18). In 1982, 30 percent of all child abuse, neglect, and injury cases reported to the Department of Health and Social Services involved native children (Alaska Natives Commission, 1994: 8).

Alcohol is frequently involved in suicides, homicides, and accidental deaths. According to a series of investigative articles published in the *Anchorage Daily News,* the rates of alcohol-related deaths for the seventeen- to nineteen-year-old age group in "bush" (rural) villages were the equivalent of 1,450 deaths per 100,000 (Toomy, 1988). Alcohol has had an enormous effect on village life in terms of fueling violent crime, domestic and child abuse, public disorder, and health problems (Alaska Natives Commission, 1994; Conn, 1982; Lonner and Duff, 1983; Shinkwin and Pete, 1983). Alcohol abuse among Alaska Natives has been called a "plague," a "health crisis," and "a social disaster" (Alaska Federation of Natives, 1989: 6; Kynell, 1981: 349). From 1980 to 1989, an average of one native suicide occurred every ten days. Almost 50 percent of all native suicides are fifteen to twenty-four years old, and 86 percent of them are male. The suicide rate for native males aged twenty to twenty-four was, by 1989, thirty times the national suicide rate for all age groups. More than 65 percent of all native suicides occurred in bush villages, and 79 percent of all native suicides were alcohol-related (Alaska Natives Commission, 1994: 9). The suicide rate in southwestern Alaska went from 5.5 per 100,000 to 55.5 per 100,000 since the 1980s (Fienup-Riordan, 1994: 40).

In Alaska, alcohol has historically been a severe social problem among both whites and natives, and Alaska ranks at or near the top of national statistics on liquor consumption (Kynell, 1981: 207). Additionally, alcohol has invariably been linked to homicide rates in the bush, even during territorial days (Kynell, 1981).

In 1999, the Bureau of Justice Statistics (BJS) published a report on Native Americans (defined as American Indians, Alaska Natives, and Aleuts) and crime, using aggregated data from 1976 to 1996. Several findings in the report differ sharply from the situation in Alaska. First, BJS found that the rate of violent crime for Indians was higher in urban and suburban areas than in rural areas (although the rural rate is more than double that for rural whites or blacks). Second, BJS found that non-Indians committed 70 percent of the violent victimizations of Indians and that these perpetrators were intimates, family members, or acquaintances (Bureau of Justice Statistics, 1999: vi, 4, 5).

In Alaska, violent crime is primarily intraracial, and the bulk of it occurs in the bush, where the majority of the population is native. This pattern of higher intraracial rural crime rates in Alaska has been demonstrated since at least 1935 (Kynell, 1981).

The BJS report found that Alaska Natives comprise only about 4 percent of the total Indian population in the United States, but they account for 10 percent of all Indian murders. Alaska Natives comprise 15.6 percent of the Alaskan population, but they account for 28 percent of all murders in Alaska (Bureau of Justice Statistics, 1999: 19). The report also states that the "typical" Indian murder occurs in an argument or a brawl with a nonnative and that alcohol is usually involved (Bureau of Justice Statistics, 1999: 21). With the exception of alcohol, this scenario is unlikely to describe native murders in Alaska, except possibly in the major urban areas of Juneau, Anchorage, and Fairbanks, areas that do not contribute heavily to the homicide rate. Barring mass out-migration of natives from the bush into urban areas, the rural/urban differences will continue in the same historical pattern.

In Alaska, violent crime and suicide are becoming increasingly racialized and ruralized as Alaska Natives consistently lose ground in numbers to nonnatives who migrated to the state, primarily in the twentieth century. In 1880, natives accounted for 98.7 percent of the population; by 1990, this figure had dwindled to 15.6 percent. In 1880, violent crime among native groups was rarely observed, except in certain geographic areas in which whites were located; even then, native crime was intraracial, and alcohol was involved (Crain, 1957; Healy, 1987; Murton, 1965; Van Stone, 1967). In 1880, Alaska Natives had aboriginal title to the entire state. In 1990, natives had title to only 10 percent of the state; 61 percent resided in rural villages, where unemployment rates can be more than 50 percent, the cost of living is anywhere from 62 percent to 165 percent higher than in urban areas, sanitation and water systems are nonexistent, education is substandard, and hopelessness thrives (Alaska Federation of Natives, 1989; Alaska Natives Commission, 1994).

CRIME CONTROL IN THE BUSH

Given the conditions of many native villages, the issue of preventing or controlling crime is crucial. Social control in rural Alaska is problematic, not only because of the harsh environment, isolation, and vast distances but also because of basic cultural differences between native and Western mechanisms used to maintain social order (Conn, 1982, 1984; Hippler and Conn, 1973). In Western society, if people persist in breaking laws, they will be processed through a system with formal procedures, the emphasis of which is punishment for wrongdoing. In Yup'ik society, if people persist in breaking the rules, they will be talked to and encouraged to confess so that they can remain useful members of the community (Fienup-Riordan, 1990). Punishment for wrongdoing was never a concept in Yup'ik culture.

Becoming subordinate to Western laws and processes that are completely alien to many natives has created conflict and confusion for them. Western social control relies on enforcement through police, a social role that never existed in Yup'ik culture. How to gain native conformity to Western norms is a question that has plagued the Department of Public Safety since before statehood; in response, the department created the village public safety officer (VPSO) program, which has a history of poor training and underfunding. The bulk of local law enforcement has fallen on the shoulders of the village VPSO, who, as a native, takes on a role that is often quite contrary to traditional cultural norms (Angell, 1981).

Some frequent complaints about VPSOs are that they do not always enforce local ordinances and that the village council is powerless in these cases. The difficulty for VPSOs is that some local ordinances violate both the state and federal constitutions. These cases often arise as a result of local prohibition laws against the importation of alcohol; dry villages would like to have every person who enters the village searched, for example, and do not understand why that is not legally permissible (Conn, 1986).

Part of the conflict surrounding the enforcement of Western norms in rural villages has to do with Public Law 280, which gives the state of Alaska jurisdiction over criminal matters. Alaska Natives argue that the state criminal justice system does not take into consideration native culture and that rural crime could best be resolved by allowing the villages to have criminal jurisdiction, but the state of Alaska is unwilling to give village councils and village courts the authority to handle local cases themselves. The Alaska Natives Commission (ANC) recommended that Public Law 280 be amended to give tribes either complete jurisdiction over crime or, at the very least, concurrent jurisdiction with the state (Alaska Natives Commission, 1994; vol. 1: 26).

Another problem lies with the issue of corrections. The jail and prisons component of the justice system incarcerates natives at the rate of 250 percent of their numbers in the general population, and many of these individuals are in prison for probation or parole violations. The state of Alaska has centered its probation and parole programs in urban areas, with the result that rural natives are assigned to probation or parole in cities rather than in their home villages. The ANC recommended that the entire state judicial and correctional system be evaluated and reformed in order to be "culturally effective" for natives (Alaska Federation of Natives, 1989: 7, 16).

The basic difficulty for the Alaskan justice system is that many natives (and especially the Yup'ik) are not assimilated into the dominant culture in spite of more than 100 years of governmental policies aimed at assimilation. Some acculturation has taken place, but when predominantly white institutions of criminal justice assume that natives understand the purpose and goals of the system and ignorance of the law is not excused, the result is the overcriminalization of natives.

THE ALASKA NATIVE CLAIMS SETTLEMENT ACT: A RECIPE FOR DISASTER

In 1971, Congress enacted the Alaska Native Claims Settlement Act (ANCSA), an agreement that many people thought generous—$962.5 million in compensation and title to 44 million acres of land. ANCSA completely extinguished all aboriginal claims to Alaskan land, as well as aboriginal hunting and fishing rights.

Prior to the enactment, natives held aboriginal title to approximately 90 percent of the state, or 365 million acres of land, over which they customarily engaged in a "subsistence" lifestyle. Upon settlement, the federal government reserved for itself 197 million acres, and the state was allowed to select 124 million acres. Ultimately, the villages of rural Alaska received title (surface only) to 22 million acres of land, an amount that was not sufficient to support subsistence.

In 1971, ANCSA was seen as a "modern land-rights and self-government" document (Jull, 1993: 13). According to the terms of ANCSA, natives would have land, capital, corporations, and economic development—an opportunity to engage in capitalism through the corporate exploitation of natural resources to which natives now had clear title. ANCSA was a departure from traditional federal mechanisms of Indian land control, but the purpose of ANCSA was to avoid a "lengthy wardship or trusteeship" (ANCSA, Section 1601 [b]) and to "bring Alaska Natives into the mainstream of American life" (Berger, 1985: 20). Most important, ANCSA revoked all reservations in Alaska except one, but it included an "opt out" clause for the other reservations that allowed them to forgo monetary payment and land selections if the reservation members wanted to retain only their former reservation lands.

ANCSA required the creation of two kinds of corporations: a regional corporation that retained subsurface title to village lands, and a village corporation that retained surface title to village lands. The act also required villages to establish state-chartered local governments. A total of thirteen regional corporations and more than 200 village corporations were established. In addition to the ANCSA corporate structure, there are nonprofit regional corporations that provide some health and social services to villages by contracting either with the state or federal government.

Prior to ANCSA, many villages had long-established forms of self-government. Some, as "traditional" councils, dated from the late nineteenth and early twentieth centuries; others were formed under the Indian Reorganization Act (IRA) of 1934, which had been amended in 1936 to include Alaskan "groups ... not heretofore recognized as bands or tribes" (Berger, 1985: 127). After ANCSA, these traditional councils and IRA governments continued to coexist with the corporations and municipalities.

The result for rural villages was confusion regarding the spheres of control and specific functions that each entity was to have. Legal questions soon arose as to land-selection boundaries between regions, revenue sharing, the eligibility of villages for certification as village corporations, battles over what constitutes subsurface resources versus surface resources, and proxy battles within corporations (Berger, 1985: 31). Millions of dollars have been spent in legal fees trying to resolve corporate disputes; village corporations have had to absorb legal fees defending themselves against civil suits filed by outside private businesses, and villages have incurred legal expenses in cases pertaining to tribal jurisdiction.

In addition to creating organizational havoc and ill will, ANCSA has placed rural natives in a position of direct conflict with the state government over the issues of subsistence and sovereignty. Because ANCSA extinguished aboriginal hunting and fishing rights, natives could no longer hunt on lands to which they did not have title, even though those lands had traditionally been used for subsistence. Natives were now even more subject to federal and state fish and game regulations. As one elder said:

> Our ancestors were hunters all year around.... Today, as a result of the Migratory Bird Treaty Act, we are being told that we can only hunt geese in certain times of the year or fish in certain times of the year.... All these ridiculous laws and regulations ... are dividing the Yup'iks. (Toksook Bay Traditional Council, 1988; cited in Fienup-Riordan, 1990: 224)

In 1980, Congress enacted the Alaska National Interest Lands Conservation Act (ANILCA), which gave the state management of all fish and wildlife but required Alaska to guarantee subsistence on public lands to rural residents (Berger, 1985: 64). This subsistence clause has never been implemented due to a decision by the

Alaska Supreme Court that a "rural preference" violated the Alaska Constitution, which outlines how these kinds of preferences are discriminatory.

As of May 1999, the subsistence issue had reached a critical point of conflict between the federal government and the state. The federal government gave the state until the end of October 1999 to implement the rural preference; otherwise the federal government would take over fish and game management on public lands in the state. The governor wanted to avoid a federal takeover, so a bill was introduced into the legislature that would have implemented the rural preference. However, this effort failed, and the federal government assumed the responsibility for fish and game management.

Another hotly contested subject is the status of natives in terms of self-government and sovereignty. ANCSA extinguished all aboriginal claims. Did that mean that tribes no longer existed, or were there tribes without any land base? Did ANCSA lands constitute Indian Country, did the village corporations have the sole authority to determine what could be done with the land, and did the council or IRA governments have any authority over the corporation or the municipality? Could the municipality restrict the village only to natives? Could contracts be made with the state to provide services or make capital improvements on a government-to-government basis? Were tribes governments?

Natives believe that they are sovereign entities, but the state believes that they are not sovereign. The general population in Alaska believes that natives want a "totalitarian government apart from the United States government" (Alaska Natives Commission, 1994; vol. 1: 75). But what does "sovereignty" mean? To native people "sovereignty" is "A word that is lived. Sovereignty is the ancestral spirits that each and every one of us carry within our hearts and within our minds, and that power and that driving force ... that forces us to stand up and fight for areas that are being threatened by the United States Forest Service.... This is what sovereignty means to us" (Testimony of Gilbert Charles Fred; Alaska Natives Commission, 1994; vol. 1: 76).

This meaning of sovereignty extends to all aspects of life, including "control over and protection of Native lands and resources and the prerogative to make their own rules and live by them" (Alaska Natives Commission, 1994; vol. 1: 76). If natives are tribes and their ANCSA land is Indian Country, then they have certain sovereign rights, which might include the above. If natives are not tribes and their ANCSA land is not Indian Country, then they have no more sovereign rights than do any other Alaska residents. The question of sovereignty cannot be considered without first determining the tribal status of Alaska Natives and the status of their ANCSA land.

The Alaska Supreme Court ruled in 1988 that there are no tribes in Alaska except for "rare exceptions" (*Stevens Village v. Alaska Management and Planning*, 757 p.2nd 32, 1988). This ruling is at odds with the opinion of the secretary of the interior, who in 1993 published a list of Alaska native tribes—groups with whom the Bureau of Indian Affairs deals with on a government-to-government basis (Alaska Natives Commission, 1994; vol. 1: 74). Since the *Stevens* decision, however, the state has refused to recognize natives as being tribes with sovereign rights.

Another blow to sovereignty fell in 1998, when the U.S. Supreme Court ruled that there is no Indian Country in Alaska (*Alaska v. Native Village of Venetie Tribal Government,* 96–1577 2/25/98). In the opinion, Venetie is referred to as a "tribe," but its land is not Indian Country because Venetie is not a "dependent Indian community." The land was transferred to a private, state-chartered corporation, the federal government does not exercise supervision of the land, and ANCSA clearly revoked all existing reservations, except Metlakatla. Venetie's argument was that its former reservation land was Indian Country because the federal government provides programs such as health and welfare to the tribe. The court flatly rejected that argument, stating that "those programs are merely forms of general federal aid" and not anything special due to tribal status. The court also stated, "Congress contemplated that non-Natives could own the former Venetie Reservation, and the tribe is free to use it for non-Indian purposes" (*Alaska v. Venetie,* 96–1577: 2).

These decisions certainly do not comport with the ideas of natives controlling and protecting their lands and resources or making their own rules and living by them. If the subsistence issue goes to court and ANCSA is found to be controlling, the last bastion of aboriginal rights will be dead.

With the extinguishments of aboriginal title and subsistence hunting rights, ANCSA fully accomplished the subordination and dependency of Alaska Natives for survival on state agencies and legal rules and regulations. Domestication and dependency are recipes for disorganization, both culturally and socially, especially when the bulk of it is accomplished in only thirty years.

RADICAL CHANGE IN THE BUSH

In 1971, ANCSA permanently altered the structures of rural villages by imposing corporations and city governments. The discovery of oil and the development of the oil pipeline in the 1970s generated huge revenues for the state, bringing the Alaskan economy into a "boom" period that produced rapid growth in construction industries and in the governmental sector. Nonnatives who moved to Alaska because of economic opportunities filled most of these new jobs. During the 1970s and 1980s, the state and federal governments spent significant amounts of money in rural Alaska, constructing new housing, building airstrips, installing electricity and telephone lines, building schools, and so on. The purpose of this investment was to stimulate the economic development premise of ANCSA (Alaska Federation of Natives, 1989: 29). Capital improvements brought modern conveniences to the bush. Daily flights to villages brought material goods and outsiders; the Western world alighted in bush Alaska with a resounding crash, almost instantaneously altering patterns of life.

Federal and state funds paid for these improvements, and these sources continue to pay for their maintenance and additional improvements. A self-sustaining private sector economy as envisioned by ANCSA has not developed in most rural villages, nor is it likely to develop. The reason is deceptively simple: there is nothing to develop or exploit. Public sector money supports villages through grants and contracts, transfer payments and salaries. By far the most important category is grants and contracts, which include health services, schools, subsidized housing, transportation facilities, utilities, energy subsidies, social services, recreational programs, and public works construction (Alaska Federation of Natives, 1989: 45). The cost of maintaining the villages is not recouped through government revenue such as local or state taxes; the state or federal government finances even local government. At least 90 percent of village economies come from the public sector (Fienup-Riordan, 1994: 40).

The future for most villages is bleak. With no basis for a cash economy, no source to generate revenues, expensive operational costs for infrastructure, and exorbitant costs of living—in addition to a rapidly expanding population that is increasingly young, undereducated, and unemployed, with high rates of child abuse, sexual assault, violent crime, suicide, and alcoholism—if state funding declines due to a loss in oil revenues (the main source of state revenue), village infrastructure and village life will further unravel.

THE LOSS OF AUTONOMY

Prior to the Alaska Native Claims Settlement Act in 1971, Alaska Natives were viewed as being more fortunate than were the Indians in the lower forty-eight because the former were never subjected to treaties and removal to reservations. This was primarily due to the commonly accepted view of whites that most of the land was worthless. The isolation of Alaska from the rest of the United States and the extreme winter weather discouraged all but the most intrepid whites from migrating to the area; many of those who did come were missionaries, intent on civilizing the native savages.

If aboriginal groups are left to their own devices, occupying lands their ancestors had inhabited for thousands of years and living a lifestyle that they had followed for generations, they might be described as "traditional." An element of being traditional is having the autonomy to live a traditional life.

When missionaries, teachers, and rough governmental structures appeared in rural Alaskan villages at the turn of the nineteenth century, these agents of change were in the minority. Although they converted natives to Christianity and introduced above-ground housing and Western clothing, food, tools, education, they were never able to completely eradicate native beliefs concerning the natural world, which were an integral part of their culture; those beliefs were imbedded in hunting, fishing, and the distribution of food (Fienup-Riordan, 1994; Wolf, 1981).

Due to contact with white cultures, native culture adapted, absorbing new ideas and technology from whites that were useful to them. However, so long as natives had the autonomy to practice their subsistence way of life and to pass that knowledge on to their children, they retained a sense of cultural identity and lived an ordered life. This situation prevailed in many rural Alaska villages until well into the twentieth century, especially among the Yup'ik of southwestern Alaska, often considered to be the most "traditional" of Alaska Natives (Fienup-Riordan, 1990: 221).

In legal terms, Alaska Natives lost autonomy when Alaska became a territory in 1867 and then a state in 1959. In cultural terms, Alaska Natives lost autonomy in 1971, when aboriginal hunting and fishing rights were curtailed. In that ninety-year period, it is impossible to pinpoint the exact decade when native anomie set in, although the Alaska Natives Commission argues that "indicators of serious social and behavioral health breakdown began to multiply throughout the 1960s and 1970s" (1994; vol. 1: 22). The degree to which subsistence is seen as a core of native culture is evident in the commission's statements that "Many Natives have willingly faced arrest and imprisonment rather than give up one of the last remaining pillars of their aboriginal cultures" and "subsistence is more than economics.... It provides people with productive labor, personal self-esteem, strong family and community relationships and a cultural foundation that can never be replace or duplicated by any other arrangement" (Alaska Natives Commission, 1994; vol. 1: 61, 62).

Whether young natives can practice subsistence may be a good indicator of anomie associated with the loss of traditional norms and controls. Prior to 1976, rural native children were removed from their villages and sent to boarding schools, with the result that many of these children became alienated from their culture. As one mother said: "When my older children used to go away for high school, they didn't learn to think like Eskimos. They'd come back to the village and they didn't know what it was to be Eskimo. They didn't fit here. I want my children to stay here, to learn to think and be like an Eskimo" (Kleinfeld, McDiarmid, and Hagstrom, 1985: 62).

Boarding schools were blamed for a problem that existed in villages before the construction of rural schools in 1976—young, unemployed native graduates who were known for "just hanging around the village complaining they have nothing to do" and drinking.

> The reason young adults just hung around home after high school, the argument went, was that the boarding schools had taken them out of the village during the crucial adolescent years. Students acquired tastes for modern conveniences at boarding school, but they did not acquire the skills and dispositions necessary to satisfy these tastes. Because they were away from the village during adolescence, the students had not learned subsistence skills. Many were caught between two cultures—but were comfortable or competent in neither. (Kleinfeld, McDiarmid, and Hagstrom, 1985: 140)

Local education in rural villages has not solved this problem. A Yup'ik mother said of her children: "My high school children come home to our one-room house. They are here, but a partition exists between us. They are losing our language and way of life, yet there really is not an alternative lifestyle other than subsistence for many years to come. They now have needs and wants based on the white man's way" (Kawagley, 1989: 17; cited in Fienup-Riordan, 1994: 362).

According to the Alaska Natives Commission, native students graduate from local high schools with abysmally low achievement scores—so low that they are guaranteed to fail in urban universities. White teachers dominate the rural education system, and their Western method of teaching does not teach young natives how to survive on their own. The ANC argues that "children and young adults who are deprived of self-respect by a culturally alien school system and then sent into society as functional illiterates without marketable skills cannot improve their economic status" (Alaska Natives Commission, 1994: 3).

These students return to the village and hang out, just as they did prior to 1976. There is "a pronounced generation gap with English-speaking young people increasingly unwilling and even unable to take the advice of their Yup'ik speaking elders" (Fienup-Riordan, 1990: 206). The rejection of native culture by young people was spoken of again and again in testimony taken by the Alaska Native Review Commission of 1983, and the general state of cultural alienation is exemplified in these words:

> In a few years, maybe twenty or thirty years, the Arctic Slope ... will have as many fields developed to the enormity of Prudhoe Bay. They're starting up now in small areas but cumulatively the total will have a devastating impact on our culture because we are a hunting culture. And that frame of mind has not left our people, even though we have been immersed into a cash economy.
>
> But when you look at the total package, money has spoken above all of those, and that money is being used against them. You see, the oil-lease sales are taking place in areas where our people have deep, sacred ancestral feelings. Well, oil development in the Arctic is destroying those feelings quite rapidly. You can see it in the loss of language that our younger generations are now experiencing. It's visible in the way our schoolchildren living today have an "I don't care" attitude. Why should we learn? What's the future of learning? You see generation gaps developing where there never used to be any, and language barriers developing between grandparents, parents, and grandchildren. That is quite evident; all you have to do is approach one of our families. You'll find the eldest, who may speak only Inupiat and on the other hand, their grandchildren speak only English. So, we are presently in the Arctic Slope experiencing a very different form of a degeneration of our society—physically, mentally, economically, spiritually, and culturally. The damage is evident, you just have to look at it. (Berger, 1985: 17)

Natives in Alaska no longer have control over most aspects of their lives, including their children. The proliferation of Western laws, rules, regulations, and government agents; limitations on subsistence; substandard education; and lawsuits between corporations and between villages and the state have caused havoc. In Alaska, natives do not have the autonomy to be natives; they are merely corporate citizens of the state. People drink to drown out the misery of their lives, thereby increasing their misery and supporting the state's position that natives cannot possibly manage themselves.

REMEDIES

No doubt public policy has been destructive of Alaska Natives' autonomy and their right to be culturally different. The question is, what can be done to reverse the cultural disintegration already taking place? The Alaska Natives Commission states, The "true nature of the sickness … throughout the Native villages is the state of dependency which has led to the loss of direction and self-esteem" (1994: 3). Operating from the position that dependence causes dysfunction, the commission made recommendations based on three "overarching principles: self-reliance, self-determination, and integrity of Native cultures" (4). Thirty-four of the recommendations are the principal policy proposals of the report and deal with social needs, employment, law enforcement and justice, education, physical and behavioral health, subsistence, and tribal governance. These principal proposals are extremely important in terms of the wide-ranging effects they would have on the state and federal structures. For this reason, they are included here for the reader's information.

Social Service and Needs

1. Federal and state laws, regulations, and procedures should give maximum local powers and jurisdiction to tribes and tribal courts in alcohol importation/control, community/domestic relations, and law enforcement.

2. Federal and state governments should stop developing new nonnative agency programs and research on native social pathologies until natives themselves can design effective approaches in their own communities.

3. Obstacles to native employment in rural Alaskan extractive resource industries should be identified and removed.

4. Federal and state regulations should permit tribal design and management of income support programs (e.g., AFDC, food stamps, State General Assistance, BIA General Assistance).

5. Tribal governments should be permitted to design and operate local "workfare" programs that (a) require able-bodied recipients to give productive community labor in return for transfer payments and (b) provide training, child care, and support services.

Law Enforcement and Justice

1. Tribes should establish culturally appropriate institutions and procedures for local dispute resolution (including tribal courts), and federal and state governments should support the same, with training and technical assistance.

2. The state government should negotiate formal agreements with all tribal councils, delineating those offenses within the domain of tribal courts and those under state law and specifying that VPSOs will enforce tribal ordinances as well as state statutes.

3. In addition to advocating tribal status, jurisdiction, and powers, native organizations should identify ways in which existing governmental entities can address village problems and goals effectively.

4. State parole and probation programs should be reformed by implementing them in the offenders' home villages and fully involving local people and traditional values in monitoring, support, rehabilitation, and healing.

5. The state should establish alternative corrections programs, supported by effective alcohol treatment services and operated by local native organizations, for all but the most violent native offenders.

Education

1. Local control of schools in native areas should be strengthened by (a) changing village advisory boards to policymaking bodies and (b) delegating, within five years, operating authority from the Rural Education Assistance Administration to tribal governments in partnership with the State Department of Education.

2. The state government and local school districts should significantly increase the number of native teachers and administrators through affirmative hiring, alternative certification, and other means.

3. Federal and state governments should create an Alaska Native Heritage Trust, granting funds to tribes for programs that promote parental/community involvement and the educational enhancement of native languages/cultures.

Physical and Behavioral Health

1. Federal and state governments should fully fund rural water/sewer projects, as recommended by the Alaska Sanitation Task Force, involving local residents in all funding, construction, maintenance, and repair.

2. The entire native health care system, now concentrated on secondary and tertiary care, should be reformed to emphasize health education and primary prevention—stressing community involvement, changing attitudes, and encouraging healthy lifestyles.

3. Congress and Indian Health Services should establish and finance an improved, timely system of diagnosis/screening for serious disease and other disorders, providing adequate travel funds for village residents to obtain same.

4. Unorganized, ineffective data gathering by federal, state, and municipal governments should be reformed into a single, comprehensive, statewide system for assessing native health needs and evaluating services.

5. Substance abuse programs for natives should be reformed to emphasize community-based, family-oriented, culturally relevant strategies developed by villages. Public funds for such programs should be directly granted to councils and other native organizations.

Subsistence

1. Congress should repeal its 1971 extinguishments of aboriginal hunting and fishing rights in Section 4 (b) of ANCSA.

2. Congress should maintain Alaska National Interest Lands Conservation Act's rural preference as the minimum acceptable level of subsistence protection in federal law, resisting all state and private pressures to remove or weaken it.

3. Congress should conduct oversight of Title VIII implementation by the state and by federal agencies and should draft alternative language that provides more adequate protection of subsistence by all Alaska Natives.

4. During dual management, federal jurisdiction should be maximized to include, at least, all public lands (including all marine/navigable waters), all conveyed ANCSA lands, all selected/unconveyed state and ANCSA lands, and extraterritorial regulatory reach off public lands.

5. Administering federal agencies should fully implement regional advisory councils and options for comanagement, contracting with native communities and organizations, and the state should regionalize its Fisheries and Game Boards for greater local control of subsistence.

6. The Alaska legislature should adopt a constitutional amendment allowing state subsistence law to comply with federal law, using language that will conform to an improved federal preference; it should adopt laws mandating comanagement agreements, effective regional advisory councils, and thorough reform of its regulatory system.

Tribal Governance

1. Congress should adopt policies supporting and strengthening Alaska's tribal governments, starting with the repeal of all legislative disclaimers disavowing its promotion of the federal relationship with these tribes.

2. The secretary of the interior should withdraw Solicitor's Opinion M-36, 975 and clarify the federal position on the Indian country jurisdictions of Alaskan tribes through participation in pending court cases.

3. Native communities should have the legal power to transfer freely the ownership of their ANCSA lands between corporations, tribes, individuals, and other Native organizations, and to govern such lands for tribal and subsistence purposes, regardless of institutional ownership.

4. State and federal governments should strengthen tribal financial bases by such measures as federal tax credits for tribal taxes paid and state funding for tribal communities equal to those with municipalities.

5. By executive order or legislative enactment, the state government should recognize the existence of Alaska Native tribes (Alaska Natives Commission, 1994: 4–7).

Many of the issues and recommendations in the 1994 ANC report were first discussed in 1985, when Thomas Berger wrote *Village Journey: The Report of the Alaska Native Review Commission.* He recommended the comanagement of fish and game resources as well as recognition of tribal status by the state, implementation of Title VIII of Alaska National Interest Lands Conservation Act, and recognition of Indian Country in Alaska by the state. Since 1985, the state of Alaska has refused to recognize tribes and has failed to implement Title VIII. The existence of yet another commission report is unlikely to change the state's position.

Muddying the waters in terms of sovereignty is the *Venetie* decision. There is no Indian Country in Alaska except for Metlakatla. Villages that transferred their land from village corporations to tribal governments, such as Akiachak and Venetie, have not gained sovereign rights over the land, as Berger thought, nor do they have sovereign immunity as to control of the lands on which they live. For all practical purposes, unless ANSCA is repealed entirely and the land is restructured as reservations, this issue is moot. The 1994 report never suggests this as a possibility, perhaps because the commission was convinced that Indian Country existed in Alaska. In the lower forty-eight, of course, reservations are perceived as the epitome of paternalism, a system that breeds dependency and interference by outside agencies.

The 1994 report goes well beyond anything that Berger recommended in 1985. In urging the present recommendations there seems to be an implicit but unstated understanding that all of these reforms will be paid for by public sector money. Indeed, the recommendations call for even more state and federal funding. Using such money will not eliminate the "unhealthy dependency" of which the commission speaks, but it will transfer the control and management of programs and public funds almost exclusively into native hands. If most of rural Alaska will never have a self-sustaining cash economy, what happens when public funds dry up?

The Alaskan economy is driven by the exploitation of nonrenewable re-sources. Economic diversification should be a primary concern, as black gold is beginning to peter out and public funds are dwindling. The commission does not speak to this issue, but the dependency of natives is on public money. One of the most significant questions in terms of self-reliance, self-determination, and cultural integrity is how Alaska Natives can become self-sustaining people without relying on public funds. But that is the dilemma of many Native American groups—at one point in history, they were all self-reliant and autonomous.

Beyond this dilemma, a serious consequence of colonialism has been the increasing criminalization of natives. The Western economic and governmental system has made them part of a vast underclass, a surplus population that can be imprisoned. If Western and native behavioral norms are so diametrically opposed that conflict is inevitable, then the five law enforcement and justice proposals might mitigate some of these cultural differences.

Additional recommendations for law and justice were proposed in the report, including "cultural evaluation/reform of state judicial system regarding natives" and "revised state goals for punishment, rehabilitation, and protection" (Alaska Natives Commission, 1994: 7). Taken together, the recommendations seem to point in the direction of a bifurcated justice system, one for natives and one for everybody else. At the same time, however, the report calls for the state to sup-port—through funding and law—all alternative native justice entities, procedures, programs, and local ordinances.

As discussed earlier, the state of Alaska has a constitution that prohibits making distinctions between citizens on the basis of race. Theoretically, all people in Alaska are to be treated the same. This applies just as much to benefits (the receipt of the permanent fund dividend, for example) as it does to burdens (such as being prosecuted for crimes). Because of these constitutional provisions, it is doubtful that the state judicial system would institute reforms that would treat natives differently from other criminal defendants. Even if tribal courts were the norm in Alaska, a native committing an armed robbery in Anchorage would be tried in Anchorage; the defendant would not be diverted from Anchorage courts to a tribal court just because he is native.

This issue really concerns jurisdiction. In non–Public Law 280 states with reservations, federal law takes precedence for felonies committed on reservations, although tribal courts may have jurisdiction over misdemeanors and child welfare matters. Tribal jurisdiction is not absolute, since it can be changed by congressional legislation. Although Alaska Natives might prefer this arrangement, it does not fit the Alaskan situation because there are no reservations and there is no Indian Country.

Another question regarding the ANC recommendations has to do with punishment. Jurisdiction over misdemeanors could easily be given to tribes, as punishment is limited anyway. Control over felonies is an entirely different matter; many Alaska Natives are doing time for serious crimes such as murder and the sexual assault of children. Diversion out of the judicial and/or correctional system for these offenders would not garner much support from the state.

Yet another issue has to do with the commission's recommendation regarding state support of village ordinances. There have been many problems with village ordinances because they violate either state or federal constitutional rights—rights that are not suspended at the borders of rural villages. Neither the state or the federal government will support local laws that violate constitutional rights, yet that is being recommended.

In summary, there are several areas where agreements between natives and the state justice system would be beneficial. Tribal courts with jurisdiction over misdemeanors and child welfare matters make sense; local justice should be available, and currently it is not. Probation and parole programs in villages are sensible as well. Native felons being released on parole or probation should not be forced to live in Anchorage, Fairbanks, or Juneau because those are the only locations where services are available.

Other recommendations that violate constitutional rights or depend on state recognition of tribal status are not likely to be given serious consideration by the state. In fact, the question of tribal status will no doubt have to be settled in federal court, as was the issue of Indian Country. Nevertheless, natives are seeking ways in which to regain some of their lost autonomy, and this is a good beginning.

IV

Conclusion

16

Integrating the Past, Present, and Future

Larry Gould and Jeffrey Ian Ross

When cultures intersect, a complex set of issues must be addressed. Then add into the mixture the general feeling of superiority of one culture—particularly that emanating from individuals of European extraction—the issues become even more complex (Gould, 1999a). A very recent example of this includes the efforts of both Canadian and U.S. customs to prohibit the transportation of eagle feathers, used in spiritual ceremonies by the Blackfoot tribe, across the border from Montana to Alberta and back. At the same time, there was no attempt to prohibit the transportation of Bibles, Jewish prayer shawls, rosary beads, or other implements of European-based religions.

This is clearly insensitive and discriminatory behavior on the part of both governments, a behavior born from feelings of white European superiority over other cultures and societies. In part, as a result of the negative attitudes of the federal and state governments that led to policies of theft, genocide, kidnapping, rape, and murder, understanding and decoding the complex relationship between native peoples and the criminal justice system involves a long-term commitment to such work—the very type of work illustrated by the contributors to this volume.

The preceding chapters represent a collection of thoughts and the hard work of some of the leading scholars, activists, and policymakers working in Indian Country today. At the very least, their writing is ostensibly about how Western constructs (including deviance, crime, criminal justice, and law) have been applied, many times with negative consequences, to Native Americans. This text also presents numerous examples of how native communities, in their own unique ways, have not only responded to Eurocentric laws, policies, and practices, but also developed their own methods of dealing with individuals and groups who stray from accepted cultural norms. This body of work also presents some of the unique solutions to the cultural conflicts that have arisen from the oppressive policies of the U.S. government over the last 225 or so years. Thus, not all reporting that comes out of Indian Country is of a negative or depressing nature.

This chapter attempts to tie up the loose ends of this book and also offers brief suggestions about future research and policy directions. It is broken into six areas: neglected topics, enduring dilemmas, the integration and adoption of technology, funding, blind spots, and the ownership of the problem.

Neglected Areas

It would be an impossible task, in a single volume, to include all the past and present issues that have been neglected. Ideally we would have included chapters that focus on crime in the context of national borders, how Native Americans structure and run community corrections programs, gangs on native reservations, and resource theft by both corporations and federal/state governments. Significant native populations live on both sides of the Canadian American and Mexican American borders. Many of them do not recognize the formal border and are protected by such legal mechanisms as the Jay Treaty. In recent years, cross-border crime has captured media attention, and we have learned that some of these crimes have taken place with the assistance of Native Americans/Canadians. This problem was highlighted by the Oka standoff on the Mohawk (Akwesakne) reserve (near Oka, Quebec) in 1990–1991. Additionally, many native communities are taking their first steps in trying to design and implement community-based correctional programs. Many of these are tied to the local indigenous judicial system. What is clearly lacking in this area is an evaluation of these kinds of programs. Finally, although juveniles have been covered, what is lacking is an extensive discussion of Indian gangs.

The Basic Dilemma

In some respects, the problems Native Americans experience are no different than those of a stranger entering a foreign community. However, in this case, the strangers were the Europeans, and their goals and motivations were ostensibly malicious. Consciously or unconsciously, the foreigners invaded, murdered, exploited, and conquered Native Americans and practiced one of the longest-lasting genocides in world history.[1] Europeans imposed a different political and legal system, replacing one that, on further scrutiny, was perfectly logical to begin with. Whether those individuals were Europeans in colonial Africa, or are Americans in twenty-first-century Afghanistan or Iraq, the types of emotions felt by both parties can range from fear to distrust to cooperation. The initial reactions generally result from the foreigners' tendencies to impose their ways, wills, and morals on the people they encounter (typically referred to as colonialism) and their reluctance to change their approach when they are among their hosts. There may be periods of experimentation with indigenous ways and methods, and there will also be an integration of new patterns of thinking. Not only are Native Americans looking to their cultures and thus back into their past to see if there are concepts and methods that have merit for their own contemporary justice systems but they are also consulting with other tribes to see how successful they have been.

All of this has led to a complex and sometimes contradictory set of laws, legislation, and rulings that have at times helped and at other times increased the suspicion on the part of native peoples concerning the motives of the late-arriving Europeans. There is also, at the most basic level of understanding of how the universe works, a difference in how the world is perceived. At times this means that the frame of reference used by each culture has little or no substantive overlap, which makes conversation about issues a complex as justice and social control almost impossible to hold. This thought is the thread that holds this book together—the vastness of the divergence of thought between native peoples and those of European-based ancestry.

TECHNOLOGY

As new kinds of technology and procedures are developed and introduced, we will be able to make critical leaps in terms of knowledge and communication. These tools and processes will be available to consumers both in the public and private sector. It is not clear whether or how native communities will accommodate or integrate those devices and procedures, some of which are intended to make their lives easier or allow them to better operate inside and beyond Indian Country. Doing so will require not only adequate training but also the injection of necessary funds. More importantly, it will require the development of cultural mechanisms to deal with issues presented by new technology. For example, some might suggest that the introduction of television to some reservations can be directly linked to a loss of culture, an increase in gang activity, alcoholism, and other issues destructive of the native culture (personal conversation between Gould and several Navajo elders).

LIMITED FUNDING

The lack of adequate resources has had an intergenerational impact on native communities. It has almost completely destroyed the culture of Native Americans.

Increasingly, the federal government—through the programs of the Department of Justice and especially since the prodding by the Clinton administration and, to some extent, the second Bush administration—have been interested in the quality of justice in Indian Country. At the same time both administrations have done little to solve the issue of misspent or stolen funds entrusted to them for safekeeping. Still, there is much more that needs to be done to correct problems that are centuries old. In post–9/11 America, resources are tight, and the focus is on new external problems rather than on long-term, internal difficulties. There will be a tendency to spend money on such things as the border patrol, which has already lead to clashes with native communities that live close to or straddle the border. In cases like this, government priorities need to be cautiously reexamined and alternative sources of funding need to be found. In this case, the private sector may be helpful.

BLIND SPOTS

The provision of criminal justice services for Native Americans in urban areas appears to be a blind spot, both in a policy sense and as a research topic. Similarly, injustices that have been perpetrated against Native Americans need to be righted. A changed focus on urban issues opens up the possibility that the lens of victimization studies, now so popular in criminology and criminal justice, can now be turned on Native Americans. It also raises the possibility of a financial reconciliation similar to what is currently being debated in the African American community, particularly through the demands for reparation.

WHO OWNS THE PROBLEM?

There is no single answer to this question. The suppressionist and oppressionist policies and practices originated during the trading post era (1825–2003) and continue to this day. For example, even today entrepreneurs acquire Kachina dolls from Hopi artists at ridiculously low prices. The trading posts or other buyers in Flagstaff, Scottsdale, Sedona, or Phoenix generally pay about $30 to $40 to an artist for a doll that they, in turn, will sell for about $400. Our infinite ability to suppress any religion or belief that is not connected to the Judeo-Christian one is pervasive. It included the practice whereby native children were abducted and sent to boarding schools so that they could be brainwashed with Judeo-Christian mythology, policies that prohibit healing ceremonies in prisons, evangelism practiced on reservations, and forced labor required to help missionaries.

We acknowledge that the theoretical and policy problems where Native Americans and the criminal justice system meet run deeper in some states (and cities) than others. The public, policymakers, and politicians should, however, not be lured into thinking that these matters are the narrow purview of the state and local governments. In reality these should be interpreted as national problems. Americans who care about democracy, equality, and social justice should realize that the abuse of Native Americans, particularly through the criminal justice system, is an issue for everyone, not simply those who can afford high-priced lawyers and politicians backed by well-funded corporate interests.

Native Americans have proven, time and time again, that they are fully capable of handling their own criminal justice issues in their own way, if two things occur. First, there must be sufficient resources to fund the system or infrastructure of their own design. Second, they must be left to design, implement, and test their systems in their own way, rather than be forced to abide by the somewhat arbitrary standards set by external review. Chapters 8, 10, and 14 reflect on some of the issues addressed above, providing reference to how the European-based system negatively impacts Native Americans and how even minimal efforts on the part of the justice system to allow for Native American practices can have positive effects.

Chapters 2, 3, 4, and 5 provided a theoretical context for understanding the difference between European-based views and those of native peoples—in particular, the ties of native peoples to the land and resources, the differing definitions of crime and criminal, and the understanding of the human mind in a culturally different context. One might ask, since it is unlawful in some places for native peoples to take eagle feathers for ceremonies, should it not also be unlawful to cut trees to print Bibles or to hue rare wood to make elaborate crosses to place in churches?

There is nothing in Indian Country that is simple or straightforward. Whether the issue is resources, law, crime, punishment, definitions, sovereignty, or education, it is always related to cultural definition. Most native peoples understand this; it is more often than not individuals from the dominant European-based society who do not.

NOTES

1. Long forgotten from the history books, however, is the fact that the Hopi, Navajo, and Seminoles have never signed a peace treaty with the United States.

Bibliography

Aamot-Snapp, E. W. 1995. "When Judicial Flexibility Becomes Abuse of Discretion: Eliminating the 'Good Cause' Exception in Indian Child Welfare Act Adoptive Placements." *Minnesota Law Review* 79, no. 5: 1167–1196.

Alaska Federation of Natives. 1989. "The AFN Report on the Status of Alaska Natives: A Call for Action." Anchorage, AK: Author.

Alaska Natives Commission. 1998. "Report of the Alaska Natives Commission: Executive Summary." Vol. 1. Anchorage, AK: Author.

Alaska v. Native Village of Venetie Tribal Government. 1998. U.S. Supreme Court, 96–1577.

Albanese, Catherine. 1980. "The Poetics of Healing." *Soundings* 63, no. 4 (Winter): 381–406.

Albrecht, P. G. 1974. "The Social and Psychological Reasons for the Alcohol Problem among Aborigines." In B. S. Hetzel, M. Dobbin, L. Lippmann, and E. Eggleston, eds., *Better Health for Aborigines: Report of a National Seminar at Monash University.* St. Lucia, Australia: University of Queensland Press, pp. 31–41.

Alexander, K., ed. 1990. "Aboriginal Alcohol Use and Related Problems: Report and Recommendations Prepared by an Expert Working Group for the Royal Commission into Aboriginal Deaths in Custody." Phillip, Australia: Alcohol and Drug Foundation.

American Indian Religious Freedom Act, 42 U.S.C. 1996.

Anderson, Gary C. 1986. *Little Crow: Spokesman for the Sioux.* St. Paul: Minnesota Historical Society Press.

———. 1999. "Indian Gaming: Financial and Regulatory Issues." In Troy R. Johnson, ed., *Contemporary Native American Political Issues.* Walnut Creek, CA: Alta Mira Press, pp. 163–173.

Anderson, Gary C., and Allan R. Woolworth, eds. 1988. *Through Dakota Eyes.* St. Paul: Minnesota Historical Society Press.

Angell, John. 1981. *Public Safety and the Justice System in Alaskan Native Villages.* Cincinnati, OH: Anderson Publishing.

Apsanahkwat. 1999. Testimony presented before the NGISC Subcommittee on Indian Gaming, Seattle hearing, January 7. Available at http://www.indiangaming.org/library/studies/1062_Menominee_Apsanahkwat.pdf.

Arbogast, D. 1995. *Wounded Warriors.* Omaha, NE: Little Turtle Publications.

Archambeault, W. G. 2002. "Academic Neglect of Crime and Justice Issues Affecting Native America: A Continuing Story." Paper presented at the forty-fourth annual Western Social Science Association conference, Albuquerque, New Mexico, April 11.

————. 2003a. "The Web of Steel and Heart of the Eagle: The Contextual Interface of American Corrections and Native Americans." In W. G. Archambeault, ed., *Prison Journal*, Special Edition, "Native Americans and Corrections" (April).

————. 2003b. "Soar Like an Eagle, Dive Like a Loon: Human Diversity and Social Justice in the Native American Prison Experience." In Jeffrey Ian Ross and Stephen C. Richards, eds., *Convict Criminology*. Belmont, CA: Wadsworth/Thompson, pp. 287–308.

Armstrong, T. L., M. H. Guilfoyle, and A. P. Melton. 1992. *Native American Delinquency: An Overview of Prevalence, Causes, and Correlates, and Promising Tradition-Based Approaches to Sanctioning*. Rockville, MD: National Criminal Justice Reference Service.

————. 1996a. "Native American Delinquency." In Marianne O. Nielsen and Robert A. Silverman, eds., *Native Americans, Crime, and Justice*. Boulder, CO: Westview Press, pp. 75–88.

————. 1996b. "Traditional Approaches to Tribal Justice." In Marianne O. Nielsen and Robert A. Silverman, eds., *Native Americans, Crime, and Justice*. Boulder, CO: Westview Press, pp. 46–51.

Austin, Raymond. 1993. "ADR and the Navajo Peacemaker Court." *Judges' Journal* 32, no. 2 (Spring): 9–11.

Avalon Project. 1996. *The Treaty of Westphalia*. Available at http://www.yale.edu/lawweb/Avalon/westphal.htm.

Axtman, Kris. 2002. "Texas Closing Down Indian Gaming Bonanza." *Christian Science Monitor*, April 24, p. 3.

Bachman, J. G., J. Wallace, P. O'Malley, L. Johnston, C. Kurth, and J. Neighbors. 1991. "Racial/Ethnic Differences in Smoking, Drinking, and Illicit Drug Use among American High School Seniors, 1976–1989." *American Journal of Public Health* 81, no. 3: 372–377.

Bachman, Ronet. 1992. *Death and Violence on the Reservation*. New York: Auburn House.

Barker, Michael L. 1998. *Policing in Indian Country*. New York: Harrow and Heston.

Barker, M., and K. Mullen. 1993. "Cross-Deputization in Indian Country." *Police Studies* 16, no. 4: 14–32.

Barlett, Donald L., and James B. Steele. 2002a. "Wheel of Misfortune." *Time*, December 16, pp. 44–58.

————. 2002b. "Playing the Political Slots." *Time*, December 23, pp. 52–63.

Barsamian, David. 2000. "Interview with Winona LaDuke: Being Left—Activism On and Off the Reservation." Available at http://www.nettime.org/Lists-Archives/nettime-1-0007/msg00092.html.

Barton, Winifred W. 1990. *John P. Williamson: A Brother to the Sioux*. Clements, MN: Sunnycrest Publishing.

Beauvais, Fred. 1992. "Trends in Indian Adolescent Drug and Alcohol Use." *Journal of the National Center* 5, no. 1: 1–2.

Becker, H., and H. Barnes. 1961. *Social Thought from Lore to Science*. New York: Dover Publications.

Benedict, Jeff. 2000. *Without Reservation*. New York: Harper Collins.

Berger, Lawrence, and Judith Kitzes. 1989. "Injuries to Children in a Native American Community." *Pediatrics* 84: 152–156.

Berger, Thomas. 1985. *Village Journey*. New York: Hill and Wang.

Berman, H. 1983. *Law and Revolution: The Formation of the Western Legal Tradition*. Cambridge, MA: Harvard University Press.

Bernstein, Alison. 1991. *American Indians and World War II.* Norman: University of Oklahoma Press.

"Big Chief Pataki." 2002. *Wall Street Journal,* March 1.

Black Elk. 1988 [1932]. *Black Elk Speaks.* Lincoln: University of Nebraska Press.

Blagg, Harry. 1997. "A Just Measure of Shame: Aboriginal Youth and Conferencing in Australia." *British Journal of Criminology* 37, no. 4 (Autumn): 481–501.

Blauner, R. 1972. *Racial Oppression in America.* Chicago: University of Chicago Press.

Bloom, Harold, ed. 1993. *Implementation of the Indian Gaming Regulatory Act: Survey Report and Audit Report.* Washington, DC: U.S. Government Printing Office.

Bodley, J. 1982. *Victims of Progress.* 2nd ed. Palo Alto, CA: Mayfield Press.

Bohannon, J. 1967. "The Differing Realms of the Law." In P. Bohannan, ed., *Law and Warfare: Studies in the Anthropology of Conflict.* Garden City, NJ: Natural History Press, pp. 43–58.

Boldt, Menno, and J. Anthony Long. 1984. "Tribal Traditions and European-Western Political Ideologies: The Dilemma of Canada's Native Indians." *Canadian Journal of Political Science* 17, no. 3: 537–553.

Bond-Maupin, Lisa. 1996. "Who Made the Code in the First Place? Delinquency and Justice in an American Indian Community." *Crime, Law, and Social Change* 25: 133–152.

———. 1998. "Self-Determination? Juvenile Justice in One American Indian Community." *Journal of Contemporary Criminal Justice* 14, no. 1: 26–41.

Bond-Maupin, Lisa, Carol Chiago Lujan, and M. A. Bortner. 1995. "Jailing of American Indian Adolescents." *Crime, Law, and Social Change* 23: 1–16.

Bourgois, P. 1989. "In Search of Horatio Alger: Culture and Ideology in the Crack Economy." *Contemporary Drug Problems* 16, no. 4: 619–649.

Brady, M., and K. Palmer. 1984. *Alcohol in the Outback: A Study of Drinking in an Aboriginal Community.* Darwin: Australian National University, Northern Australia Research Unit.

Bresette, W. 1992. "Remarks from a Watershed Conference on Mining and Treaty Rights." Tomahawk, WI.

Brewer, E. 1978. *The Dictionary of Phrase and Fable.* New York: Avenel Books.

Brooke, J. 1997. "Military Ends Conflict of Career and Religion." *New York Times,* May 7, p. A16.

Brown, Joseph Epes. 1982. *The Spiritual Legacy of the American Indian.* New York: Crossroad Publishing.

Buffalo, Henry M., Jr. 2002. "Indian Gaming Success in the North." In *Oklahoma Supreme Court Sovereignty Symposium 2002: Language and the Law.* Oklahoma City: Supreme Court of Oklahoma, III 22–III, p. 40.

Bullard, R. 1994. *Dumping in Dixie: Race, Class, and Environmental Quality.* 2nd ed. Boulder, CO: Westview Press.

Bureau of Indian Affairs. 1993. *Casting Light upon the Waters: A Joint Fishery Assessment of the Wisconsin Ceded Territory.* 2nd ed. Minneapolis, MN: Author.

Bureau of Justice Statistics. 1999. *American Indians and Crime.* Washington, DC: U.S. Government Printing Office.

Burgard, Matt, and Rick Green. 2002. "More Arrests in Loan Scheme: Casino Patrons Are Victimized." *Hartford Courant,* March 13.

Bynum, T. 1982. "Release on Recognizance: Substantive or Superficial Reform?" *Criminology* 20: 67–82.

California Nations Indian Gaming Association Newsletter. 2003. "Tribal Sovereignty Works," pp. 1–24.

Carter, C. 1976. "The Policing of the Indian Reserve," master's thesis, University of Ottawa.

Churchill, Ward, and Winona LaDuke. 1992. "Native North America: The Political Economy of Radioactive Colonialism." In M. Jaimes, ed., *The State of Native America: Genocide, Colonization, and Resistance*. Boston, MA: South End Press, pp. 241–262.

Coconino County Juvenile Action no. J-10175, 153 Ariz. 346, 736 P.2d 829 (Ariz.App. 1987).

Cohen, F. G. 1986. *Treaties on Trial: The Continuing Controversy over Northwest Indian Fishing Rights*. Seattle: University of Washington Press.

Collmann, J. 1979. "Social Order and the Exchange of Liquor: A Theory of Drinking among Australian Aborigines." *Journal of Anthropological Research* 32, no. 2: 208–224.

Colorado, Pamela. 1986. "Native American Alcoholism: An Issue of Survival." Ph.D. diss., Brandeis University.

Committee on the Social and Economic Impact of Pathological Gambling and Committee on Law and Justice, Commission on Behavioral and Social Sciences and Education, National Research Council. 1999. *Pathological Gambling: A Critical Review*. Washington, DC: National Academy Press.

Conn, Stephen. 1982. "Town Law and Village Law: Satellite Villages, Bethel, and Alcohol Control in the Modern Era—The Working Relationship and Its Demise." Paper delivered to the American Society of Criminology, Toronto, Ontario.

———. 1984. "Bush Justice and Development in Alaska: Why Legal Process in Village Alaska Has Not Kept Up with Changing Needs." Paper delivered to Northern Development Session, Western Regional Science Association.

———. 1986. "No Need of Gold: Alcohol Control Laws and the Alaska Native Population." In *Alaska Historical Commission Studies in History* 226. Anchorage: University of Alaska School of Justice.

Cooter, R., and W. Fikentscher. 1992. *Is There Indian Common Law? The Role of Custom in American Indian Tribal Courts*. Working Paper no. 92–3, Working Paper Series, Program in Law and Economics. Berkeley: Center for the Study of Law and Society.

Cornell, Stephen, and Joseph P. Kalt. 1992. "Reloading the Dice." In *What Can Tribes Do?* Los Angeles: American Indian Studies Center, UCLA.

Cortese, A., et al. 1994. *Second Nature Partnership Training Manual*.

Coulter, Cynthia. 1993. "Midline Cerebral Dysgenesis: Dysfunction of the Hypothalamic-Pituitary Axis, and Fetal Alcohol Effects." *Archives of Neurology* 50: 771–775.

Crain, Melvin. 1957. "Governance for Alaska: Some Aspects of Representation." Ph.D. diss., University of Southern California.

Cryderman, Brian K and Chris N. O'Toole. 1986. *Police, Race, and Ethnicity*. Toronto: Butterworths.

"A Curse upon the Unborn." *Anchorage Daily News*, January 13, 1988.

Cutter, T., and N. Perkins. 1976. "Drinking Patterns of Aborigines in the Northern Territory." *Australian Journal of Alcoholism and Drug Dependence* 3, no. 3: 74–76.

Dale, M. J. 1991. "State Court Jurisdiction under the Indian Child Welfare Act and the Unstated Best Interest of the Child Test." *Gonzaga Law Review* 27, no. 3: 353–391.

Danziger, E. J. 1990. *The Chippewa of Lake Superior*. Norman: University of Oklahoma Press.

Davis, R., and M. Zannis. 1973. *The Genocide Machine in Canada*. Montreal: Black Rose.

De Laszlo, Violet, ed. 1959. *The Basic Writings of C. G. Jung.* New York: Modern Library.

De La Torre, Joely. 2003. "American Indian Gaming: A Brief History of Its Evolution and the Political Debate." Available at http://www.humbolt.edu/~go1/kellogg/gaming.html.

Deloria, Vine, Jr. 1994. *God Is Red: A Native View of Religion.* Golden, CO: Fulcrum.

Deloria, Vine, Jr., and Clifford M. Lytle. 1983. *American Indians, American Justice.* Austin: University of Texas Press.

Devitt, Steve. 1999. "Death and Detox in Indian Country." *Weekly Wire,* August 16, 1999.

De Witt, Dana. 2000. "Incident at White Clay: An Exploration of Factors Related to Crime, Racial Tension, and Justice on the Pine Ridge Reservation." Paper presented at the annual meeting of the Western Social Sciences Association.

Diamond, Jared. 1992. *The Third Chimpanzee: The Evolution and Future of the Human Animal.* New York: Harper Collins.

———. 1997. *Guns, Germs, and Steel.* New York: W. W. Norton.

Dickson-Gilmore, E. J. 1996. "Finding the Ways of the Ancestors." In Marianne O. Nielsen and Robert A. Silverman, eds., *Native Americans, Crime, and Justice.* Boulder, CO: Westview Press, pp. 261–270.

DNA–Peoples Legal Services. N.D. "Native American Youth Law Project" (pamphlet).

Donnermeyer, I. F., R. W. Edwards, E. L. Chavez, and F. Beauvais. 1996. "Involvement of American Indian Youths in Gangs." *Free Inquiry in Creative Sociology* 24, no. 2: 167–174.

Donovan, Bill. "Reservation Teens Turn to Youth Groups." *Arizona Republic,* January 20, 1997, pp. B1, B3.

Dosman, Edgar J. 1974. *Indians: The Urban Dilemma.* Toronto, ON: McClelland Stewart.

Dryzek, J. 1993. "From Sciences to Argument." In F. Fischer and J. Forester, eds., *The Argumentative Turn in Policy Analysis and Planning.* Durham, NC: Duke University Press, pp. 10–15.

Dufour, M., D. Bertolucci, and H. Mailin. 1985. "Differential Alcohol-Involved Proportionate Mortality among Oklahoma Indians: A Tribal Comparison." Paper presented at the Public Health Conference on Records and Statistics, Washington, D.C.

Dumont, James. 1993. "Justice and Aboriginal People." In *Aboriginal Peoples and the Justice System: Report of the National Roundtable on Aboriginal Justice Issues.* Royal Commission on Aboriginal Peoples.

———. 1996a. "Justice and Native Peoples." In Marianne O. Nielsen and Robert A. Silverman, eds., *Native Americans, Crime, and Justice.* Boulder, CO: Westview Press, pp. 20–33.

———. 1996b. "Cultural Emergence of Two Distinct Justice Systems." In Marianne O. Nielsen and Robert A. Silverman, eds., *Native Americans, Crime, and Justice.* Boulder, CO: Westview Press.

Durkheim, Emile. 1966. *Suicide: A Study of Sociology.* Trans. John A. Spaulding and George Simpson. New York: Macmillan.

Eadington, William, and Judy Cornelius, eds. 1998. *Indian Gaming and the Law.* Reno: University of Nevada Press.

Eckermann, A. K. 1977. "The Binge: Some Aboriginal Views." *Aboriginal Health Worker* 1, no. 4: 49–55.

Eisler, Kim Isaac. 2001. *Revenge of the Pequots.* New York: Simon and Schuster.

Ellickson, R. 1991. *Order without Law: How Neighbors Settle Disputes.* Cambridge, MA: Harvard University Press.

Etheridge, David. 1977. "Law Enforcement on Indian Reservations." *Police Chief* 44 (April): 74–77.

Evans, T. D., F. Cullen, R. G. Dunaway, and V. S. Burton, Jr. 1995. "Religion and Crime Reexamined: The Impact of Religion, Secular Controls, and Social Ecology on Adult Criminality." *Criminology* 33: 195–217.

Evans, William N., and Julie H. Topoleski. 2002. "The Social and Economic Impact of Native American Casinos." National Bureau of Economic Research Working Papers 9198. Available at http://netc.mcc.ac.uk/WoPEc/data/Papers/nbrnberwo9198.html.

Executive Committee for Indian Country Law Enforcement Improvements. 1997. *Final Report to the Attorney General and the Secretary of the Interior.* Washington, DC: U.S. Government Printing Office.

Exxon Corporation. 1983. "Forecast of Future Conditions: Socioeconomic Assessment, Crandon Project." Prepared for Exxon Minerals by Research and Planning Consultants, October.

Fagan, B. 1984. *Clash of Cultures.* New York: W. H. Freeman.

Fairbanks, Kathy. 2003. "Casino San Pablo Fate To Be Debated Friday in Federal Courtroom in Sacramento." *PR Newswire,* March 5.

Farella, John. 1984. *The Main Stalk: A Synthesis of Navajo Philosophy.* Tucson: University of Arizona Press.

"FBI Agent to Meet with Kiowas." 2000. *Tulsa World,* July 1.

Feinman, Clarice. 1986. "Police Problems on the Navajo Reservation." *Police Studies* 9 (Winter): 194–198.

———. 1992. "Women Battering on the Navajo Reservation." *International Journal of Victimology* 2, no. 2: 131–146.

Ferguson, R., and N. Whitehead. 1992. *War in the Tribal Zone.* Santa Fe, NM: School of American Research Press.

Fienup-Riordan, Ann. 1990. *Eskimo Essays.* New Brunswick, NJ: Rutgers University Press.

———. 1994. *Boundaries and Passages: Rule and Ritual in Yup'ik Eskimo Oral Tradition.* Norman: University of Oklahoma Press.

Fine, Glenn A. 2001. "Review of Indian Gaming Crimes." Office of the Inspector General, Report Number I-2–1–06, July 3.

Fischer, F., and J. Forester. 1993. *The Argumentative Turn in Policy Analysis and Planning.* Durham, NC: Duke University Press.

Fisher, L. 2001. "Indian Religious Freedom: To Litigate or Legislate?" *American Indian Law Review* 26.

Fisher, Robin. 1992. *Contact and Conflict: Indian-European Relations in British Columbia, 1774–1890.* Vancouver: University of British Columbia Press.

Fixico, D. L. 1988. "Chippewa Fishing and Hunting Rights and the *Voigt* Decision," in D. L. Fixico, ed., *An Anthology of Western Great Lakes Indian History.* Milwaukee: University of Wisconsin Press, pp. 481–519.

———. 1998. *The Invasion of Indian Country in the Twentieth Century: American Capitalism and Tribal Natural Resources.* Boulder: University Press of Colorado.

Fleras, Augie, and Frederick J. Desroches. 1986. In Brian K. Cryderman and Chris N. O'Toole, eds., *Police, Race, and Ethnicity: A Guide for Law Enforcement Officers.* Toronto, ON: Butterworths.

Fleras, Augie, Frederick J. Desroches, Chris O'Toole, and George Davies. 1989. "'Bridging the Gap': Towards a Multicultural Policing in Canada." *Canadian Police College Journal* 13, no. 3: 153–164.

Flood, J. 1995. *Archaeology of the Dreamtime: The Story of Prehistoric Australia and Its People.* Rev. ed. Pymble, New South Wales: Angus and Robertson.

Fogelson, Robert M. 1977. *Big City Police.* Cambridge, MA: Harvard University Press.

Forslund, M. A., and R. Meyers. 1974. "Delinquency among Wind River Indian Reservation Youth." *Criminology* 12, no. 2: 97–106.

Forslund, M. A., and V. A. Cranston. 1975. "A Self-Report Comparison of Indian and Anglo Delinquency in Wyoming." *Criminology* 13, no. 2: 193–197.

Francis, David R. 2003. "Costs versus Benefits of Betting." *Christian Science Monitor,* January 21.

French, Laurence A., ed. 1982a. *Indians and Criminal Justice.* Totowa, NJ: Allenheld Osmun.

———. 1982b. "Prison Survival Schools." In Laurence A. French, ed., *Indians and Criminal Justice.* Totowa, NJ: Allanheld Osmun.

———. 2000. *Addictions and Native Americans.* Westport, CT: Praeger.

French, Laurence A., and Jim Hornbuckle. 1982. "Indian Alcoholism." In Laurence A. French, ed., *Indians and Criminal Justice.* Totowa, NJ: Allanheld Osmun.

Gallagher, B. D. 1994. "The Indian Child Welfare Act of 1978: The Congressional Foray into the Adoption Process." *Northern Illinois University Law Review* 151: 81–106.

Gallaher, Margaret. 1992. "Pedestrian and Hypothermia Deaths among Native Americans in New Mexico." *JAMA* 267: 1345–1348.

Galliher, John, F. L. Patrick Donovan, and Daniel L. Adams. 1975. "Small-Town Police: Troubles, Tasks, and Publics." *Journal of Police Science and Administration* 3 (March): 19–28.

Gedicks, A. 1991. "Racism and Resource Colonization in Ceded Territory of the Wisconsin Chippewa." Paper presented at the American Indian History and Culture Conference, Green Bay, Wisconsin.

———. 1993. *The New Resource Wars: Native and Environmental Struggles against Multinational Corporations.* Boston, MA: South End Press.

General Accounting Office. 2000. "Impact of Gaming." GAO/GGD-00–78 (April): 1–68.

Gibbs, James T. 1988. *Young, Black, and Male in America: An Endangered Species.* Dover, MA: Auburn House.

Gibson, Arrell. 1980. *The American Indian: Prehistory to the Present.* New York: D. C. Heath.

Godel, C. 1992. "Smoking and Caffeine and Alcohol Intake during Pregnancy in a Northern Population: Effect on Fetal Growth." *Canadian Medical Associate Journal* 147: 181–188.

Goldberg, Carole E. 1997. "Overextended Borrowing: Tribal Peacemaking Applied in Non-Indian Disputes." *Washington Law Review* 72 (October): 1003–1019.

Goldberg-Ambrose, Carole. 1994. "Of Native Americans and Tribal Members: The Impact of Law on Indian Group Life." *Law and Society Review* 28: 1123–1148.

———. 1997. *Planting Tail Feathers: Tribal Survival and Public Law 280.* Los Angeles, CA: American Indian Studies Center, UCLA.

GoodTracks, Taka X. 1999. "Myths, Methodology, and the Legend of American Indian Crime: An Analysis of One American Indian Nation." Masters thesis, University of New Mexico.

Gorman, Tom. 1998. "Stakes Are High in Indian Casino Debate." *Los Angeles Times,* October 13.

Gough, Robert P. W. 1980. "A Cultural-Historical Assessment of the Wild Rice Resources of the Sokaogon Chippewa." In *An Analysis of the Socio-Economic and Environmental Impacts of Mining and Mineral Resource Development on the Sokaogon Chippewa Community.* Madison, WI: COACT Research.

Gould, Larry. 1998a. "Winslow Intoxicated Street People Project." Report funded by the U.S. Department of Justice, Office of Community-Oriented Policing Services. Washington, DC: U.S. Government Printing Office.

———. 1998b. "The Dilemma of the Navajo Police Officer: Traditional versus European-Based Means of Social Control." *Proceedings of the Eleventh International Congress Commission on Folk Law and Legal Pluralism.*

———. 1999a. "Youth Risk Survey: Hualapai Nation." Report funded by the U.S. Department of Justice, Office of Community-Oriented Policing Services. Washington, DC: U.S. Government Printing Office.

———. 1999b. "The White Male Experience in America." In Marianne O. Nielsen and Barbara Perry, eds., *Investigating Difference: Human and Cultural Relations in Criminal Justice.* New York: Allyn and Bacon, pp. 27–44.

———. 2000. "The Impact of Working in Two Worlds and Its Effect on Navajo Police Officers." *Journal of Legal Pluralism and Unofficial Law:* 53–71.

———. 2002. "Indigenous People Policing Indigenous People: The Potential Psychological and Cultural Costs." *Social Science Journal* 39: 171–188.

Grana, Sheryl, and Jane C. Ollenburger. 1999. *The Social Context of Law.* Upper Saddle River, NJ: Prentice-Hall.

Grant, B. A., and F. J. Porporino. 1992. "Are Native Offenders Treated Differently in the Granting of Temporary Absences from Federal Correctional Institutions?" *Canadian Journal of Criminology* 34 (July): 525–532.

Graves, T. D. 1967. "Acculturation, Access, and Alcohol in a Tri-Ethnic Community." *American Anthropologist* 69: 307–321.

———. 1970. "The Personal Adjustment of Navajo Indian Migrants to Denver, Colorado." *American Anthropologist* 69: 306–321.

Great Lakes Indian Fish and Wildlife Commission. 1993. *A Guide to Understanding Chippewa Treaty Rights.* Odanah, WI: Great Lakes Fish and Wildlife Commission.

———. 1993. *Seasons of the Chippewa.* Odana, WI: Great Lakes Fish and Wildlife Commission.

Green, Donald E. 1999. "The Contextual Nature of American Indian Criminality." In Troy R. Johnson, ed., *Contemporary Native American Political Issues.* Walnut Creek, CA: Alta Mira Press, pp. 179–196.

Greenfeld, Lawrence A., and Steven K. Smith. 1999. *American Indians and Crime.* NCJ 173386. Washington, DC: U.S. Department of Justice, Office of Justice Programs, Bureau of Justice Statistics.

Grenier, L. 1998. *Working with Indigenous Knowledge: A Guide for Researchers.* Ottawa, ON: International Development Research Centre.

Griffin-Pierce, Trudy. 1992. *Earth Is My Mother, Sky Is My Father.* Albuquerque: University of New Mexico Press.

Griffiths, Curt T. 1994. "Policing Aboriginal Peoples: The Challenge of Change." In R. C. Macleod and David Schneiderman, eds., *Police Powers in Canada.* Toronto, ON: University of Toronto Press, pp. 121–164.

Griffiths, C., and C. Belleau. 1995. "Addressing Aboriginal Crime and Victimization in Canada: Revitalizing Communities, Cultures, and Traditions." In Kathleen Hazelhurst, ed., *Popular Justice and Community Regeneration*. New York: Praeger, pp. 165–186.

Grim, Charles. 2002. "Responding through Collaborations." Report delivered at the Tribal Leader Summit on Alcohol and Substance Abuse, Albuquerque, New Mexico.

Grinols, Earl L., and David B. Mustard. 2001. "Measuring Industry Externalities: The Curious Case of Casinos and Crime." Working paper, Department of Economics, University of Illinois. Available at http://www.terry.uga.edu/~dmustard/casinos.pdf.

Grobsmith, E. 1989. "The Relationship between Substance Abuse and Crime among Native American Inmates in the Nebraska Department of Corrections." *Human Organization* 48: 285–298.

———. 1994. *Indians in Prison: Incarcerated Native Americans in Nebraska*. Lincoln: University of Nebraska Press.

———. 1996. "American Indians in Prison." In Marianne O. Nielsen and Robert A. Silverman, eds., *Native Americans, Crime, and Justice*. Boulder, CO: Westview Press.

Guidelines for State Courts, Indian Child Custody Proceedings. 1999. 44 Fed. Reg. 67,583–67,595.

Hagan, William T. 1966. *Indian Police and Judges: Experiments in Acculturation and Control*. New Haven, CT: Yale University Press.

Haile, Father Berard. 1943. *Soul Concepts of the Navajo*. The Vatican: Tipografia Poliglotta Vaticana.

———. 1982. *The Upward Moving and Emergence Way: The Gishin Biye' Version*. Lincoln: University of Nebraska Press.

Harring, Sidney L. 1982. "Native American Crime in the United States." In Laurence A. French, ed., *Indians and Criminal Justice*. Totowa, NJ: Allanheld Osmun, pp. 93–108.

———. 1994. *Crow Dog's Case: American Indian Sovereignty, Tribal Law, and U.S. Law in the Nineteenth Century*. New York: Cambridge University Press.

Hasteen, Klah. 1942. *Navajo Creation Myth*. Trans. Mary C. Wheelwright. Santa Fe, NM: Museum of Navajo Ceremonial Art.

Hauswald, L. 1988. "Child Abuse and Neglect: Navajo Families in Crisis." *Diné Be'iiná': A Journal of Navajo Life* 1, no. 2: 37–53.

Havemann, Paul. 1988. "The Indigenization of Social Control in Canada." In Bradford W. Morse and Gordon R. Woodman, eds., *Indigenous Law and State Law*. Dordrecht: Foris Publications, pp. 71–99.

Hawkins, D. F., ed. 1995. *Ethnicity, Race, and Crime*. Albany: State University of New York Press.

Healy, M. A. 1987. *Report of the Cruise of the Revenue Steamer Corwin in the Artic Ocean, 1885*. Washington, DC: U.S. Government Printing Office.

Henderson, Eric, and Scott Russell. 1997. "The Navajo Gaming Referendum: Reservations about Casinos Lead to Popular Rejection of Legalized Gambling." *Human Organization* 56: 294–301.

Henry, Mark. 1999. "Morongo Indians Get Crime-Fighting Grant." *Press-Enterprise*. Available at http://www.wibarchives.net/october_1999/morongo_indians_get_crime.htm.

Hickman, Matthew, and Brian A. Reaves. 2002. "Census of State and Local Law Enforcement Agencies, 2000." Washington, DC: U.S. Department of Justice, Bureau of Justice Statistics. NCJ 194066.

Hill, L. 1999. "Youths Plead for Congressional Support: Gangs, Inhaling, Juvenile Crime, All on Increase." *Indian Country Today,* June 14, pp. AI–A2.

Hill, Rick. 2000. "Letter to the Editor." *Boston Globe,* December 20.

Hill, T. 1990. "Peyotism and the Control of Heavy Drinking: The Nebraska Winnebago in the Early 1900s." *Human Organization* 49: 225–265.

Hippler, Arthur E., and Stephen Conn. 1973. "Northern Eskimo Law Ways and Their Relationship to Contemporary Problems of 'Bush Justice': Some Preliminary Observations on Structure and Function." Institute of Social, Economic and Governmental Research Occasional Paper no. 10. Anchorage: University of Alaska.

Hirschi, T. 1969. *Causes of Delinquency.* Berkeley: University of California Press.

Hirschi, T., and R. Stark. 1969. "Hellfire and Delinquency." *Social Problems* 17: 202–213.

Hoebel, E. A. 1954. *The Law of Primitive Man: A Study in Comparative Legal Dynamics.* Cambridge MA: Harvard University Press.

Horn, Scott T. 1997. "Casinos and Crime: Don't Bet on It." Salem College Report no. STH-0797–0001. Winston-Salem, NC: Wake Forest University.

Hostetter, George, and Javier Erik Olvera. 2003. "Casinos Expand Quest for Riches." *Fresno Bee,* March 3, p. A1.

Hughes, Polly Ross. 2003. "Texas Comptroller Takes Gamble for Revenue." *Houston Chronicle,* April 4, p. 32.

Hunter, E., W. Hall, and R. Spargo. 1992. "Patterns of Alcohol Consumption in the Kimberley Aboriginal Population." *Medical Journal of Australia* 156: 754–768.

Hutchings, S. 1993. "The Great Shoe Store Robbery." *Oceania* 63: 345–361.

"Indian Casinos Today." 2002. *Wall Street Journal,* April 4.

Indian Child Welfare Act of 1978, 25 U.S.C. § 1901–63.

Institute for Natural Progress. 1992. "In Usual and Accustomed Places: Contemporary American Indian Fishing Rights Struggles." In M. Annette Jaimes, ed., *The State of Native America.* Boston, MA: South End Press, pp. 217–239.

Jaimes, M. A., ed. 1992. The State of Native America: Genocide, Colonization, and Resistance. Boston, MA: South End Press.

Jayewardene, C. H. S., and C. K. Talbot. 1990. *Police Recruitment of Ethnic Minorities.* Ottawa, ON: Canadian Police College.

Jennings, Francis. 1975. *The Invasion of America: Indians, Colonialism, and the Cant of Conquest.* New York: W. W. Norton.

Jilek-Aall, Louise. 1981. "Acculturation, Alcoholism, and Indian-Style Alcoholics Anonymous." *Journal of Studies of Alcoholism* 9: 143–158.

Joe, J. R. 1988. "Breaking the Navajo Family: Governmental Interference and Forced Relocation." *Diné Be'iina': A Journal of Navajo Life* 1, no. 2: 1–21.

Johnson, Broderick H., ed. 1977. *Stories of Traditional Life and Culture by Twenty-Two Navajo Men and Women.* Tsaile, AZ: Navajo Community College Press.

Jones, B. J. 1997. "The Indian Child Welfare Act: In Search of a Federal Forum to Vindicate the Rights of Indian Tribes and Children against the Vagaries of State Courts." *North Dakota Law Review* 73, no. 3: 395–457.

Josephy, Alvin M. Jr. 1991. *The Indian Heritage of America.* Boston, MA: Houghton Mifflin.

Jull, Peter. 1993. "Indigenous Self-Government: Emerging First World Experience." Paper presented at the International Conference on Indigenous Politics and Self-Government, Tromso, Norway, November.

Jung, Carl. 1968. *Analytical Psychology: Its Theory and Practice.* New York: Vintage Books.

———. 1973. *Memories, Dreams, Reflections.* New York: Pantheon Books.

Kahn, M. W. 1982. "Cultural Clash and Psychopathology in Three Aboriginal Cultures." *Academic Psychology Bulletin* 4: 553–561.

Kamien, M. 1978. "The Measurement of Alcohol Consumption in Australian Aborigines." *Community Health Studies* 2, no. 3: 149–151.

Kass, Anne. 1993. "Peacemaking." *New Mexico Bar Bulletin* 32, no. 2 (January 14).

Kawagley, Oscar. 1989. "Yup'ik Ways of Knowing." Unpublished manuscript. Vancouver: University of British Columbia.

Kelley, Matt. 2000. "BIA Head Apologizes for Legacy of Racism." *Great Falls Tribune,* September 9, p. 119.

Kleinfeld, Judith S., G. Williamson McDiarmid, and David Hagstrom. 1985. *Alaska's Small Rural High Schools.* Anchorage: University of Alaska, Institute of Social and Economic Research.

Knox, M. 1993. "Their Mother's Keepers." *Sierra Magazine* 78, no. 2: 50.

Kraus, R. F., and P. A. Buffler. 1979. "Sociocultural Stress and the American Native in Alaska: An Analysis of Changing Patterns of Psychiatric Illness and Alcohol Abuse among Alaska Natives." *Culture, Medicine, and Psychiatry* 3: 111–151.

Kunesh, P. H. 1996. "Transcending Frontiers: Indian Child Welfare in the United States." *Boston College Third World Law Journal* 161: 17–34.

Kuttner, Robert, and Albert B. Lorinez. 1967. "Alcoholism and Addiction in Urbanized Sioux Indians." *Mental Hygiene* 51: 530–542.

———. 1970. "Promiscuity and Prostitution in Urbanized Indian Communities." *Mental Hygiene* 54: 79–91.

Kynell, Kermit Sypple. 1981. *A Different Frontier: Alaskan Criminal Justice, 1935–1965.* Ph.D. diss, University of Michigan.

Lac Courte Oreilles Band of Lake Superior Chippewa Indians et al. v. Voigt (1983) and *U.S. v. State of Wisconsin,* Nos. 78–2398 and 79–1014, U.S. Court of Appeals, Seventh Circuit (January 25, 1983). *Federal Reporter,* Vol. 700 F2d; *Cases Argued and Determined in the United States Courts of Appeals in the United States Courts of Appeals and Temporary Emergency Court of Appeals.* Saint Paul, MN: West Publishing, pp. 341–365.

Ladd, John. 1957. *The Structure of a Moral Code.* Cambridge, MA: Harvard University Press.

LaDuke, Winona. 1993. "A Society Based on Conquest Cannot Be Sustained." Foreword in A. Gedicks, *The New Resource Wars: Native and Environmental Struggles against Multinational Corporations.* Boston, MA: South End Press.

———. 1999. *All Our Relations: Native Struggles for Land and Life.* Boston: South End Press.

LaFree, G. 1995. "Race and Crime Trends in the United States, 1946–1990." In D. F. Hawkins, ed., *Ethnicity, Race, and Crime.* Albany: State University of New York Press, pp. 169–193.

Lamarine, Roland. 1998. "Alcohol Abuse among Native Americans." *Journal of Community Health* 13: 143–155.

Landau, Tammy. 1994. "Policing and Security in Four Remote Aboriginal Communities." Ph.D. diss., University of Toronto.

———. 1996. "Policing and Security in Four Remote Aboriginal Communities: A Challenge to Coercive Models of Police Work." *Canadian Journal of Criminology* 38, no. 1.

LaPrairie, Carol. 1995. "Seen But Not Heard: Native People in Four Canadian Inner Cities." *Journal of Human Justice* 6, no. 2: 30–45.

LeClaire, Thomas L. 1999. "Statement of Thomas L. LeClaire, Director of Tribal Justice, before the Committee on Indian Affairs, U.S. Senate, Concerning Indian Country Budget for Fiscal Year 2000." Washington, DC: U.S. Department of Justice.

Lee, John Alan. 1981. "Some Structural Aspects of Police Deviance in Relations with Minority Groups." In Clifford Shearing, ed., *Organizational Police Deviance.* Toronto, ON: Butterworths, pp. 49–82.

LeResche, Diane. 1993. "The Reawakening of Sacred Justice." *Clearinghouse Review* 27, no. 8 (December): 393–399.

Lesieur, Henry R. 1998. "Testimony for Expert Panel on Pathological Gambling." National Gambling Impact Study Commission, Atlantic City, New Jersey, January 22.

Leubben, R. A. 1964. "Anglo Law and Navajo Behavior." *Kiva* 29, no. l: 66–75.

Levy, Jerrold E. 1998. *In the Beginning: The Navajo Genesis.* Berkeley: University of California Press.

Levy, J. E., and S. J. Kunitz. 1971. "Indian Reservations, Anomie, and Social Pathologies." *Southwest Journal of Anthropology* 27: 97–128.

———. 1974. *Indian Drinking: Navajo Drinking and Anglo-American Theories.* New York: Wiley Interscience.

Levy, J. E., S. J. Kunitz, and M. Everett. 1969. "Navajo Criminal Homicide." *Southwestern Journal of Anthropology* 25, no. 2: 124–152.

Lex, Barbara. 1985. "Alcohol Problems in Special Populations." In J. H. Mendelson and N. K. Mello, eds., *The Diagnosis and Treatment of Alcoholism.* 2nd ed. New York: McGraw-Hill.

Longclaws, Lyle, Gordon E. Barnes, Linda Grieve, and Ron Dumoff. 1980. "Alcohol and Drug Use among the Brokenhead Ojibwa." *Journal of Studies on Alcohol* 411: 21–36.

Lonner, Thomas, and Edward Duff. 1983. *Village Alcohol Control and the Local Option Law.* Anchorage: University of Alaska School of Health Sciences, Center for Alcohol and Addiction Studies.

Lorber, Leah. 1998. "States Should Stop Encroaching on Tribal Sovereignty." In Rod L. Evans and Mark Hance, eds., *Legalized Gambling: For and Against.* Chicago: Open Court Publishing, pp. 277–306.

Lowman, B. 1978. *220 Million Custers.* Anacortes, WA: Anacortes Publishers.

Lujan, Carol. 1989. "Profile of Abused and Neglected American Indian Children in the Southwest." *Child Abuse and Neglect* 13, pp. 449–461.

Luna, Eileen. 1997. "Community Policing in Indian Country." *Church and Society* (March–April).

———. 1999. "Law Enforcement Oversight in the American Indian Community." *Georgetown Public Policy Review* 4, no. 2: 149–164.

Lurie, Nancy O. 1971. "The World's Oldest Ongoing Protest Demonstration: North American Indian Drinking Patterns." *Pacific Historical Review* 40: 311–332.

MacEachron, A. E., N. S. Gustavsson, S. Cross, and A. Lewis. 1996. "The Effectiveness of the Indian Child Welfare Act of 1978." *Social Service Review* 70, no. 3: 451–463.

MacLeod, William C. 1937. "Police and Punishment among Native-Americans of the Plains." *Journal of the American Institute of Criminal Law and Criminology* 28: 188–201.

———. 1967. "Celt and Indian: Britain's Old World Frontier in Relation to the New." In P. Bohannan and F. Plog, eds., *Beyond the Frontier: Social Process and Cultural Change.* Garden City, NY: Natural History Press, pp. 25–42.

MAGNA Management Consulting. 2000. Arizona Department of Gaming Public Hearings on Indian Gaming. Available at http://www.gm.state.az.us/report.htm.

Maguire, Brendan, William Faulkner, Richard Mathers, Carol Rowland, and John Wozniak. 1991. "Rural Police Job Functions." *Police Studies* 14, no. 4: 180–187.

Malinowski, Bronislaw. 1926. *Crime and Custom in Savage Society.* London: Routledge and Kegan Paul.

Mall, P. D. 1984. "American Indian Alcoholism: What Is Not Being Done?" *IHS Primary Care Provider* 9, no. 3: 1–5.

Mall, P. D., and S. Johnson. 1993. "Boozing, Sniffing, and Toking: An Overview of the Past, Present, and Future of Substance Use by American Indians." *American Indian and Alaska Native Mental Health Research Journal* 5, no. 2: pp. 1–33.

Mancall, Peter. 1996. *Deadly Medicine: Indians and Alcohol in Early America.* Ithaca, NY: Cornell University Press.

Mander, J. 1991. *In the Absence of the Sacred: The Failure of Technology and the Survival of Indian Nations.* San Francisco: Sierra Club Books.

Manlove, James S., Jr., Susan Warren, and Thomas Holgate. 1993. "Jail Conditions on the Navajo Reservation: A Case Study." *Clearinghouse Review* 27, no. 8.

Mann, C. R. 1993. *Unequal Justice: A Question of Color.* Bloomington: Indiana University Press.

Maracle, Brian. 1994. *Crazywater: Native Voices on Addiction and Recovery.* Toronto, ON: Penguin.

Marenin, Otwin. 1992a. "Explaining Patterns of Crime in Native Villages in Alaska." *Canadian Journal of Criminology* 34, nos. 3–4: 339–368.

———. 1992b. "Policing the Last Frontier: Visions of Social Order and the Development of the Village Public Safety Officer Program in Alaska." *Policing and Society* 2: 273–291.

———. 1994. "Conflicting Perspectives on the Role of the Village Public Safety Officer in Native Villages in Alaska." *American Indian Quarterly* 18, no. 3: 297–319.

Marenin, Otwin, and Gary Copus. 1991. "Policing Rural Alaska: The Village Public Safety Officer (VPSO) Program." *American Journal of Police* 2: 1–26.

Maricopa County Juvenile Action no. A-25525, 136 Ariz. 528, 667 P.2d 228 (Ariz.App. 1983).

Maricopa County Juvenile Action no. JD-6982, 186 Ariz. 354, 922 P.2d 319 (Ariz.App. Div.1 1996).

Maricopa County Juvenile Action no. JS-8287, 171 Ariz. 104, 828 P.2d 1245 (Ariz.App. 1991).

Martinez, F. 1996. "Conflicting Cultures." In Marianne O. Nielsen and Robert A. Silverman, eds., *Native Americans, Crime, and Justice.* Boulder, CO: Westview Press, pp. 36–37.

Mason, W. Dale. 2000. *Indian Gaming.* Norman: University of Oklahoma Press.

May, Philip A. 1982a. "Susceptibility to Substance Abuse among American Indians: Variations across Sociocultural Settings." In *Problems of Drug Dependence, 1981.* NIDA Research Monograph no. 41. Washington, DC: Department of Health and Human Services, pp. 34–44.

———. 1982b. "Substance Abuse and American Indians: Prevalence and Susceptibility." *International Journal of the Addictions* 17, no. 7: 1185–1209.

Mayers, J., and R. Seely. 1990. "Conflict Tugs on State Resources." *Wisconsin State Journal.*

McCarthy, R. J. 1993. "The Indian Child Welfare Act: In the Best Interests of Child and Tribe." *Clearinghouse Review* 27, no. 8: 864–873.

McCone, R. 1966. "Cultural Factors in Crime among Dakota Indians." *Plains Anthropologist* 27, no. 97: 144–151.

McCue, Julia. 2003. "Differing Views." *Maine Sunday Telegram,* March 16, p. 6A.

McNeley, James. 1981. *Holy Wind in Navajo Philosophy.* Tucson: University of Arizona Press.

Mead, M. 1967. "The Rights of Primitive Peoples: Papua New Guinea—A Critical Instance." *Foreign Affairs* (January): 304–318.

Medcalf, Linda. 1978. *Law and Identity.* Beverly Hills, CA: Sage.

Mendenhall, Barbara, and Troy Armstrong. 1997. "Finding and Knowing the Gang Nayee': Navajo Nation Youth Gangs and Public Housing." Paper presented at the American Society of Criminology annual meeting, San Diego, California, November.

Merton, R. 1938. "Social Structure and Anomie." *American Sociological Review* 3: 672–682.

———. 1957–1968. *Social Theory and Social Structure.* New York: Free Press.

Messner, S., and R. Rosenfeld. 1994. *Crime and the American Dream.* Belmont, CA: Wadsworth.

Metteer, C. 1998. "Hard Cases Making Bad Law: The Need for Revision of the Indian Child Welfare Act." *Santa Clara Law Review* 38, no. 2: 419–472.

Metz, Sharon. 1990. "A Legacy of Broken Promises." *Sojourners* (June): 16–20.

Meyer, Jon'a F. 1998. "History Repeats Itself: Restorative Justice in Native American Communities." *Journal of Contemporary Criminal Justice* 14, no. 1: 42–57.

———. 1999. "Reintegration Is Traditional: An Evaluation of the Navajo Nation's Yaa D'Ya (Young Adjudicated Adult Upward Bound) Program." Report presented to the Navajo Nation Judicial Branch, December.

Michalowski, R. 1990. "A Critical Model for the Study of Crime." In D. Kelly, ed., *Criminal Behavior: Text and Readings in Criminology.* 2nd ed. New York: St. Martin's.

Midwest Treaty Network. N.D. "Wisconsin Treaties: What's the Problem?" (pamphlet).

Mihesuah, Devon. 1996. *American Indians: Stereotypes and Realities.* Atlanta, GA: Clarity Press.

Minnis, M. S. 1963. "The Relationship of the Social Structure of Indian Community to Adult and Juvenile Delinquency." *Social Forces* 41: 395–403.

Mischke, James A. 1981. "Evil, Society, and Navajo Culture." *Anima* 8 (Fall): 33–36.

Mississippi Band of Choctaw Indians v. Holyfield, 490 U.S. 30, 1989.

Mollison, Andrew. 2003a. "Life without Casino Isn't Easy for Alabama-Coushatta Indians." Cox News Service, available at http://www.indiangaming.org.

———. 2003b. "Casinos Lift Indians Closer to Other Americans." Cox News Service, available at http://www.indiangaming.org.

Moncher, Michael, Gary Holden, and Joseph Trimble. 1990. "Substance Abuse among Native-American Youth." *Journal of Consulting and Clinical Psychology* 58, no. 4: 408–415.

Moon, Sheila. 1970. *A Magic Dwells.* Middletown, CT: Wesleyan University Press.

Morita, Jennifer K. 2002. "Application for Placer County, Calif., Indian Casino Land Headed for Approval." *Sacramento Bee,* January 18.

Morris, B. 1996. "How the Federal Government Crushes Indian Religion." *Crosswinds* 8, no. 9: 18–19.

———. 1997. "How the Feds Crush Indian Religion: Part II. *Crosswinds* 9, no. 5: 5.

Moses, L. G., and Raymond Wilson, eds. 1993. *Indian Lives: Essays on Nineteenth- and Twentieth-Century Native American Leaders.* Albuquerque: University of New Mexico Press.

Muir, Douglas. 2003. "Casinos in Maine: A Costly Choice." Available at http://kitterycitizens.org/Gaming_Economics.htm.

Mullis, Angela, and David Kamper, eds. 2000. *Indian Gaming: Who Wins?* Los Angeles, CA: American Indian Studies Center, UCLA.

Murphy, Sean P. 2002. "Poll of Massachusetts Voters Shows Support for Indian-Owned Casino." *Boston Globe,* February 15.

Murton, Thomas O. 1965. "The Administration of Criminal Justice in Alaska, 1867 to 1902." Ph.D. diss., University of California, Berkeley.

Nader, L., and C. Shugart. 1980. *Old Solutions for Old Problems: No Access to Law—Alternatives to the American Justice System.* New York: Academic Press.

Nathanson, Donald. 1992. *Shame and Pride: Affect, Sex, and the Birth of the Self.* New York: W. W. Norton.

National Gambling Impact Study Commission. 1999. *Final Report.* Washington, DC: U.S. Government Printing Office.

National Indian Gaming Association. 2003. Library and Resource Center. Available at http://www.indiangaming.org.

National Indian Gaming Commission. 2003. "Tribal Data." Available at http://www.nigc.gov.

National Indian Justice Center. 1995. *Child Sexual Abuse.* National Institute of Justice/National Criminal Justice no. 167686. Washington, DC: U.S. Department of Justice, Office of Justice Programs, Office for Victims of Crime.

"Native American Gaming and Organized Crime." *Gamble Tribune,* December 20, 2002. Available at http://www.GambleTribune.org.

The Native American: U.S. Indian School, Phoenix, Arizona, 1916. Phoenix, AZ: Native American Press (printed by the students).

Navajo Nation. N.D. "Proposal for the Navajo Nation Hozhojhi Youth Diversion Project."

Navajo Nation Department of Criminal Investigations. 2000. "Major Crime Summary, 1990–2000."

Navajo Nation Department of Law Enforcement. 1995. "Gang Activities in the Navajo Nation." March 27.

Navajo Nation, Division of Diné Education. 1999. "Diné Education Statistics, 1998–1999: A Presentation." Window Rock, AZ: Division of Diné Education.

Navajo Youth Crime Prevention Coalition. N.D. Various documents.

Neesham, R. "Exxon Emerging as a Major Mining Firm." *Engineering and Mining Journal* 179, no. 7: 55–60.

Newton, N. J. 1984. "Federal Power over Indians: Its Sources, Scope, and Limitations." *University of Pennsylvania Law Review* 132: 195.

Nielsen, Marianne O. 1996. "Contextualization for Native American Crime and Criminal Justice Involvement." In Marianne O. Nielsen and Robert A. Silverman, eds., *Native Americans, Crime, and Criminal Justice.* Boulder, CO: Westview Press, pp. 10–19.

———. 1998. "A Comparison of Canadian Youth Justice Committees and Navajo Peacemakers." *Journal of Contemporary Criminal Justice* 14, no. 1: 6–25.

Nielsen, Marianne O., and Robert A. Silverman, eds. 1992. *Aboriginal Peoples and the Canadian Criminal Justice System.* Toronto, ON: Harcourt Brace.

———. 1996. *Native Americans, Crime, and Criminal Justice.* Boulder, CO: Westview Press.

Nielsen, Marianne O., James W. Zion, and Julie A. Hailer. 1998. "Navajo Nation Gang Formation and Intervention Initiatives." In Kayleen Hazlehurst and Cameron Hazlehurst, eds., *Gangs and Youth Subcultures: International Explorations.* New Brunswick, NJ: Transaction, pp. 141–163.

Nies, J. 1996. *Native American History: A Chronology of a Culture's Vast Achievements and Their Links to World Events.* New York: Ballantine.

"No Slots for Tracks." *Arizona Daily Star,* February 17, 2002.

North Carolina Criminal Justice Analysis Center. 1999. "Crime and Victimization among North Carolina's American Indian Population." *SystemStats* (Summer): 1–12.

Northern Plains Indian Law Center. 2003. "Tribal Gaming Quick Facts." Available at http://www.law.und.nodak.edu/NPILC/quick.html.

Oakes, Maud, Jeff King, and Joseph Campbell. 1943. *Where the Two Came to Their Father.* New York: Pantheon Books.

O'Brien, S. 1988. "Cultural Rights in the United States: A Conflict of Values." *Law and Inequality* 5: 267–358.

Oetting, E. R., and F. Beauvais. 1985. "Epidemiology and Correlates of Alcohol Use among Indian Adolescents Living on Reservations." Unpublished manuscript.

Ohr, Bruce G. 2001. "Statement Presented to the Senate Committee on Indian Affairs, Oversight Hearing on the Indian Gaming Regulatory Act, July 25." Available at http://www.usdoj.gov/otj/statementbrucegohr.htm.

Park, R., and E. Burgess. 1921. *Introduction to the Science of Sociology.* Chicago: University of Chicago Press.

Parry, J. H. 1967. "Spanish Indian Policy in Colonial America: The Ordering of Society." In John J. TePaske, ed., *Three American Empires.* Durham, NC: Duke University Press, pp. 109–126.

Paulson, Michael. 2001. "Casino Bid Faces Religious Protest: Church Leaders Cite Danger to the Poor." *Boston Globe,* August 5, p. B1.

Peak, K., and L. Spencer. 1987. "Crime in Indian Country: Another Trail of Tears." *Journal of Criminal Justice* 15: 485–494.

Pedigo, J. 1983. "Finding the Meaning of Native American Substance Use: Implications for Community Prevention." *Personnel and Guidance Journal* 61: 273–277.

Peele, Thomas. 2001. "Indian Casino Pact Gives San Pablo More Power." *Contra Costa Times,* April 11.

Peregoy, R. M., W. R. Echo-Hawk, and J. Botsford. 1995. "Congress Overturns Supreme Court's Peyote Ruling." *Native American Rights Fund Legal Review* 20, available at http://www.narf.org/archives.

"The Peril Remains." 1989. *Anchorage Daily News,* January 15.

Peroff, Nicholas C. 1982. *Menominee Drums: Tribal Termination and Restoration, 1954–1974.* Norman: University of Oklahoma Press.

———. 2001. "Indian Gaming, Tribal Sovereignty, and American Indian Tribes as Complex Adaptive Systems." *American Indian Culture and Research Journal* 25, no. 3: 143–159.

Peterson, L. P. 1984. "Pregnancy Complications in Sioux Children." *Obstetrics and Gynecology* 64: 519–523.

Pfohl, S. 1994. *Images of Deviance and Social Control: A Sociological History.* 2nd ed. New York: McGraw Hill.

Pima County Juvenile Action no. S-903, 130 Ariz. 202, 635 P.2d 187 (Ariz.App. 1981).

Podger, Pamela J. 2003. "Casino Foes Talk Options in Sonoma." *San Francisco Chronicle,* May 30, p. A21.

Podolefsky, A. 1985. "Rejecting Crime Prevention Programs: The Dynamics of Program Implementation in High-Need Communities." *Human Organization* 44: 33–40.

Pratt, J. 1996. "Colonization, Power, and Silence: A History of Indigenous Justice in New Zealand Society." In Burt Galaway and Joe Hudson, eds., *Restorative Justice: International Perspectives.* Monsey, NY: Willow Tree Press.

Prucha, F. P. 1985. *The Indians in American Society.* Berkeley: University of California Press.

Quinault Tribe and Queets Band of Indians, et al. v. Washington. 1974. Civ. No. 9213 U.S. District Court for the Western District of Washington, Tacoma Div. 384F. Supp. 312.

Quinney, Richard. 1991. "The Way of Peace: On Crime, Suffering, and Service." In Harold E. Pepinsky and Richard Quinney, eds., *Criminology as Peacemaking.* Bloomington: Indiana University Press, pp. 3–13.

"Racism Cited in Fishing Dispute," *Milwaukee Sentinel,* April 11, 1986.

Ramirez, O. 1992. "The Year of the Indigenous Peoples." *Social Justice: A Journal of Crime, Conflict, and World Order* 19, no. 2: 78–86.

Randazzo, Ryan. 2003. "Casinos Bring Change to California Backroads." *Reno Gazette-Journal,* June 8.

Reasons, C. 1972. "Crime and the American Indian." In H. M. Bahr, B. A. Chadwick, and R. C. Day, eds., *Native Americans Today: Sociological Perspectives.* New York: Harper and Row, pp. 319–326.

Reaves, Brian A. 1996. "Local Police Departments, 1993." NCJ 148822. Washington, DC: U.S. Department of Justice, Office of Justice Programs, Bureau of Justice Statistics.

Reaves, B. A., and A. L. Goldberg. 1999. *Law Enforcement Management and Administrative Statistics, 1997.* Washington, DC: Bureau of Justice Statistics.

Reed, L. R. 1989. "Native Prisoners." *Rights Committee News* (June).

Reed, L. R., ed. 1993. *The American Indian in the White Man's Prisons: A Story of Genocide.* Taos, NM: Uncompromising Books.

Reichard, Gladys A. 1970. *Navajo Religion: A Study of Symbolism.* Princeton, NJ: Princeton University Press.

Reina, Edward. 2000. "Domestic Violence in Indian Country: A Dilemma of Justice." *Domestic Violence Report* 5, no. 3: 33–48.

Rennison, Callie. 2001. *Violent Victimization, 1993–1998: A Special Report.* NCJ 176354. Washington, DC: U.S. Department of Justice, Office of Justice Programs, Bureau of Justice Statistics.

Reno, Ronald A. 1999. "Gambling and Crime." *CitizenLink,* December 27. Available at http://www.family.org.

Rezendes, Michael. 2000. "Big-Money Draw Spurs Corruption." *Boston Globe,* December 13, p. A1.

"Rising Crime Blamed on Gambling." *Detroit News,* November 1, 2000.

"A River of Booze." 1988. *Anchorage Daily News,* January 14.

Roberts, Chris. 2001. "Texas Battling Tribal Casino." Associated Press Online, December 15. Available at http://elibrary.bigchalk.com.

Roberts, S. 1983. "The Study of Dispute: Anthropological Perspectives." In John Bossy, ed., *Disputes and Settlements: Law and Human Relations in the West.* Cambridge, UK: Cambridge University Press, pp. 1–25.

Robbins, S. 1985. "Commitment, Belief, and Native American Delinquency." *Human Organization* 44, no. 1: 57–62.

Robinson, C. M., III. 1995. *A Good Year to Die: The Story of the Great Sioux War.* New York: Random House.

Robyn, L. 1992. "State-Corporate Crime and the Issue of Chippewa Treaty Rights." Unpublished manuscript.

Rose, Arnold. 1954. *Theory and Method in the Social Sciences.* Minneapolis: University of Minnesota Press.

Rosenbaum, S. I. 2002. "Casino Foes Watch, Wait as Proposal Resurfaces." *Providence Journal,* February 18, p. B4.

Ross, Jeffrey Ian, ed. 1998. *Cutting the Edge: Current Perspectives on Radical/Critical Criminology and Criminal Justice.* Greenwood, CT: Praeger.

———. 2000a [1995]. *Controlling State Crime: An Introduction.* 2nd ed. New Brunswick, NJ: Transaction.

———. 2000b. *Varieties of State Crime and Its Control.* Monsey, NY: Criminal Justice Press.

———. 2004 [1995]. *Violence in Canada: Sociopolitical Perspectives.* 2nd ed. New Brunswick, NJ: Transaction.

Roundtable. 1999. "Indian Youth Gangs, Violence, and Suicide in Indian Country." Various documents. December 13–15, 1999. Washington, D.C.

Rousseau, Jean-Jacques. 1998 [1762]. *The Social Contract.* Trans. Maurice Cranston. London: Penguin Books.

Rowley, C. D. 1974. *The Destruction of Aboriginal Society.* Harmondsworth, UK: Penguin.

Royster, Judith V., and Rory SnowArrow Fausett. 1988. "Fresh Pursuit onto Native American Reservations: State Rights to Pursue Savage Hostile Indian Marauders across the Border." *University of Colorado Law Review* 59 (Spring): 191–287.

Ryser, R. C. 1991. "Anti-Indian Movement on the Tribal Frontier." Occasional Paper 16. Kenmore, WA: Center for World Indigenous Studies.

Sagan, E. 1995. *At the Dawn of Tyranny: The Origins of Individualism, Political Oppression, and the State.* New York: Vintage.

Saggers, Sherry, and Dennis Gray. 1998. *Dealing with Alcohol: Indigenous Usage in Australia, New Zealand, and Canada.* Cambridge, UK: Cambridge University Press.

Sanders, Donald. 1979. *Navajo Symbols of Healing.* New York: Harcourt Brace Jovanovich.

Sanders, Douglas. 1989. "The UN Working Group on Indigenous Populations." *Human Rights Quarterly* 11: 406–433.

Sansom, B. 1980. *The Camp at Wallaby Cross: Aboriginal Fringe-Dwellers in Darwin.* Canberra: Australian Institute of Aboriginal Studies.

Satz, R. 1991. *Chippewa Treaty Rights: The Reserved Rights of Wisconsin's Chippewa Indians in Historical Perspective.* Madison: Wisconsin Academy of Sciences, Arts, and Letters.

Schevill Link, Margaret. 1956. *The Pollen Path.* Palo Alto, CA: Stanford University Press.

Schwartz, Maureen. 1997. *Molded in the Image of Changing Woman: Navajo Views on the Human Body and Personhood.* Tucson: University of Arizona Press.

Shattuck, Petra T., and Jill Norgren. 1991. *Partial Justice: Federal Indian Law in a Liberal Constitutional System.* New York: Oxford University Press.

Shaw, C. R., and H. D. McKay. 1942. *Juvenile Delinquency and Urban Areas.* Chicago: University of Chicago Press.

Shelburne, Walter. 1988. *Mythos and Logos in the Thought of Carl Jung: The Theory of the Collective Unconscious in Scientific Perspective.* Albany: State University of New York Press.

Sheridan, T. E. 1995. *Arizona: A History.* Tucson: University of Arizona Press.

Shinkwin, Ann, and Mary C. Pete. 1983. "Homes in Disruption: Spouse Abuse in Yup'ik Eskimo Society." Anchorage: University of Alaska.

Shusta, Robert M., et al. 1995. *Multicultural Law Enforcement.* Englewood Cliffs, NJ: Prentice-Hall.

Siedschlaw, K. D. 1996. "Do Indians 'Do Time' Better?" Paper presented at the Western Social Sciences Association, Reno, Nevada.

Silk-Walker, Patricia 1998. *Alcoholism, Alcohol Abuse, and Health in American Indians and Alaska Natives.* American Indian and Alaska Native Mental Health Research monograph no. 1, pp. 65–67.

Silverman, Robert A. 1996. "Patterns of Native American Crime." In Marianne O. Nielsen and Robert A. Silverman, eds., *Native Americans, Crime, and Justice.* Boulder, CO: Westview Press, pp. 58–74.

Singer, M. 1985. "Family Comes First: An Examination of the Social Networks of Skid Row Man." *Human Organization* 44: 137–141.

Skoog, Douglas M. 1996. "Taking Control: Native Self Government and Native Policing." In Marianne O. Nielsen and Robert Silverman, eds., *Native Americans, Crime, and Justice.* Boulder, CO: Westview Press, pp. 118–131.

Skoog, Douglas M., S. Roberts, and M. Boldt. 1980. "Native Attitudes towards the Police." *Canadian Journal of Criminology* 22.

Snake, Reuben, George Hawkins, and Steve La Boueff. 1976. *Report on Alcohol and Drug Abuse: Final Report to the American Indian Policy Review Commission.* Washington, DC: U.S. Government Printing Office.

Snider, Z. K. 1996. "Self-Determination and American Indian Justice." In Marianne O. Nielsen and Robert A. Silverman, eds., *Native Americans, Crime, and Justice.* Boulder, CO: Westview Press, pp. 38–45.

Snipp, Matthew C. 1989. *American Indians: The First of This Land.* New York: Russell Sage.

Snyder, Howard N., and Melissa Sickmund. 1995. *Juvenile Offenders and Victims: A National Report.* Washington, DC: Office of Juvenile Justice and Delinquency Prevention.

Snyder, M. C. 1995. "An Overview of the Indian Child Welfare Act." *St. Thomas Law Review* 7, no. 3: 815–843.

Snyder-Joy, Z. K. 1996. "Self-Determination and American Indian Justice: Tribal versus Federal Jurisdiction on Indian Lands." In Marianne O. Nielson and Robert A. Silverman, eds., *Native Americans, Crime, and Justice.* Boulder, CO: Westview Press.

Solomon, Chris. 2002. "Two Tribal Casinos Get Approval from Washington Gambling Commission." *Seattle Times,* January 11, p. B1.

Spradley, J. P., ed. 1969. *Guests Never Leave Hungry.* New Haven, CT: Yale University Press.

Stark, R., D. P. Doyle, and L. Kent. 1982. "Rediscovering Moral Communities: Church Membership and Crime." *Journal of Research in Crime and Delinquency* 19: 4–24.

"State Doesn't Need New Casino." 1999. *Wisconsin State Journal,* July 11.

Stern, S. J. 1993. *Peru's Indian Peoples and the Challenge of Spanish Conquest.* Madison: University of Wisconsin Press.

Stevens Village v. Alaska Management and Planning, 757 P. 2nd 32, 1988.

Stewart, Iryne (Greyeyes). 1980. *A Voice in Her Tribe: A Navajo Woman's Own Story.* Socorro, NM: Ballena Press.

Stewart, O. 1964. "Questions Regarding American Indian Criminality." *Human Organization* 23, no. l: 61–66.

Stiffarm, D. L. 1995. "The Indian Child Welfare Act: Guiding the Determination of Good Cause to Depart from the Statutory Placement Preferences." *Washington Law Review* 70, no. 4: 1151–1174.

Stitt, G. 2000. *Effects of Casino Gambling on Crime and Quality of Life in New Casino Jurisdictions.* Washington, DC: U.S. Department of Justice.

Strayer, J. 1970. *On the Medieval Origins of the Modern State.* Princeton, NJ: Princeton University Press.

Strickland, Rennard, Stephen J. Herzberg, and Steven R. Owens. 1990. "Keeping Our Word: Indian Treaty Rights and Public Responsibilities—A Report on a Recommended Federal Role Following Wisconsin's Request for Federal Assistance." Unpublished manuscript, University of Wisconsin-Madison School of Law.

Sutherly, Ben. 2003. "Gaming Complex Dicey, Official Says." *Dayton Daily News,* February 7.

Task Force on Federal, State, and Tribal Jurisdiction. 1976. *Final Report to the American Indian Policy Review Commission.*

Taylor, Jonathan B., Matthew B. Krepps, and Patrick Wang. 2000. "The National Evidence on the Socioeconomic Impacts of American Indian Gaming on Non-Indian Communities." Available at http://www.ksg.harvard.edu/hpaied/pubs/pub_010.htm.

Thomas, W. I., and F. Znaniecki. 1920. *The Polish Peasant in Europe and America.* Chicago: University of Chicago Press.

Thompson, William N., Ricardo Gazel, and Dan Rickman. 1996. "Casinos and Crime in Wisconsin: What's the Connection?" Milwaukee: Wisconsin Policy Research Institute, pp. 1–20.

Tinker, G. 1993. *Missionary Conquest: The Gospel and Native American Cultural Genocide.* Minneapolis, MN: Fortress Press.

Tittle, C. R., and M. R. Welch. 1983. "Religiosity and Deviance: Towards a Contingency Theory of Constraining Effects." *Social Forces* 61: 653–682.

Toomy, S. 1988. "Akakanuk's Suicide Epidemic." *Anchorage Daily News,* p. A1.

Travis, R. 1983. "Suicide in Northwestern Alaska." *White Cloud Journal* 3: 23–30.

Tribal Nation. 2003. "Tribal Nation." Available at http://www.tribalnation.com/about.html.

Trigger, Bruce G. 1976. *The Children of Aataensic: A History of the Huron People to 1660.* 2 vols. Montreal: McGill-Queens University Press.

Tso, Tom. 1992. "Moral Principles, Traditions, and Fairness in the Navajo Nation 'Code of Judicial Conduct.'" *Judicature* 76, no. 1 (June–July): 15–20.

Umbreit, Mark S. 1994. *Victim Meets Offender: The Impact of Restorative Justice and Mediation.* Monsey, NY: Criminal Justice Press/Willow Tree Press.

Underhill, R. M. 1979. *Papago Woman.* New York: Holt, Rinehart, and Winston.

Unger, Steve, ed. 1977. *The Destruction of American Indian Families.* New York: Association on American Indian Affairs.

Ungerleider, C. S., and J. McGregor. 1991. "Police-Challenge 2000: Issues Affecting Relations between Police and Minorities in Canada." *Canadian Journal of Criminology* 33: 555–563.

U.S. Census Bureau, Population Estimates Program, Population Division, 1999. "States Ranked by American Indian Population in 1998." Available at http://www.census.gov/population/estimates/state/rank/strnktb3.txt.

U.S. Department of Health and Human Services. 1987. "Sixth Special Report to the U.S. Congress on Alcohol and Health, Public Health Service, Alcohol, Drug Abuse, and Mental Health Administration." Rockville, MD: National Institute on Alcohol Abuse and Alcoholism.

U.S. Department of Justice. 1992 *Sourcebook of Criminal Justice Statistics,* 1992. Washington, DC: U.S. Government Printing Office.

Useem, Jerry. 2000. "The Big Gamble: Have American Indians Found Their New Buffalo?" *Fortune,* October 2.

Utter, Jack. 2001. *American Indians: Answers to Today's Questions.* 2nd ed. Norman: University of Oklahoma Press.

Vaillancourt, Meg, and Hilary Sargent. 1999. "Reilly Denounces Casino Gambling: Law Chief Warns Crime in Massachusetts Will Rise." *Boston Globe,* March 17.

Valencia-Weber, G. 1994. "Tribal Courts: Custom and Innovative Law." *New Mexico Law Review* 24, no. 2.

Van Stone, James W. 1967. *Eskimos of the Nushagak River.* Seattle: University of Washington Press.

Vecsey, C. 1997. "How the Feds Crush Indian Religion: Part II." *Crosswinds* 9, no. 5: 5.

Vecsey, C., ed. 1991. *Handbook of American Indian Religious Freedom.* New York: Crossroad.

Volpe, Maria R. 1991. "Mediation in the Criminal Justice System." In Harold E. Pepinsky and Richard Quinney, eds., *Criminology as Peacemaking.* Bloomington: Indiana University Press, pp. 194–206.

Wachtel, David. 1982. "Indian Law Enforcement." In Laurence A. French, ed., *Indians and Criminal Justice.* Totowa: NJ: Allanheld Osmun, pp. 109–120.

Waddell, Jack. 1980. "Similarities and Variations in Alcohol Use in Four Native American Societies in the Southwest." In Jack Waddell and Michael W. Everett, eds., *Drinking Behavior among Southwestern Indians: An Anthropological Perspective.* Tucson: University of Arizona Press, pp. 227–237.

Wakeling, Stuart, Mirium Jorgensen, Susan Michaelson, and Manley Begay. 2001. *Policing on American Indian Reservations.* A Report to the National Institute of Justice. Washington, DC: Office of Justice Programs.

Waldram, J. B. 1996. "Aboriginal Spirituality in Corrections." In Marianne O. Nielsen and Robert A. Silverman, eds., *Native Americans, Crime, and Justice.* Boulder, CO: Westview Press, pp. 239–254.

Walker, Douglas M. 2001. "Kimpt's Paper Epitomizes the Problems in Gambling Research." *Managerial and Decision Economics* 25: 197–200.

Walker, Samuel, and Molly Brown. 1995. "A Pale Reflection of Reality: The Neglect of Racial and Ethnic Minorities in Introductory Criminal Justice Textbooks." *Journal of Criminal Justice Education* 6, no. 1: 61–77. Available at http://www.faculty.de.gcsu.edu/~dwalker/PDF%20articles/MDE.pdf.

Ward, J. A. 1984. "Preventive Implications of a Native Indian Mental Health Program: Focus on Suicide and Violent Death." *Journal of Preventive Psychiatry* 2: 371–385.

Washburn, W. 1984. "A Fifty-Year Perspective on the Indian Reorganization Act." *American Anthropologist* 86: 279–289.

———. 1988. *Handbook of North American Indians: History of Indian-White Relations.* Washington, DC: Smithsonian Institution.

Wellford, Charles. 2001. "When It's No Longer a Game: Pathological Gambling in the United States." *National Institute of Justice Journal* (April): 15–18.

Western Australia Task Force on Aboriginal Social Justice. 1994. "Report of the Taskforce on Aboriginal Social Justice—Two Volumes and Summary." Perth: Government of Western Australia.

Western Navajo Juvenile Services Coordinating Council. N.D. Various documents.

Wexler, L. 2001. "Tribal Court Jurisdiction in Dissolution-Based Custody Proceedings." *University of Chicago Legal Forum:* 613–652.

Whaley, R. and Walt Bresette. 1994. *Walleye Warriors: An Effective Alliance against Racism and for the Earth.* Philadelphia, PA: New Society Publishers.

Wheeler, David L. 1999. "A Surge of Research on Gambling Is Financed in Part by the Industry Itself." *Chronicle of Higher Education* 60: 17–18.

White, Richard. 1983. *The Roots of Dependency.* Lincoln: University of Nebraska Press.

Whittaker, J. O. 1982. "Alcohol and the Standing Rock Sioux Tribe: A Twenty-Year Follow-Up Study." *Journal of Studies on Alcohol* 43, no. 3: 191–200.

Wichner, David. 2002. "Indians' Income Going Up." *Arizona Daily Star,* May 25, p. A1.

Wilkins, David E. 2002. *American Indian Politics and the American Political System.* Lanham, MD: Rowman and Littlefield.

Wilkins, David E., and K. Tsianina Lomawaima. 2001. *Uneven Ground: American Indian Sovereignty and Federal Law.* Norman: University of Oklahoma Press.

Wilkinson, C. F. 1987. *American Indians, Time, and the Law.* New Haven, CT: Yale University Press.

Williams, Larry E. 1979. "Antecedents of Urban Indian Crime." Ph.D. diss., Brigham Young University.

Williams, Larry E., Bruce A. Chadwick, and Howard M. Bahr. 1979. "Antecedents of Self-Reported Arrest for Indian Americans in Seattle." *Phylon* 40, no. 3 (Fall): 243–252.

Williams, Robert A. 1990. *The American Indian in Western Legal Thought: The Discourses of Conquest.* New York: Oxford University Press.

———. 1991. "Columbus Legacy: Law as an Instrument of Racial Discrimination against Indigenous Peoples' Rights of Self-Determination." *Arizona Journal of International and Comparative Law* 8, no. 2: 51–75.

Wilson, J. 1997. *Moral Judgment: Does the Abuse Excuse Threaten Our Legal System?* New York: Basic Books.

Winfree, L. Thomas, Curt Griffiths, and Christine Sellers. 1989. "Social Learning Theory, Drug Use, and American Indian Youths: A Cross-Cultural Test." *Justice Quarterly* 6, no. 3: 395–417.

Witherspoon, Gary. 1974. "The Central Concepts of Navajo World View (I)." *Linguistics* 119: 41–59.

———. 1975. "The Central Concepts of Navajo World View (II)." *Linguistics* 161: 69–84.

Wolf, J. 1951. *The Emergence of the Great Powers, 1685–1715.* New York: Harper and Row.

Wolf, Robert J. 1981. "Norton Sound/Yukon Delta Sociocultural Systems Baseline Analysis." Technical Report no. 71. Washington, DC: U.S. Department of Interior, Bureau of Land Management.

Yazzie, Robert. 1994. "'Life Comes from It': Navajo Justice Concepts." *New Mexico Law Review* 24, no. 2: 176–190.

———. 1995. "The Traditional Navajo Dispute Resolution in the Navajo Peacemaker Court." *Forum* 27 (Spring): 5–16.

———. 1997. "Criminal Justice: Technology and Traditional Navajo Peacemaking." Paper presented at Indigenous Renascence: Law, Culture, and Society in the Twenty-First Century conference, St. Thomas University, Miami, Florida, March 13–14.

Young, Thomas J. 1990. "Native American Crime and Criminal Justice Require Criminologists' Attention." *Journal of Criminal Justice Education* 1 (Spring): 111–116.

———. 1991. "Medical Resources, Suicides, and Homicides among Native Americans." *Corrective and Social Psychiatry and Journal of Behavior Technology Methods and Therapy* 37, no. 3 (July): 38–41.

Young, Thomas, and Lawrence French. 1997. "Homicide Rates among Native American Children: The Status Integration Hypothesis." *Adolescence* 32, no. 125 (Spring): 57–59.

"Youth's Despair Erupts." 1988. *Anchorage Daily News,* January 12.

Zatz, M. S., C. C. Lujan, and Z. Snyder-Joy. 1991. "American Indians and Criminal Justice: Some Conceptual and Methodological Considerations." In M. J. Lynch and E. B. Patterson, eds., *Race and Criminal Justice.* New York: Harrow and Heston, pp. 100–112.

Zehr, H. 1995. *Changing Lenses.* Waterloo, ON: Herald Press.

Zion, James. 1994a. "Stories from the Peacemaker Court." *In Context* 38: 1.

———. 1994b. "The Navajo Peacemaker Court: Deference to the Old and Accommodation to the New." *American Indian Law Review* 11, no. 1: 89–109.

Zion, J., and R. Yazzie. 1997. "Indigenous Law in North America in the Wake of Conquest." *Boston College International and Comparative Law Review* 20, no. 1: 55–84.

Index

About the Editors
and Contributors

Thom Alcoze is from the Cherokee Nation and is an associate professor of forestry with the College of Ecosystem Science and Management at Northern Arizona University in Flagstaff. His teaching and research interests involve traditional ecological knowledge and the application of First Nation practices to contemporary environmental issues. The results of his research demonstrate that indigenous nations of the Americas practiced ecologically sound methods of natural resource management and conservation, which are now being incorporated into the fields of ecological restoration, conservation biology, and management. He has been instrumental in the development of culture-based science curriculum materials in collaboration with the National Science Foundation and the Apache, Diné (Navajo), Hopi, and Zuni nations.

William G. Archambeault is a professor and criminologist with the School of Social Work, Louisiana State University in Baton Rouge. His current research focuses on traditional Native American healing and justice issues, and he teaches courses dealing with Native American crime, justice, and social work practice issues. Most of his previous works (books, articles, and research projects) focused on criminal justice as it related to computers and correctional management and comparative justice issues, including research on the cost-effectiveness and comparative safety of privately operated versus state-operated prisons in Louisiana. He is a former chair of the Department of Criminal Justice at LSU, former member of the Louisiana Board of Pardons, former chief probation officer, and former jail consultant. He is of Chippewa, Cherokee, and Sioux ancestry and has spent much time doing fieldwork, especially among the Chippewa.

Lisa Bond-Maupin received her doctoral degree in justice studies from Arizona State University in 1992. Her dissertation analyzed the legal processing and jailing of youth in one southwestern Indian reservation community. Her subsequent research has focused on juvenile justice in minority communities in the southwestern United States and depictions of crime, gender, and justice on reality-based crime television. She is an associate professor in the Department of Criminal Justice at New Mexico State University.

Tracy M. Bouvier was born and raised in the Southwest. She received her master's degree in criminal justice from Northern Arizona University in 1999. Her primary research interest is child maltreatment. For the past seven years, she has served as a court-appointed special advocate in Coconio County, Arizona, advocating for victims of child abuse and neglect. She received her bachelor's degree in the legal assistant program at Northern Arizona University in 1979 and has ten years' experience as a paralegal.

Dorothy H. Bracey is professor emeritus of anthropology at John Jay College of Criminal Justice and professor emeritus of criminal justice at the Graduate School of the City University of New York. She has carried out research in a number of countries and has written extensively on topics of comparative and international criminal justice. She has a doctoral degree in anthropology from Harvard University and a master of studies in law from Yale Law School. She has been visiting professor at the University of Illinois at Chicago, distinguished scholar at American University, and holder of the George Beto Chair at Sam Houston State University in Texas. She has served as president of the Academy of Criminal Justice Sciences, where she was named academy fellow and was given the 1995 Founders Award as well as the 2005 G. E. O. Mueller Award for Contributions to Comparative Criminal Justice.

Duane Champagne is a member of the Turtle Mountain Band of Chippewa from North Dakota. He is Professor of Sociology and American Indian Studies. Professor Champagne has authored or edited over one hundred publications. His research interests focus on issues of social and cultural change in both historical and contemporary Native American communities.

Taka X. GoodTracks, who passed away in 2005, received his bachelor of criminal justice (1997) and master of criminal justice (1999) from New Mexico State University, and was a Ph.D. student there. His thesis analyzed major crimes within one American Indian community and focused on problematic issues related to counting crime within American Indian communities.

Larry Gould is a professor of criminal justice and associate dean of the College of Social and Behavioral Sciences at Northern Arizona University. He received his bachelor's and master's degrees in criminal justice from Louisiana State University and a doctorate in sociology with emphases in experimental statistics and criminal justice from Louisiana State University in 1991. He served for fifteen years as a police officer in Louisiana. Most of his research interests focus on the adaptation of police officers to their environment and the impact the policing environment has on the officer. He is continuing his work with the Navajo Nation police as a project evaluator on a federally funded, community-oriented policing project.

Marilyn Holly is professor emeritus of philosophy at the University of Florida in Gainesville. She is a specialist in social and political philosophy and teaches and conducts research in Native American philosophy. She spent a postdoctoral year at the Carl Jung Institute in Zurich, Switzerland studying Jungian theory and methods. Holly has also held an adjunct appointment in psychology at the University of Florida. She has published articles in a number of academic journals, including *International Journal of Philosophy, Teaching Philosophy, Small Group Behavior, Radical Therapist,* and *Journal of Religion and Health.*

Nella Lee is currently a researcher for the Washington State Department of Social and Health Services. She is the past director of research for the Washington State Sentencing Guidelines Commission and was an associate professor of criminal justice at Portland State University. From 1993–1994, she was a senior Fulbright research scholar to the Arctic Research Centre at the University of Lapland in Rovaniemi, Finland. She was the author of *Crime and Culture in Yup'ik Villages* (Edwin Mellen, 2000), which was selected to be in the permanent collection on American Indian history at the University of Illinois (Chicago) Newberry Library.

Eileen Luna-Firebaugh is associate professor of American Indian Law and Policy at the University of Arizona at Tucson. She is Choctaw and Cherokee. She holds a J.D. and an M.P.A. from the Kennedy School of Government at Harvard University. She an appellate justice for the Colorado River Indian Tribal Court and a faculty member of the U.S. Department of Justice–funded National Tribal Judge College. She was principal investigator for the National Institute of Justice evaluation of STOP Violence against Indian Women programs and for a National Institute of Health study of family violence programs in Australian aboriginal communities. She is a consultant to the Harvard CIRCLE Project, a joint DOJ and tribal project on juvenile justice, a member of the Board of Directors for the National Center for Responsible Gaming, the Harvard Medical School Division on Diversions Project on Pathological Gambling, and the Southwest Center on Law and Policy. She is the author of a number of criminal justice articles focusing on American Indian tribal police, family violence, and tribal governments. She is the author of a forthcoming book, *Policing Indian America: The Juncture of Sovereignty and Justice,* from the University of Arizona Press.

James R. Maupin received his M.P.A. from Southwest Missouri State University and his Ph.D. in political science from Arizona State University in 1990. He is an associate professor and head of the Department of Criminal Justice at New Mexico State University. He has published several articles on decisionmaking within the juvenile justice systems of the southwestern United States.

Marianne O. Nielsen is an assistant professor in the Department of Criminal Justice at Northern Arizona University in Flagstaff. She is the coeditor with Robert A. Silverman of *Native Americans, Crime, and Criminal Justice* (Westview, 1996) and *Aboriginal Peoples and the Canadian Criminal Justice System* (Harcourt Brace, 1992). She coedited with James W. Zion *Navajo Nation Peacemaking* (University of Arizona Press, 2005). Her work has also appeared in *Law and Anthropology, Journal of Contemporary Criminal Justice, Canadian Journal of Administrative Sciences, Canadian Journal of Ethnic Studies,* and *Journal of Criminal Justice Education* and as chapters in numerous books. Her current work focuses on the structures, processes, survival, and success of indigenous-operated justice organizations.

Nicholas C. Peroff holds a bachelor of science in American history (1966), a master's degree (1972), and a doctoral degree in political science (1977), with a minor in urban and regional planning from the University of Wisconsin at Madison. He attended the U.S. Naval Officer Candidate School in Newport, Rhode Island, in 1966 and served as a line officer in the Vietnam War from 1967 to 1969. He joined the public administration faculty at the University of Missouri at Kansas City in 1974. He has served as an instructor at Haskell Indian Nations University in Lawrence, Kansas, and taught internationally at the Professional Training Center, Ministry of Economics, Hsin Chu, Republic of China; Kiemyung University, Taegu, South Korea; and the University of the Western Cape, Bellville, South Africa. Significant community service and other activities include serving as president of the Western Social Science Association (2002–2003), a member of the board of directors of the Kansas City Heart of America Indian Center (1997–2004), and a participant in a range of exchange activities between the Bloch School of Business and Public Administration and the faculty of the School of Economics and Management Sciences at the University of the Western Cape in South Africa. He serves as the faculty coordinator for the Bloch School's interdisciplinary doctoral program in public affairs and administration. He is currently engaged in the development and application of complexity theory in American Indian policy analysis and is writing a second book on Indian policy and the Menominee Indian Tribe of Wisconsin.

Linda Robyn is from the Ojibwa Nation and is an associate professor in the Department of Criminal Justice at Northern Arizona University. She teaches a variety of criminal justice topics as well as environmental justice and indigenous studies. Her area of interest and research agenda is utilizing indigenous knowledge as it relates to the criminal justice system, environmental justice and people of color, and corporate and government crime.

Jeffrey Ian Ross is an associate professor in the Division of Criminology, Criminal Justice, and Social Policy and a fellow of the Center for Comparative and International Law at the University of Baltimore. He has conducted research, written, and lectured on national security, political violence, violent crime, political crime, corrections, and policing for over fifteen years. His work has appeared in many academic books as well as articles in popular magazines in Canada and the United States. Ross is the author of *Making News of Police Violence* (Praeger, 2000), *The Dynamics of Political Crime* (Sage, 2002), and *Political Terrorism: An Interdisciplinary Approach* (Peter Lang, 2005). He is the editor of *Controlling State Crime*

(Garland Publishing, 1995; Transaction, 2000), *Violence in Canada: Sociopolitical Perspectives* (Oxford University Press, 1995; Transaction, 2003), *Cutting the Edge: Current Perspectives in Radical/Critical Criminology and Criminal Justice* (Praeger, 1998), and *Varieties of State Crime and Its Control* (Criminal Justice Press, 2000). Ross is coeditor with Stephen C. Richards of *Convict Criminology* (Wadsworth, 2003) and coauthor of *Behind Bars: Surviving Prison* (Alpha, 2002). Ross received his doctoral degree from the University of Colorado. In May 2003 he was awarded the distinguished chair in research award by the University of Baltimore.

Samuel Walker is professor emeritus of criminal justice at the University of Nebraska at Omaha, where he has taught since 1974. He is the author of eleven books on policing, criminal justice history and policy, and civil liberties. His current research involves police accountability, focusing primarily on citizen oversight of the police and early warning (EW) systems. The research on citizen oversight is published in *Police Accountability: The Role of Citizen Oversight* (Wadsworth, 2001).

James W. Zion is the solicitor to the courts of the Navajo Nation, an adjunct professor in the Department of Criminal Justice of Northern Arizona University, a justice planner, and a writer. He has taught traditional Indian justice at the University of New Mexico at Gallup, Northern Arizona University, and at conferences of the National Indian Justice Center. He holds a bachelor's degree from the University of Saint Thomas (1966) and a law degree from the Columbus School of Law of Catholic University (1969). He began a career in Indian justice by participating in the occupation of the Bureau of Indian Affairs building in 1968.

DATE DUE

		WITHDRAWN	

DEMCO 38-296

Please remember that this is a library book,
and that it belongs only temporarily to each
person who uses it. Be considerate. Do
not write in this, or any, library book.